John M. Sawada.

Controlling Interest

DIANE FRANCIS

Controlling Interest

Who Owns Canada?

Macmillan of Canada
A Division of Canada Publishing Corporation
Toronto, Ontario, Canada

First Printing, August, 1986
Second Printing, September, 1986
Third Printing, October, 1986

Canadian Cataloguing in Publication Data
Francis, Diane, date.
        Controlling interest : who owns Canada?
ISBN 0-7715-9744-4
1. Corporations – Canada. 2. Canada – Economic
conditions – 1945-   . 3. Elite (Social sciences) –
Canada. 4. Business enterprises – Canada. I. Title.
HD2809.F73 1986   338.7′4′0971   C86-093811-5

Design by Don Fernley

Macmillan of Canada
A Division of Canada Publishing Corporation
Toronto, Ontario, Canada

Printed in Canada

CONTENTS

This is dedicated
to my parents,
Paul and Mary Davis.

INTRODUCTION

EVEN BUSINESSPEOPLE are beginning to be alarmed about the degree of concentration in Canada. "In a number of years there will be six groups running this country," warns Bernie Ghert, president of Cadillac Fairview Corp., the country's second-largest development company.

"We must grapple with the problems of concentration of substantial economic power in Canada in the hands of a new aristocracy consisting of twenty or thirty powerful families and the Canadian banks," says Henry Knowles, a Toronto lawyer and formerly Canada's top securities watchdog. But bankers like Richard Thomson, chairman of the Toronto-Dominion Bank, are also concerned, from a different viewpoint. "I worry about the political backlash if it is not dealt with. This could lead to socialism."

Concentration is an issue of vital importance to all Canadians and their political leaders. And it is more pervasive and more serious than I thought when I began my research. Unbridled, concentration forces Canadians to overpay for many goods and services, removes job opportunities, hurts small investors, taxes the poor to help the rich, weakens our competitive position as a trading nation, and ultimately threatens our democratic process.

Controlling Interest profiles Canada's thirty-two wealthiest families who, along with five conglomerates, already control about one-third of the country's non-financial assets, nearly double what they controlled just four years before. Combined, their revenues in 1985 were nearly $123 billion, far greater than the federal government's income of around $80 billion. Just one member of this élite group, Bell Canada Enterprises, had a cash flow of $3.2 billion in 1985, greater than that of either the Canada Pension Plan or the Caisse de dépôt et placement du Québec. By comparison, in the U.S. the 100

1

largest firms, few of which are controlled by individuals, own one-third of the non-financial assets.

Canada has become a collection of family dynasties and management fief-doms, with more billionaire families per capita than the United States. While their actual net worth is unknown, Canada probably has six billionaire fami-lies: the Reichmanns, the Irvings, the Eatons, Edgar and Charles Bronfman, the Westons, and the Thomsons. The rest of the families profiled in this book are each worth not less than $100 million in net terms, and they control enter-prises with at least $1 billion in assets and/or sales.

In the U.S., by comparison, there are only a dozen billionaire families in an economy twelve times as large. The wealthiest man in America is Sam Moore Walton, sixty-seven, an Arkansas-based department store entrepreneur worth US$2.8 billion, according to a *Forbes* magazine report in 1985. But all indi-cations are that K. C. Irving and the Reichmanns are also worth that much. Because both empires are private fortunes headed by tight-lipped individuals, we may never know.

The thirty-two profiles in this book are not a definitive list of the country's thirty-two richest families. The McConnells of Montreal, for instance, are wealthier, in net terms, than many profiled here. They control some $400 million, half of which is locked away in a trust fund for the eleven grand-children of J. B. McConnell, who made his money in publishing, the stock market, and sugar. That money is invested in hundreds of different companies as a form of private pension plan for family members. The family does not hold controlling interest in any corporation. Its remaining $200 million was put by J. B. McConnell into two charitable foundations, the Griffith Founda-tion and the McConnell Foundation, which collectively contribute more money to charities in Canada than any other single entity, roughly $11 million in 1985.

The McConnell family, like others, is worth more than, say, Conrad Black and his brother, Montegu, but its money is passively invested, not leveraged to gain control over a corporate empire considerably greater in value. Similar-ly, others with considerable means who have invested their huge sums of money in small or passive ways include the Siebens family, rumoured to be worth some $300 million to $400 million, and families such as the Southams and the Atkinsons, whose empires are large, but divided among dozens of heirs, some of whom take little, or no, interest.

Canada's inordinately high degree of concentration means that all kinds of goods and services — everything from your glass of orange juice in the morning, to the clothes you put on, to the office where you work, to the department store and mall where you shop, to that after-work beer and a night at the ball game — are likely to be produced by these families and conglomerates. Concentration has become so significant that the country is hurtling towards a new form of economic and political feudalism, a twentieth-century version of Upper Canada's Family Compact back in the 1800s, when agrarian Ontario was politically and financially controlled by the few.

Canada has come full circle. What began as an area controlled by the Hudson's Bay Company and the North West Company has ended up as a country that is little more than a collection of financial franchises. Competition among Canadian capitalists rarely breaks out in the absence of any meaningful combines laws within or foreign rivalry from without. This means that instead of a lively, competitive marketplace yielding jobs, innovations, or opportunities for new entrepreneurs, Canada has far too many cash cows controlled by far too few proprietors. The result is that, whether buying beer or tranquillizers, gasoline, eyeglasses, or shopping centre space, Canadian consumers pay too much. Like economic serfs, we are paying private-sector surcharges, levied by a diminishing number of families and faceless conglomerates, on just about everything.

By far the most heated competition in Canada has been to buy the fiefdoms themselves, as conglomerates and families spent most of the 1970s borrowing millions against what they already owned to acquire more. At the last count by federal officials, some 4,685 takeovers had been made between 1974 and 1984, compared with 3,464 significantly smaller takeovers in the ten previous years. The concentration continues, hurtling us towards an even more closely held economic oligarchy than already exists. Tragically, the issues do not have top political priority, even though controlling interest in the entire country is at stake, and so are political freedoms.

Ottawa has never blocked a specific takeover but did ban briefly all takeovers during 1981 — for good reason. Some $14 billion left the country in "Canadianizations" in the first eight months, encouraged by the Liberals' ill-fated National Energy Program. "The takeover thing had gone haywire," recalls Rowland Frazee, chairman of the Royal Bank of Canada. "The banking system was running out of capital. I told MacEachen he had to order an end to it."

On July 29 he did just that. Canada teetered that month on the edge of a currency collapse, a banking crisis, and full-scale bankruptcies, thanks to corporate Canada's takeover frenzy and a government that understood little about economics. Not surprisingly, what was a recession in the United States became a depression here, as unemployment soared and the economy virtually ground to a halt. It was the year of the near-miss, but nothing was learned. It was a year that left corporate Canada with an enormous mortgage, but nothing has changed. And we are still paying the price for 1981.

In the absence of rules, ours has been a financial system fashioned after our national sport of hockey, but without referees or penalty boxes. Unchecked, "free-enterprisers" destroy their own system, mopping up all opportunities and pushing political leaders towards socialist alternatives. Unbridled, free enterprise devours its young as surely as an unofficiated hockey game sidelines the most talented players in the game, if they are small.

Calgary entrepreneur Rob Vanderham can tell you what concentration is all about. As president of Peyto Oils Ltd., an oil and gas exploration company, he felt more keenly than most about his job — after all, he had helped found the company in 1970 and had built it, by 1980, into an enterprise with sales of some $10 million and assets of more than $70 million. Then, in January 1980, while sunning himself in the Caribbean, he got a call from the office. Someone was snapping up the stock, trading had been suspended, and he and his company were no longer players. Now they were pucks. Only a few days earlier an Eastern broker had rounded up 38 per cent of Peyto's stock from its largest institutional shareholders and peddled them to Westburne International Industries Ltd., a Calgary-based conglomerate, for $31.8 million. Vanderham, a Dutch immigrant with 10 per cent of Peyto's stock, recalled, "As soon as that first call came, I knew it was all over. I put the phone down and felt as though somebody had just stolen my baby."

Economists measure two types of concentration: the accumulation of assets in industries that may not be related (by conglomerates or passive holding companies), and the increase of market share within a sector by a few firms. Both types of concentration have relentlessly accelerated in Canada, and both are economically harmful. Only 20 of Canada's 400 largest public corporations are widely held. Some 380 have a shareholder with at least 15 per cent of the stock and in 374 of these, controlling interest of at least 25 to 30 per cent is held by a family or conglomerate. By comparison, only 75 of the companies in the American Standard & Poor's 500 stock index have a large shareholder.

Of Canada's 100 largest public companies, which represent as much as half of the country's corporate assets, 25 per cent of the total sales and assets are family-controlled, 25 per cent are in the hands of widely held conglomerates, such as Bell, 25 per cent are foreign-controlled, and 25 per cent are public enterprises, such as Crown corporations, utilities, or co-ops. But by far the most aggressive acquisitors are the families.

"We don't need to worry about family wealth," says Hal Jackman, a Toronto tycoon with extensive insurance and trust company assets. "For most, it will be shirt-sleeves to shirt-sleeves in three generations." While that is true for some, the new reality is that changes to tax and securities laws brought in during the 1970s permit the creation of dynasties and fiefdoms, able to reign for as long as they wish. This means the country will be run by a royalty of rich families, ensconced for generations if they wish.

Of course, not all concentration is harmful. If a company is going to fight its way into a bigger foreign market for a few years before it gets a first order, it needs to be big. To compete abroad, a company must have long production runs to reduce unit costs, special technology developed by investing millions in research, as well as millions of dollars to finance expansion. Such gearing up for export often means Canadian companies are oversized within Canada's relatively small economy (it is smaller than California's). However large they may loom here at home, these companies are often tiny compared with their foreign rivals. This is why many argue against concentration curbs: they maintain that lessening competition at home will sabotage success abroad.

But only a handful of Canadian companies have used monopoly positions as springboards into the international big leagues: the big five chartered banks, Canadian Pacific, and Northern Telecom, Canada's greatest corporation. What Canada needs, and lacks, is ten Northern Telecoms. Instead, we have ten companies like Argus Corporation, a notably ugly conglomerate that bled Massey-Ferguson for years, steadfastly refusing to give it cash transfusions for research. Argus lent nothing to the company in the way of operations; it was a passive controlling shareholder, extracting dividends and refusing to allow the company to issue more shares because it did not want to invest more or be diluted. Massey eventually borrowed itself into huge debts it could not afford and a government bail-out in 1979. Then Argus chairman Conrad Black, who inherited the mess, sensibly walked away. But just a few years later, in 1985, Black's Argus jettisoned another of its troubled assets, Dominion Stores — selling out when stormy weather hit and patience, expertise, and cash were needed.

Instead of building world-class contenders, corporate Canada is preoccupied with collecting unrelated assets back at home and gobbling up the accomplishments of other players in unrelated fields, through the cunning use of tax avoidance and the games only paper entrepreneurs can play. It is a parasitical game that will not make the economic pie grow. It will shrink, as the pieces change hands and workers are thrown out of jobs because of duplication.

And this acquisitiveness affects every single Canadian. As if they weren't rich enough already, Canadian billionaires drive trucks through tax loopholes, leaving ordinary Canadians to ante up more to pay for government services, or do without.

The profiles of Canada's thirty-two wealthiest families reveal a great deal about Canada's power élite. For a goodly portion of the 1970s, most have been playing Monopoly with the money of average Canadians. Finding that inflation suddenly gave them enormous borrowing power, they borrowed Canadian savings socked away in Canadian banks that behave, at times, like open-ended slush funds for the tycoons sitting on their boards.

Not only can these families and conglomerates raise huge bank loans for takeovers, but they are also able to raise "free" equity money easily. The successful ones have become masters of what could be dubbed Canada's monetary merry-go-round — an economic anomaly created after the Second World War when the government required that at least 90 per cent of all Canadian pension, life insurance, and trust funds must be invested in Canada. Up to 10 per cent could be invested elsewhere, but it was carefully restricted to certain conservative types of investments. Designed to provide capital to develop the country and increase the nation's wealth, this rule has single-handedly fostered more concentration of power than has anything else.

And it will continue to fuel the merry-go-round until every single one of the country's public companies falls into the hands of a few families or conglomerates, probably by the end of the decade. For instance, the Reichmanns in the spring of 1986 made a successful $3.3-billion takeover bid for the gigantic Hiram Walker distillery and energy conglomerate. To make their bid, they used Gulf Corp., an energy and paper conglomerate in which the family has an 80-per-cent stake. Gulf's bid resulted in Hiram's common shareholders getting a handsome capital gain, which is why virtually all the shares were sold, mostly those held by "institutional investors" such as pension plans, mutual funds, or life insurance and trust companies.

Eager to take profits, the managers of these massive funds must turn around and find new investments. And that has become even more difficult, for two reasons. They continue to be deluged with cash. In 1985, public pension plans like the Caisse de dépôt et placement du Québec as well as private schemes totalled $238 billion — equivalent to Ottawa's entire national debt by 1985 and enough to buy half of all the shares of every company on the Toronto Stock Exchange. Even more dramatic, they were growing by $60 million a day, or $19 billion a year. Indications are that this trend will not slow down. In addition, fund managers are faced with a decreasing number of shares to buy, because of the thousands of takeovers that have occurred.

This is how the resulting merry-go-round works: eventually, perhaps months or even years later, the Reichmanns will pay for the $3.3-billion Hiram takeover by selling shares in Gulf to the very same institutional investors who have just sold their Hiram common shares. These institutional investors will gladly buy such paper instruments, because they are captive in Canada and desperately need new "paper." They will also buy the new Gulf shares because the shares' underlying value will be the same sound, profitable Hiram assets that led them to buy Hiram common shares in the first place.

And so institutional investors have become locked into a system that offers them fewer and fewer investment choices and is rigged to reward the paper entrepreneurs. Used in this way, the hundreds of billions of dollars of Canadian savings contribute little to the nation's wealth. In fact, the system results in greatly inflated stock prices in Canada for what little stock is left on exchanges, as more and more pension dollars chase fewer and fewer stocks. This is very harmful because it means foreign investors, bringing fresh capital, are not easily attracted. It also means Canadian savings have been increasingly invested in stocks at inflated prices, which will yield disappointing results for Canadians in their collective old age.

Japan also limits pension investments outside the country, but the big difference is that Japan's captive pool of capital has been wisely utilized, because that country has many more real entrepreneurs, capable of putting the money to good use. The money has been loaned or invested to individuals and companies that have created export empires, creating jobs and new goods and services in order to increase profits and the nation's wealth.

Not all forms of concentration can be curbed, nor should they be. Only big players who cause injuries or prevent other players from getting onto the ice to participate must be disciplined. However, even big players who play by the rules and are hugely successful raise questions. Canada's biggest empire, Bell Canada Enterprises, has a telephone monopoly in Ontario and Quebec and large stakes in a number of companies. In 1983, Bell convinced federal regulators to allow it to embark on a "diversification" strategy, and since then it has bought controlling interest in a major corporation every year. Now Bell and its affiliated companies have combined market values that are equivalent to about 9 per cent of the entire Toronto Stock Exchange float.

Bell's success is based on three things: it does not have to compete, its management is obviously good at negotiating highly beneficial telephone rates before federal communications regulators, and it shops the takeover market carefully. The question is, given its awesome size, do advantages such as these deserve such enormous rewards, or is it not time to let Bell share its monopoly position, particularly long-distance services, with new, possibly more innovative entrants? Or perhaps Bell should prune its profits, passing along more benefits to phone users rather than to its shareholders and those of companies it takes over.

Another example of questionable success of a big player is the Canadian Pacific empire, which is second only to Bell. The base upon which this huge conglomerate grew is largely the land and sub-surface rights — equivalent in size to Nova Scotia — given by the fledgling government of Canada to the railway's original developers. Little wonder that CP owns Canada's most profitable and successful oil exploration company because it has the choice of so many lands to explore and no royalties to pay, as well as one of its wealthiest real estate development companies, with valuable acreage in the downtowns of most Canadian cities. CP is profitable mostly because of such ancient gifts — combined with a railway that operates mostly like a utility with guaranteed profits. Beginning in the early 1970s, with tax changes paving the way, CP leaped into the takeover game, but it has had problems with most of its acquisitions. CP may be a conglomerate that has become unwieldy, a financial dinosaur roaming too far afield.

Some say conglomerates are beneficial because they provide additional financial muscle when trouble hits one subsidiary or another. Conversely, however, the conglomerate structure also means that when a subsidiary is in trouble, it drags down the other, well-run operations. Conglomerates are only as strong as their weakest links, and they concentrate decision-making into fewer and fewer hands. When mistakes are made, the amplification is dramatic.

An example of a conglomerate gone awry is the Dome Petroleum empire, which contributed mightily to Canada's near-miss in 1981. Dome's aggressive managers had built the company with foolishly expensive takeovers, always being bailed out by international oil price hikes. But in 1981, they decided to pay $4 billion for a company they could not afford. Not only did Dome Pete shareholders lose their proverbial shirts as a result, ending up with a negative equity value five years later, but Dome Pete raped the shareholders of its sister company, Dome Mines, in which it had a controlling interest of 40 per cent.

By July 1981, Dome Petroleum faced soaring interest rates on its huge debt and plummeting stock values, a disaster in light of the fact that it hoped to swap its stock to buy the other half of Hudson's Bay Oil shares. In a vain attempt to shore up its sagging stock price, Dome Petroleum directors lobbied the board of Dome Mines to borrow up to $125 million and buy Dome Pete stock. The mining company, which already owned 27 per cent of the oil giant, actually spent $75 million. "Thank heavens we only took up three million shares," says former Dome Mines president Malcolm Taschereau. "Even that ran up to a cost of $75 million and eventually resulted in Mines having to dispose of other assets."

The stock swap was never accepted by the market, and Dome went to the wall. The new Dome Pete shares held by Dome Mines were worthless, wiping $75 million in value off the company's books. It was a case of a controlling shareholder harvesting a company for its own ends rather than for the good of all shareholders. In 1982, Dome Mines was dragged even further into the mess when it was forced to sign a $225-million loan guarantee to the Toronto-Dominion Bank to support Dome Petroleum. Taschereau became increasingly uncooperative about executing his board's decisions and resigned in mid-1983.

Eventually, Dome was bailed out by its bankers, who stretched out loan repayments to avoid embarrassment and loan loss provisions on their books. But Dome Mines was a sorry lesson that he who lives by the conglomerate dies by the conglomerate. Despite that publicly aired display of disaster management, current examples of potentially dangerous interlocking directorships and financial arrangements exist throughout corporate Canada, particularly in the heavily debt-laden Edper empire of Peter and Edward Bronfman, which is the subject of the lengthiest family profile in this book.

Apologists say that concentration is the natural result of tariffs and foreign ownership restrictions needed to create jobs and buy back the country. Of course, foreign ownership proscriptions have backfired because tariffs and other restrictions also protect foreign-owned outfits already operating inside the country, many of whom enjoy near-monopolistic privileges as a result.

In addition, foreign ownership restrictions in Canada's resource and manufacturing sectors are unnecessary. Resources are already owned by the people, and owners of companies exploiting those companies must pay royalties, regardless of nationality. As for manufacturing, the Auto Pact, a special bilateral treaty, already enshrines job protection in the only significant manufacturing field in Canada.

Throughout our history, concentration, and what to do about it, has been the black hole of Canadian economic policy. Our leaders do not understand the importance of concentration, cannot define it, and have no tools with which to measure it. This is not surprising, given that Canada is a newly industrialized country with its own populist traditions. In the U.S., regulators monitor the biggest players and penalize them when they use bullying tactics. Big is bad, according to American populist tradition. It must be watched.

An example of where all of Canada might be headed can be seen in one province, New Brunswick, where the Irving empire reigns supreme. In fact, the Irving family virtually *is* New Brunswick's private sector, apart from a few notable competitors like the wealthy McCains. Former New Brunswick premier Louis Robichaud recalls that one of K. C. Irving's sons told him, "My father's never lost a New Brunswick election in his life," even though Irving never sought public office. But for years, Irving could make or break politicians, a chilling fact in a country where thirty-two families control an inordinate portion of the economy. Even worse, the extent of family wealth is unknown because disclosure requirements are lax or non-existent in Canada, in contrast to other industrialized countries.

While unassailed and misunderstood in Canada, the concentration issue has nonetheless nagged. Countless royal commissions and regulatory hearings have been held into concentration's various manifestations, most notably in the oil and newspaper businesses. The Royal Commission on Corporate Concentration concluded in 1978 that concentration was a necessity. But the commission listened principally to the business community and failed miserably to fulfil its mandate.

Concentration of power has grown like cancer, spreading rapidly while one federal consumer minister after another wrestles with reforms of the toothless Combines Investigation Act. The Americans, on the other hand, have recognized the importance of having tough anti-trust laws. Their system pits business against business, for small and medium-sized firms can blow the whistle on big marketplace bullies when necessary, thus protecting the fastest-growing and most innovative businesses in any economy. Perhaps the Americans are more attuned to this because of their respect for individual freedoms. Restraint of trade and other anti-competitive abuses destroy an individual's right to ply his chosen trade.

Cartels also rob consumers of choices and bargains. The best example of such marketplace abuse occurred in 1986, when Canadian motorists were deprived for months of the benefits of collapsing oil prices, benefits that American motorists enjoyed immediately. Only under the glare of publicity and after Opposition battering did Canadian oil companies begin to reduce gasoline prices. But prices for diesel fuel and home heating oil actually increased in many parts of the country to make up for lower gasoline prices.

In March 1986, following a series of articles I had written in the *Toronto Star*, criticizing these and other pricing practices, Imperial Oil and Petro-Canada spokesmen actually admitted to me that they had sold Canadian gasoline to Americans for up to 7.5 cents a litre less than they were charging Canadians. PetroCan chairman Wilbert Hopper subsequently said this was a slip-up by an "overenthusiastic salesman in Vancouver" that would never happen again. But Imperial's chairman Arden Haynes said plainly, "Why would we sell to competitors? And if we used it ourselves to reduce prices, we'd end up taking market share away from someone who would drop their prices and get that market share back from us." In other words, Haynes is a perfect example of Canada's cartelists, who live in fear lest competition ever break out.

Industry-wide explanations during the period between December 1985 and March 1986, when oil prices were falling by 60 per cent, were no more satisfactory. Canadian oil companies said it took eighty days for crude to be transported and processed for consumption, and because of this delay they could not afford to pass along immediate savings without massive losses. The Americans did not use excuses, but competed almost immediately. Canadian explanations were feeble defences for cartelism, while the Americans competed because their government has understood for years how markets work and how to police them to ensure that they work.

The result is that about 40 per cent of U.S. gasoline stations are independents, compared with Canada's paltry 20 per cent. The American wholesale and refinery sectors are characterized by literally dozens of independents in many regions, while in Canada five major refiners reign over 86 per cent of the country's entire marketplace: Petro-Canada, Imperial, Shell Canada,

Texaco Canada, and Irving Oil. Because they dominate refining, they also dominate gasoline stations, because they supply them with products although they also own competing gasoline stations. This is a conflict of interest that should never have been allowed: refiners are at once competitors and suppliers to independents, which allows them to ensure that their competition never enjoys pricing advantages.

The U.S. government jealously guards competition, a cornerstone of capitalism. When Texaco's parent company took over Getty Oil in 1984, the U.S. marketplace watchdog, the Federal Trade Commission, forced Texaco to sell off much of its wholesale and refinery operations in New England, because the takeover had resulted in four firms controlling 70 per cent of the market. When Gulf was taken over by Chevron in 1985, the commission ordered Chevron to divest several thousand gasoline stations and several refineries in certain regions because of concentration levels. Whether in oil or in other industries, what is intolerable in the U.S. is the norm in Canada.

Canadians have yet to understand that competition creates jobs and opportunities and enhances a nation's economic well-being, because it imposes economic efficiencies.

It is Canada's misfortune that most Canadian politicians have been concerned with how to hand out money and win votes, rather than with how to create economic wealth. Pierre Trudeau, whose wealth was the result of his father selling a chain of gasoline stations to Imperial Oil, said shortly after becoming prime minister that if he had to choose between the growth of the GNP and an improvement in the quality of life, he would disregard the economics. Unfortunately, he followed through.

Without regulation, Canada's corporate barons have played fast and loose with tax and securities laws, and sometimes their actions have bordered on theft. Canada has not come to grips with securities rules that address the level of concentration that exists. This is due to lack of knowledge on the part of most Canadians. And it is hardly surprising. Nearly one out of three Canadians works for a non-profit enterprise (mostly governments, their agencies, and Crown corporations). That means one-third of all Canadian workers do not live under bottom-line discipline. And Canada's history has not been dogged by the strings of financial scandals that led to consumer movements after America's industrialization. Canadians simply do not have experience dealing with crooks, nor do they have a heritage of fighting for economic rights. So they do not understand these rights. Neither does Parliament or the courts.

Not surprisingly, certain politicians, the churches, and grass-roots organizations have taken the matter into their own hands, fighting concentration on an ad hoc basis. This has given rise to Canada's unique forms of "people's capitalism," such as credit unions and cooperatives. Uniquely Canadian counterweights to the concentration of power in the hands of the banks or grain merchants, they have been joined by 1,000 Crown corporations, aimed at stemming foreign investment or central Canada's industrial and monetary power.

In some cases, public enterprise in Canada has been necessary to fill the vacuum created by a Canadian private sector almost totally populated by paper entrepreneurs, who are uninterested in projects that add to the nation's wealth. But in many other cases, the managers of our public enterprises put politics before economics, creating useless schemes or feather-bedding government services as make-work mega-projects.

Lacking a vibrant, open, and competitive marketplace, Canada has created jobs by spending billions providing top-notch government services, entitlements, schools, hospitals, airports, and roads. But a nation without potholes is a nation of pothole-fillers — and huge mortgages. The tragedy for Canada is that far too large a portion of our economy is run about as efficiently as our post office. And the rest is run for the sake of a handful of wealthy, family-owned mutual funds.

This book is a bid for change, to curb abuses and steer our entrepreneurs towards activities that will make the pie as a whole grow, not just encourage the trading back and forth of pieces. Right now, it is a hockey game with no referees in sight. Without new rules, we hurtle towards financial feudalism, with our children as economic serfs. It is feudalism or socialism. The choice is ours.

1

THE DYNASTIES

THE IRVINGS

NEW BRUNSWICK is a company town, and its proprietor is K. C. Irving. The name may not be a household word outside the province, but it should be, because Kenneth Colin Irving is quite possibly the richest Canadian in the world. Some 400 Irving companies ring up an estimated $2 billion a year in sales, have up to $8 billion in assets, and employ 25,000 persons, or one out of every twelve workers in the province. Irving's empire represents 25 per cent of the gross provincial product, the total of all goods and services produced in New Brunswick. And K. C. owns the whole shooting match.

While the Reichmanns and the Bronfmans may control more assets, Irving is personally richer, as the sole owner of shares in an empire with very little debt. He is also more politically powerful. As he built his empire from 1924 onwards, he functioned as a private-sector potentate with a great deal of influence over politicians. In the 1960s, Liberal premier Louis Robichaud took on K. C., eventually losing at the polls to Irving-endorsed Tory Richard Hatfield, but not before leaving a legacy of government provisions that permanently clipped Irving's corporate wings. These included campaign contribution limits and disclosure requirements, designed to curb his influence.

However, Irving still has power that few tycoons possess because his virtual media monopoly in New Brunswick lets him shape public opinion. And even more importantly, his companies are so pervasive in New Brunswick that he has positioned himself to become the principal instrument of regional development in the province. Inescapably, and regardless of who is in office, it remains true that what is good for the Irving empire is good for New Brunswick.

"K. C. *is* New Brunswick's private sector," says John Rocca, a lawyer and owner of the Rocca Group, a real estate development company in Saint John. "Irving is the last of the great nineteenth-century industrialists. His is the only empire in Canada not built on illegal booze, stolen money, stock markets, or land speculation. He's a builder. One of North America's greatest industrialists and probably its richest man."

While admirable in a business sense, the Irvings have been questionable corporate citizens. Their prosperity has been based, in some measure, on an ability to lobby politicians, an aggressive desire to erect barriers against competitors, and an absence of social responsibility on specific issues such as pollution — all of which may produce great profits, but raise troublesome questions for a society.

Since 1971, K. C. has been a 181-days-a-year Canadian, living the rest of the year in tax-free Bermuda. It is a self-imposed exile, designed to save the Irving dynasty hundreds of millions of dollars in capital gains taxes. And even though his three middle-aged sons run day-to-day operations of his 400 companies, he is the sole shareholder and is consulted on all major decisions.

Annual meetings of the largest company, Irving Oil Ltd., are held quietly in the Golden Ball Building in Saint John. Chevron Corp. of San Francisco has been Irving's partner in this company for more than two decades; it is a mutually beneficial match. But the involvement in Irving Oil is a noticeable departure of policy for this multinational giant because K. C. has the upper hand and owns 51.2 per cent of Irving Oil's shares. The board of directors includes three representatives from Chevron, Irving's three sons — Jim, John, and Arthur — and two Irving executives. Every year, the routine is the same: K. C. sits outside the boardroom until the directors' meeting is completed, then he comes in and sits down, and the shareholders' meeting begins.

Nicknamed "Gassy," "Oily," and "Greasy" as youngsters during the Depression, the three sons delegate very little to others along the way. James operates the family's dry-dock and marine businesses, Arthur, its oil companies, and John, the rest. "Jim is a smart man and very nice," says Louis Robichaud, "but the other two I don't care to comment on."

Observers say the Irving sons are not as cunning nor as dynamic as their father, who was once spotted at a Montreal airport carrying on three conversations at three separate phone booths. However, there's little evidence of any dynastic decay. Despite their billions, the Irvings are still imbued with the Protestant work ethic. The sons live in modest homes, draw small salaries, and are listed in the Saint John telephone book. They travel mostly by

commercial airline and lead low-key lives. It's a family that does not have —
and would not tolerate — high-livers, playboys, or layabouts.

"He trained his sons and grandsons to be workaholics like him," says
Rocca, who owns a Saint John weekly, the only newspaper in the province not
owned by Irving. "There are three grandsons, and apparently the most interesting one is Jim's son, John, who has a Harvard MBA. Apparently he's
tireless, like the old man. Some Irving people told me he was working on a
company project in Cape Breton Island til nine o'clock one night. He and the
others decided to go to a party, but he left at eleven and drove around the area
checking out all the Irving gas stations."

The empire's six-storey headquarters opens onto a graveyard, where rest
the remains of United Empire Loyalists who settled here after the American
Revolution. Irving employees often picnic in this square, eating sandwiches
on pastel park benches surrounded by decaying tombstones. Beside the building is a familiar Maritime landmark: a red-white-and-blue Irving gasoline station. Across the street are the offices and press rooms of the only daily
newspapers serving this sea-swept city of 135,000 (owned by Irving). Next
door to this are the studios of Irving's lucrative television station. Irving's
presence is simply everywhere: his cranes dominate Saint John's port and
skyline. And the name IRVING, spelled out on white storage tanks, stretches
for a mile or more along the route between the city and its airport, welcoming
visitors.

The Irving group of companies is big by anybody's standards. It includes
the country's largest shipyard and dry-dock facilities. Irving Oil is one of
Canada's ten largest oil companies, with 3,000 service stations in Atlantic
Canada and the Ottawa Valley, the country's largest refinery, as well as untold
holdings in oil and gas discoveries in western Canada. K. C.'s forestry business is world-scale, including half a dozen pulp and paper mills and sawmills
and title to 1.5 million acres of timberlands in New Brunswick and Maine, an
area equivalent in size to Prince Edward Island. These land holdings, which
he owns outright, make him the largest private landowner in the Maritimes.
He also owns fleets of ships, trucks, buses, and railway cars, most of the
media in the province, stores selling cars, food, hardware, drugs, and
construction materials, and factories spewing out everything from pre-fab
houses to concrete, steel, and hundreds more products.

It is hard to get an exact picture of the scope of the Irving empire. None of
the companies are publicly owned, and the Irvings fiercely protect their

privacy through a complicated and impenetrable corporate structure. In 1971, the Seafarers International Union failed to negotiate contracts for seamen on six ships in the Irving fleet because the provincial labour board couldn't untangle the complex Irving corporate ownership to find out who the actual owner of the ships was. Disclosure could have been forced through the courts, but the union decided it was not financially worthwhile and gave up.

Secrecy is sacrosanct, regardless of cost. The Royal Commission on Corporate Concentration came close to suing the family in the mid-1970s for failing to provide basic financial information, saying its run-in with the Irvings "is a vivid illustration of the deficiencies in the law, which should be remedied." And in 1982, answering a subpoena to testify before the Restrictive Trade Practices Commission's inquiry into oil competition, Arthur Irving stonewalled when asked for information, under oath.

"No," he said to the first query, when asked to confirm Irving Oil information, according to transcripts.

Asked why not, he replied: "Why should I?" and said he wouldn't return to the inquiry. And he didn't.

Since 1952, Irving has owned all the province's newspapers, but he kept this secret until 1965, when the revelation was made by Senator Charles McElman, formerly Robichaud's executive assistant. This sparked a number of probes into the Irving media empire. In 1969 the Senate Special Committee on Mass Media described Irving's media monopoly as "about as flagrant an example of abusing the public interest as you're likely to find in Canada."

Meanwhile, federal combines investigators were poring over company documents; they eventually laid charges of anti-competitive practices against the company. The case came to court in 1975 and lasted for nearly a year. At the end, the Irvings were convicted, fined $150,000, and ordered to sell two of their newspapers. However, the litigious Irvings fought all the way to the Supreme Court of Canada, and in 1976 the conviction was overturned.

Some years later, the Royal Commission on Newspapers, under Tom Kent, took another look at concentration of ownership in the media, commenting that "Irving papers are noteworthy for their obeisance to every industrial interest. They are not known for probing investigations into pollution, occupational health dangers, industrial wastes, or any of the other darker consequences of industrial power."

Kent commissioners were particularly upset at media cross-ownership in New Brunswick, where the Irvings control newspapers, television, and radio.

At the time, Arthur Irving warned the commission: "I own 40 per cent of CHSJ [television station] and I intend to keep it. It is our privilege to own it, and nobody in this God-given room is going to take it away from us."

The Liberals placed a restriction on the Irvings in 1982, when the cabinet ordered the Canadian Radio-television and Telecommunications Commission to refuse licence renewals to television stations owned by newspaper companies in the same market. The Irvings took the government to court over this directive, challenging its legality. Continuing the action became unnecessary in June 1985 when the federal Tory cabinet revoked the directive.

The legendary Irving litigiousness is rooted in their father's Presbyterianism: K. C. and the boys don't drink, smoke, or swear. But more importantly, they are imbued with the moral certainty of Calvinists and the conviction to fight the good fight, no matter how large or trifling the issue. Fearlessly, and with the fervour of Richard Lion-Heart, K. C. Irving has taken to task giants such as Imperial Oil, Canadian National, and the government. Once a lawyer advised him to settle a case against a gigantic multinational out of court, and he said, "I don't believe I asked you for a verdict. I was inquiring if you'd care to represent me."

Likewise, he has never hesitated to go after small fry and will do so without concern about costs or about accusations that he is being a bully: the principle is the thing to K. C. Irving. People in New Brunswick still talk about an incident back in 1948 when thousands of Irving logs, heading down the St. John River towards Irving's pulp mill, broke up in a storm. Winds and waves scattered the logs far and wide along the coast, and a few locals began salvaging wood and reselling it. Two men were charged for "stealing" fifty-four logs, according to Russell Hunt and Robert Campbell in their book *K. C. Irving: The Art of the Industrialist*.

Even as recently as 1985, Irving's newspapers blared headlines that a new invisible ink was being applied experimentally to Irving trees so that culprits stealing them could be caught. Such feistiness may seem unduly harsh in some instances, but scrappiness has served Irving well. He has usually won against the giants, and has also avoided a great many more battles because he has taught would-be rivals that he means business.

And when it comes to guts, few can match K. C. In 1951, he nearly died when his plane burst into flames and crashed on take-off. But witnesses say he crawled out of the wreckage with singed hair and went back to the office. He was similarly unimpressed during a labour strike when he saw a truck driver balk at passing through the picket lines. "You may be big, but I'm bigger," he told the strikers, and the next day, when a non-striking truck driver refused to cross, Irving took the wheel himself and plowed through. The union laid charges against him for reckless driving but withdrew them after the dispute was settled.

His first major fight involved Imperial Oil, Canada's largest oil company, in his home village of Buctouche, an Acadian village that lived on oyster fishing and rum-running during Prohibition. K. C. was born there in 1899, one of James Irving's four children. A Scottish immigrant, his father made the first family fortune by running a general store and small sawmill. K. C. was an indifferent student, but an enterprising youngster.

More significantly, however, K. C. had a fascination for making things work, and spent many hours taking his father's car apart and putting it back together again. He never finished university, but trained as a pilot during the First World War. He nearly emigrated, with a buddy, to make his fortune — a choice that many New Brunswick entrepreneurs have made, such as Lord Beaverbrook, movie magnate Louis B. Mayer, and Sir James Dunn. But, heading for Australia, he got only as far as Vancouver. He returned to sleepy Buctouche in 1923 and decided to sell cars. By 1924, he had his own dealership.

That led to the car repair business and eventually to selling gasoline, which he bought from Imperial and resold. But the oil giant pulled the rug out from under Irving and suddenly gave his franchise to a "full-time" operator — mostly to satisfy complaints from his father's business rivals that they resented dealing with the son of a competitor.

Bankrolled by his father, K. C. went out and built the prototype for his chain of service stations. "It was beautiful to behold," he said once in a rare interview. "I still think there's something beautiful about an Irving service station."

As he began to build more stations, he created a construction company, and when it ran out of stations to build, it began building houses. In 1937, with his chain prospering, Imperial caused more trouble and talked Canadian National Railways into applying a little pressure on Irving, who was eating into Imperial's gasoline market. CNR hiked its transportation rates and told Irving to stop shipping his oil by boat up the St. John River. Not only did he refuse, but he stopped dealing with CNR altogether and built his own fleet of barges and trucks. That eventually led, in the 1950s, to his purchase of a shipbuilding company as well as plants to make his own trucks, buses, tires, steel, and components. Another string added to his bow was a fleet of ocean-going vessels he accumulated to bring him oil products so that his gas stations would not be dependent upon domestic oil companies for supply. He also made a partnership deal with Chevron Corp. of San Francisco (then known as Standard Oil of California), and the two built their own refinery in Saint John.

Irving also parlayed his father's sawmill business into one of the largest forestry businesses in Canada. His father died during the Depression, leaving his three daughters and two sons a general store, a sawmill, and 7,000 acres of timberlands. The others, including K. C.'s brother John, who became a Montreal stockbroker, sold out. K. C. expanded the firm greatly and in 1941 bought control of New Brunswick Railway, solely to get its million acres of timberlands. He built mills, trucks, and barges to transport his logs, and in 1938 he bought a bankrupt veneer plant. With an ample supply of wood products sewn up, he began buying up his own customers such as newspapers, hardware stores, and building-supply factories. Sometimes he created a customer, as he did when he started a pre-fab housing company.

The Second World War was good for the Irvings, as wood prices jumped. But more importantly, his veneer plant landed plum defence contracts from Britain, compliments of his good friend Lord Beaverbrook, who served as a wartime minister in Winston Churchill's cabinet. Beaverbrook tossed such a sizeable bone Irving's way that Canadian Veneers was the world's biggest veneer plant for many years to follow.

Sometimes Irving ran roughshod over people without an ulterior motive. Hunt and Campbell's book describes the construction of a steel plant by Irving in the 1960s, which ignored zoning requirements, cutting off streets and access to a fish store. Irving was never prosecuted or reprimanded, even though the store had to throw out its entire inventory for five days in a row until construction ended.

It was business as usual for the Irvings until 1960, when Robichaud, a feisty country lawyer, was elected premier. Ironically, K. C. had supported Robichaud and personally congratulated him on the night of his election. But the "honeymoon" period lasted only two years, until the premier made a deal with Belgian-owned Rothesay Paper, giving it land for a pulp and paper mill that Irving had wanted for his own use.

"He tried to prevent Rothesay Paper from coming in at all, but we accommodated both by giving Irving the land he wanted for his dry dock and giving more land, farther away, to Rothesay," Robichaud recalls. "But the land was only part of the reason why Mr. Irving didn't want them in. He was the sole buyer of pulpwood in the area and the sole supplier of the finished product too. He had a monopoly."

The next problem came when Robichaud used generous land concessions to entice an Italian firm to build another pulp and paper mill in the province. Irving was furious, but his anger is shown in subtle ways. "Kenneth never threatens you directly, but you know from his newspapers what he thinks. And there were certain private conversations with him and his executives that shall forever remain private," says Robichaud.

Another irritant arose when Robichaud launched a royal commission into the province's municipalities and recommended an end to the types of tax concessions and grants the Irving companies had so successfully extracted over the years. There were many examples of thirty-year tax freezes and multi-million-dollar grants.

"His papers went berserk against me because the commission recommended that all concessions be ended retroactively. I never felt that way, but he wouldn't listen and then it was war," recalls Robichaud. "I had my words twisted around by his newspapers. The damage was so severe in terms of the misunderstanding that a team of my ministers had to travel across the province to get our point to the people. I got on his television station, but had to pay for it."

The final straw came in 1965, when Robichaud stopped an Irving squeeze play involving the building of a smelter in Bathurst by Brunswick Mining & Smelting. "I wanted it developed, the province had put $40 million into the project, but there were terrible cost overruns," says Robichaud. "Some 196 of Irving's companies were involved in the construction and supply of the whole thing. At the same time, he was buying the company's shares as it was going downhill."

Robichaud helped Noranda take over Brunswick. Irving lost out, sued, and won $10 million for unfulfilled contract obligations. Despite that high settlement, Irving was furious. His newspapers jumped all over Robichaud's government, he threatened to shut down the province, and he even ordered the removal of both Robichaud's name and that of another critic from two ships already christened. And to this day, there are two no-name ships in the Irving fleet that are testimony to his anger. On their hulls are numerals instead.

In 1967, Irving became determined to remove Robichaud, and to do so he recruited a former federal Tory member of Parliament, Charles Van Horn, away from his home in Arizona. Van Horn's candidacy enraged Robichaud, as did remarks by Arthur Irving, who crowed, according to Robichaud, "My father's never lost a New Brunswick election in his life."

Robichaud beat Van Horn in 1967, but he lost the next provincial election in 1970 against Tory Richard Hatfield, supported by Irving. Van Horn also won in the 1970 provincial election, and briefly became one of Hatfield's cabinet ministers.

"But he was fired by Hatfield and charges of influence-peddling were laid. That's why I fought like crazy against him in 1967 for the sake of New Brunswick. He was a menace to democracy, and if he was elected it would have been Irving's fault," says Robichaud. (Van Horn left the province and has not been tried on the influence-peddling charges.)

With Robichaud removed, the Irvings settled back to business. In 1974, Irving Oil landed a lucrative $212-million oil-supply contract with the province's utility. Irving officials argued the deal was necessary to pay for an expansion of his refinery. Over the years, he had also extracted many tax concessions and grants out of the government for his refinery, always maintaining it made very little, if any, profit. But Senator McElman pointed out this anomaly in a Senate speech during expansion talks.

"The price [of oil] is so high that the poor refinery operation is in trouble. Some years it cannot even show a profit or pay the national wage rate to its employees. Other years it can squeeze out a small profit and pay a correspondingly small corporate tax to the federal government. It is really to be pitied.

"It is very interesting to note at this very point in time [1973] this refinery, because of this arrangement, either loses money on paper or pays a very small tax. At this very moment it is in the process of almost tripling its production capacity, at the expenditure of many millions of dollars, from 50,000 barrels a day to 135,000 [now it is 300,000] — presumably in order to lose more money."

Just before this deal, in 1972, K. C. had moved to Bermuda, where there are no corporate income taxes, in order to get around capital gains taxes. Other Canadians didn't follow their assets to Bermuda, but merely set up Bermudian companies. Not K. C.: he became a Bermuda resident because directors of Bermuda companies must be residents and, while some people would feel confident appointing "trustees" such as local lawyers to act as directors, that isn't the Irving style.

What followed was a Revenue Canada probe into Irving Oil and its Bermuda connection, culminating in a massive reassessment in 1979 of Irving Oil's taxes. Revenue officials claim Irving Oil made $142 million more in profits between 1971 and 1975 than it declared in Canada, for tax purposes. Profits were understated, said the government, because Irving purposely paid its Bermuda subsidiary $142 million more for oil than it should have, so that profits would be made in Bermuda, which has no corporate taxes. (A total of $1.2 billion worth of oil flowed via Irving's Bermuda subsidiary during that six-year period.) Irving counter-sued the government over the reassessment; the case is still before the courts.

Another tax battle erupted in 1979: Irving Oil failed to report $800 million in petroleum exports — equivalent to one-fifth the gross provincial product — from its New Brunswick refinery. The federal finance minister, John Crosbie, called the reporting failure "inadvertent office error," and put the best possible face on it by saying it meant Canada's balance of payments were better than thought.

The Irving corporate track record on pollution is abysmal. For instance, in 1951 Irving decided to expand an old pulp mill he had bought in 1947. Using his $20-million plant expansion plans as bait, he extracted a concession from politicians to freeze his taxes for thirty years; he also obtained an exemption from expropriation, freedom to spill wastes into the St. John River, and immunity from "nuisance cases" in the courts over pollution or other problems. As recently as 1976, Irving was acquitted of polluting the St. John River even though tests revealed that rainbow trout died in three minutes in the Irving pulp and paper mill's sewers. Atlantic salmon died within thirty minutes. For decades, the stench of the Irving sawmill hung over Saint John, until Irving closed it in the late 1970s (not because of protests or pleas by local officials, but strictly because the mill was no longer profitable).

Such stonewalling has saved money, but the greatest wealth has been made through Irving Oil's controversial Bermuda company, called Irving California Oil. It was hard to lose money trading oil in the 1970s, when prices increased twelvefold. By the time tankers reached their destinations, prices had almost always risen.

K. C.'s partnership with Chevron enabled him to play in the big oil leagues, a feat normally impossible for a smallish, regional player from New Brunswick. The partnership provided him with contacts, muscle — in the form of protection from Uncle Sam, which looks after the interests of multinationals like Chevron — and the opportunity to share oil-trading profits with one of the Seven Sisters.

"In the 1970s he really got into the big time," says Rocca, "buying oil from Saudi Arabia with Chevron, not for the refinery but to resell on the spot market. His retained earnings went from $30 million a year in 1972 to $150 million in 1978.

The Irvings are also enormous players in exploration and production in western Canada, through their association with Chevron's Canadian subsidiary, Chevron Canada Resources in Calgary. They have invested up to $75 million a year in Chevron's drilling programs in return for a piece of the action — and Chevron is one of the country's most successful finders.

Canada's shift to world oil prices will no doubt benefit Irving Oil, but its other businesses have certainly been in the doldrums. The recession in the early 1980s forced significant layoffs in its transportation, refining, manufacturing, mining, and forestry businesses. However, the Irvings have a couple of new cards up their sleeves.

In 1980, the Irvings entered into head-to-head competition with New Brunswick's other successful family, the McCains of frozen food fame, by purchasing Cavendish Farms, with a processing plant in Prince Edward Island and an option to buy 2,400 hectares of potato land. Several thousand acres of Irving timberlands farther north have been cleared, presumably for cultivation. The price of farmland in and around McCain potato country near Florenceville has been bid up as Irving interests buy farms. The McCains are non-plussed by these moves, and as ex-Irving employees, the brothers issued a warning, Irving-style: in 1980, they sued Cavendish Farms for copyright infringement, claiming its frozen food package designs were illegally close to theirs. They withdrew the suit in 1983, but not before making a point.

It remains to be seen if there is room for two frozen food empires in New Brunswick. But the Irvings' future as industrialists might be assured with the landing of a $3-billion contract with the Department of National Defence to build frigates for the Canadian navy. In effect, the contract is vital because it will give the Irvings an opportunity to modernize their shipbuilding business as well as the chance to design a state-of-the-art high technology, which can be sold elsewhere.

In fact, as the principal instrument of regional development, the Irvings will always prosper. "He has no political power any more. Just one week after he gave $300,000 to the city of Saint John to pay for the summer games, he tendered for the city's oil contract and didn't get it," says Rocca. "But he has economic power, and that's better. He has votes. He controls a tremendous block of votes. He can't deliver it, but they have the same interests. And Irving will never be allowed to go broke but he will always have to be bailed out. He has reached an optimum size."

Robichaud disagrees. "I think economic power is powerless. Groups like the Chamber of Commerce may have some influence, but not the individual billionaires. Even if you socialize and accept contributions from them, the degree of dangerous influence depends on your own vulnerability. No vulture is going to take advantage of me. One tried and he failed lamentably."

THE MCCAINS

IT'S SAFE TO SAY that whatever the Irvings don't own in New Brunswick, the McCains do.

As you make your way up the scenic St. John River Valley on the Trans-Canada Highway, you can begin to detect McCain headquarters, tiny Florenceville, from three kilometres away. It smells like a fast-food outlet, because the village's only factory belches out steam from its french-fry cookers three shifts a day. The route to the village is lined with miles of seedlings, tiny spuds sprouting in the rust-brown soil. The highway is clogged with trucks hauling potatoes from clapboard farms to food factories. And there are the ones that got away, spuds smashed on the road's shoulder. This is potato country. This is McCain country.

McCain Foods Ltd. is a global food conglomerate. Sprouting from New Brunswick soil and generously fertilized by government grants and loan guarantees, Florenceville is the french-fry capital of the world. Harrison and Wallace McCain make more frozen french fries than anyone else in the world. The firm buys half the potatoes grown in Canada. Once the fry frenzy peaked in the mid-1970s, as a saturation point was reached, McCain expanded into other lucrative fast-food niches, and in no time it has become one of the world's biggest frozen pizza manufacturers. It buys one-fifth of the cheese produced in Ontario to ship to its pizza factories in New Brunswick. It also sells more fruit juices in Canada than any other company, after a shopping spree of acquisitions that began in 1982. Not surprisingly, to move all this stuff around the continent, McCain owns Day & Ross, eastern Canada's largest trucking company.

In addition, the family owns fertilizer and farm implement plants, sells potato-harvesting equipment and front-end loaders around the world, and operates beef cattle and dairy farms. It also steadily accumulated shares in the food giant Canada Packers — four times the size of McCain Foods — and by 1985 had 12 per cent of its shares. It sold these in 1985 because Canada Packers management refused to let it have board seats, but it may return. In 1979, the McCains nearly bought Eastern Provincial Airways and Quebecair, but lost out to another takeover artist. Since 1978, they have owned 25 per cent of Commerce Capital Corp. Ltd. of Toronto, engaged in mortgage lending, real estate, and other financial services.

The McCains have farmed the St. John River Valley since 1830, but it wasn't until the late 1940s that Andrew McCain, a teetotalling Baptist who nonetheless gambled on the stock market, hit it big. And unlike his father, Hugh McCain, who speculated in hay during the Boer War and lost a bundle, Andrew left Harrison, Wallace, and his four other children a small fortune that became the grub-stake in 1957 for a food empire. He also left them with a lucrative seed potato export business, hundreds of acres of land in this fertile potato country, and a triple-A credit rating among fellow-farmers, many of whom he had propped up during the Depression.

"It's a lot of satisfaction to have a large number of people working and to drive around the countryside here and look at the quality of the buildings, the automobiles, the quality of life and compare that with 1950. I'm not suggesting we deserve all the credit for the change, but we deserve some of it and the difference is enormous. Twenty-five years ago every building here leaned," said Harrison McCain, chairman of the board, in a magazine interview.

Stocky, bull-necked, and balding, Harrison McCain looks like a man who would be more comfortable atop a four-wheel-drive Massey-Ferguson than sitting in an executive's swivel chair. But Harrison and his younger brother, Wallace, were never cut out to be sons of the soil. While their two older brothers, Andrew and Robert, minded their father's potato export business, raised cattle, and farmed, the two younger sons went to university and did the only other thing that comes naturally to New Brunswickers: they worked for the pervasive Irving empire.

In no time flat, following their graduations from university after the Second World War, they became rising stars in the Irving network. By 1956, Harrison was fidgety, fed up that he couldn't own a piece in any of the hundreds of privately held Irving companies. So he took an investment dealers' extension course and toyed with the idea of buying seats on the Toronto and Montreal stock exchanges.

The success that followed was a classic case of being in the right place at the right time. Also helpful were astute political connections, acquired by marriage and all steadily cultivated with campaign contributions.

Florenceville is only a few kilometres from the Maine–New Brunswick border, and it was this proximity that gave the McCain brothers the brainstorm for their billion-dollar enterprise. "Over in Maine, General Foods had a factory doing french fries and peas. So we figured that, if they were doing it over on the American side, we can do it over here," Harrison stated.

At the time, the average consumption of frozen french fries in North America was practically zero. Now, every man, woman, and child eats eleven pounds of french fries a year, at home or out.

Encouraged by the entire family, Harrison and Wallace set about to build their frozen food empire. Robert and Andrew continued to farm and run the export business. Their two sisters, Marie and Eleanor, remained shareholders, but their husbands' careers took them away from home.

Now the company has built an impressive multinational network of nineteen processing plants in six countries, out of a low-rise headquarters in Florenceville, population 1,000. Since 1957, the company has grown from 30 employees and $152,000 in sales to 7,500 workers and nearly $1 billion a year in revenue.

Florenceville must be one of the world's unlikeliest headquarters for a global multinational. It is also an expensive place from which to operate. To save its executives time, the company had to build its own airport, buy two jets, and employ four pilots on virtually permanent stand-by. Harrison spends 140 nights a year away from home, mostly in Toronto, but has fiercely resisted the temptation to move. The brothers and their executives live in posh homes on River View Drive, perched on a hill across the river overlooking the factory and head office. At the end of the street, on McCain Lane, is the family's cemetery, where their parents and brothers are buried.

The McCains are truly civic-minded. Harrison, a lifelong Liberal Party member, has served on the boards of many charitable organizations and as a

Petro-Canada director in addition to his many corporate directorships. In the early 1980s, he organized a citizens' group to take over two failing lumber businesses, for which he took no share of profits or ownership. While laudable, this angered Harrison's former employers, the Irvings, who also sell lumber.

In fact, the Irvings and the McCains have been battling for quite a while. Sparks flew after McCain dropped Irving as an oil supplier for its hundreds of trucks in the mid-1970s. And the gloves have been off ever since. In 1977, Irving lent millions to a McCain competitor, C. M. McLean, so that he could expand in order to snare a McDonald's contract. McLean was eventually gobbled up by the Irvings, pitting the McCains and the Irvings directly against each other. Irving also got into the trucking business in a bigger way, and he has been steadily buying property in the McCains' potato country as well as clearing several thousand acres of timberlands, used for logging in the past.

But the McCains have fought back. In 1980, McCain sued McLean for copyright infringement on its packages. It dropped the action when the Irvings renamed their food company Cavendish Farms. In 1983, McCain's American subsidiary blew the whistle on the Irvings to Washington trade officials, sparking an inquiry into charges that Cavendish was dumping frozen potatoes onto the U.S. market.

The Irvings are not the only family attempting to frustrate the McCains' ambitions. Canada Packers' largest shareholder, the McLean family trusts, with 23 per cent, would not allow the McCains to have board seats despite their large shareholding. These two are also competitors, with York Farms making many of the same products that McCain makes.

Trying to beat the cunning McCains in the fast-food sweepstakes will not be easy. They are already in first place with so many products. They are also flush with cash. In 1984 alone, the firm opened a new truck terminal in Ontario and bought a Winnipeg trucking firm, a fish plant in Britain, an Ontario cheese plant, an air freight company, a competitor's pizza operation, and a plant in Maine that processes peas and broccoli from 7,000 acres.

Gregarious and charming, the McCains are nonetheless rarely interviewed. Their reluctance is similar to the secretiveness of the Irvings or the concern about safety of the security-absorbed Ghermezians, but it is due to their run-ins with the media. The family won $60,000 after suing the small rural newspaper *Farm & Country* for libel over an editorial it ran in 1977, titled "A corporate empire too big to swallow." The article, described by the New

Brunswick trial judge as "grossly disparaging," claimed that New Brunswick farmers were being ripped off by the McCains, and it upset the family greatly. A year later, in 1978, CBC's *Fifth Estate* criticized subsidies by Canadian tax-payers to help the McCains' worldwide expansion and described the extent of the family's influence on the province's political life.

As if to prove the show's point, an impressive number of the region's VIPs leaped to the family's defence and severely criticized the program. Several senators and members of Parliament and Premier Richard Hatfield were among those defending the "McCain boys." Senator Margaret Norrie, a Nova Scotia Liberal and Wallace's mother-in-law, said the show's hostess, Adrienne Clarkson, "must have had a perverted mind to work so hard to find such ugly things to say and insinuate about McCain Foods."

The truth is that the McCains are exceedingly well connected politically. Wallace is married to the Senator's daughter, and Harrison is married to the daughter of John Babbitt McNair, former Liberal premier, chief justice, and eventually lieutenant-governor. And such political connections undoubtedly played a big role in gaining huge grants for McCain along the way, an esti-mated $8 million in provincial loan guarantees and $7 million from Ottawa's Department of Regional Economic Expansion.

"In the early days we had some government support," Harrison told *Executive* magazine. "It was started with some money of our own, a $100,000 line of credit from the Bank of Nova Scotia, and $420,000 in government bonds."

Walter Stewart's 1974 book on the Canadian food business, *Hard to Swallow*, noted that Harrison and Wallace bankrolled Trudeau's 1968 Liberal leadership campaign, saying, "By one of those coincidences that never fail to astonish, the McCain company had the honour to be offered the very first grant under the Trudeau government's new Regional Development Incentives Act."

To be fair, it is not just job-hungry Canada that is more than willing to contribute a few million to people like the McCains who have a track record of bringing prosperity to a region. In 1982, the French government kicked in 25 per cent of the cost of building an $8-million french-fry plant in France, which now employs 300. Similarly, Manitoba put up half of the $14 million to entice McCain to build a plant to process local farmers' potatoes.

Despite its size, the firm is still very much a family affair. The brothers and their sister Marie's husband, J. D. Sutherland, are on the board of directors. Only two formal board meetings have been held in twenty-six years, and

Harrison, the board's chairman, attended neither. Of the twenty-four McCain offspring, only five work for the family business: Harrison and Wallace have two children each on board, Andrew has one.

But the latest family members are undoubtedly imbued with the same entre-preneurial spirit that has infused this high-rolling family for several genera-tions. Fast food is no fad, and the McCains continue to push out into other new areas: from chips to pizza to juices to desserts and fully cooked frozen diet meals. Without a doubt — and trouble from the Irvings and the McLeans aside — the McCains are well positioned to remain kings of the freezer case.

THE SOBEYS AND THE JODREYS

THE CONSTANTLY FEUDING McCains and Irvings dominate New Brunswick's economic life, but across the Bay of Fundy, Nova Scotia's two most promi-nent families — the Sobeys and the Jodreys — act like kin. In fact their unique, amiable partnership not only is a rarity, but has helped the two to fend off attacks from Upper Canadians as well as to gain footholds in companies across Canada with $10 billion in assets.

"Dad's philosophy was to take minority positions in companies with suc-cessful managements," says Donald Sobey, the lean and ginger-haired son of the first wealthy Sobey, Frank, who died in 1985 at the age of eighty-three. And Donald and his two brothers subscribe to hard work, as do the Jodreys. "I always remember reading about the original Rothschilds. What a family can do working together is fantastic. If they work apart, it's not nearly as success-ful. When a family doesn't work they lose it. I remember when we didn't have a refrigerator but an icebox. And we have raised our kids in a small town. It's better to live there in terms of perspective than living in the Bridle Path. I only come to Toronto for meetings."

Like other Maritime magnates, they are the antithesis of flamboyance. No Lear jets, Rolls-Royces, or condos for them. They drive ordinary cars, live in ordinary houses, and have ordinary summer cottages. God-fearing Christians, the current crop of Sobeys and Jodreys would be inconspicuous at a service club luncheon in Moose Jaw.

"Frank Sobey and his wife used to travel economy from Halifax to London, but then they'd go first-class all the way, with fancy hotels, limousines through Europe, and top restaurants. Back at home they'd never flaunt. They were brought up to never show off in front of the neighbours," says Harry Bruce, Halifax writer and official biographer of both the Jodreys and the Sobeys.

"Dad didn't like to show off," says Donald Sobey. "I remember he would take a new car and run it through puddles so nobody thought he was getting a big head. I guess it was his Scottish upbringing." The late Roy Jodrey was a workaholic whose idea of relaxation was to sit back and listen to the hum coming from his pulp mill and carton factory.

Both families mastermind their empires from tiny Nova Scotia villages. The Sobeys live and work in Stellarton, 130 kilometres northeast of Halifax, with a population of 5,435. This is where Donald Sobey's father, the family patriarch Frank Sobey, and his wife, Irene, raised their three sons and daughter while living over Frank's father's meat market on Main Street. Now Frank Sobey's three sons operate a vast food, drug, entertainment, resource, and real estate network through the family holding company, appropriately named Empire Inc.

The Jodreys live in Hantsport, a village of 1,395 residents, 65 kilometres northwest of Halifax. Their family holding company is called Scotia Investments Ltd. Snuggled in the scenic Annapolis Valley, Hantsport is where the late patriarch Roy A. Jodrey began by growing apples; then he moved into land, lumber, and the stock market. With the money he made before and after the Second World War, he took regular jaunts to St. James Street and Bay Street, where he made excellent contacts among bankers and brokers, becoming a master at their game. His contacts in Upper and Lower Canada's financial districts also resulted in another unique and highly profitable partnership with the Burns family of stock brokerage and insurance fame. The Jodreys and the Burnses still share a controlling interest, 46 per cent, in Crownx Inc.

Even though the Sobeys and the Jodreys operate quietly from rural bases, they definitely dominate their province's economy. In fact, what major industries they do not own either are government-owned or were attracted to Nova Scotia by Frank Sobey during the twelve years when he served as the province's unpaid ambassador in charge of getting new investment. A close friend of former premier and Tory leader Robert Stanfield, Frank Sobey was also a local politician, serving twenty-two years as Stellarton's mayor, unopposed at election time.

The Jodreys and the Sobeys both had their roots in rural Nova Scotia, but their wealth has been made in the cities. Some of their best deals have been defensive, and the two have been a feisty duo, repeatedly joining forces to repel rivals, real or imagined.

Virtually all of downtown Halifax is owned by them. Each family has 35 per cent of the shares of Halifax Developments, which, through various other companies, owns the seventeen-acre Scotia Square downtown mall, with one million square feet of office and retail space. Halifax Developments also owns 466 apartments in three towers nearby; the 312-room Château Halifax hotel; the nearby Scotia Royal Bank Tower, the Bank of Commerce Tower, and Barrington Place, including Delta's Barrington, a 203-room hotel; and two more office skyscrapers. The families also share 49 per cent of Nova Scotia Savings and Loan Co., with $600 million in assets as well as control over the province's largest employer, National Sea. And if both family empires were tallied, these Bluenose businessmen would probably have a combined net worth of nearly $1 billion, putting them among North America's richest families.

The Sobeys are third-generation Canadians. Donald's grandfather and Frank's father, J. W. Sobey, came with his parents from Britain, but the family was originally from Poland. Their surname was probably Sobij. J. W. was a butcher who started his own business in 1906, selling meats and groceries. Frank Sobey and his brother, Harold, helped their father and worked for him full-time after quitting school as teenagers.

By 1946, there were six Sobey stores. But after the war, Frank Sobey expanded rapidly as a defence against the big Eastern and American chains like Dominion Stores and A&P, who were beginning to invade the Maritimes. Loblaws attacked in another way — by accumulating 40 per cent of Sobey Stores stock during the 1960s and 1970s. But through a series of smart moves, all invaders were successfully repelled by 1980.

His first defence was an offensive. Sobey borrowed millions from investment bankers in Toronto and Montreal to expand rapidly and capture markets before his competition did. He used the same financial contacts that his friends Roy Jodrey and Roy's son, John J. Jodrey, had cultivated. Tapping central Canada for money, Sobey grew slowly and strategically.

"Father decided that rather than spreading across Canada, allowing others to own the real estate, he would just expand in the Maritimes but own the properties. That proved to be the right thing. It keeps our rents to a minimum," Donald Sobey says.

Now the Sobey chain has eighty-one supermarkets, not including other food interests such as its Lofood division, with fourteen discount outlets; nine Cash and Carry outlets; and twelve wholesale distribution centres. The family's other food interests include 13 per cent of Quebec's largest grocery chain, Provigo, 40 per cent of Food City Ltd., and 25 per cent of Hannaford Bros. Co., the largest grocery store chain in New England.

After food stores, Frank's next investment in the 1930s was to buy Stellarton's cinema. His dabbling in the world of entertainment has turned into a lucrative sideline, and the Sobeys own almost all the province's moviehouses, for a total of thirty-one, plus two dozen bowling alleys and 15 per cent of the First Choice pay-television network. After the war, Frank Sobey also began picking up drugstore chains; the Sobeys now own Empire and Lawton's Drug Stores, with about fifty outlets in the Maritimes.

The Sobeys also own pieces of just about every shopping centre and major development in Nova Scotia. Between Empire's 35 per cent of Halifax Developments and its 96 per cent in Atlantic Shopping Centres, the Sobeys own and/or operate five million gross leaseable square feet of commercial and office space plus residences — equivalent to half of downtown Toronto's gross rentable space.

Until his death, Frank Sobey lived in Bermuda on his secluded estate called Nova Estates, near others owned by K. C. Irving and Graham Dennis, the anglophile publisher and owner of the Halifax *Chronicle-Herald*, a media money machine with a stranglehold on the province. Frank Sobey and his wife had four children. William was born in 1927, David in 1931, and Donald in 1935; Donald is the only university graduate. Frank's daughter, Dianne, is a Stellarton homemaker and uninvolved in day-to-day Sobey business.

The three sons work in Empire's head office, a converted warehouse on a Stellarton railway siding. They are a close family, spending most weekends at their cottages nearby, close to their father's waterside estate. Donald and Dianne have two children each; Bill has four and David, three.

Donald is the stock market whiz and president of Empire; David is president of the family food chain; William, the oldest, is chairman of the board of Sobeys Stores. First cousin John R. Sobey (son of Frank's brother, Harold) is a vice president with Sobeys, and J. William Sinclair (son of Frank's sister, Edith) is a forestry technician. All five started in Sobey stores as meat-cutters. William's two sons, Karl and Frank C. Sobey, are involved in the family businesses, as is David's son Paul, a chartered accountant.

The close relationship between the Sobeys and the Jodreys has extended to the current generation, and in 1972 they all joined forces in another Sobey-inspired defensive move, capturing control of Halifax Developments.

In 1972, the Sobeys had 10 per cent of Halifax Developments, the Jodreys, 12.5 per cent, and Nova Scotia developer Charles MacCulloch, 10 per cent. Along the way and after a battle, MacCulloch cashed in his shares, leaving the Jodreys and Sobeys with 35 per cent each, or a total of 70 per cent.

Four years later, in 1976, the Sobeys began to diversify. They eventually acquired Atlantic Shopping Centres; 22.3 per cent of Wajax, a resource and materials-handling equipment manufacturer; 7 per cent of Dominion Textile Inc.; and 8 per cent of Jannock Ltd., a sugar, steel, and brick company. Empire also owns substantial blocks of dozens of other companies and banks, as well as two small oil exploration companies, APL Oil & Gas and Erskine Resources Ltd.; the Avis franchise for the Maritimes; and the Chrysler and Volvo-Volkswagen dealerships for Nova Scotia.

Empire has $350 million in assets, which includes the $150-million grocery store chain, but not the Sobeys' stakes in Halifax Developments, Nova Scotia Savings, and National Sea. "I've made more money out of other people's businesses than I have out of my own," said Frank in 1983, referring to his lucrative stock market portfolio.

In 1978, with help from the Jodreys, the Sobeys pulled off another stock market coup. They wanted to take over M. Loeb, a profitable Ottawa-based wholesaler, but Quebec's largest food-store chain, Provigo, wanted the company, too. The gigantic Quebec pension plan, Caisse de dépôt et placement du Québec, sided with Provigo and bought Loeb shares, which it tendered to Provigo.

Provigo wanted all the shares and proposed a "squeeze-out" offer to get the rest. But the Sobeys bought the remaining 11.7 per cent from the son of Loeb's founder, Bertram Loeb (father-in-law of former deputy finance minister Mickey Cohen). This gave Sobey a majority of the remaining stock, legally allowing him to scuttle the squeeze-out. Provigo had to make a deal and swapped a million of its shares for Sobey's Loeb stock.

The Sobeys and the Jodreys began buying and selling Provigo stock as it went from $7 to $65 in four years. By February 1982, the Sobeys owned 25 per cent. That month, the Caisse — which owned 17 per cent — offered to buy Sobey's Provigo shares, and the family sold 12 per cent for $15.8 million.

That gave the Caisse a total of 30 per cent, and the Sobeys 13 per cent, and the two agreed to remain allies on Provigo's board of directors.

In 1980, the Sobeys played hardball when they shook off the only other large shareholder in their own stores, rival Loblaws, which owned 40 per cent. That year, Loblaws refused to vote in favour of a financing resolution proposed by the family. The Sobeys staged another meeting weeks later, but notice reached the Toronto offices of Loblaws on the day the meeting was held in Halifax. The boys from Stellarton had pulled a fast one, and needless to say, the resolution passed. Loblaws cashed out to the Sobeys in 1981 for $5 million, according to Harry Bruce's Sobey biography.

The Jodreys and the Sobeys also enjoy the role of white knights, galloping to the rescue of besieged managements. In August 1983, the two families were asked to counter a takeover bid by Exco for Nova Scotia Savings & Loan Co. Exco is controlled by Moncton lawyer Reuben Cohen and his partner, Montreal lumber magnate Leonard Ellen. Cohen and Ellen bought 51 per cent of the company, and the two families bought the rest. Just a few months later, in February 1984, they rescued from bankruptcy the province's biggest employer, National Sea — one of the world's largest fishing and processing companies, with 7,000 employees and thirteen plants. The families put up $10 million each and convinced banks and governments to roll over loans.

The Jodreys operate through a privately owned family holding company called Scotia Investments Ltd. They are probably richer than the Sobeys. In a rare glimpse of their personal financial situation, figures in 1977 showed the Jodreys owned 90 per cent of Minas Basin Lumber Co., which had 40,000 acres of woodlands, assets worth $80 million, and no debts. They own at least thirty more companies. In 1973, when Roy Jodrey died, the family's fortune was estimated at $300 million, which would be worth $650 million today if invested returns matched inflation rates.

The current patriarch is John J. Jodrey, born in 1911, the only son of Roy Jodrey. The family's profits are shared by his two sisters and their heirs, a total of twelve grandchildren. Those involved are John Jodrey's son, Bruce J. Jodrey, as well as his two nephews, David Hennigar (a broker in charge of Burns Fry's Atlantic region) and C. E. Bishop, sons of John's two sisters, Florence Hennigar and Jean Bishop respectively.

John Jodrey inherited his father's frugality, passion for privacy, and business smarts. A tentative talker, he belies the image of the buzz-saw businessman, whether a fast-talking used-car salesman like Jimmy Pattison or a verbose, literary financier like Conrad Black. John Jodrey is a man of few words, making every single one all the more valuable.

The Jodreys own a variety of businesses, from pulp and paper to food and financial services. Their most recent investments have been in the food business. Besides their contribution towards National Sea, the Jodreys bought Stokely-Van Camp of Canada Inc., of Berwick, N.S., in 1983 for $15 million. The company has five plants making a variety of products under the labels of Stokely, Van Camp, Gatorade, and Graves. In addition, they have vast fruit and vegetable canning operations in the Annapolis Valley, whose products are sold and exported under the Avon brand name. Other Jodrey company brand names are Ben's bread and Moir's chocolates. In 1985, the family obtained 67 per cent of Hardee Farms, adding four canneries to the Jodrey empire and giving it a major foothold in central Canada and another $30 million in annual sales.

The rise to riches began with Roy Jodrey, son of a Gaspereau Valley cabinet-maker. He left school at thirteen, but ultimately became a director of more companies than any other man in Canada at the time — a total of fifty-six corporations, according to *Maclean's* magazine. He began as an apple farmer, but he decided there was more money in farming trees, so he began buying timberlands. In the 1920s, he founded Minas Basin Lumber and Power Co. after reading a book about hydroelectricity. He bought more land with timber and powerful rivers and built his own dam to supply cheap power for a pulp mill.

His power stations were expropriated for a small fortune by the provincial utility, and those proceeds bankrolled his first stock market investments. He was nearly wiped out in the stock market crash of 1929. During the depths of the Depression, he continued to reinvest spare cash from his farming and pulp businesses. Land bought for pennies an acre during the 1930s became the basis of another fortune. He signed a deal with Scott Paper in Pennsylvania to sell the lion's share of pulp from the Minas mill at Hantsport, which generated its own cheap electricity. Whatever Scott did not buy was made into egg cartons and paper plates and cups by Jodrey's Canadian Keyes Fibre, across the street from the pulp mill. Almost all of Canada's egg cartons are still made here, as are most of the moulded plates used by McDonald's Restaurants and others.

The Jodreys think ahead. In 1968, when Scott decided to build its own Canadian mill to cut pulp costs, the family made a bundle selling for $9 million some 300,000 acres of timberlands Roy Jodrey had assembled in anticipation of Scott's invasion. "In the 1960s, Roy Adelbert Jodrey probably owned 500,000 acres of land in the Maritimes," wrote Halifax writer Lyndon Watkins in the Montreal *Gazette*.

Roy Jodrey was a shooter in the stock market, but he was personally frugal. His idea of a good time on a Saturday night was to attend a bean supper at a hotel in nearby Wolfville. Like the newspaper magnate Roy Thomson, Jodrey kept notes in a small black book, which recorded his impressions of people and facts and figures. He was obviously a person who could size up people and prospects in a minute, and profit from both.

"Jodrey used to come to Montreal and Toronto and pick the brains of bankers and brokers, go into the men's room after a conversation, and write it all down. Then he'd go back to Hantsport and make a fortune," says Robert MacIntosh, head of the Canadian Bankers' Association.

The real extent of the Jodrey investment portfolio is unknown, held through a dozen holding companies with names like Valley Investments, Minas Investments, Minas Basin Investments, and Hants Investments. But in the mid-1970s, the Jodreys held the single largest block of shares in the Bank of Nova Scotia; today they are undoubtedly shareholders in the same dozens of blue-chip companies in which the Sobeys' Empire Inc. has holdings. (Empire is a publicly traded company and must publish its portfolio, while the Jodreys' Scotia Investments doesn't have to.)

The Jodreys' other important investment, apart from Halifax Developments, is their partnership arrangement with the Burns family. Roy Jodrey was as close to Charles Burns as he was to Frank Sobey. Burns was Jodrey's investment adviser and business partner — his eyes and ears in central Canada's concrete money canyons. And the two made a fortune on Crown Life, Algoma Central Railway shares, and many of Algoma's mining company customers in Northern Ontario, such as Mattagami Mines, Rio Algom, Denison, Dickenson, and Noranda.

The Burnses and the Jodreys share 46 per cent of the voting shares of Crownx Inc., an insurance, health services, and high-tech conglomerate. It includes Extendicare, with assets of $500 million, including 149 nursing homes with 19,000 beds, and Crown Life, selling life, health, and annuity insurance, with assets of $4 billion. Vice chairman of Crownx is David Hennigar, and chairman is H. Michael Burns, Charles's son.

Roy Jodrey had the Midas touch, and he explained his formula in his biography, written by Harry Bruce, *The Story of R. A. Jodrey.*

"You don't make money, you saves it," he joked. "Start your own business and work at it eighteen or twenty hours a day. [Stock market investments should be made only after you've] checked out the management. If they're good, anything they do must be good. Keep your eyes open. Watch for opportunities. Take advantage. Don't buy and sell. Buy a stock, put it away. Leave it alone. Let it grow. When things look blackest, buy. That's the time to get aboard, when things are deflated. Boom times may be dangerous times to do anything. Most fortunes have been made when things look blackest. My advice is worth exactly what it's costing you. Nothing."

Both the Sobeys and the Jodreys have had the golden touch, and so far it is hereditary. Like Maritimes Rothschilds, Nova Scotia's two dynasties know all about teamwork, and how co-operation will ensure their survival for generations to come.

THE MOLSONS

THE MOLSONS are "old" Montreal money. WASPy and wealthy for two centuries, they and other rich anglophones have ruled Quebec from Gothic fortresses on Mount Royal for generations. Westmount Rhodesians, they're called. There is certainly no bluer blood in the land than the Molsons, who built the country's first railway and first steamboat, founded the forerunner of the Bank of Montreal — where they printed their own currency — and, lastly, built the brewery that bears their name. The current generation lives modestly and as privately as possible, even though their name is plastered on beer bottles and billboards from coast to coast. For six generations they have quietly brewed millions of barrels of beer and discreetly handled family scandals or squabbles. The family has a sense of *noblesse oblige*, and most Molsons have immersed themselves in good works, giving away millions.

"We're not rich," Eric Molson, current head of the household, once told a worker. "We are merely guardians of wealth."

The Molson Companies Ltd. is still family-controlled. Following an ambitious diversification strategy, it is now a beer, chemical, and retail conglomerate with 11,000 employees, nearly $1 billion in assets, and about $2 billion a year in sales. No one in Canada makes more beer — Molson has nearly 40 per cent of the domestic market — and its retail operations include Beaver Lumber, with 176 stores coast to coast (also operating under the names Biltrite, Saveway, and Aikenhead hardware), as well as stationery retailer

Willson Office Specialty Ltd. Its profitable chemicals division includes Diversey Corp., a Chicago-based multinational with forty-nine sanitation plants in thirty-five countries and 5,600 employees. In addition, Molson owns the Montreal Canadiens hockey team.

It all began two centuries ago, in 1786, when John Molson, a twenty-three-year-old English orphan, began making beer in Montreal. In just a few years, the venture was making so much money that he began to branch out into transportation and banking.

The Molson's Bank had 125 branches and merged with the Bank of Montreal in 1925. It was founded by John Molson in 1796 because he was making so much money that he could make loans and issue his own currency. Glass-encased "Molson money" is on display in the firm's fourth-floor boardroom on Notre Dame Street in Montreal. The first Molson also built the first railway in North America, a 22-kilometre line, and owned a fleet of steamboats until 1862, shuttling passengers and products between Montreal and Quebec City.

Currently in charge is Eric Herbert Molson, forty-nine, deputy chairman of the Molson Companies and the biggest single shareholder. He is the oldest son of the late Thomas Henry Pentland Molson, who died in 1978. Eric was the heir apparent, chosen by his father and his uncle, Liberal senator Hartland de Montarville Molson, who ran the company together from 1953 to 1966. His two aunts — Dorothy (Mrs. H. C. MacDougall) and Elizabeth (Mrs. N. L. Mather) — weren't involved in the business.

Eric's father and uncle took Molson from a regional brewery to a national brewery with huge export sales. The two brothers continued to play active roles as directors from that point onwards, but had built a talented team of managers who looked after the family firm and diversified even further, making profitable retailing and chemical acquisitions.

Eric is a good-looking, quiet, and unassuming chemist who controls 37.45 per cent of the voting stock of the company. He directly or indirectly owns 23.7 per cent of the voting interest and has control over another 13.75 per cent from his father's estate. He heads the "brewery line" of Molsons. He has a brother, Stephen, and two sisters; none of them has taken an interest in the family business, but they remain his loyal backers.

In 1975, when Molson made a number of takeovers and paid for them by issuing treasury shares to sellers, Eric and his siblings found their interest was diluted. So the four swapped more valuable non-voting shares from key employees for ones with votes, at a cost of $1 million, in order to bring their share to 55 per cent, absolute control, according to *The Molson Saga* by Shirley E. Woods, Jr. The subsequent takeover of the profitable Diversey Corp., followed by the purchase of BASF Wyandotte Corp., another U.S. chemical company, reduced Eric's family interest to 37.45 per cent once more.

Eric became president in 1980 at the age of forty-three; it was the first time in fourteen years that a member of the company's founding family was at the helm. Eric was a brilliant student; he attended Princeton University where he earned an honours degree in chemistry. He joined the company on the technical side as an apprentice brewmaster. Always the heir apparent, he never pulled rank as the boss's son. He even postponed his own honeymoon for several weeks until his supervisor could spare him.

In 1978, he took over brewing operations. A Montreal *Gazette* profile by Philippe Deane Gigantes quotes a schoolmate from Eric's school-days who "could not remember anything positive, negative, or anecdotal about Eric H. Molson." While his family has given away $15 million since 1957, Eric is thrifty, having his shoes rebuilt as many as three times at Tony's on Greene Avenue in Montreal.

Like most members of Montreal's dynasties, he lives in Westmount; his is a three-storey greystone townhouse, one block from the Forum, where the Canadiens play. He and his wife, Jane, daughter of a well-known Sherbrooke judge, have three sons. Not only do they live near the Forum, they also have a hockey room in their basement, complete with two hockey nets, lines on the hardwood floor for face-offs, real athletic lockers, and a gym-style shower room.

The couple were childhood sweethearts who met at a dance at his private school, Selwyn House. Jane once described what it was like to be married to Eric Molson: "There are clear advantages: we can travel much more than other people. We can have our children educated anywhere we want. It would be easy to slip into being decadent and doing nothing much besides having a good time. So, one must be disciplined and public-spirited, have a sense of responsibility. Ric [Eric] has that very much, a sense of *noblesse oblige*."

The Molsons are fiercely Québécois. Eric insists on bilingualism within the organization and resisted moving the head office to Toronto, where the company's actual centre of gravity is. Eric commutes, spending Tuesday to Thursday in Toronto, living in an apartment in the city. He returns to Montreal every Thursday, and often he and his family head for weekends at their country home in the Eastern Townships.

Eric, his younger brother, Stephen, and his uncle, Senator Molson, have offices at the Notre Dame Street brewery, opposite the fourth-floor board-room, which is lined with the portraits of six generations of Molsons. The office is on the original site of John Molson's first brewhouse, in a square stone structure surrounded by modern facilities.

While Eric looks after the family's business interests, his brother and two sisters are involved mostly in volunteer or charitable pursuits. Stephen works for the Molson Family Foundation, a charitable organization. Sister Deirdre married Robert Stevenson, now dean of students at McGill University, and is an active volunteer with the Montreal Museum of Fine Arts, and other museums. Cynthia graduated Phi Beta Kappa from Wellesley College and married a former *Financial Post* journalist, Clive Baxter. Now widowed, she lives with her three sons in Ottawa and has a part interest in a bookstore.

Stephen, unlike his brother, did not go to Princeton, following instead the well-worn Westmount route: Selwyn House, Bishop's College School at Lennoxville, and McGill University. He was an average student who flunked out of McGill in his third year, returning to graduate a year later. Following university he was hired by the Bank of Montreal as a management trainee, but he left banking four years later, which upset his father. He bought a fish hatchery in the Eastern Townships, which subsequently went broke. Then in 1971, when Stephen was thirty-one, his father asked him to run the Molson Foundation, a charity that sponsors the Molson Prizes and special projects.

The Senator is still the patriarch of the family. A charming mustachioed gentleman who looks, and acts, like an English aristocrat, the Senator was a hero and fighter pilot during the Second World War. Outspoken at times, he once said hockey players were "overpaid and overprivileged." As a Liberal, he also acted as unofficial spokesman for the many anglophone Montrealers who felt disenfranchised when provincial laws demoted their mother tongue to second-class status. He supported bilingualism, but spoke out eloquently against separatism.

The Senator, a chartered accountant who wrote many of Canada's tax laws as a volunteer for the Liberal government of the day, is still a director of the company, and a widower. He has a daughter, Zoe Anne, who lives in Eng-land. On most weekends he goes to the Molson compound in the Laurentian village of Ivry — 1,200 acres of forests surrounding three lakes that have been in the family since the turn of the century.

The Senator's late older brother, Tom, had four children who became the "brewery line." At the time of his death, Tom was the largest shareholder in the company and divided his estate into five portions, giving his two daughters and son Stephen one portion each, but Eric, the oldest, two shares. Another reason Eric and his family are in charge is that their cousins cashed in their chips in a complex deal involving the Canadiens team. The deal upset the Senator deeply and caused a permanent rift within the family.

John Henry Molson, first cousin of Tom and the Senator, had four children: Mary, William, David, and Peter. In the early 1960s, David was recruited by the Senator as an assistant, but he gravitated towards the family's hockey team, and in 1964 became a director. Two years later he also became a director of Molson Breweries to represent his family's interests in the firm.

In 1966, David offered to buy Canadian Arena Company, which owned the team and the Forum, for $3 million. He said he and his two brothers would sell their Molson stock to pay for the firm. At the time, David was president of the Canadiens, Peter's sporting goods venture had flopped, and Bill was a broker. In the summer of 1968, the Senator and his brother agreed to sell Canadian Arena to the three brothers for $3 million, only 50 per cent more than they had paid for it in 1957, even though they had just spent $10 million to increase seating and install air conditioning at the Forum. Presumably this was to keep the team in friendly, family hands.

The brothers listed their new company on the Montreal Stock Exchange and began to declare hefty dividends annually. In 1971, Molson director and brother-in-law Tommy MacDougall (a senior partner with Montreal broker MacDougall MacDougall & McTier) was called by David Molson. He was holidaying at Ivry, and the Senator was in Jamaica. MacDougall was told that Peter and Edward Bronfman were about to make a $13-million takeover bid for Canadian Arena Company.

The sale was executed two days before Canada's first capital gains taxes were to come into force, and the three brothers cleaned up, making a profit of $10 million. When Hartland returned from holiday, he had a picture showing his three cousins and himself the day they bought the team permanently removed from his office. And as if to add insult to injury, John Bassett, who was a partner of the Bronfmans in the deal, within months jacked up the cost to Molson Breweries of the television rights by $500,000. Naturally, the family was stunned and angry.

Today William Molson, known as "Billy," has a seat on the Montreal Stock Exchange and is a founding partner of Molson Rousseau Inc. Peter is an insurance broker, and David owns Continental Galleries Inc. on Drummond Street and spends most of his time living in Florida on his seventy-two-foot diesel yacht, *Nahanni*.

In 1978, the Bronfmans offered the Molsons a chance to buy back the team, only this time it cost $20 million, plus a larger amount for a thirty-year lease at the Forum. Ironically, these proceeds helped bankroll the Bronfmans' purchase of Brascan, with its controlling interest in the Molsons' brewery rival, John Labatt Ltd.

Similarly, Hartland MacDougall, the Senator's nephew and Tommy MacDougall's son, profited from a relationship with the Bronfmans, rising to vice chairman of the Bank of Montreal in great part because of his closeness to them. In 1984, MacDougall left the bank and became chairman of Royal Trustco, also part of the Bronfman empire.

Despite such setbacks, the Molsons are not Westmount Rhodesians who got out while the getting was good. They stayed in their beloved Montreal to look after their cherished business. And barring any dramatic takeover attempts, theirs appears to be a dynasty that will stay around for a while as the current "brewery line" is imbued with the Protestant work ethic.

THE BRONFMANS (CHARLES AND EDGAR)

AS THE STORY GOES, when the volatile Sam Bronfman, founder of the Seagram fortune, heard about the newest appointments to the Senate in 1955, he erupted angrily, according to Peter Newman's *Bronfman Dynasty*, "It should have been mine. I bought it! I paid for it! Those treacherous bastards did me in!"

Sam sought a senatorship through political contributions to enhance the prestige of his family, which was definitely not a member of the establishment. The Bronfmans had been bootleggers during Prohibition. Like Boston's Joseph Kennedy, who also ran rum and made a fortune, Sam wanted credentials and prestige. Joe Kennedy paid millions to help his son Jack win a senatorship and finally the U.S. presidency, despite Joe's shadowy past and his

Roman Catholicism. Similarly, Sam Bronfman wanted to be the first Jewish senator in Canadian history. Both goals eluded Bronfman during his lifetime, and despite the good works undertaken by his children, the name Bronfman is still not in the best social directories, either in Canada or in the United States.

The Bronfmans are in Canada's billionaire big league along with the Irvings, the Westons, the Thomsons, the Reichmanns, and the Eatons. Through their family holding company, called CEMP (for Sam's four children, Charles, Edgar, the late Minda, and Phyllis), they have controlling interests in three of Canada's largest corporations — Seagram Co., Cadillac Fairview Corp., and Warrington Inc. Added together, these companies would be Canada's fifth-largest corporation, ahead of Imperial Oil Ltd. Combined, they have $10.4 billion in assets — mostly liquor and land — and $3 billion in sales.

That includes Seagram's major $3-billion investment, made in 1980, when it bought 22.5 per cent of E. I. du Pont de Nemours of Wilmington, Delaware, one of the world's largest corporations. In 1981, Seagram and du Pont were enmeshed in a bidding war for the oil giant Conoco. Seagram gave du Pont its Conoco shares in return for du Pont treasury shares. While a seemingly small percentage, this holding means the Bronfmans indirectly are the largest shareholders, owning more than the founding du Pont family.

Du Pont is as big as Canada's largest corporation, Hydro-Québec; it has $25 billion in assets and sales of $36 billion, nearly half the Canadian federal government's tax revenues annually. "After they bought it, Charles [Bronfman] and some of his executives went down for a one-week chemistry course. Can you imagine that? The company makes $3 billion a month," says Lorne Webster, a close friend of Charles and fellow-shareholder in the Montreal Expos.

Bronfman companies are pervasive in the consumer field. Whenever you take a sip of Crown Royal, Jameson Irish Whiskey, Chivas Regal, Myers's rum, Mumm's champagne, or Amaretto liqueur, whenever you buy Bauer skates, Hush Puppies, Kodiak boots, a Teflon-coated pan, Lucite acrylic, or the drug Percodan for a headache, you are contributing to their far-reaching empire.

Through Cadillac Fairview, the Bronfmans also own large portions of Toronto commercial landmarks such as the Toronto-Dominion Centre, the Eaton Centre, Cedarbrae Plaza, half of Fairview Mall, and Warden Woods. In retail space alone, they control about 750,000 square metres (eight million square feet), equivalent to nearly 300 football fields. They also own large tracts of land in California and other Sun Belt states.

Sam and his children may never have captured Senate seats, but Liberal politicians have heaped honours onto their proxies: their business adviser, Leo Kolber, is a senator, as is long-time Bronfman lawyer Lazarus Phillips, a courtly Talmudic scholar who arranged for Pierre Trudeau to get his first nomination to run for Parliament.

Kolber and Phillips have sought former politicians as advisers, extending the family's influence and political power. John Turner was a director of their huge distillery, Seagram Co., and CEMP's chief legal counsel. Former Ontario premier Bill Davis is on Seagram's board, his close adviser Eddie Goodman is on Cadillac's, and former Liberal finance minister Donald Mac-donald is on Du Pont Canada's board.

Charles Bronfman, Seagram's second-in-command, often entertains prime ministers and politicians in the owners' box at the Big "O" stadium, where the Montreal Expos and the Concorde play. The box overlooks third base and is well equipped with a wet bar. It has a cantilevered concrete balcony with seats for thirty, a butler and a chef, plus comfortable couches with television sets relaying the game indoors. Charles put up half of the $10 million to buy the Expos baseball franchise in the early 1970s, as a favour to Montreal mayor Jean Drapeau. Similarly, he put up most of the money to bail out the city's Canadian Football League franchise, the Concorde, after the Alouettes went bust.

In fact, Charles's relationship with Trudeau is so cosy that he was accused in the House of Commons in 1982 of asking the prime minister at a social gathering to guarantee $34 million in loans to the family firm of his friend and fellow Expos investor Sydney Maislin. Trudeau denied the guarantees were a favour to friends, and a year later, Maislin Transport went bust.

Politics is important to the Bronfmans because politics made them as rich as they are today. Sam and his three brothers were running a sleazy hotel in Winnipeg when Prohibition came along in the 1920s. Canada followed, but hypocritically never made it illegal to manufacture and transport alcoholic beverages to the border. Warehouses all over Canada were filled to the brim with Bronfman booze destined for shipment south of the border. They started simply shipping the stuff, then set up distilling operations.

"We loaded carloads of goods, got our cash, and shipped it. Of course, we knew where it went, but had no legal proof. And I never went to the other side of the border to count the empty Seagram's bottles," Sam told the *New York Times* once.

Since Sam died in 1971, his sons have run Seagram, while the caustic Senator Kolber has run CEMP. A short, bespectacled man from a middle-class milieu, the Senator has a penthouse office in Montreal that looks like a smart salon at Versailles and could accommodate a dozen desks and secretaries. He serves guests coffee, poured from a silver service, in china cups and saucers and loves nothing more than to talk about his passion, the opera.

Bronfmans are so wealthy that they could have dominated Canadian business life if they had joined the takeover games here, as their cousins Peter and Edward Bronfman did with the help of aggressive advisers. But Sam and his children have always been sensitive to politics. When economics and emotions may have dictated otherwise, they have spurned investing too much in Canada to avoid negative political controversy over concentration of wealth, anti-Semitism, or both.

"My father used to hate the Bronfmans," says Larry Zolf, a CBC broadcaster who grew up Jewish in Winnipeg in the shadow of this powerful family. "He hated them because they made the Gentiles drunk, and because they got too rich and made the Gentiles hate the Jews."

For instance, in the mid-1970s, when others were making huge takeover bids for Canadian assets, Bronfman-controlled Cadillac Fairview had the largest stake in Canadian Pacific and toyed with the idea of taking it over. But Kolber consulted his contacts and was assured there would be political trouble, so Cadillac sold to Paul Desmarais.

Charles and his older brother, Edgar, have turned Seagram into the world's biggest distillery, but their two sisters were uninvolved. In separate trusts, the four siblings or their heirs own 38 per cent of Seagram, but the holdings of Phyllis and of Minda's estate have slid to a total of only 7 per cent.

Edgar Bronfman is chairman of the Seagram board. An able executive with an arrogant streak, he earned more money in 1985 than any other Canadian executive, about $1.2 million in salary and bonus. An urbane jet-setter, he is exceptionally well plugged in as president of the World Jewish Congress, giving him access to Ronald Reagan and other heads of state.

But Edgar's life has been tumultuous. He is a naturalized American citizen and lives permanently in New York City. He has been divorced four times (twice from the same woman) and has five children. Twice his personal problems have been amplified into headlines around the world. In 1974, he asked the courts to annul his marriage to a beautiful English aristocrat, Lady Carolyn Townshend. He won, but only after a sensational case in which his sex life, or lack of it, titillated the public for weeks. Testimony indicated that they had pre-marital sex, but that she refused to consummate the match on their wedding night and slept instead at her psychiatrist's house. The scandal was embarrassing for the whole Bronfman family. Carolyn was ordered to return $2.5 million in gifts and cash to Edgar, and he was ordered to pay her $40,000 annually until 1985.

In 1975, just before Edgar's marriage to Georgiana Eileen Webb, a former British barmaid, his son, Sam II, was kidnapped. The wedding was postponed until Sam was rescued. Two men were subsequently apprehended and tried for kidnapping and extortion. There followed a sensational trial at which the accused alleged that Sam was a homosexual and an accomplice. The jury disregarded that allegation, and the two men were convicted.

Edgar has led the family along its aggressive and acquisitive path. But his father's investment in the oil business turned out to be a bigger winner than distilling. In 1979, Seagram sold its oil interests for $2.7 billion in cash and began to shop for more. The family considered, then rejected, buying Gulf Canada Ltd., control of which was bought in 1985 by the Reichmanns for $2.8 billion. After several failed takeover attempts, Edgar made his deal with du Pont.

The four Bronfmans grew up rich during the Depression in Montreal's posh Westmount. Charles, Edgar, and their two cousins, Peter and Edward, shared a playground on a lot between their Montreal mansions, which contained a baseball diamond and a hockey rink. Born in 1929, Edgar was a spirited young man and was asked to leave a number of private schools. Similar in personality to his father, he clashed constantly with Sam. "My father was a tremendous personality," Charles told the *Globe and Mail*. "My older brother and I took opposite roads when it came to dealing with him. My brother would fight him all the time and I would shake."

Charles is soft-spoken and shy. Born in 1931, he has two grown children, is divorced, but has remarried. For years, he and his family lived in a mansion with gold-plated heating baseboards and a swimming pool with a retractable roof for indoor and outdoor swimming. The home sold for $2.7 million in 1983. Charles is a frustrated jock who often dons a uniform to work out with the Expos at training sessions. In 1981, he even missed his first directors' meeting at du Pont because he didn't want to pass up a key Expos game.

Phyllis Bronfman-Lambert is more comfortable in a hard hat than a tiara. An artist turned architect, she works fourteen hours a day on projects and causes. She spends at least one day a week in bed, and she has cruised the Aegean Sea every summer for the past fifteen years. She commutes between her Montreal and Los Angeles offices, but home is the loft of a three-storey converted and renovated peanut factory in Montreal's old quarter. Between holidays and a career, she has led many crusades to save historically valuable buildings in Montreal and elsewhere. And in 1985, the Canadian Centre for Architecture opened, a project that culminates years of work and was made possible mostly because of her donations of time and money.

She told the *Globe and Mail* her interest in the centre is due to her feeling that architecture is "how people live and how they relate to each other. It can be hideous or very edifying. People need to know more about architecture." An independent woman, she led a protest in 1983 against a Cadillac Fairview scheme in Montreal. She was married briefly to Jean Lambert, a French-American businessman, but never had children. Her sister, Minda, who died in 1985, was married to a French banker, Baron Alain de Gunzburg. He is a Seagram director. They moved from Paris to New York in the late 1970s, along with their capital, just before French banks were nationalized and assets frozen.

Although they grew up with Peter and Edward Bronfman, Sam's children have little to do with their cousins. Relations have been cool since Sam bought the cousins' Seagram stock for $15 million, in a take-it-or-leave-it offer below market prices in order to pave the way for his sons' succession at Seagram. But being a Bronfman is almost a sure-fire guarantee of success. As Edgar once said: "Turning $100 into $110 is hard work. Turning $100 million into $110 million is inevitable."

THE DESMARAIS

IT WAS hot and cold running politicians on New Year's Eve, 1983, at the spectacular villa of Paul Desmarais. Brian Mulroney, Pierre Trudeau, and Bill Davis tripped the light fantastic with tycoons and citizens of Tinsel Town at the Palm Beach manse of this Montreal magnate. Trudeau and singer Dinah Shore stayed several days in two of Desmarais's three lavish guest-houses in the chic Florida coastal town. Mulroney entertained guests with his favourite,

"When Irish Eyes Are Smiling," sung in his twenty-Camels-a-day voice. Others invited to the spectacular villa, Le Pavillon, were perfume executive Estée Lauder and Hollywood star Douglas Fairbanks, several Liberal and Conservative senators, and Trudeau confidant Jim Coutts.

The one-storey cream stucco-and-stone mansion, with tall arched windows and yellow-and-white décor, took seven years to design and two years to build. By all accounts, it is one of the finest homes in Palm Beach. The New Year's party guests are all good friends of Desmarais, chairman of a huge empire appropriately called Power Corp. of Canada. Desmarais is the richest French Canadian in the world, one of just two who have made it into the multibillion-dollar business big leagues. The other is Robert Campeau.

The two are also unusual because they have established dynasties, not inherited them. Both men have scaled the heights in much the same way: they rode a wave of new francophone power with the elevation of Pierre Elliott Trudeau as prime minister in 1968 and his enshrinement of bilingualism. By using French connections in the political sphere, and financial aggressiveness, both men more than made up for not attending Upper Canada College, Harvard, or any of the other traditional institutions where rich anglos learn how to get richer.

Desmarais controls a $15.8-billion media, oil, financial services, and forestry empire. A holding company, Power Financial Corp., controls Montreal Trustco Inc., Credit Foncier, Investors Group of Winnipeg, and others with about $4 billion in assets on deposit, and Canada's third-largest life insurance company, Great-West Life Assurance of Winnipeg, with $9 billion. He also owns Canada's largest French-language daily newspaper, *La Presse*, the weekly business publication *Les Journaux*, and the country's sixtieth-largest enterprise, Consolidated-Bathurst Inc., with $1.6 billion in forestry, oil, and high-tech assets. "Connie-Bathurst," as it is called, has big stakes in the laser pioneer Lumonics, in one of Canada's ten biggest oil and gas producers, Sulpetro Ltd., and in C.B. Pack, which makes more aluminum cans and bottles than any other company in the country.

Like Campeau, Desmarais was born in Sudbury. His father was a prosperous — but not rich — lawyer and businessman. He graduated from the University of Ottawa and started out in business twenty-five years ago at the helm of a nearly bankrupt bus company in which his father had a small interest. He spent long hours rebuilding the business. A forerunner of Voyageur Colonial, it is the largest intercity bus service in eastern Canada (now no longer in Desmarais's hands). To save money, he did the maintenance himself on his fleet of nineteen buses and sometimes paid his drivers in bus tickets when there was not enough cash. But a strike in the 1960s made him realize how vulnerable his bus business was, so he expanded into other areas, including financial and investment enterprises.

Desmarais was breaking new ground and knew it. "Before, a French Canadian became a doctor, a lawyer, a priest, or a teacher. French Canadians were afraid of the system, of the English-language banking institutions."

By 1960, his bus company had grown into a large, profit-making outfit. He met Louis Lévesque, a fellow–French Canadian from New Brunswick, who sold bonds for Desmarais's bus company, giving him the cash to buy another, larger bus company in Montreal. Most importantly, this deal brought Desmarais away from his backwater home town, Sudbury, to the middle of the action in Montreal.

Once there, his path to success was paved during the 1960s with the new French political reality. As bilingualism became an urgent provincial priority, then a national one, Desmarais and other francophone tycoons were sought out as directors of major corporations. What began as tokenism became an opportunity for Desmarais to rise to the top as a major player. Prestigious directorships more than made up for the lack of Upper Canada College contacts. It led to deals and relationships that would reap him riches.

In 1965, he rolled his various interests into a fifteen-company conglomerate called Trans-Canada Corporation Fund. He formed another partnership in 1967, which bought eight small newspapers. But in the spring of 1968, he found the ultimate vehicle for his ambitions: cash-rich Power Corp., a holding company with $152 million in its treasury, obtained mostly from selling its B.C. utilities to the government. The money was sitting there, waiting to be invested. And Desmarais went for it, rolling everything else he owned into Power Corp. in return for 50 per cent of Power's shares. He increased this later to 68.9 per cent.

(The identical formula was used by Peter and Edward Bronfman, who took over cash-rich Brascan Ltd. in 1978, with its $400 million in cash garnered from selling its Brazilian utilities.)

In 1970, Desmarais continued growing, giving two banks some of Power Corp.'s treasury shares in exchange for their shares in Investors Group, which at the time had highly profitable mutual funds and small interests in Montreal

Trustco and Great-West Life. He had his eye on acquiring control of the other two, but Peter and Edward Bronfman had the same idea. The brothers beat him to it, at least temporarily, by making a takeover bid for Great-West Life.

Great-West's besieged management, led by David Kilgour (father of a Tory member of Parliament from Edmonton and brother-in-law of Liberal leader John Turner), convinced Ontario securities officials to suspend the stock for five days. That gave Desmarais time to borrow $76 million, and he outbid the Bronfmans, ending up with 51 per cent.

Friends like investment counsellor Stephen Jarislowsky cannot understand such overweening ambition. "I guess he had an insecure childhood or something," he says. "You can only live in so many houses and wear one suit and pair of shoes at a time. It's crazy to me."

Desmarais's physical presence isn't exactly commanding, although his psychological one certainly is. Tall and shy, he has suffered off and on from serious asthma. That may be why he's always worked in spurts, putting in long hours for days, then taking time off, although he's never completely free of business.

"There's a shyness, but he's hard-nosed," says Gus Van Wielingen, chairman of Sulpetro Ltd., the Calgary oil giant that is controlled by Consolidated-Bathurst. "He's 'le patron,' the boss. There's never any doubt."

Desmarais is a fiercely private man, a devoted husband and father of four. His lavish parties — such as the wedding celebration in 1984 of his daughter Sophie — sometimes catapult him into the news. On that occasion, a crowd gathered as 350 guests arrived, including Trudeau, prime minister-elect Brian Mulroney, Jean Chrétien, Governor General Jeanne Sauvé, and business and entertainment world-beaters like Conrad Black, his cousin Ronald Riley, vice president of Canadian Pacific Ltd., Charles Bronfman, Winnipeg's George Richardson, Rowland Frazee, chairman of the Royal Bank of Canada, Jean de Grandpré, chairman of Bell Canada Enterprises, as well as Dinah Shore, Maureen Forrester, and Estée Lauder. John Turner, prime minister at the time, and his wife, Geills, were invited, but did not attend.

His wife, Jacqui, is also Franco-Ontarian, a stunning brunette with an eye for art. The couple have one of the country's best collections of Krieghoffs and Group of Seven works. They have beautiful homes in Montreal, the Laurentians, and Palm Beach. Once a year, Desmarais makes a West Coast appearance to keep in touch with Western contacts like former U.S. president

Gerald Ford, and he golfs at the exclusive Eldorado Golf Club in Palm Springs, California, the members of which pay a $50,000 initiation fee and must be invited to join.

The couple have two daughters, Sophie and Louise, and two sons, Paul Jr. and André. Paul Jr., born in 1955, is second in command, and more conservative than his father. Younger brother André joined Power in 1984 after living in Paris as an investment banker with Richardson Greenshields Investments, owned by George Richardson's family.

Desmarais has been an inspiration for other French Canadians, who have to overcome a traditionally poor self-image. "I thought if a shy, stuttering French Canadian can make it, the rest of us should stop complaining," said a French-Canadian director who taped him for a CBC series.

As if to symbolize new-found French financial power, Desmarais took aim in 1975 at Toronto's financial heart and boldly bid $148 million to take over Argus Corp., whose traditional owners had just been replaced by Conrad Black and his young Upper Canada College crowd. Black had only a mere toe-hold in the empire E. P. Taylor and Bud McDougald had created and could not have outmuscled Desmarais. But amid alarms about undue concentration of power, Ottawa stepped in and set up the Royal Commission on Corporate Concentration.

Similarly, Desmarais toyed with taking over the country's biggest private-sector corporation, Canadian Pacific Ltd., through a clever partnership with Quebec's gigantic pension plan, the Caisse de dépôt et placement du Québec. In essence, Desmarais gave the Caisse the shares it desired in Domtar Ltd. (of which it now owns 30 per cent) in return for an option to buy the Caisse's Canadian Pacific shares.

In 1982, Desmarais announced he would buy 20 per cent of CP, but once more, this sparked action from the federal cabinet. Ottawa politicians, worried about Desmarais's partnership with the Caisse (and the Caisse's control by the Parti Québécois), proposed a bill to limit individual ownership of transportation companies like CP to 10 per cent, without stating this purpose. The bill never passed.

"They'll end up owning this country. Everybody is looking for a Boardwalk and a Park Place," said Richardson Greenshields analyst Leo Soenen at the time. "This will play into the hands of the socialists."

Such sentiments and the huge amount of money necessary made Desmarais back off. He sold out his CP shares in 1985, leaving the Caisse with 11 per cent.

Besides taking care of business, Desmarais has consistently been one of the country's biggest political donors. He gave Mulroney $10,000 in 1976 for his first leadership bid, and in 1982, he gave the Liberals $62,000 and the Tories $30,000. His cosy connections have caused embarrassment; in 1981, for instance, Trudeau's chief adviser, Jim Coutts, took a free ride on a Power Corp. jet to and from Washington for a private visit with Desmarais and a party at the Canadian embassy.

Power executives and directors are politically plugged in, too. Vice presidents include John Rae, a Liberal fund-raiser although his brother is Ontario NDP leader Bob Rae, and Senator Michael Pitfield, former confidant of Trudeau. One of Power's directors is another aggressive acquisitor, William E. Simon, former U.S. treasury secretary.

His political connections are also personal ones. Over the years, he often entertained the Chrétiens. In 1981, his son married Chrétien's daughter in Ottawa, and the reception was held in the West Block of Parliament Hill in Ottawa. It was a match made in heaven, symbolizing more than any Desmarais deal an ability to match Power with power.

THE WEBSTERS

THE WEALTHY Websters are scattered far and wide, but whenever they invest together they remain an awesome economic force. They are so rich they can afford to give away $5 million a year. Only Montreal's McConnells are more generous; they donate $11 million annually.

The Websters' patriarch, Senator Lorne Webster, owned 250 companies by the time he died. Some Websters are still chips off the old block, but all Websters invest as a unit. The result is that the family is still worth hundreds of millions of dollars.

Websters work in mysterious ways. They own pieces of many companies ranging from the Toronto Blue Jays to the Montreal Expos and the Concorde; from Murray's Restaurants to *Saturday Night* magazine; from a large chunk of $2-billion Union Enterprises Ltd. to a piece of the company that rents miniature television sets to patients in just about every Canadian hospital. Websters have helped high-tech greats like Mitel Ltd. and Canadian Velcro become enormously successful.

They are not industrialists but financiers, buying and selling everything from the Schick razor giant in the U.S. to 10 per cent of Maclaren Power and Pulp Co., Ronalds-Federated, and the *Globe and Mail*. One Webster created the $1-billion conglomerate Burns Foods and sold out, but still owns the largest cattle ranch east of the prairies. In addition, Websters own thousands more acres of real estate in the United States; a Detroit furrier, stevedoring operation, and skyscraper; and many buildings in Canada.

"Unless you're stupid, money doesn't go away," explains Lorne Webster, the gregarious and witty chairman of Prenor Group Ltd. in Montreal, who personally runs several financial services companies with $500 million in assets. He owns 10 per cent of the Montreal Expos and the Concorde with his pal Charles Bronfman. Lorne's uncle, R. Howard Webster, owns 45 per cent of the Toronto Blue Jays, in partnership with the Eaton family and John Labatt Ltd., part of the Brascan empire of Peter and Edward Bronfman, Charles Bronfman's cousins. The Eatons became involved in the Blue Jays because a Webster is married to John Craig Eaton.

Collectively at least $400 million today, net of debts, the Websters' wealth was accumulated by Lorne's grandfather and namesake, the Senator. He inherited a small coal business, started by his father in 1858, and turned it into a monolith with a stranglehold on energy in Quebec and eventually Ontario. In the Depression, when Seagram was still just a twinkle in Samuel Bronfman's eye, the Senator's company, Canadian Import, had a virtual monopoly on coal and heating oil in most of Quebec and was convicted of uncompetitive practices. The scandal left many Quebeckers suspicious of anglo tycoons like Webster and others. By the time he died in 1941, he had carved out an industrial empire with 250 companies, and left his five sons and one daughter a vast energy, insurance, fur, steel, sugar, and lumber fortune.

Like the McConnells, the Websters were strictly Westmount: theirs was Old Montreal money, made when the port held the key to the continent's interior. Their iron grip over the port, both as coal and oil importers and as owners of dockside and stevedoring facilities, reaped them huge riches. The Westmount wealthy reigned over Canada's economy like kings. And Montreal was the seat of their power. But the construction of the St. Lawrence Seaway in the 1950s profoundly changed that. The Seaway brought transportation access to the Canadian and American midwests. Industry and enterprise moved there. Those who did not go west withered. Unlike the McConnells, the Websters have survived as major business forces.

The richest is R. Howard Webster, one of the Senator's six children and a tenacious tycoon who has bought and sold more companies on behalf of the family and himself than his father did. Equally prominent businessmen are two nephews, sons of his brother Colin: Lorne and Donald C. ("Ben") Webster. These brothers were Argus Corp. shareholders, with Conrad Black and his well-heeled group.

Ben is one of Canada's most remarkable businessmen and one of its few venture capitalists. He is among that rare breed of businessmen who have the nerves of a gambler, the instincts of a soothsayer, and the curiosity of a sleuth. Ben finds and backs baby companies and inventions, then raises them to adulthood. He is the best and biggest in Canada and has many phenomenal success stories to his credit, like Mitel and the world rights to Velcro.

Another prominent Webster is Norman Webster, Howard's nephew (the son of his brother Eric). He is editor-in-chief of the *Globe and Mail*, an author, and a patron of *Saturday Night* magazine and its various publishing divisions.

The Senator's six children — R. Howard, Colin, Richard, Eric, Stewart, and Marian — had thirty-eight children among them. Born in the 1920s and 1930s, they have pursued a variety of careers such as accountancy, teaching, charitable activities, architecture, and farming.

The Senator left his children equal shares in the family's umbrella holding company, Imperial Trust, as well as in Canadian Import, the coal business. Most of the brothers, and Marian's husband, worked in the fuel business until it was sold in 1969. Howard did his own thing, and ran Imperial Trust on behalf of the family. He has branched out into other ventures over the years, always inviting family members to participate. He keeps 51 per cent of the action in these ventures, and splits the remaining 49 per cent evenly among relatives who invest.

As the Montreal *Gazette* pointed out in 1980, on the eve of a big business decision and a Webster family reunion: "In true Webster fashion, [Howard's] plan [about what to do with Ronalds-Federated shares] is to be ratified amid festivities this weekend at his 7,000-acre Prince Edward Island cattle ranch. Directors of a family holding company will meet Saturday morning before Webster's yearly steak-and-lobster barbecue."

Howard has not shared everything with his relatives. He personally controlled Burns Foods and swapped that for preferred convertible shares in the $2-billion energy and utility conglomerate Union Enterprises Ltd. Acting as a white knight to Union's besieged management in 1985 when the company was captured by George Mann, Webster got a beautiful deal: preferred shares with a hefty dividend and the ability to convert his preferred shares into 20 per cent of Union's common shares.

Howard was born in 1910. He married once, at fifty-three years of age, but stayed married only for weeks. Fiercely private, he lives alone with two servants near the Royal Montreal Golf Course. His speech, like that of most Websters, is staccato. They talk like Gatling guns and think faster. Most are well co-ordinated jocks, devoted to athletics, both as owners of sports teams and as participants. The Senator's sons were brought up to be fiercely competitive on and off the playing field. Howard was Canadian intercollegiate golf champ twice at McGill University. Lorne is an outstanding athlete, with many trophies earned as an amateur squash player. Ben, Norman, and the others can claim comparable achievements.

Howard is eccentric. For instance, he has not written a letter in decades, preferring to do his deals by phone or in person. "He wrote one a couple of years ago to a guy he was involved in a dispute with," says Lorne. "It had been carefully drafted by a lawyer because it was a matter that might have gone to court. Howard had a male secretary type it up. But Howard thought he'd add a little bit to this carefully drafted letter. In tiny print at the bottom of all this, he added the words 'You rat.' He took the rat reference out and never sent the letter."

He is extremely reclusive. On the night in 1955 when Howard bought the *Globe and Mail* for $10.9 million, he refused to be photographed by the *Globe*'s photographers. One of Canada's largest papers did not even have a picture of its new owner on file. Ever aloof, Howard did not arrive in Toronto to meet his management until one week after the takeover.

In 1969, the family sold its family coal firm to Shell Canada Ltd. for tens of millions. It was selling 1.1 billion gallons of oil a year, which today would be a $2-billion-a-year business. That year, Lorne went on his own. He had already made a pile of money on the Growth Oil & Gas mutual fund with Stephen Jarislowsky, the glib, German-born owner of the country's largest investment counsellor, Jarislowsky & Fraser. Its shares went to $120 from $3.50 in months. Lorne hunted for financial companies.

Lorne began with a small private land company called St. Lawrence Diversified, owned by an Egyptian developer called Joseph Bardo, a Webster coal customer. Bardo asked Lorne in; he invested and eventually took over. Then he bought life and casualty insurance companies, but sold them in the 1970s when the Parti Québécois set up provincially operated automobile insurance. He also bought Trust générale, Quebec's fifth-largest trust company, to help a financially troubled friend, André Simard. In 1983, with the clandestine help of Quebec's pension plan, the Caisse de dépôt et placement du Québec, Simard gained control of its board of directors and pushed Lorne out. But Webster made $46.5 million in profit from selling his shares.

Lorne's holding company, the Prenor Group, includes the $178-million mutual fund Bolton Tremblay; 30 per cent of Toronto's Vanguard Trust, with an option on 21 per cent more; a mortgage company and properties. He is also a partner with Montreal's ebullient John Dobson in Formula Growth Fund, a smallish mutual fund whose shares have gone from $100 to $3,000 in twenty-five years.

Lorne has seven children, and interests of his own in South America, the Caribbean, and Europe. He and his brother Ben share a country place in Quebec and a château in France, complete with vineyards.

Ben left Montreal for Toronto in 1955, and pursued his many and varied interests. For three decades, he has combed the world in search of excellence. Along with big-buck backers drawn from his family, friends, and pension funds, Ben invests in companies and ideas. Helix Circuits Inc. has fifty small companies in its stable at any given time. Some become big enough to go public, selling shares to the public and becoming listed on stock exchanges. Between 1981 and 1984, Helix brought four to market: two high-tech companies, Orcatech Inc. and Helix Circuits Inc., and two medical technology firms, Sterivet Laboratories Limited and Novametrix Medical Systems Inc.

Ben was one of the first behind Mitel, Toronto television station CITY-TV, and Canadian Velcro, which owns the world rights to the Swiss invention. Intensely curious, he took a medically supervised LSD trip in 1960; he has investigated reported instances of telepathy, clairvoyance, and reincarnation and has flown seers and mediums to Toronto to entertain friends.

He, his wife, Madaline, and five children live in Toronto's posh Forest Hill and are neighbours of the Eaton brothers, Jimmy Kay, George Mann, and Douglas Bassett.

Norman, his wife, Pat, and their six children occupy a Georgian lakefront estate in Oakville, west of Toronto. Shortly after moving in, they decided the in-ground pool should be where the tennis court was, and vice versa, so they had them moved. And the children's $10,000 tree-house is a sight to behold, with miniature cutlery and plates and several rooms cradled in a magnificent oak tree.

The Websters are indeed interesting, and very, very rich. They control several billions in assets, and are collectively worth $400 million or more. How much, they decline to disclose.

"'Are you a millionaire?' a lawyer once asked me," Lorne recalls. "'What do you mean?' I said. 'In lira, yen, pounds?' I didn't answer it. Rather than punch him, I told him I have assets and I have debts, too, and on a good day, the assets are ahead.'"

THE IVANIERS

THE SECOND WORLD WAR gave Canada the Ivaniers, a talented family of European industrialists like the Bentleys, the Batas, and the Reichmanns. For several generations, the Ivaniers were tycoons in Romania, where they employed hundreds at their steelworks. Then the storm-troopers arrived. Fortunately, the Ivaniers, like many Romanian Jews, were protected and survived the Holocaust. But they lost all their possessions and remained disenfranchised after Romania was "liberated" by the Soviets. They immigrated to Canada in 1949 and in a little over three decades became one of the richest families in their adopted country, accumulating $5 billion in assets in one of the world's toughest businesses, steelmaking.

In 1948, the undaunted Isin Ivanier left Romania with his wife, Fancia, and children and went to Paris. A year later, the family immigrated to Canada, with a modest amount of money. Isin chose Canada rather than the United States, where some Ivanier relatives lived, "because we heard good things. We didn't know anything else about the place. We just heard nice things about it," explains Paul Ivanier, Isin's oldest son, who was born in 1933.

Because they spoke French, the family went to Montreal, where Isin immediately set up a small wire mill. Born in 1907, he is a brilliant industrialist, described by some as a technological genius. He's a man who still enjoys nothing more than to spend most days on the shop floor in his mills.

Unlike most of Canada's richest families, who are investors or paper entrepreneurs, the Ivaniers are mostly builders. What's more, they have triumphed in a so-called sunset industry operating from a province that has become one of the economic backwaters of North America. But they are successful because they are both technological innovators and takeover artists, combining the genius of a Thomas Edison with the brains of an investment banker like J. P. Morgan.

This rare combination has enabled them to turn a modest Montreal mill into North America's foremost secondary steelmaker. Primary steelmakers like Algoma or Bethlehem Steel make steel out of iron ore. The Ivaniers make specialized products out of steel and scrap metals. Their $2-billion steelmaking conglomerate is called Ivaco.

Through in-house technology and a head-spinning series of acquisitions that began only in 1969, Ivaco has become the world's largest maker of nails and one of North America's biggest suppliers of wire. Its mills turn steel slabs into wire used in fences, reinforced concrete, pipeline cages, and cables and ropes for bridges, elevators, and vehicles. They also make everything from axe blades to nuts, bolts, and other fasteners used in the automobile and construction industries.

Ivaco is as much an American as a Canadian operation. Some 84 per cent of its products are sold in the U.S., with the rest in Canada. The company has become North America's eleventh-largest steel company, in a field dominated by monoliths like U.S. Steel and Bethlehem Steel. By 1984, Ivaco was Canada's seventy-third-largest company, with sales of $1.2 billion and assets of $1.1 billion. It also owned the largest single stake, 12 per cent, of the Hamilton steelmaker Dofasco Inc., Canada's forty-eighth-largest company, with nearly $2 billion in sales. That same year, Dofasco and Ivaco were two of only four steel companies in North America that made profits. The others lost money and blamed imports from Third World countries, which flooded the U.S. market until protectionist action was imposed.

In 1985, Paul Ivanier continued to blaze a trail of takeovers, buying 51 per cent of Canron Inc., a steelmaker with assets of $223 million and sales of $387 million. Later that year, he also bought 54.3 per cent of the AHL Group Ltd. of Toronto, a privately owned maker of automobile and construction products with sales of $145.9 million in 1984.

The Ivaniers' success story should not be a surprise. After all, it is hardly a patch on what they have already surmounted. This is a family to whom adversity has become second nature, and that has forged an ability to be worldbeaters in one of the toughest businesses around. Even more important, the second generation picked up where the first left off, dovetailing each other's gifts.

"It takes a certain kind of person to start a business as my father did, and quite another to take it along to the next level," says Paul.

Paul is the family's driving force — Isin's oldest son and Ivaco's lepre-chaun-like president. An acquisitions specialist and dealmaker, Paul oversees the company's direction, while his brother Sydney, his fourth cousin Jack Klein, and his uncle Michael Herling are operations executives, in charge of important divisions. The five own a total of 61 per cent of Ivaco's stock, worth at least $250 million, in more or less equal proportions.

"They are all driven to succeed and excel," observes Don Lawson, a direc-tor and shareholder since 1970, who heads the Toronto brokerage firm Moss Lawson. "The father is a technical genius, who has a tremendous number of patents on the development of the steelmaking process. He has been a real innovator. Michael Herling has a lot of the financial expertise. Syd runs an important division, and Jack Klein has done a tremendous job in his role."

Paul is all of five-foot-three, a tiny, hyperactive chartered accountant. A graduate of McGill University and an art patron, he lives for competition. With the alacrity of a sportscaster, he snaps off his company's stats: "Eleventh-largest steelmaker in North America. Seventy-third-largest company in Canada by sales, eighty-fourth by income, and ninety-fourth by assets. Nine thousand employed in thirty-seven plants, twenty in the U.S. and seventeen in Canada. Thirty-seven per cent compounded growth rate per annum. I'm told this has never been done before. You haven't heard about it? We don't flaunt. You don't build the kind of business we've built and give interviews."

Paul Ivanier's Sherbrooke Street office overlooks Montreal's Mount Royal and the Samuel Bronfman Building. His office is filled with Group of Seven paintings. The beige suede walls and elegant furnishings are set off with dramatic sculptures. Beside his stunning brass desk is an autographed picture of his son, Philip, with former Israeli prime minister Menachem Begin. Across the office beside a sofa is an autographed picture of one of his closest friends, the late Nelson Rockefeller, former governor of New York, with whom he did business.

Paul is a dynamo, who speaks Romanian, English, French, and German fluently and describes himself with characteristic immodesty as "a salesman at heart and industrialist by aptitude. I have an understanding of people and am good at dealmaking."

He is also a philanthropist who is active in several charitable organizations, a member of the acquisitions committee at the Montreal Museum of Fine

Arts, and a director of several universities. "I feel you have to do more than the people who just write a cheque. It's good for the soul."

Even though his business takes him all over North America and many of his assets are elsewhere, he remains devoted to Montreal. He and his wife, Lilly, live in the city but have a country place in the Laurentians, where he enjoys an occasional game of golf and goes skating often in the winter.

The rapid rise of Ivaco began in December 1969 — twenty years after Isin launched the enterprise in Canada. It all sounds too simple the way Paul describes it, with his rapid-fire delivery and slight accent. "There were five partners — my dad, me, my younger brother Syd, my uncle Michael Herling, and my cousin Jack Klein. I told my partners: we had $11 million in sales at the time and three small plants we all built together. I spent until two in the morning explaining what I wanted to do with the business and how I would do it and they said go. And it went from $11 million to $1.2 billion in sales and twenty-three acquisitions later. We will hit $1.5 billion in sales in 1986 after two more deals. And I'm talking yours truly. This has been most successful."

In order to grow, he convinced them that shares had to be sold to the public to raise more capital. And within weeks, Paul made his first — and most important — acquisition. Ivanier merged his company with Ingersoll Machinery in Ontario, which was owned at the time by Don Lawson's father, Frank Lawson. It was a marriage made in heaven and the courtship was whirlwind.

"I called Lawson Sr. and said, 'You don't know me, but I'd like to come by,'" recalls Paul. "I called him from California, where I was vacationing with my wife, and asked for fifteen minutes of his time. We flew to Toronto first thing in the morning. I left my wife in the hotel and said to Lawson, 'How about making our companies partners? Look at the situation: we're producing 80 per cent standard [regular-size fasteners like nuts and bolts] and 20 per cent specials [custom-made]. And you're making the other way round. If we combined we could do all the standards in one plant and all the specials in another. And your warehousing network is strong in the West and we're strong in the East.' It was a perfect fit."

Four hours later he called his wife; they returned to Montreal that day with a deal. Shares were exchanged on a one-for-one basis even though Ivanier's company had fewer assets. "Ingersoll put us on the map," says Paul. "I had ambition, vision, less assets, but they trusted me. And they've made a fortune." Those shares sold for $6 apiece and had increased sevenfold by 1985 to $42 apiece.

Along the way there have been twenty-five acquisitions, and only two that got away. But there has also been internal growth through innovation and special marketing skills. "Growth by expansion. Acquisitions are a short cut in our expansion program. If it would take ten years to grow to a certain level of sales and only three if we buy someone out, we will attempt an acquisition," says Paul.

In 1985, the Ivaniers pulled off a stock market coup and sold $191 million worth of Ivaco preferred shares, exchangeable into the Dofasco shares that Ivaco had bought for $60 million. But to postpone the exchange Ivaco will pay these shareholders 8.5-per-cent dividends during the first five years and after that, whatever dividend Dofasco pays on its shares plus 4 per cent. That way, Ivaco gets to have its cake and eat it too: it reaps the capital gains of its Dofasco shares by not selling them.

Of the $191 million, $60 million was used to pay off the bank loans taken out to buy Dofasco in the first place and the rest is on deposit, being invested. Even more clever, these proceeds are not taxable until shareholders exchange their holdings for Dofasco shares down the road — which gives Ivaco about $6 million a year in sheer profit from investing the proceeds.

"It was absolutely brilliant, one of the smartest deals I've ever seen," says Lawson. "From an investment standpoint, best success is always with owner-managers. There's no question that the Ivaniers spend twenty-four hours a day at what they're doing. I don't think Paul's brain ever stops."

Ivaco is very much a hands-on operation, but nepotism is non-existent. Like Dylex, it is decentralized in structure, and it usually keeps the entrepreneurs who started the companies it takes over. As a result, there are a dozen or more "presidents" besides Paul Ivanier.

As with other dynasties, the biggest challenge is succession. By all reports, Paul's son, Philip, has inherited his grandfather's technological genius, but has applied this gift to computers. He built his first computer on his own at eleven, and at nineteen became a highly paid consultant to Apple Computers while still a university student. Paul's daughter Janet obtained an MBA and lives in Florida; he has another daughter, Shirley. His brother Syd has a teen-aged son and daughter.

But the indefatigable Monsieur Ivanier promises to be around for quite some time, inspiring everyone around him that one can accomplish anything, "if you are a realist and don't disappoint people."

He has proven his philosophy. At Ivaco's 1983 annual meeting, Paul

Ivanier reminded shareholders he had met a ten-year target stated at Ivaco's 1973 meeting: that the company would reach $1 billion in sales. He went on to set another target, promising sales would reach $2 billion by 1993.

And not a soul in the audience that day doubted the tiny tycoon. They considered it done.

THE STEINBERGS

MITZI DOBRIN was the first woman to sit on the board of directors of the country's largest bank, the Royal Bank of Canada, an exclusive gentlemen's club where excellent food and excellent contacts are served for lunch. She is the unlikeliest feminist you'll ever see. Slightly less than five feet tall in heels, she has a Montreal office that looks like the boudoir of a teenaged girl, minus the stuffed animals. It is decorated in shades of pink and beige with paintings by Henri Masson and Gingras. Two pink-beige-and-white loveseats occupy a corner, along with pictures of her father, husband, and two grandsons. Her father groomed her husband to run the family business because he thought his daughters belonged at home. Nonetheless, she is now a dynamic business-woman and is executive vice president of Steinberg Inc., the $1-billion company her late father, "Mr. Sam" Steinberg, founded.

Steinberg Inc. is Canada's twenty-fifth-largest enterprise, with sales of $3.3 billion and 32,600 employees. Steinberg now has 216 supermarkets; a few dozen department stores; 93 Valdi discount stores; La Maisonée, a chain of 67 convenience stores; a catalogue showroom company called Cardinal Distributors Ltd.; half interest in Quebec's Pharmaprix drugstore chain; sugar refiner Cartier Sugar Ltd.; Phenix Flour Ltd.; 164 fast-food outlets; Smitty's, the largest grocery chain in Phoenix, Arizona; and real estate developer Ivanhoe Inc., with dozens of shopping centres.

Mitzi did not join the family business until 1973, when her children were grown. Mitzi is the oldest daughter and her husband, a chartered accountant named Melvyn Dobrin, was taken under her father's wing, eventually becoming president in 1969 and chairman of the board when Mr. Sam died in 1978. Shortly after his funeral, Melvyn was quoted as saying, "He gave me 99.99 per cent of what I have," including a wife.

While uninvolved in day-to-day operations, Mitzi was always her father's confidante. "My father always discussed business with me. But he never thought I'd go into business. My parents' attitude was when I'd marry, my husband would come into the business," says Mitzi.

In 1969, she went to law school, over her father's protest. "It was the stimulus I needed while raising my young family. Maids have never looked after my children. I went to school because studying gave me an excuse to stay home and look after them. I studied law — not to be a lawyer, but to develop expertise. I decided when I finished law school that I would do legal aid. Life was good to me and I wanted to help others less fortunate."

In July 1973, Mr. Sam turned to her for help when the company began heading for financial trouble, accosting her at Montreal's Elmridge Golf Club, where she was lunching with friends.

"My dad came up to me. He was pale. I asked what was wrong, and he said he was disgusted with Miracle Mart's results. Our year ends in July. He said, 'I want you to come into the business.' At the time I had finished law school and didn't want to be tied down. He said, 'Be in my office tomorrow morning.' I was, and he made me an offer I couldn't refuse. I took the job. My father didn't discuss it with my husband. I was rather surprised he came to me because my parents felt daughters should get married and shouldn't work."

Sam's attitude towards his daughters was all the more surprising considering that his own mother had started the enterprise. Ida Steinberg opened her carriage trade store on St. Lawrence Boulevard in 1917, offering charge accounts and delivery from a horse-drawn cart. A few years later, she became the first grocer in the city to offer self-service meat. Singlehandedly she supported her six children, while her religious husband "spent all of his time in the synagogue and didn't really work," says Mitzi.

They eventually separated. All six children stayed in the business, but Sam was the clear leader. He finished Grade Seven and was running things by the age of fourteen, expanding the firm into the real estate and retail conglomerate it is today.

But his strong, dynamic personality cowed many executives who worked for him, and that was why in 1973 when the firm hit troubled waters he turned to his strong-willed daughter Mitzi. With an almost uncanny business sense and the full support of her father, she gained the respect of those around her, playing an important role in turning around Steinberg's struggling department store chain, called Miracle Mart. The stores were the first major diversification the firm had made away from the food business. And the results were disastrous. The department stores were badly run, and their losses were eating up the precious capital needed to meet the needs and new challenges of the grocery business. By 1976, they were profitable again.

"We had to completely rethink our business," she says. "Everything my father did was to enhance his supermarkets. Real estate was a natural outgrowth; similarly he went into department stores. He thought of it as an adjunct to support the food business rather than thinking about the needs of getting into the general merchandise business. In retrospect, it wasn't a mistake. Miracle Mart turned around in two years," she says.

The trouble was more deep-seated than just the Miracle Mart stores. The seeds for problems to come were sown in 1969 on the food side of the business when Steinberg decided to become a discount grocery store chain, to grab a bigger market share in Quebec. To pick up forfeited revenues, the company slashed maintenance and training programs. By 1973, these problems were coming home to roost, as stores began looking tatty and good people within the firm were getting hard to find. The company also cut costs by advertising goods from the suppliers who offered them the biggest advertising rebate, rather than from those that offered customers the best products.

Politics, too, were a factor in Quebec; some 130,000 anglos left for Ontario and elsewhere in Canada where they felt more welcome. The market was also shrinking for other reasons. Because of changing work patterns and family structures, people were shifting to fast foods, convenience stores, and delicatessens for their needs. Competing grocery stores, like Provigo, were franchise operations, with significantly lower costs because they were not unionized. Besides all that, the smallest independents had a big edge in Quebec because they were allowed to remain open on Sundays, have extended hours, and sell beer, liquor, and wine.

"In the early 1970s, we were left alone as the only pure supermarket in Quebec, and we had the highest wages in the business," she says. "Independents had sprung up, there were co-ops and franchise operations. Dominion had disappeared. We had too many stores, too close together."

Steinberg closed less profitable grocery stores, and those that remained were upgraded, with delicatessen, fast food, bakery, boutique, and bulk-buying departments added. Since 1984, the company has been experimenting with warehouse no-frills grocery stores and quality fruit and vegetable markets. And attempts are under way to renegotiate with the unions. In 1984, Steinberg lobbied successfully for the right to sell beer and wine in any of its outlets located in shopping centres.

Some department stores were closed, too, and Mitzi had to determine the proper niche for those that remained. Some stores catered to the budget-conscious, others to more upscale shoppers. Mitzi decided the right niche lay in upgrading merchandise and making all of the stores' buying policies uniform. That would help people identify what a Miracle Mart was.

"We turned that business around in two years. It was hard to get good new people because it was such a losing operation. It was losing a tremendous amount of money, but I saw a niche for Miracle Mart. And it was to target the buying to specific customers."

Not all problems were overcome, she adds. "My father made commitments and got carried away, and it's been a terrible drain. I tried to stop him, but couldn't. We have a Windsor store and two in Quebec that lose $300,000 a year, but we can't close them because we can't break the lease."

Steinberg's chain in Arizona and its real estate business continue to reap rewards, contributing most of the profits since 1980.

Now Mitzi and her husband have offices kitty-corner from each other in Steinberg's executive offices, across the street from the Montreal Forum. Melvyn Dobrin, born in 1923, joined Steinberg as store manager in 1950 and was made president nineteen years later. The firm's operation is still a family affair. Sam's brother, Nathan, is vice chairman of the board, and Nathan's son, H. Arnold Steinberg, is executive vice president, finance and development. Of the five top executives only one, Steinberg president Irving Ludmer, is not a family member. His appointment is the beginning of the end of family management — a switch in philosophy that most dynasties must make at some point in time as heirs lose interest.

"You must ensure that those with talent are not blocked. The family is given opportunity, but not at the expense of others," Mitzi says. "The proof is that our president is not a member of the family. He got the job because he was the best."

Mitzi is the only one of Mr. Sam's four daughters to get involved in the company. One sister died, and the others, Evelyn Alexander and Marilyn Cobrin, have remained homemakers. Their father's 51-per-cent controlling interest in the form of special voting shares is divided equally between the four daughters or their heirs. The only non-family shareholder with the special voting shares is the Quebec pension plan, Caisse de dépôt et placement du Québec, with 3 per cent. The rest of these shares are held by the heirs of Mr. Sam's four brothers and one sister.

The sisters each had three children, but only one is involved in the company. Mitzi and Melvyn's youngest son, an MBA, is a store manager, and their other two children — a son and daughter — are both Montreal-based lawyers. Mitzi remains close to her sister Marilyn, who manages the family trusts, but not to Evelyn.

The Dobrins live in Westmount and spend weekends playing tennis or golf or jogging and skiing at their 10,000-square-foot house in Saint-Sauveur in the Laurentians, about an hour from Montreal. Scenic and secluded, the home has an indoor pool, a tennis court, and a sauna. They also travel a great deal, when they're not attending company social functions, and have one of the country's best Group of Seven collections.

"I'm close to paradise when I'm jogging in the country," says the wiry grandmother of two. "We're also art collectors, and have a few hundred paintings. We have some of the finest Lawren Harrises, Emily Carrs, Frank Johnstons, and Varleys and some good Quebec artists. Our kids are collectors, too. And we have a democratic way of buying paintings. We give the kids the vote."

As for the future, it is doubtful that the children and grandchildren of Mr. Sam will continue to hold onto their controlling interest. The Dobrins have certainly not forced their children to become involved in the family firm and there appears to be little interest.

"You never know about the future. At the moment we've got control, but things change," says Mitzi. "My sisters never took an active role in the business."

Like so many families, the Steinbergs must find an heir apparent to run things. Cousin Arnold Steinberg is the likeliest candidate but only time will tell.

THE BATAS

OUT OF ITS Don Mills, Ont., headquarters, Bata Shoes masterminds a global empire that shoes a barefoot world. Roughly one out of every ten persons in the world buys a pair of Bata shoes every year. One million pairs a day spew forth from the company's ninety-six factories in as many countries, representing one out of every twelve pairs of shoes sold in the world. In several African countries, the word for shoe is "bata." And while only 5 per cent of Bata's production is in Canada, worldwide headquarters remain here because that is where its chairman of the board, Thomas G. Bata, lives when he is not in airplanes visiting his far-flung empire.

The Batas are another of Canada's transplanted dynasties. In 1939, only twenty-five years old, Thomas Bata dismantled his father's shoemaking factory in Czechoslovakia and smuggled out the machinery in hundreds of cases, along with a hundred key employees and their families. Now it is a mom-and-pop operation on a mega-scale: Thomas Bata and his Swiss-born wife, Sonja, run Bata Shoes with its 85,000 employees, travelling together and amicably dividing duties. He is in charge of technical and administrative matters. She is an architect and heads the company's design teams, creating footwear fashions, advertising images, or new interiors in Bata's 6,000 stores. Their son, Thomas Jr., a Harvard Business School graduate, became chief executive officer in 1984, at the age of thirty-seven.

Thomas Bata was born in 1915 in Zlin, Czechoslovakia, the only child in a family of shoemakers. Like ten generations of Batas before him, he was blessed with a "cobbler's thumb" — a digit that curves half-way back to the wrist. The cobbler's trade had been transformed forever by his father, also named Thomas. The Henry Ford of cobblers, he brought the assembly line to shoe manufacturing. By 1932, when the elder Thomas Bata's life ended prematurely in an airplane crash, his sleepy Moravian village had become one of Europe's bustling factory towns, as Bata Shoes grew from fifty employees to 20,000. Now his son is the world's foremost cobbler, one of its most successful industrialists and undoubtedly one of its wealthiest.

Bata has continued his father's strategy: to mechanize the craft in order to reduce costs and to make shoes close to the markets where they will be sold. This process has not been trouble-free. Bata plants have been nationalized, burned, and bombed. Local ambitions have resulted in partial nationalization, seizure, or sales of shares to the public at thirteen of his overseas outfits. In Uganda, Idi Amin seized the Bata plant three times and gave it back to the family three times. In 1977, Sudan returned 51 per cent of the operation it had only just nationalized but couldn't run.

"All over the world after the war, governments thought they should get involved in business, but subsequently this changed. We were nationalized three times in Uganda, but were one of the first to get our companies back," says Bata. "We do not participate in political activities in any country. We always continued to give support and services even though the assets were taken over. We are running a business, not accumulating wealth. Our experience is usually that, whatever the government, they gradually come to an understanding of the facts of economic life and find it necessary to follow those laws of nature."

The changing world economy, with tariff barriers and other forms of protectionism, posed other challenges. In January 1984, Bata closed its fifty-year-old Jamaican operations because of mounting financial losses. Problems were compounded by chronic shortage of hard currency, making imports of machinery or raw materials difficult; in addition, the footwear industry suffered because Jamaicans simply ignored import controls and smuggled in shoes.

Paradoxically, protectionism has also helped improve Bata's bottom line. Competitors faced with tariff barriers to imports and without a global network of plants hire Bata factories to produce their shoes, too, as a means of surmounting trade obstacles. In many countries, Bata factories also produce footwear for Adidas, Sears Roebuck & Co., and dozens of other companies.

Bata and his raven-haired wife, Sonja, are the only husband-and-wife team among Canada's wealthiest families. Inscribed over the gates of the first Bata factory was the motto "Work is a moral necessity," and the family still lives by it. Despite enormous wealth, they continue to work long hours on and off the road. Thomas and Sonja married in 1946 and had three daughters and one son very soon afterwards. But Sonja decided not to stay at home. She decided that the only way she could be with her globe-trotting husband was to join the firm.

"Many of the company's plants were destroyed during the Second World War," she told a magazine. "Rebuilding meant a tremendous amount of travelling. I had a choice, either travel with [Thomas] and then become a working member of the team, or stay at home. So I decided to make a career in his business."

"Ours is a highly decentralized business," explains Bata. "We provide new techniques and new training, but we are proud at how decentralized things are. Our managers in each plant make 95 per cent of decisions on their own, and that's a very exciting situation."

Thomas and Sonja also generously contribute time and money to charities worldwide. She is chairman of the World Wildlife Fund and Canadian Junior Achievement Club, among other organizations. They often travel to the Galapagos and Melanesian islands to observe wildlife, photograph, and dive.

Twelve years younger than he, she enjoys helicopter skiing in the Bugaboos and is a pilot, who first soloed at the age of fifteen.

The senior Batas are celebrated everywhere they travel; they are on a first-name basis with more world leaders than any of Canada's prime ministers. This is because Bata means jobs. As Bata explains, "We quickly generate jobs directly and indirectly. We will encourage someone, for instance, to go into the lacemaking business so we can buy laces locally. This will occur with other suppliers, so that if there are import restrictions we won't be held to ransom."

As the largest employer in Kenya, after the government, and among the largest in Uganda, India, South Africa, and dozens of other countries, Bata is often consulted on government policy by anxious leaders. The result is that the Batas and their executives function like a private-sector version of world government, juggling export ambitions, import restrictions, and government policies with the alacrity of diplomats. Bata even couches his comments in language more like that of an ambassador than a hard-driving capitalist: "This world is so marvellously varied that it could be the government in, say, Brazil that decides all shoe machines will be made in Brazil. Then there is no way for our company there to do anything but buy Brazil-made machines."

The Bata International Centre in Don Mills is where technological innovations, shoe machinery modifications, courses, conferences, marketing, and publications for the worldwide empire originate. In addition to factories and stores, Bata owns tanneries, hosiery factories, textile plants, rubber plantations, rubber-processing plants, and an engineering company to design patented shoemaking equipment.

The Batas and their executives log millions of miles annually, and in the company's headquarters hangs an enormous map with executive name-tags pinned all over it. The tags of executives on holiday are put on ice in Greenland. "Because we have no plants there," he explains. Banks of clocks give the office a newsroom aura, with labels underneath like Paris, Singapore, and Toronto.

Like some potentate of profits, Bata must stay tuned to the world's current problems. "I listen to the BBC World Service news at breakfast, because that gives me a broad spectrum of international events," Bata says. "I'm in Toronto about 40 per cent of the time and the rest of the time I'm travelling."

The story of Bata and its products reads like a current events course in school: it made boots for GIs in Vietnam, it has become embroiled in Canada in controversy over how it treats its 3,500 South African workers, and its Lebanese operations have been shelled and evacuated. Some $500,000 in ransom money was paid to free a kidnapped Bata executive in South America. Even so, the hot spots aren't always bad for the bottom line. "Our Nicaraguan company has done even better since the Sandinistas took over," Bata told a Toronto newspaper.

All his factories provide him with weekly profit and loss reports in Toronto, with figures broken down in detail so that Bata can see at a glance whether problems, or profits, are the result of the retail or manufacturing ends of the business. "Some say he can sit in Toronto and pinpoint a mistake in India that has had local executives biting their nails for months," said a Bata executive.

Thomas Jr., the new CEO, has never been interviewed; all the Batas avoid publicity whenever possible. By most accounts, however, he is more cautious in business than his father.

The story of Bata, Canada's most successful multinational, began in 1939, when the last German ship to dock in Canada before the war delivered a number of machines and components smuggled out of his father's factory. "The ship left without clearance, and fortunately our alert RCMP stopped it with a thirty-foot launch and got the cargo unloaded."

The year before, as Hitler's army encroached on Europe, twenty-five-year-old Thomas was plotting a way out. Canada was a likely first choice because the company owned 1,500 acres of land for future development as a factory site on the Trent Canal in southern Ontario. Besides that, he had had a childhood fascination with Jack London and books about the Yukon gold rush, and he had gained a respect for Britain, its institutions, and the Commonwealth after attending schools in the U.K. So in 1939, he went to Ottawa and convinced the Canadian government to let him in, without any financial help. And by mid-1939, the first of several hundred crates of patented Bata shoemaking equipment arrived in Canada, labelled SHOES FOR EXPORT.

"Canada appealed to me because since I was a child I had read stories by London and Zane Grey about the North and stories about the Bay and the adventures of gentlemen traders. The first head of Hudson's Bay was a Czech king," says Bata. "I used to import Peterborough canoes to Czechoslovakia in the '30s. I had a certain psychological affinity to Canada and having gone to school in Britain, it looked British and was next to the U.S. To me, it was the best of both worlds, and I have not been disappointed."

Young Bata had also obtained permission from Ottawa for a hundred Czech families to immigrate. These people became the nucleus of his new venture in Canada, which he named Batawa. It was, and remains, a feudal-style company town with neat houses, schools, churches, library, store, and a community centre. Back in 1964, employees paid a mere $10 a week to rent company houses. Most now own their own homes.

There was a great deal of opposition to Bata's settling in Canada, mostly from shoe manufacturers. "The shoe industry then was in the same state as it is now. I was not welcomed by that industry with brass bands. They made insinuations about my politics because I was fair game. There was no FIRA in those days, but immigration regulations. The prime minister set up a cabinet committee, the only cabinet committee on economics since, and that was the best thing that could have happened because by the time war broke out the government knew everything about us and accepted us as part of the Canadian participation in the Allied cause."

In 1940, he lived in a worker's cottage, knew all his employees personally, played defence on the company's old-timers' hockey team, ate in the cafeteria, and worked harder than anyone else in the plant. Besides being a superb shoemaker, he is also a master mechanic.

The young industrialist also benefited from the war. Batawa's factories were devoted to machinery and manpower for the war effort, making anti-aircraft equipment and ammunition-inspecting machines. A remnant from those days is Bata Engineering, which still sells about $40 million a year of ammunition and tank parts.

Meanwhile, his uncle Jan A. Bata had set up a similar operation in Maryland, but the two had bitter business disagreements. Jan waged an unsuccessful court case against Thomas for portions of the family business. In 1962, the two sides settled. Jan Bata later died in Brazil.

Unchallenged king of the shoe business, Bata Sr. is husky and tanned with thick grey hair. His speech is somewhat clipped and his accent is as much London as Prague. He is fluent in most European languages, knows some African dialects, and has studied Japanese. He and his wife make their home in an artwork-laden house in Toronto's posh Bayview Avenue area, a John Parkin–designed bungalow on a high hill overlooking the local Bata factory. They also have a flat in London, a place owned by Sonja's family in St. Moritz where they ski, and scores of company guest-houses where they and their executives stay.

His office, like his personal style, is spartan. There are no family memorabilia or knick-knacks decorating his office credenza or desk. He loves tennis and chess, ballet and opera, and every year he takes a party of friends to the opening of the Stratford Festival.

As with many industrialists who learned at the knees of their nineteenth-century fathers, Bata's management style is too Victorian for some. Smoking in head office has been banned since 1978, and in the developed world workers find his company-owned towns stifling. But elsewhere they are a form of private-sector paternalism that may be passé, but is a godsend in the Third World.

In his twenties, Bata was known to go into rages: he had a demoralizing habit of bawling out employees. One Batawa man talked back in the 1950s and was sent home without pay for three months. These days, in the era of wrongful dismissal, such management relations would be considered Neanderthal. "I holler and they holler back," he says. But he has toned down accordingly. In more recent years, while touring a plant he tore the top off a shoe and asked the foreman, "Is this quality?" The foreman asked Bata for his shoe and promptly tore its top off. "I, too, have strong hands, Mr. Bata," he said, and Bata walked away without comment.

But there is a sensitivity to the social needs of his workers in Thomas Bata, missing from today's multinational-bound MBAs, as this remark to *Executive* magazine reveals: "We know what kind of a social shock it is when a plant closes in Canada. Yet in Canada we have unemployment insurance and all kinds of welfare and alternatives. But in most of the developing countries, it's a question of life and death for these people. They have uprooted themselves from an agricultural society and come to a town to work in an industry. They've brought their relatives with them because, working in industry, their earnings are so much higher. Thus a large group of relatives are dependent upon them."

His unceasing ambition and push for constant perfection was forged by his father, who prized self-reliance. When young Tom was only seven, his father stopped the car during a trip through Czech countryside and gave him some cash and the address of a friend 30 kilometres away. Then he drove off. The heir made the trip without spending any of the money.

Vacations were spent working in his father's shoe factory. By age eighteen, he had earned a master shoemaker's certificate, and his father sent him to sell in Switzerland and to open another factory there. In 1932, his father's airplane crashed en route to the factory, killing him instantly.

Setbacks and even tragedy haven't deterred that remarkable son and his talented workmate, Sonja. While others may have relaxed, the Batas persist despite the pervasiveness of their empire. They recently decided to expand in the United States, buying a chain of 600 retail outlets in addition to their four factories there. As one of the two biggest sponsors for the World Cup of soccer, the world's biggest sporting event, Bata is making a big push into sports shoes sold under the Power label. In fact, Power outsells Nike, Adidas, and all others in that field. As he told *Financial Post Magazine* in an interview: "We are hard pressed to find any new geographical locations, but we still have an enormous reservoir of bare feet in areas where we currently operate. So the opportunities really are unlimited."

THE POSLUNSES

ONE DOLLAR out of every ten spent on clothing in his country is earned by Dylex, a publicly traded company controlled by Toronto tycoons Wilf Posluns and Jimmy Kay. In just two decades, Dylex has grown into a collection of specialty fashion store chains, catering to many ages and income ranges, that now outsells Canada's monolithic department store chains like Eaton's or The Bay.

For Wilf Posluns and the rest of his family, it is certainly a far cry from the "shmatta" (Yiddish for rags) business where they have worked for three generations as clothing manufacturers. Back in 1966, the Posluns family discovered the rich vein of retailing when they joined forces with Kay, a high-flying Winnipeg financier. And on the back of a placemat, over lunch at Toronto's Lord Simcoe Hotel, a partnership deal was struck that would make fashion history.

They called their partnership Dylex, the name of one of Kay's many companies and an abbreviation for Damn-Your-Lousy-Excuses. Kay is Dylex's chairman, Wilf Posluns is its president, and his brother, Irving Posluns, is vice president and treasurer.

Wilf is an intense, good-looking man, who rarely smiles. His muted green office is half the size of Kay's, but he controls the company with 50.1 per cent of the voting shares. Kay, on the other hand, is an ebullient entrepreneur who enjoys sailing close to the wind even if he sometimes gets wet. He's considerably more aggressive than Wilf, is ten years older but looks younger.

The two are like chalk and cheese. Their relationship became somewhat strained in 1981 when Kay's non-Dylex business affairs monopolized his time; Posluns worried that companies affiliated with Peter and Edward Bronfman would move in and take Kay's shares. At that time, Kay was borrowing money from Hees International and Continental Bank, both controlled by the Bronfmans, and the two companies had liens against all of Kay's assets. Posluns snapped up more shares to give himself 50.1 per cent of votes and undisputed control over Dylex.

While such concerns have worried and occasionally angered Posluns, the situation has not affected the operations of Dylex. And despite differences in style and philosophy, Posluns and Kay certainly are a winning combination.

Their Dylex formula is unique and, ironically, was born out of the fact that neither the Posluns brothers nor Kay knew anything about retailing when they first decided to get involved.

Posluns and Kay snapped up successful retail chains over the years, but kept on staff the entrepreneurs who made the stores successful by offering generous profit-sharing schemes. Profit-sharing appeals to them because Dylex offers them a chance to call their own shots but grow more quickly because they are plugged into a bigger organization.

"More than half our guys make more money than Jim or I do, and some draw triple the money we do, $1.5 million or so," says Wilf. "For instance, in the case of Bi-Way [a discount chain] we have an agreement that executives will get 10 per cent of anything over and above $4.5 million in profits, which is what the chain made the year we bought it. In 1984, the company made $19 million, and the $1.9 million was split among three or four key people."

The strategy of buying and keeping entrepreneurial retailers and having the chains operate in so-called competition against one another is unique. Dylex's 1984 sales surpassed $1 billion and doubled in 1985 with the acquisition of two large U.S. fashion chains. Dylex's 1,100 stores in Canada operate under a variety of names: Town and Country, Suzy Shier, L.A. Express, Thrifty's, Rubys Shoes, Fantasia, Feathers, Diva, Fairweathers, Tip Top, B.H. Emporium, Big Steel Man, Bi-Way discount, Braemar, Daniel Hechter, Harry Rosen, and Drug World. In 1984, Dylex began an aggressive foray into the

United States and acquired 36-per-cent interest in two chains, Foxmoor and Brooks, with 1,460 stores. And under the terms of that deal, Dylex has an option to get another 36 per cent.

The meteoric growth of bank credit cards freed cashless customers from having to shop at the big department stores, which had their own card systems, and the company has aggressively moved into shopping centres. It operates out of a handsome, eight-storey building topped off by a TIP TOP TAILOR sign on Toronto's Lakeshore Boulevard. Inside, the art deco styling has been tastefully preserved, complete with vaulted ceilings and frescoes. In fact, it was the Poslunses' interest in this building, as a manufacturing facility, that led to their involvement with Kay.

Until 1967, the building and Tip Top Tailors were owned by the Dunkelman family. Heir apparent was Dan Dunkelman, who had returned to Toronto after the Second World War and ran Tip Top like the army: discipline was tough and the pecking order rigid. By the mid-'60s the company was starting to lose money and was up for sale. In 1966, Kay decided to try to buy Tip Top. "But he couldn't even get an appointment," says Wilf, whose family were occasional suppliers of Tip Top and knew the Dunkelmans socially.

Kay's accountant knew the relationship between the Dunkelmans and the Posluns family, who were also his clients, and he suggested Kay and the Poslunses get together. Just months before, wheeler-dealer Kay had bought an eight-store women's clothing chain, not in order to get involved in the riches of retailing, but because he was involved in real estate and wanted a chain as a secure large tenant. The Poslunses were interested in Tip Top's building to house their manufacturing operation. So Wilf and his father, Louis Posluns, and two brothers joined forces with Kay.

Kay was born in 1921 in Winnipeg, the only child of an American immigrant who ran a profitable business recycling rags and wiping cloths. His mother was an heiress whose family lost everything in the stock market crash of 1929. "I've always kidded my mother that she's the only woman in the world who went from riches to rags," says Kay.

After university and a stint in the Royal Canadian Air Force during the Second World War, he returned to Winnipeg to help run his father's textile business. In 1948 he started his own plastics business, producing polyethylene, first used during the war by the military. It was a tremendous success.

In 1959, he sold out to the British chemical giant International Chemical, eventually becoming president of its Canadian subsidiary, CIL Ltd. Undoubtedly, Jimmy was on the fast track and heading for the big jobs in the United Kingdom. But in 1963, at age forty-one, he decided to marry and settle down in his wife's home town of Toronto.

"Raising kids in a multinational means at least twelve moves. I had roots and I wanted my kids to have them," he says of his decision. He has three daughters and one son.

Louis Posluns died in 1982 and Jack Posluns in 1984, leaving Wilf and Irving to carry on a family tradition started by their grandfather, Abraham Poslanitz, who began sewing women's cloaks in a Toronto garage after fleeing Poland's pogroms. Louis and his three brothers built this into a large manufacturing operation, but Wilf, Jack, and Irving bought out their cousins in the 1950s.

Wilf finished university in 1955 and became a Bay Street broker. He was successful until 1961, when he was accused of wrongdoing and suspended by the Toronto Stock Exchange. He and others were partners of Morton Shulman, a well-known doctor, financier, and politician, but Shulman lost them a bundle, causing a partner, a Peterborough dentist, to go bust. The dentist went after Shulman and Wilf Posluns. The TSE held an in-camera session, and Posluns's employer was forced to dismiss him for alleged "conflicts of interest."

His pride and pocketbook hurt, Posluns took on the establishment, eventually spending $250,000 to fight the case all the way to the Supreme Court of Canada. "Being Jewish, I was sensitive to the discrimination that existed heavily in the securities business. The TSE was a private club: Jewish people weren't even allowed to have a seat on the exchange in those days, or join fancy stockbrokers or law firms. Here I was, young and Jewish and making lots of money. And I had no choice, but they forced me to defend myself. I lost [in court] everywhere, but I won."

In all the cases, the courts decided the TSE was not guilty of illegal acts, but chastised it for behaving as it had. In fact, the Supreme Court decided to hear the case in order to establish how self-governing "clubs" operating in the public sector (which includes law societies and medical associations) must adhere to the "rules of law," such as proper notice of a hearing, the right of an accused to attend the hearing, and a requirement to keep transcripts of such proceedings.

"The reason I say I won is that it is no longer possible to have a private club operating in the public sector, as the TSE did. It's been worth it because the system's changed, and my case is the most important case in the British empire on private clubs," Posluns says. "I became determined as hell to prove I was a good businessman."

There is no doubt about that now.

Wilf and the estate of his late brother Jack own 50.1 per cent of Dylex's voting shares, and Kay has 39 per cent. Irving Posluns sold his shares to Wilf. In addition, Wilf and Kay control Strathearn House Group, a separate public company with a mixed bag of operations, from furniture to plastics to chemicals, and $48.4 million in assets.

Kay has bought and sold businesses all his life. At one time he was heavily involved in real estate development, construction, and fast-food franchises. But he cashed in most of his real estate interests in the 1970s, and huge losses cost him control of his franchise conglomerate, called Foodex, to Hees International, one of the Brascan stable of companies. He still owns 10 per cent of North Canadian Oils, a medium-sized oil and gas company.

"That's my investment portfolio, but Dylex is my active portfolio," he says. "The problems with Foodex were due to the fact that I had a guy running the company who didn't know a thing about how to run a business."

The Posluns brothers have proven to be the appropriate counterbalance to the go-go Kay, who readily admits he would have bought the Foxmoor and Brooks chains outright for more than $300 million, rather than buy into the companies slowly, as Posluns preached. But Kay has always lived on the business edge. In fact the Posluns family had to lend him the money to close their partnership deal back in 1966 because he was strapped for cash.

"When it was time to close we had to put up $200,000 each, and he didn't have the money to close, so we said, 'Okay, don't worry,'" recalls Wilf. "He paid us in a few weeks."

Conservatism is the watchword for the Poslunses because of their father's advice. "Once my dad got in deep with the banks and he became upset because they thought they could call the shots in his clothing business," says Wilf, who personally owns about $100 million worth of real estate, mostly without mortgages. "He became so upset he went out and prepaid every account and supplier so all these cheques would hit the bank at once. The banker called him and Dad said, 'If you don't like it, buy me out.' There's a fear in me of having banks run my life. I don't owe a nickel. I could be three times the size I am with leverage, but it isn't worth it to me to lose what I have."

Some members of the second generation have gotten involved in Dylex. Richard Posluns, son of Wilf's older brother, Jack, is involved, but his sister is not. Irving's three children are in other businesses. Wilf's older daughter is a tax lawyer, but his younger daughter is an assistant store manager. His son, David, lives in Philadelphia, where he works for a merger and acquisitions company, Financo, specializing in retail deals. "The Brooks and Foxmoor thing happened when my son called me on the telephone for a routine friendly call and I asked him what he was up to," recalls Wilf. "He said, 'We've just tied down this big retailer, and it's quite exciting.' I said to him, 'Maybe we'd be interested,' and my son said to me, 'Don't bother, Dad, it's too big for you.' I thought maybe he's wrong. He wasn't. It was too big for us alone, but we bought it in a unique way with partners."

Dylex formed a company with a group of lenders and the managements of the two U.S. chains. In the Brooks deal, the family that sold has reinvested its money and will operate the chain. In the Foxmoor case, the chain had been losing money after going through four presidents in five years. So Dylex enticed a wealthy retailing entrepreneur out of early retirement to become president. The U.S. operations have been somewhat troubled and it remains to be seen whether the Posluns-Kay magic will defy the difficulties of retailing in the United States, difficulties that have all but sunk other Canadian success stories such as Canadian Tire Corp., owned by the Billes family.

Wilf commutes between his Toronto home, his four-bedroom Lake Simcoe cottage just north of the city, and his apartment in Pompano Beach, Florida, where he and his wife like to go once a month for a four-day weekend.

Kay's spare time is spent dabbling in sidelines and charities. He also sits on a dozen boards of directors. Chalk and cheese, the partnership has worked.

"As conservative as I am, I need some jogging at times," admits Wilf. "But I may restrain Jim's over-aggressiveness."

THE EATONS

FOUR GENERATIONS AGO, Irish immigrant Timothy Eaton founded his dynasty of merchant princes with this motto: "Early to bed, early to rise, never get tight, and advertise." While the current generation of Eaton brothers are not strict Methodists like their great-grandfather Timothy, they continue to rule the empire Timothy built. The T. Eaton Company Limited operates 306 stores with sales of $2 billion — the largest privately owned department store chain in North America. And while religion has no direct bearing on its continuing retail triumphs, the family's success has been due in great part to a goodly dose of the Protestant work ethic mixed with a Methodist's disdain for debt.

The Eatons are, quite simply, the nation's best shopkeepers. They also have made fortunes in real estate and the media. The T. Eaton Realty Company owns large chunks of the country's biggest and best downtown malls. The Eaton-Bay Trust Company is one of the country's largest trust, mutual fund, and insurance companies. And the Eatons own controlling interest in Baton Broadcasting, which owns the Toronto television station CFTO, radio stations, and one of the world's most successful production studios, Glen Warren Productions.

The currently reigning princes are eight years apart in age, starting with John Craig, born in 1938, followed by Fredrik, George, and Thor. All are handsome and happily married, and they work and play together. The four are jocks, continuing to enjoy the outdoors together on weekend jaunts as they did in their childhood, fishing and hunting with their father. A squash racquet in a kit bag slumps beside Fredrik's briefcase in his smallish nineteenth-floor office.

"You don't have to be a playboy to enjoy life," says Fred, the slightly shy, second-born Eaton who is chairman, president, and chief executive officer of the retail operations. "We enjoy our jobs, getting a sense of accomplishment, just like anybody else."

Atop the retail company is a holding corporation called Eaton's of Canada Ltd. John Craig is chairman, Fred is president, George, executive vice president, and Thor, vice president. By most accounts, Fred is the brightest — the only direct descendant from Timothy Eaton to finish university — and the most hard-working.

The brothers are the first generation of Eatons to share the family firm. Timothy Eaton had only one son, an earlier John Craig. He, in turn, had four sons and two daughters, but stipulated in his will that trustees must select the most suitable son to run the firm and to buy out all the others, once the youngest was twenty-seven years of age. John David Eaton, the second-born, was selected. His older brother, Timothy, who was passed over as heir apparent, devoted his life to building model railway trains.

But in this generation, a single successor was never chosen by trustees, and John David's four sons share the company "more or less in equal portions," says Fred. This prospect never bothered their father, who once said: "Some people will tell you that a partnership never works, but Smith Brothers sold a hell of a lot of cough drops."

Eaton money is old money. Like the Richardsons, the Websters, and the McConnells, the Eatons made their first fortune before the arrival of income taxes. And while every new generation has swelled the family's ranks and reduced individual inheritances, to live the life of an Eaton is to travel in million-dollar jets, spend weekends in cottages with Group of Seven paintings, lavish $1 million worth of jewellery on your wife, and sit in the owners' box at Blue Jays games. It is fishing and hunting with monarchs and being surrounded by limos, yachts, helicopters, gadgets, and servants.

George, asked if there was a problem being rich, said, "Are you kidding? I'm what everybody in the world would like to be — a rich kid. The word 'need' simply never has existed for me, in a material sense anyway." At six-teen, he got a Karmann-Ghia.

The Eatons run their affairs conservatively, perhaps a throwback to Meth-odist Timothy, who didn't believe in extending credit to his customers because of his religious beliefs. Today, credit is a way of life for everyone and the Eatons gladly give it. But the four brothers do not believe in borrowing. This philosophy makes for an amazingly debt-free balance sheet, with nearly $2 billion in assets. It is a philosophy that has cushioned the blow of recessions. But it has certainly sidelined the Eatons from the type of feverish takeover game that has been under way in Canada since the Royal Commission on Cor-porate Concentration declared open season in 1978 by saying big wasn't bad. While others have grown meteorically, the Eaton philosophy has stubbornly remained: grow assets, don't grab them.

"As a family company we have not done the kinds of things others have done, like lever ourselves up to buy somebody else. This is principally because we like to use our own resources," explains Fred. Profits are pri-marily reinvested in improvements or innovations, not in providing down payments for takeovers. The family's only public vehicle, its 53-per-cent ownership in Baton Broadcasting, reveals this operating philosophy. It is virtually debt-free.

Eaton's flagship is the $250-million Eaton Centre, which outdraws Niagara Falls as Canada's biggest tourist attraction, with one million visitors weekly. It is a three-block-long atrium-focused monolith that has been copied by its developer, Cadillac Fairview Corp., around North America. It is the prototype for most downtown malls, the company's greatest triumph, and the brainchild of John David Eaton, who died in 1973 and never saw it finished.

The Eatons own 20 per cent of the mall, one-third of Vancouver's Pacific Centre, and one-third of Ottawa Centre. The only property the firm owns is what is "beneath the stores," says Fred. It has not diversified into property development for development's sake.

"We've stuck to our knitting," says Fred. "One of the biggest challenges we face is staying flexible. You can find you get into things and go down with them. You've got to be able to get in and get out."

The family business has certainly changed since Timothy Eaton's time. The son of a poor Irish farmer, Timothy surpassed rivals by pioneering ideas like selling for cash only, eliminating bartering by fixing prices, and enacting a popular policy of "goods satisfactory or money refunded." He also launched the country's first catalogue in 1884; using it, homesteaders could order a seven-room house for $999.77. The catalogue was so successful that it became unpopular among small merchants, many of whom ran the frontier post offices; Eaton's had to send them out in plain brown wrappers.

Now the firm is strictly a storekeeper, its nationwide chain employing 50,000 persons. Expansion continues, but never into the United States. Canada is dominated by a handful of department store chains, while in the U.S. competition is ferocious. "It's a big, rich country, and retailers and everyone else are as aggressive as hell," says Fred. "We wouldn't have that special position Eaton's enjoys in Canada. It just wouldn't translate."

It didn't translate here either, for a while. Eaton stores suffered a costly identity crisis in the mid-1970s. The fashion image suddenly swung from frumpy to far-out. A chain of discount stores, called Horizons, flopped. The catalogue operation began to bleed red ink, its once-monopoly position eroded by Sears and Consumers Distributing. There were clashes inside the executive suite over who the store's customers were, or should be.

The family closed its catalogue division at a huge loss, turning over some $70 million in severance pay to 9,000 workers. In 1982, amid layoffs during the recession, the Eatons felt they could no longer justify spending $500,000 a year on their world-famous Santa Claus parade in Toronto and dropped out of sponsorship.

The Baton investment evolved out of a deep friendship between John David Eaton and media tycoon John Bassett Sr. Highly profitable, it racked up $100 million in profits in seven years, starting in 1978, and is simply the latest in a long-standing partnership between the Eaton and Bassett families. In 1952, John David helped his friend John Bassett purchase the Toronto *Telegram* for $4.25 million by co-signing Bassett's half of the loan. The Telegram Corp. was set up as a holding company for these and other assets, such as the Toronto Argonauts. The three Bassett sons eventually cashed in their chips, beginning in the mid-1970s, but John Bassett Sr. remains chairman of the board of Baton, and his son Douglas Bassett is its chief executive officer and president.

The Eatons have made millions, and have given away millions to charities over the generations. Timothy's son, John Craig, owned two Rolls-Royces and a 172-foot ocean-going yacht, which slept five and had a crew of ten. He gave it to the navy in the First World War and it was sunk. He also returned to the government all profits his company made on war contracts. In 1915, he was knighted.

During the Second World War, his wife, Lady Eaton, converted her French-style château and 700-acre country estate north of Toronto into a home for evacuated British children and convalescing seamen. Eventually the entire estate was given to the public; it is now part of the campus of Seneca community college. Today the Eatons give time and money to charities, but have a passion for privacy — understandable, after unsuccessful kidnapping and extortion attempts in the 1970s.

Fred is sociable. He has a country house in Caledon, north of Toronto, flies to Lyford Cay, shoots at Griffith Island and Long Point, and owns the 1950 Rolls-Royce that once belonged to Sir James Dunn, founder of Algoma Steel in Sudbury. The four brothers often car-pool to work because they live within blocks of one another.

"We tend to be rather quiet people who go away on weekends with our families and mix with ourselves," says Fred Eaton.

George Eaton had a highly successful seven-year career as a Grand Prix racing driver. He and his brother Thor had a successful entertainment booking business, but sold it in the early 1980s. Thor is a loner who enjoys riding and racehorses. Eaton Hall Farm's silks are red, white, and blue. And the family steeds are strictly blue-ribbon. In November 1984, an Eaton horse called Billy Bessarabian won $200,000 at the Meadowlands, in New Jersey.

John Craig is fascinated with politics. He and Conrad Black backed Claude Wagner's Tory leadership bid. A heavyweight in provincial Tory circles, he called Bill Davis directly about issues.

But the Eatons deny they have any political pull, even though they are on a first-name basis with finance ministers, premiers, and prime ministers. In November 1982, the Davis cabinet overturned a decision that would have made it easy for gravel operators to open pits next to estates owned by three members of the Eaton family and many others in Caledon. This action followed a petition by Caledon council and the Eatons.

However, when it came time to obtain a rezoning for the Eaton Centre, the city council in Toronto wrangled for years over details. This led John David Eaton, worth an estimated $400 million at the time, to say: "If I were powerful, the Eaton Centre would be a going concern."

Now it is a whopping success. But, as in any other family business, the future depends on the next generation. The four Eaton brothers have a dozen children, but so far only one heir is working full-time in the store.

In the 1950s, there were rumours that the chain was for sale, but president Sir John Craig Eaton, the founder's son, said, "There's not enough money in the whole world to buy my father's name."

"This firm has never been for sale," says Fred. "As for going public, that's all speculative, but I suppose nothing's written in stone."

THE ROMANS

STEPHEN BOLESLAV ROMAN is one of that rare species among Canada's rich: he's a self-made man and an ideologue, who fiercely believes in Catholicism, capitalism, the emancipation of Slovakia, Denison Mines, and Roman Corp. — more or less in that order. Born in 1920, he came to Canada when he was sixteen and worked for his older brother for 50 cents a day. His brother, George, once traded his services for a few weeks in order to pay for a horse. But from those humble beginnings, Roman has built a $2-billion energy and financial empire.

And Roman wasn't built in a day. He is complex and contradictory: a hard-nosed capitalist and devout Christian; a devoted democrat politically, but an autocratic executive; a grateful immigrant who would shut the doors on many newcomers. He has gone from being a farmer to a soldier to a munitions factory mould-maker and finally to a Bay Street promoter. Now he owns controlling interest in two huge companies — Denison Mines and Roman Corp.

These companies, in turn, own the world's second-largest uranium mine, in

Elliot Lake, Ont.; wells that produce $1 million a day worth of natural gas, sulphur, and crude oil; potash and coal mines in Canada; one of the country's largest cement companies; a fleet of ships; oil exploration companies operating in several countries around the world; the country's largest boxboard manufacturer; Lawson Mardon, one of its largest printing companies; and Standard Trustco, a trust company with twenty branches and $1 billion in deposits.

A capitalist emperor, Roman even has an ocean-going tanker and a mountain of coal in British Columbia named after him. Short and dumpy, he looks more Japanese than Slovak, his round face containing slits for eyes. He has run twice for political office, losing badly both times. He has had ferocious political run-ins with two Liberal prime ministers, Lester Pearson and Pierre Trudeau. He once called the mild-mannered Pearson a "son of a bitch" to his face after a confrontation in his Ottawa office.

However, Roman's relationship with former Ontario premier William Davis (whom he calls "Billy") was a love affair. Little wonder: in the 1970s, Roman's Denison Mines got a thirty-one-year sweetheart uranium deal from Billy's own Crown corporation, Ontario Hydro, worth $7.3 billion. The deal included a $340-million interest-free loan, no cancellation until the early 1990s without sizeable penalties, and a guaranteed, undisclosed price for the uranium. It saved Denison from financial problems, allowed Roman to borrow in the big leagues, and paid for his massive expansion into more oil and mining ventures.

Lester Pearson once described Roman as "fifty years behind the apes" for his élitist views on immigration, expressed in Roman's book *The Responsible Society*. Written with a fellow Slovak émigré, it was a treatise on economics and social policy. The two believed immigrants should be allowed into the country, given a test run, and deported if not up to scratch.

The book has been just one of several ways in which this complicated captain of industry has sought a high-profile platform for his beliefs. In addition to running for political office, he has lectured shareholders at annual meetings on the threats of socialism and once bid $13 million to buy the Toronto *Telegram*, then a major metropolitan daily.

Most of Roman's annual meetings and Christmas parties are like feasts, with sumptuous buffets, fountains spewing drinks, and good-looking women scattered through the group. But during the festivities, Roman will lecture his assemblage on the perils of the political situation. In 1980 he said, "We in the

West have started down the slippery slope into the first step of that benevolent kind of slavery euphemistically called socialism. The question is whether we can muster the will to reverse the trend, before we are trapped in the tentacles of real slavery, to be found at the bottom of the pit."

Not surprisingly, the politically minded Roman ran as a Progressive Conservative candidate in two federal elections, in 1972 and 1974, outspending all other candidates by forking out $92,103, only to have Liberal Barney Danson beat him four-to-one in 1974. He also was the biggest spender in the 1972 federal election.

His political proxy is his nephew, Tony Roman, a successful politician who ran as an independent but is now a Tory member of Parliament in Ottawa. Before that he was regional chairman in Markham, and four-time mayor of Markham, a wealthy suburb of Toronto. Roman was appointed regional chairman by his uncle's close friend Bill Davis, who hosted a $1,300-a-plate dinner to honour Tony and to raise money for the Tories. Davis is now a director of Mardon Packaging International Ltd., controlled by Roman Corp.

Davis's cabinet also approved Denison's contract with Ontario Hydro. And in 1978, when Ontario Hydro suggested it might buy Denison, Davis and his cabinet were cool. "The contract was no gift," says Roman. "Ontario refused to give me a permit to export my uranium. I had a better deal signed with the French and for more money. They forced me to sign with Ontario Hydro."

Stephen Roman's other great political passion is his pursuit of freedom for his homeland and the preservation of the Slovak culture. He is head of the Slovak World Congress, and his wife, Betty, has the best collection of Slovakian music in the world, some 5,000 records. The couple support many artistic groups and are building a $13-million, 750-seat cathedral on their farmland for Slovaks of the Byzantine Rite in Canada.

He has a private mass read in the Greek liturgy every Sunday afternoon in his house, and he was the first and only Canadian lay auditor to the Vatican Ecumenical Council in Rome. In September 1984, Pope John Paul II made a special side trip during his visit to Canada to lay and bless the foundation stone for the new cathedral. The property was valued at $550,000; Roman gave it to the church for $10.

Roman is a tycoon, but also a country boy at heart; around his farm he wears a suit, tie, and straw fedora. In 1953, when he first hit it big after finding oil in Alberta, he bought six operating farms and two more adjacent properties in Markham, which he assembled into a 1,200-acre estate called

Romandale. Roman and his brother George had studied at agricultural college in Slovakia before immigrating to Canada, and the two have built Romandale into one of the finest Holstein breeding farms in North America. In 1985, Roman paid a record $1.4 million at an auction for one bull. His "farm" house is a seventeen-room pseudo-Tudor mansion, thirty-five minutes from downtown. The elegant interior has marble walls and a chandelier that was formerly owned by an Indian maharajah.

Roman and his brother, then twenty-seven, arrived in Canada from eastern Slovakia in 1937 with $1,500 in their pockets. With that modest grub-stake they put a down payment on a farm on Scugog Island, near Port Perry, Ont. The Romans had been leaders in the farming villages of Velky and Ruskov. "My father had a net worth at the time of $25,000, if he had sold everything. What a farm that would have been. My father went to the U.S. three times and was interested in immigrating there, but my mother would never leave our village," says Roman. Another brother immigrated to the U.S., but Stephen and George decided to go to Canada because it was easier to get in "and close to the U.S."

In 1940, Stephen joined the army, but he was invalided out and worked in a foundry as a mould-maker in a munitions factory. While there, he began playing penny mining stocks and lost practically his entire savings of $2,000 on a deal. After the war he worked as editor of the *Slovak Voice*, a small Slovakian newspaper published in Oshawa, and moonlighted for a stock brokerage firm. He saved his money and switched from journalism to the market. In 1946, he raised $10,000 by organizing a twenty-partner syndicate and struck oil in Alberta's Leduc. In 1953, Roman cashed in his shares for $2 million, which provided the grub-stake for his farming venture and his next stock market coup.

He began to buy Denison Mines stock for 8.5 cents a share and had control by 1954. That year, he bought some claims in Ontario's uranium-rich Algoma valley that had been turned down by uranium king Joe Hirshhorn (a Brooklyn Jew who made a fortune in Canada and left one of the world's most valuable art collections, some 6,000 pieces housed in a museum on the Mall beside the Washington Monument). Roman paid only $30,000 and 500,000 Denison shares for Hirshhorn's discarded claims, but these contained the richest vein of uranium ore in the area. By 1955, Roman had opened the first of many shafts there.

Uranium was in big demand, particularly after 1956, when the Suez crisis underscored the volatility in the Persian Gulf and the potential for oil supply problems. But the boom turned to bust in the 1960s, because of a number of new developments. Uranium peddling became strictly a political affair.

The slowdown in the arms race and growing concerns about safety and the environmental dangers of nuclear power dried up the market. There was also increased competition from new mines opening in foreign currency-starved undeveloped countries. There were worries about nuclear proliferation. But the biggest crunch came in 1965 when the U.S. prohibited uranium imports. The embargo was designed to prop up its domestic mining industry as well as to ensure that U.S. utilities did not become dependent upon foreign sources of supply. That left the largest market in the world off limits to the world's largest producers.

Prices plummeted. By 1967, all but three of Canada's twenty-two uranium mines were shut down, with production only 24 per cent of the 1959 peak. Even that was only sustained by a government stockpiling program. Earlier, in 1965, Roman had made a deal with the French government to sell Denison's $700 million of uranium, but Pearson, under pressure from U.S. president Lyndon Johnson, blocked the transaction. Denison's purchase would have given the French a secure supply of uranium, and the Americans did not want France's General Charles de Gaulle to join the "nuclear club."

"It was awful. It was not in Canada's interest, but in the Americans' interests. The French would sign a non-proliferation treaty regarding our uranium, but then Canada was pushed by the U.S. to insist it had to sign a blanket non-proliferation treaty regarding everybody else's uranium it bought," says Roman. "The French would have paid us $95 million, we would have bought two more companies in the U.S. Instead, with their $95 million, the French explored for uranium in Africa, found some — and three years later they were our competitors."

Then in 1970, still struggling, Roman decided to swap his interest in Denison in return for 18 per cent of Conoco (then Continental Oil Co.) of Wilmington, Delaware. Trudeau intervened and blocked the sale by announcing a retroactive law limiting foreign ownership in a uranium company to only 33 per cent. The law was passed years later. Roman, rightly angry, told the Toronto *Telegram* in 1970, "I'll quit Canada if they do this to me." Instead, he sued the prime minister and the energy minister for $100 million. The case was eventually dismissed. "They were so stupid they didn't realize that it was a reverse takeover bid. Here I was, a Canadian company, taking over one of the world's biggest oil companies, Conoco. It would have benefited Canada over the years as dividends flowed this way."

Denison shares plummeted because the law made the company unsaleable, and Roman threatened to shut down Elliot Lake. Unsure whether he meant it, the government made a deal at the end of 1970, to buy nearly $30 million of uranium and stockpile it to keep Denison's mine going.

Caught in a squeeze play, Canada and its uranium producers joined a cartel formed with Australia, South Africa, and France. From 1972 to 1975, uranium prices went from $4 to $5 a pound, thanks to the cartel. Canadians involved were Denison, Gulf Minerals, Rio Algom, Eldorado Nuclear, and Uranium Canada.

But in 1976, Rio Algom was sued for $600 million by Westinghouse Electric for breach of contract. Westinghouse had sold reactors to the Tennessee Valley Authority utility and had promised it would also supply cheap uranium. Westinghouse claimed it was suddenly locked into artificially high cartel prices, in violation of the U.S. Sherman Anti-Trust Act and the Wilson Tariff Act. It sought triple damages.

The cartel was abandoned, and Ottawa granted immunity to the politicians involved. By 1981, lawsuits were settled out of court with Westinghouse and others, but Canadian anti-trust officials are still prosecuting Gulf, Denison, and Rio Algom for anti-competitive practices.

Roman still runs his own show, riding around the world regularly in his company's twelve-seat jet. But he is gradually withdrawing from operations; in 1985 he appointed two new presidents for his two firms and named his eldest child, Helen Roman-Barber, vice chairman of Roman. He is a clean-liver and devoted family man, who occasionally drinks rye on the rocks, doesn't smoke, and doesn't gamble, except in business. At lunchtime he eats in his company's private dining room, and his favourite meal is his wife's stuffed peppers and cabbage rolls. He is superstitious, and Friday the thirteenth is his lucky day. Whenever possible, he stages events or board meetings and makes decisions or announcements on the thirteenth of the month.

Next to uranium, his oil properties have yielded the most profits, particularly interests in Greek and Sicilian oilfields with enormous potential. In 1984, he opened the $950-million Quintette Coal mine, which he shares fifty-fifty with Japanese investors. But cost overruns during development and production problems afterwards have worried many investors, including Roman, who suddenly fired president Cliff Frame in the spring of 1985.

Denison's head office is on the thirty-ninth floor of Toronto's Royal Bank Plaza, and Roman's office is entirely separate, through carved double doors. Off the pentagonal lobby of his private suite are the office of Helen, a bright, dynamic, Parisian-trained corporate lawyer; that of his son Stephen, his special assistant; and that of his nephew, Frederic Roman, treasurer of Roman Corp. and other companies. Also involved as directors are his nephew Tony Roman and his son-in-law, Bertram Willoughby. In all, Roman has seven children who have equal interests in his private company, Sagamore Ltd., which in turn holds the family's shares in Denison and Roman Corp. Besides Helen and Stephen, the others are Peter, who works for Denison's Quintette coal mining operation in B.C.; Paul, who lives in Houston and is in the oil business; David, a university student; Angela, who runs the family's private holding company; and Ann, who "keeps very busy running my parents' lives," according to Helen.

"The seven of us are very close and are interested in the business," says Helen, the unofficial head of the next generation. Her husband, Michael Barber, runs a high-tech company called EDA Instruments Ltd. "We all get along and I guess that's unusual. And my father and I get along about 364 days out of the year. He sometimes gets upset whenever I take a vacation. He doesn't believe in too many." As Stephen Roman passes through those portals daily, the hard-working chairman of Denison can be assured that his family's involvement means his Roman empire will last and not be squandered, perhaps the ultimate wish granted to a remarkable man.

THE LOVES

RECLUSIVE REAL ESTATE TYCOON G. Donald Love is the one who got away. In 1981, his huge company, Oxford Development Group, was about to be gobbled up by one of Canada's giant empires. In those dark days of takeover fever, Love sought help from Dick Thomson, chairman of the Toronto-Dominion Bank. Love's problem was that he had sold so many shares over the years to other investors that he had only a 10-per-cent toe-hold in the company he began in 1960. The TD gave Love $327 million, and he made a dramatic pre-emptive bid to buy all the outstanding shares before someone else snapped them up: he bid $26 for shares trading at only $16. He gave shareholders twenty-four hours to accept. It worked.

Love not only kept control, but ended up with 60 per cent of Oxford. The TD got 40 per cent of Oxford — a sweet deal for the bank, because the partnership ensures Oxford will be a captive customer. The marriage also catapults Canada's fifth-largest chartered bank into the real estate big leagues. The Toronto-Dominion Bank, it could be said, is one of North America's five largest real estate developers, directly and indirectly, thanks mostly to its partnership with Love. In partnership with other developers, the bank also owns 15 per cent of Toronto's Eaton Centre, one-third of Vancouver's Pacific Centre, and 30 per cent of Edmonton Centre.

Love and Thomson are Canadian capitalism's odd couple — an aggressive, risk-taking entrepreneur and a cautious, conservative banker. But it is a match made in heaven because money is as essential a raw material to real estate developers as is land. Developers borrow money to buy sites, they borrow to build projects, and they borrow once more after they are finished and until buildings can be sold, or rented, or both. Undoubtedly, the TD's support has helped Love build a company able to ride through recessions and rise above rivals. Oxford now weighs in at a staggering $3 billion in assets.

Not a great deal is known about G. Donald Love. "G" stands for Gordon, his late father's name, but he never uses it. Letters addressed to "Don Love" or beginning "Dear Don" are tossed out unread. What his father did for a living is unknown; however, he must have been an overriding influence for his photograph is prominently displayed in Love's office.

Love is both president and chairman of Oxford. A loner, he's been described as very much a hands-on president. He started Oxford from scratch and it has been his whole life. He is not the kind of guy who goes and sits on the beach. He is an unusually hard-driving proprietor, and Oxford has a high turnover rate to prove it. In 1984, four senior vice presidents in charge of a $250-million development in Minneapolis came and went. So did the development.

He is very private and generally refuses to have his photograph taken or to be interviewed. He told *Maclean's* in 1977 that he was convinced that a fellow developer who had had his photo taken had died as a direct result of public ridicule after his picture, and the accompanying story, were printed. This reclusiveness makes it hard to verify reports that he has worked as an oil scout and a used-car salesman. Or that he started Oxford on a shoestring of $309 in 1960. Or that his wife's father was wealthy and bankrolled him.

Oxford is owned by a holding company called 91922 Canada Ltd. The TD has two representatives on Oxford's board and Love has four: his wife, Marilyn, two sons, John and Noble, and himself. John is in charge of Canadian operations, and Noble, U.S. ones. Another son, Jeff, is in university, and a daughter, Kathleen, is married to a doctor and lives in the U.S.

Love owns 60 per cent of 91922 Canada, and TD Capital Corp., a wholly owned subsidiary of the bank, owns the rest. However, bank spokesmen are always quick to add that TD Capital has only 5 per cent of voting shares in 91922 — an important factor that allows the bank to get around restrictions in the Bank Act limiting bank ownership in companies to no more than 10 per cent.

Love works hard and is in the office by eight, regularly staying until five-thirty. He talks to the TD's Thomson daily and often lunches with him at the bank, whenever he's in town. He never takes work home with him. At Oxford, he and a private secretary work in a separate suite, sealed off from the rest of the operation by double doors. Inside is Love's panelled office, a reception area for his secretary, a washroom, kitchen, and boardroom. This office-within-an-office is sacrosanct, and executives are not allowed to enter unless invited. A couple of years ago, when finishing touches were being put on the suite by workers on two occasions, Love had the locks changed both times. "He says the private suite is because he doesn't want staff to feel his presence," says a former employee. "It's really because he doesn't want them to know what he's doing."

His wife, Marilyn, is a tiny woman, blonde, with a pleasant smile. She is not involved in Oxford's day-to-day affairs and participates only as a director. The two sit at opposite ends of the boardroom during directors' meetings, like a couple entertaining dinner guests. Her main preoccupation, now that the couple's four children are grown, is charity work, particularly setting up the Maredon Foundation (the name stands for Marilyn and Don), an exclusive treatment centre in Edmonton for emotionally disturbed children.

Love was born in 1926 and keeps himself in good shape by doing exercises on a miniature trampoline in his home. He drives a dark grey Porsche — a Father's Day gift from his wife several years ago. He travels constantly, in an eight-seat Citation jet, and is personally involved in all the company's deals.

"You can have all the reports and studies in the world done," he once told a U.S. magazine. "I've never read a Chamber of Commerce report on a city yet that doesn't say it's the greatest city in the world. A gut-feeling assessment is something that's almost as important as anything."

He is a fidgety person, with a nervous habit of clipping his nails while talking to executives or anyone else in his office. He is sometimes abrupt, inclined to point his finger at a cup of cold coffee and say to a secretary, "Cold," instead of requesting a new cup of coffee.

The Loves left their beloved $2-million ranch outside Edmonton to move Oxford's head office to Toronto in 1984. They bought two $600,000 adjoining condominiums, which they renovated into one large, luxurious home, decorated in shades of blue with a big white grand piano. The Loves entertain rarely, because of his travelling and preference for early nights. For recreation they go down to their island off Naples, Florida. They have another condominium near the island for their children to use.

Like so many of Canada's fabulously wealthy families, Love is concerned a great deal about safety, perhaps more than others because of the kidnapping in 1983 of fellow–Edmonton entrepreneur Peter Pocklington. Love's $2-million farm outside Edmonton had intricate electronic security surrounding it. So do his condos.

Love is a Westerner by birth, growing up as an only child in Calgary. But he went east to make his fortune, graduating as a mechanical engineer from McGill in Montreal. He stayed in the East as a young adult and worked as a broker for Dominion Securities. In the late 1950s, he was able to return to the West; he opened a brokerage branch for Dominion in Edmonton. Those were the days when the West was beginning to boom, and Love — like so many other Alberta entrepreneurs — formed his own company in 1960 and began to do real estate deals for himself on the side.

One of Love's gifts has been to make a go of partnerships. His first partners — John and George Poole, who founded PCL Construction — taught him a great deal about designing and constructing projects. Then he attracted a group of insurance companies and other institutions, which gave him the financial muscle to do bigger deals and move into the United States. And finally, his unique marriage to a Canadian chartered bank affords him financial freedom and the opportunity to found a family dynasty.

By the end of the 1970s, the biggest backer was Great-West Life Assurance of Winnipeg, with 29 per cent — part of Paul Desmarais's gigantic Power Corp. In fact, it was concern that Oxford would be gobbled up by Desmarais or others that led to Love's gutsy buy-out with TD's help.

A power struggle erupted between Great-West and Love over his perceived aggressiveness. The insurers felt Oxford was over-extending itself. In

December 1979, Great-West and several other insurance companies — with a total of 60 per cent of Oxford's share — informed him they would be selling. That was when he turned to the Toronto-Dominion rather than cash in his chips.

"Back then, when we took over a couple of companies, someone made a joke. They said, 'You'd better watch out, Love. One of these days you're going to walk in and there'll be another guy in your chair.' That twitched me a bit. They can't do that now," he told an interviewer after the buy-out in 1981.

Like all of Canada's big developers, Love went south in a big way in the 1970s. He explained this to *Businessweek*: "The conditions are right for development in U.S. central cities. We're not afraid of them. It's really very simple. In Canada, there are nine population centres with more than 500,000 people. In the U.S., there are ninety."

Oxford formed a partnership with Denver oilman and billionaire Phil Anschutz; now it has 70 per cent of $1 billion worth of property there and 13 per cent of all Denver office space. In Minneapolis, Oxford has a staggering 36-per-cent market share of office space. It has huge projects in a dozen more cities.

However, some critics believe that Oxford, and other Canadian developers, sank too much money into the U.S. Sun Belt and oil patch, where many values declined during the early 1980s. For instance, some maintain Oxford's Republic Plaza in Denver, built for $100 million, would be worth considerably less if resold.

Not that Love and Thomson plan to flip the properties they develop. The idea has been to build for cash flow and asset appreciation. It is a formula that can be played out forever, as long as the bank is there with that vital raw material: money.

The odd couple have been happy, but they have certainly been through some tough times. In 1980, they became part of the gang of a dozen who acted as white knights for Royal Trustco to fend off a $453-million takeover bid by development rival Campeau Corp., owned by Robert Campeau. When the trust company asked Thomson for help, he also enlisted Love's. Campeau withdrew his bid after the gang tied up 55 per cent of Royal's stock by spending $200 million. Love and Thomson held 19.8 per cent of the block.

It turned out to be a pyrrhic victory, because the trust company was eventually gobbled up by the Brascan empire of Peter and Edward Bronfman. In addition, the Ontario Securities Commission punished all the white knights for their roles by forcing them to pay for a lengthy and embarrassing public hearing.

In 1984, Love and Thomson took Campeau on again over his project to build a $380-million office tower in Toronto for the Bank of Nova Scotia. Oxford and the TD were furious, because the new building would contribute to the already growing glut of office space. The TD's Thomson took the gloves off in mid-May, spending $120,000 in full-page newspaper ads, lobbying city councillors and telling the press how Campeau's project would create a planning nightmare. Campeau eventually won.

The odd couple have certainly proven to Campeau, and anybody else, that they are quite willing to throw their weight around. But the unique relationship between these two may not translate into future prosperity for Love and his huge family business.

As one of Love's many former executives puts it: "The big question is this: Love wants the dynasty to carry on, but will his two sons be able to do it? When his son John was put in charge of Canada at the age of twenty-nine [1985], a lot of people began looking around for other work."

So G. Donald Love might be the one that got away, but his sons may not be as lucky.

THE JACKMANS

HAL JACKMAN once parked his decaying Lincoln in the lot at 10 Toronto St. to attend a meeting of the Argus Corp., headed by the articulate and verbally mischievous Conrad Black.

"Jackman bought that car used and then beat it up," says Black. "He's so absent-minded he can't drive, and he bumps into hydrants and things."

Another Argus director, Fredrik Eaton, president of Eaton's of Canada Ltd., arrived late to the same meeting in a chauffeur-driven limousine. "Eaton came in and said, 'Did you see that wreck in the parking lot? I've had it towed,'" Black says. Jackman, a multimillionaire financier who obviously does not carry cash, says he had to borrow a subway token from Eaton's chauffeur to get home after the meeting. Hal Jackman is not your typical Toronto tycoon.

He is the Canadian establishment's eccentric, an iconoclastic businessman who has inherited millions and made millions more. Yet he lives modestly.

"When you've inherited wealth, you don't feel that you have to spend money to impress anyone. I used to have a 1971 Ford station wagon, which I stopped driving because it literally fell apart. So then I bought a 1969 Lincoln for $2,000, even though it had started to rust. I hate taking cars in for repairs because the garages charge too much. My wife doesn't have a fur coat, but Conrad's a conspicuous spender. Have you seen his house? It's really something. And he's got another one in Florida. I've got one house."

But Black cautions against taking Jackman's comments too literally. "He's acquired a certain affection for his own caricature [tight-fistedness]. And he sometimes gets carried away."

Besides sharing with Black the best vocabulary this side of Upper Canada College and a flair for verbal jousting, Jackman is different from other Toronto businessmen for other reasons. He has an abiding passion for politics and, like Stephen Roman, has run unsuccessfully for office. James Richardson is the only big-league Canadian dynasty member to win office, but there are plenty of others who have thought about it, for obvious reasons. As Richardson said once, the federal cabinet is "the ultimate board of directors."

Instead, Jackman plays a significant back-room role within the Tory party. He is the most successful fund-raiser for the Big Blue Machine in Ontario and a confidant to Joe Clark and others. Jackman is also one of the few financially powerful men in Canada to openly bash establishment icons, such as the hallowed chartered banks. "The banking system is not in the country's best interests," says Jackman, whose trust company, National Victoria & Grey Trustco, is in competition with those banks.

Jackman believes that Canada's banks are actually bust, bailed out through a number of accounting tricks. He also says laws should be changed to allow more competition. As for politics, he says, "I raise a lot of money for the Tories and enjoy the excitement. Politics is a fascinating thing: nowhere else is mediocrity rewarded or superb performances stomped on."

Jackman's father, Harry, held the Rosedale riding in Toronto for the federal Tories from 1940 to 1949, but election success eluded Jackman and his brother Eric, who has run as an independent. Jackman lost three times to Liberal Donald Macdonald, who occupied the Rosedale riding from 1962 to 1978. "If I were young and had been elected, I might have had a political career, but I can't do both now. I couldn't be an MP and keep my business under the rules."

And what a business to give up.

From a tenth-floor office on Toronto's University Avenue, Jackman straddles a financial empire with $10 billion worth of assets, started during the Depression by his entrepreneurial father. "Like my dad, I get kicks out of saving money and making it grow," he explains.

A practising lawyer for a few years with a partner, Jackman took over the reins of his father's sizeable portfolio. He now functions as a professional shareholder, buying stakes in dozens of companies through his maze of corporate entities. He is never involved in the daily operations of any of the companies he controls and employs just two secretaries. Because of his investments, he is a director of a record-breaking twenty-five companies and another five charities. His life is one long string of meetings and six-dollar cigars.

He owns the majority of shares in a collection of closed-end investment funds — which in turn own shares in other companies as investments — and also controls Canada's third-largest trust company, National Victoria, and Algoma Central Railway and Empire Life Insurance.

"Jackman has a byzantine collection of companies, which he calls independent, but they are about as independent as Lithuania is within the Soviet Union," Black says. "Jackman's like a crocodile. He seems to be sleeping, but he isn't and suddenly he'll pounce on companies. He's a genius."

Black delights in taking shots at Jackman, such as one made during another Argus meeting, after the Tory convention in Winnipeg where Joe Clark's leadership was tested. "We passed a resolution that Jackman could not continue to embarrass us after he made a spectacle of himself on television at the convention," says Black. "He was shown standing on a chair with his jacket off, screaming 'Joe, Joe, Joe.'"

Jackman and Black were fellow-shareholders in Argus until 1983 when Jackman cashed in his chips, some 15 per cent of Black's private holding company, Ravelston. Black bought 5 per cent and the Webster brothers, Ben and Lorne, bought the rest. In 1985, Black eventually bought out all his Argus partners, including his brother, G. Montegu Black.

Despite jibes, the two are very close friends, sharing a passion for Shakespearean verse and Napoleonic war games. They often send each other handwritten notes. When Black asked Jackman if he was interested in an investment, Jackman wrote: "That you do love me I am nothing jealous." When the two were dickering over cost, Black quoted Falstaff back, saying, "Who steals my purse steals trash."

In the basement of his Rosedale home, Jackman has toy soldiers and an elaborate playing field. Black often comes over, Jackman says, and they conduct troop manoeuvres.

Physically, Jackman is as large as a pro football player, with bushes for eyebrows and long, slender fingers. Despite his size, he has never been enticed into jockmanship. The only exercise he gets is walking from his home to work most days, swimming in the summers in his pool, and "those damn Air Force exercises every night."

His office is spacious, occupying the corner penthouse of one of his companies. It is big enough to accommodate a group of fifty and is furnished like a Rosedale drawing-room, complete with antiques, fabrics in muted tones, and a bust of Churchill. An en-suite secretary's office is there, complete with a miniature kitchen. When asked about his financial worth, he ducks the question. Some estimate it at as much as $100 million, net of debts.

The Jackmans, their two sons and three daughters, three cats, and two dogs occupy a large home in Rosedale, complete with an outdoor pool. His wife, Maruja, has taught philosophy at York University and the University of Toronto. While Jackman says "business and politics are my life," Maruja has other interests but is a director in some of his companies.

"My wife's not turned on by politics, and in the last election I ran, people said, 'Why isn't your wife coming to the teas?'" Jackman recounts. "I said, 'She's got a baby and is teaching and is working on her PhD. She's not interested in coming to this and just being decorative or something.' And I wouldn't relish going to a faculty dinner with my wife. I would be hard pressed to tell you what her PhD thesis was all about."

Jackman, born Henry, is the oldest of four children, but the others "sold out" their inheritance. Eric is a psychologist, Edward, a Roman Catholic priest; when asked what his sister, Nancy, does, Jackman curiously described her as "a feminist." His own family history is the reason he discounts concern about concentration of economic power in the hands of a few families.

"Families are not a form of concentration to be concerned about, because they come and they go. What ever happened to Lord Strathcona and his fortune, which would be equivalent to several billion dollars nowadays? Take me: I have five kids. How do I know any one of them will be interested in doing what I do? Family wealth doesn't last."

Black says the whole family is eccentric.

"When Eddy announced he was going to become a priest, Harry [their father] disowned him, saying there were two vows with which he was never comfortable — poverty and chastity. Mary [Hal's mother] has always wondered exactly what she'd gotten into. For instance, Harry dragged them all off to Japan for six months, so he could learn to play the Tokyo Stock Exchange. The man never lost money at anything he did."

Harry Jackman began his career as an investment analyst with Sun Life Assurance Co. in Toronto. As a sideline, during the Depression, he began buying insurance companies and mutual funds for pennies per share that turned out to be worth a fortune because they had solid assets. His oldest son, Hal, was born in 1932. He became a lawyer, practised law, and worked as an executive assistant to a Tory cabinet minister in John Diefenbaker's government. In the 1960s, he took over the reins of Empire Life and the other companies his father had accumulated, under the family umbrella of Dominion and Anglo Investment Corp. Ltd. Then he began accumulating financial assets, insurance, mutual funds, and trust companies.

Most unusual of all — but hardly surprising, given that he is a competitor — is Jackman's attitude towards the banks. He has stated publicly that the entire system totters on the brink of collapse. Banks are only in business because they use an accounting technique — the five-year loan loss provision — to blunt the impact of their bad loans, Jackman says. This makes them appear more profitable than they are and keeps stock values high, attracting investors who furnish the funds to buy more shares that eventually more than cover the bad loans. He also says consumers and taxpayers have been keeping Canadian banks solvent by buying bank stock, paying higher interest rates than necessary, and funding bail-outs of troubled corporations.

Black, a Canadian Imperial Bank of Commerce director, observes that Jackman's bank-bashing "gets a little carried away" at times, leading him to make "flim-flam statements." But Jackman is adamant that banks are to blame for much of the country's economic trouble. His outspokenness has a great deal to do with being a rival of the banks, but it is also refreshing to hear from a tycoon when so many others are frightened to speak up, even if they feel the same.

He wants an end to the 10-per-cent ownership rule on banks because he feels it has entrenched bank management so firmly that shareholders cannot organize even when poor track records should result in management removals. He also decries the practice of having dozens of the banks' biggest customers sitting on boards of directors as the corporate equivalent of monkeys guarding the bananas. Some of his ideas about opening up banking to individuals and limiting the size of chartered bank boards were recommended in the 1985 Green Paper proposed by the minister of state for finance, Barbara McDougall. In fact, some even dubbed it "the Jackman paper."

It is his political dimension that makes him so interesting. Hal Jackman may not be Canada's richest man, but he is among the few who possess real political influence. Because of his loyal service as a fund-raiser, back-room strategist, and former candidate, he has the ear of the Tory party. That is not actual power, but it certainly gives him the kind of leverage few tycoons possess.

THE WESTONS

ON A SUNNY DAY in August 1983, six gunmen from the Irish Republican Army skulked around the Irish castle and estate of Galen Weston, one of the wealthiest Canadians in the world. Galen, his wife, Hillary, and their two children live in Toronto during the school year but spend summers commuting between their stately homes in Ireland and England. The kidnapping was foiled by a police ambush, thanks to a tip-off. Weston was not even there. He was at his eighteenth-century English estate, playing polo with Prince Charles.

Galen and his older brother Garry head empires that, in just three generations, have grown to be among the world's biggest food businesses. The family's first fortune was made by their grandfather, George Weston, an eighteen-year-old baker's apprentice who bought his own bread delivery route in 1882 and made business history. The family's North American vehicle, George Weston Ltd., weighs in along with North America's heavyweights, like General Mills and Beatrice Foods. It is Canada's sixth-largest corporation and one of North America's five biggest bakers and five biggest supermarket chains.

Unlike other conglomerates, such as the eclectic Brascan empire of Peter and Edward Bronfman, the Weston empire has stuck to its trade, beginning with bread, moving into stores to sell the bread, and finally making more products to sell in the grocery stores. The Westons have not dabbled in other enterprises, but not for want of trying. In 1979, Galen bid $550 million for The Bay, with its billions in assets, but backed off after being outbid by the Thomson family.

The family owns the W. Garfield Weston Foundation (U.K.) and the Garfield Weston Foundation. Galen is chairman of George Weston Ltd. in Toronto, which invests in North America, and Garry is chairman of Associated British Foods Group of London, England, which invests everywhere else. The two companies posted combined sales in 1984 of $12 billion worldwide, more than the $8.5 billion in taxes collected by Canada's four Atlantic provinces. The Toronto company alone had sales of $8.2 billion, with $2.2 billion in assets; it was bigger in sales than Alcan Aluminium Ltd., Canadian National Railways, or Shell Canada Ltd. Associated British Foods had sales of nearly $5 billion. Together the two employ 45,000 workers worldwide.

As a corporate entity, George Weston Ltd. may not be a household word in Canada, but it has been the darling of Bay Street investors for a number of years because of its enormous profits. In 1984, it made $92 million—$6.76 per share — and cash flow (actual cash made before paper write-offs for tax purposes) was nearly $250 million. The company is so prosperous that it is poised for expansions or takeovers — or both — during the 1980s.

The Weston products and stores, on the other hand, are household words in Canada. Weston owns 403 Loblaws stores and supplies 1,370 franchised stores with names like Ziggy's, Save Easy, No Frills, National Grocers, Shop Easy, OK Economy, Super Value, Dominion Fruit, Canal Villere, Gordons, and others. It also has chains in the U.S. such as National Tea Co. and Peter J. Schmitt Co. Inc., with hundreds more stores.

The company is one of Canada's biggest food processors. It makes Weston breads, Golden Dawn frozen juices, McCormick's cookies, Country Harvest breads, Wheat Thins, and confections like Wagon Wheels, Sweet Maries, Jersey Milk, Crispy Crunch, and Neilson chocolates. Its resources group is in fishing and forestry: B.C. Packers sells canned salmon, tuna, and other seafood under the well-known Clover Leaf, Connors, Brunswick, Connoisseur, and other brands; and its E.B. Eddy Forest Products Co. makes the famous wooden matches of the same name, as well as White Swan paper products.

Associated British owns supermarkets and department stores in Ireland, the U.K., and Australia, and processes everything from frankfurters to Popsicles through 140 subsidiaries in a dozen countries. It owns Twinings Tea and Ryvita, whose products are found in North America, and also the world-famous caterer to the carriage trade, London's Fortnum & Mason.

The Weston empire began in the nineteenth century like the Eaton, Webster, Molson, and Richardson fortunes. But it was the dynamic son of the founder, W. Garfield Weston, who combined food with high finance and snapped up companies by the score. When George Weston died in 1924, twenty-seven-year-old Garfield inherited a string of Ontario bakeries and biscuit factories that employed a mere 400 workers. At his father's graveside, Garfield said, "I'm not going to build a costly monument to my father — I'm going to make his name known around the world." He began his campaign, here and abroad, and moved to England in 1935, setting up his second food empire, Associated British.

Like so many Canadian tycoons of his era — such as Roy Thomson, Max Aitken, and James Dunn — Weston was an anglophile and felt that England, not the United States, was the land of business opportunity. Britain was the big time. After a period of head-spinning growth, Garfield stopped shopping because of the Second World War and served as a British Tory member of Parliament. During that time he established close ties with the royal family and Britain's power élite — ties that still bind.

Galen and Garry have been involved in the family business since they were teens. Their seven siblings have not. However, indications are that the other Westons share the proceeds. Sisters Miriam, Nancy, and Gretchen are married and live in the U.S.; Barbara, Wendy, and Camilla live in Toronto. The oldest brother, Grainger, spurned the family business and is operating a real estate company in Texas.

Garry was born in 1927 and is second-oldest. Galen, the youngest of the nine children, was born in 1940. Galen attended seventeen schools as his father searched the world for companies. Their lives were filled with horses, mansions, and servants, but their most frequent address was Wittington House, the family estate on the Thames River. Wittington was eventually given by the family to the Salvation Army.

Wittington is also the name of one of the family's holding companies; it owns 56 per cent of George Weston Ltd. and is controlled by Galen. Associated British is controlled by Garry.

Their father was a great philanthropist and personally handed over millions of pounds to England's chancellor of the exchequer; some went to help restore St. Paul's Cathedral after a bombing attack, other funds to build jet fighters. He was even asked to become a director of the Bank of England, but he telexed back, "There must be a mistake. I'm a baker, not a banker."

Galen cultivates those British roots by spending summers at his Irish and English castles. There he and his family ride horses, play polo with princes, and drink tea (Twinings, no doubt) with England's aristocracy. Galen's eighteenth-century English estate, called Fort Belvedere, is actually on the grounds of one of the royal family's country palaces, and was purchased from the late Duke and Duchess of Windsor. Its grand sitting-room was where the duke signed the documents that legally allowed him to abdicate the throne as King Edward VIII so he could marry an American divorcée.

Galen Weston is as much an Englishman as a Canadian. Toronto is home, but he speaks with a clipped, mid-Atlantic accent. He has the fair-haired, peaches-and-cream look of a slowly aging English schoolboy. His wife is Irish, a model named Hillary Frayne. They were married in 1966, and wedding guests wore 1890s Klondike costumes and were ferried in a vintage steamboat, complete with ragtime band, up and down the Thames.

(Equally flamboyant was the 100th-anniversary party he threw in 1982 for 20,000 employees, friends, and relatives to celebrate the founding of the business. He rented Canada's Wonderland amusement park, north of Toronto, for an entire day at a cost of $300,000.)

Naturally friendly and open, Galen has gone underground since the kidnapping incident, declining interviews with the press and ducking public functions whenever possible. Garry is stocky, balding, and mustachioed. He is a British subject and rarely comes to Canada. Like his father, he sits on some of Britain's most prestigious boards of directors, travels constantly, and is a confidant and private-sector adviser to the country's titled, elected, or otherwise powerful.

Galen and Garry became company directors in their teens, but the entrepreneurial Galen left the fold to launch his own business in Ireland between 1961 and 1972. He ended up with the largest supermarket chain and second-largest department store group there, now part of Associated Foods. Along the way, he also acquired the family's interest in a large supermarket chain in Germany, called Manns, whose founder sits on the board of George Weston Ltd.

By the mid-1960s, the Weston-Loblaw group was Canada's biggest company, but it was heading for serious trouble. It was bloated with too many stores at a time when consumers were shifting towards shopping at specialty food stores as well as eating out. In 1970, the company had financial problems and Galen moved back to Toronto to mind the stores. He moved his wife, two children, five polo ponies, and two jumping horses to Toronto and sorted out the family firm. He turned the company around — its 2,000 stores were chopped to fewer than 500 — and by 1979, was solvent enough to make his bid for The Bay.

Robert Kidd, Weston's senior vice president and chief financial officer, remembers well those dark days before the turnaround. "The company was doing too many things and did not have enough cash to do any of them well. He [Galen] decided to change priorities and to concentrate on doing those things we do well. Anything — whether it was a brand name or a store — that was third, fourth, or fifth in its market was closed. His philosophy was that only first and second succeed, and losers usually lose you a lot more than winners ever make you. About one-third of the entire company was trimmed."

Unlike other gigantic retailers such as the Steinbergs, the Eatons, and the Sobeys, the Westons never got into real estate, buying and developing stores or malls. "We feel renting is cheaper than building," says Kidd. "For instance, we feel a lot of retailers, like The Bay, were stuck with undesirable retail sites developed by their real estate divisions."

"He enjoys doing something well," says Kidd, who works closely with Galen and accepts interviews on his behalf since the IRA made him gun-shy. "He likes to build and have employees happy with steady jobs. He has a personal interest in people. You are more likely to see him in a store than on Bay Street or in a bank chairman's office. He keeps a low profile for safety reasons and also because of the decentralized nature of the company. He lets his operations guys speak for themselves."

He does not rub shoulders with Toronto's business or political élite as often as many of his peers do. Galen, like George Weston's headquarters, is slightly removed from the heart of downtown Toronto. He spends most of his time with his family, and also puts in long hours at work and helping charities. Weston's headquarters, removed from the Albany, York, and Toronto Clubs, are located at St. Clair and Yonge Streets, across from the Unicorp penthouse offices of George Mann, a Forest Hill neighbour. Socially, he is friendly with the Eatons, with whom he has obvious common interests, but he does not do the Toronto–Palm Beach–Lyford Cay circuit. And if home is where the heart is, he has many homes.

Galen and Garry are extremely talented businessmen. By all accounts, they are nice guys who happened to inherit a great deal of money, but who work as hard as their forbears ever did. They have also accomplished a great deal in their own right and are imbued with the type of work ethic that will guarantee future accomplishments.

THE BLACKS

CONRAD BLACK'S name may be a generic term in Canada for capitalist. He may be the most celebrated and visible of the country's financiers. And he may also be one of our most interesting and entertaining businessmen. But he is far from the richest. He once said he had only two ambitions in life: to escape Canada's horrible winters and to make $100 million. By 1985, at the age of forty-one, Black had achieved both goals. As if to celebrate, that summer he became the sole proprietor of the Argus empire, buying out all but a small fraction of his partners, including his older brother, George Montegu Black.

Black lives an exceedingly extravagant lifestyle. He is a complex, brilliant businessman with a flair for turns of phrase and eloquent, Faulknerian sentences, laced with references from literature and the classics. He devours several books a week, has an almost photographic memory, and cherishes a tremendous collection of miniature soldiers. He plays complicated war games, lasting for weeks, with friends like Hal Jackman. While fawning journalists have made more out of his accomplishments than is justified, the fact is that Black is one of Canada's most clever financiers.

Since 1978, Conrad Black has been chairman of the Argus empire, launched after the Second World War under the skilful guidance of Bud McDougald and E. P. Taylor of Toronto. Argus acquired toe-holds in seven corporate giants: Labrador Mining, Noranda Mines, Hollinger-Argus, Standard Broadcasting, Dominion Stores, Domtar, and Massey-Ferguson Ltd. The old guard's philosophy was simple. "We buy the biggest piece of the biggest piece," explained Taylor, who was once plucked — with Conrad Black's father — from a lifeboat in the Atlantic after their ship had been torpedoed during the war. George Black was to become president of Taylor's Canadian Breweries, and a small shareholder in Argus's total empire.

Blessed with a silver-spoon start, Black nonetheless deserved accolades in 1978 when he successfully plotted the Argus takeover. Dubbed "Black magic" by the *Economist* of London, he and his shareholders bought controlling interest in Argus from the aging widows of the two men his father had worked for. Only thirty-three years old but going on sixty, Black raised money for the purchase by inviting well-heeled friends to participate. Once he had put together an élite partnership, the banks fell in line and lent him the rest with little or no down payment.

"That's Conrad's genius, how a young guy like that could fool all those bank presidents into lending him the money," says his good friend Jackman, who was an Argus partner until 1983.

The only thing the Blacks were really interested in was the "royalty stream," or dividends, from North America's best iron ore bodies, operated by the Iron Ore Co., former employer of Brian Mulroney. Iron Ore runs the mines and ships out ore and billions of dollars of royalties to the shareholders of Hanna Mining of Cleveland, including Argus companies and some of the biggest steel companies in the U.S. The rest of the Argus empire, which included profitable companies with radio stations, paper mills, and grocery stores, was just icing on the cake. Eventually, it became excess baggage as everything but the mining companies was jettisoned.

What followed were a number of complex machinations that allowed Black to turn $7 million into $100 million by 1985. Along the way he also made his partners richer than they already were — a blueblood collection of scions of his father's friends or young lions he met at Upper Canada College. While he is nowhere near as wealthy as most of the families profiled here, he remains powerful because he singlehandedly controls a hefty resource empire with nearly $1 billion in assets. In 1986, Black became a partner of Peter and Edward Bronfman by swapping his control stake in Norcen Energy Resources Ltd. for $170 million in cash and 16 per cent of Hees International Corp., eventually reduced to 5 per cent.

His former Argus partners were his first cousin Ron Riley, a vice president of Canadian Pacific Ltd.; Fredrik Eaton; Douglas Bassett, who runs Baton Broadcasting for the Eatons; Lorne and Ben Webster, linked to the Eaton family by marriage; Ralph Barford, a London-based financier with a fistful of directorships in Hal Jackman's stable of companies; Glen Davis, who inherited dozens of companies worth millions in assets from his father, Ohio financier Nelson Davis, who had served as Black's mentor and ally in the Argus takeover; and Argus executives such as Dixon Chant, John Finlay, Peter White, and David Radler. These four still own some shares.

For seven years, Conrad ran his Argus empire as though it were a gentlemen's club: a network of partners and pals, a fraternity of middle-aged financiers who work, play, and get richer together. Even the Argus corporate jet is a replica of the Toronto Club, complete with leather-studded chairs and walnut panelling. Conrad functions as the chief frat brother.

Black is still on top, but his star has lost its sparkle for a number of reasons.

He may have made himself exceedingly rich along the way, but three of his six original companies were sold, or given away, after falling into disarray. In 1979, there was the Massey-Ferguson mess; it was inherited from the old guard and Black wisely walked away from it. In 1984, Dominion Stores began hemorrhaging red ink, so Black eviscerated the chain, by selling 75 per cent of the stores to rival A&P for $134 million. In 1985, Standard Broadcasting's takeover of a California cable company turned profits into losses, so Black grabbed the first offer for Standard that came along, from media magnate Allan Slaight, and sold out.

But Black and his Argus shareholders never billed themselves as builders. They are Canada's inheritors. They are not entrepreneurs, but investors who learned from their fathers how to decipher cash-flow ratios and price/earnings multiples. They also learned there is a time to buy and a time to sell, but never any time to run things. They are financiers — or parasites, as Marxists would call them: a cluster of Canadians straddling the country's economy, who, for the most part, will never invent a better mousetrap. But once there is one on the market, they may take it over.

On the positive side, Black also sold Domtar and Noranda for good prices and acquired Norcen Energy Resources Ltd., a well-run oil company. Between these business benchmarks were a number of restructurings and share swaps among companies in his stable, designed to avoid taxes and get dividends to flow upward towards his private holding company, Ravelston. This made him and his fellow-shareholders rich, but turned off many outsiders.

Overall, Black and his shareholders have done well. According to internal figures he supplied to me, anyone buying Argus common shares in 1979, when he did, made a profit by 1985 of 43 per cent (capital gains plus dividends); Argus Class C preferred shares made 87 per cent; Hollinger, 71 per cent; Dominion, 31 per cent; and Standard, 44 per cent. These increases are understated, considering that dividends are more valuable than capital gains, because companies in Canada pay no tax on dividends and individuals pay virtually none.

However, along the way, Black has swapped or shifted his companies to maximize his profits and returns. Black has not "grown" a company, nor will he. He buys companies that were started and nurtured by others. He does not put seed capital into fledgling companies. That is why when Dominion hit heavy weather, he cashed in his chips. The antithesis of a Lee Iacocca who turned around a troubled Chrysler by attracting new cash and revamping operations, Black sold off profitable portions to A&P and closed down the rest of the chain. He is strictly a financier, who buys and sells, but does not run, companies.

"Maybe he's just a good liquidator," comments astute investment counsellor Stephen Jarislowsky.

Black's reputation was bloodied in 1983 following his unsuccessful 1981 attempt to take over Hanna Mining in Cleveland. The battle became bitter, and both sides agreed to a "standstill" deal, limiting Black to 26 per cent of Hanna's shares. But the fighting was rough and dragged Black's name through the mud as Sam Wakim, a streetfighting lawyer for Iron Ore Co. and Mulroney's best friend, pulled out the stops. Legal officials on both sides of the border were alerted to so-called transgressions. Hanna's management laid charges of "racketeering" against Black and Norcen's board of directors.

The takeover led to two investigations by Toronto police and the Ontario Securities Commission. Charges were not laid by either body, but the incident provoked Black into verbal pique, as he lashed out at members of the political establishment. He attacked Ontario's attorney general, Roy McMurtry, describing him as having "scrambled around for a year like an asphyxiated cockroach trying to explain away the impropriety of his people," and saying that Toronto police had conducted a "witch hunt" and were "either negligent or malicious" in their methods. He also said his private detective agency, Canadian Protective Services, had swept his phones for listening devices, and Black accused the police of illegally tapping his lines.

Eventually, the U.S. Securities and Exchange Commission slapped Black's wrist, but the headlines led to police and securities probes here. Investigations centred on a notice of intention sent to Norcen shareholders in October 1981 that stated the board did not intend to make any major changes. Norcen board minutes indicated a takeover was being planned. The notice of intention was an offer to buy Norcen shares from its shareholders, and between October and February some 340,000 shares were sold by unwitting shareholders.

This interested the Ontario Securities Commission, because securities laws require disclosure of such major plans to shareholders so that they may make informed decisions. To police, the affair required scrutiny because the discrepancy in the documents smacked of forgery, or intent to deceive or defraud shareholders.

Black and other directors swore that the minutes were inaccurate and that definite plans to take over Hanna did not exist. In April 1983, the securities commission decided against taking action, saying that to disclose half-baked plans would be as disruptive to stock markets as to withhold definite plans. In June, the police, in consultation with Crown attorneys from McMurtry's office, announced the matter would be dropped for lack of evidence of intent to defraud or deceive. That should have closed the case. It didn't.

A storm of controversy developed when *Maclean's* magazine found out that the commission's own investigators had strongly urged laying twenty-six charges against Black and others. But it was all a tempest in a teapot. Criminal charges would have been impossible to prove, and the securities breaches were so minor that the headlines were punishment enough. However, the tarnish has yet to wear off.

The Blacks are definitely on the wane as a financial force, particularly now that the brothers are no longer partners. A rift developed over Montegu's handling of both Standard's and Dominion's business affairs, according to most reports. Although they may be on friendly terms, there is nothing like division to destroy a dynasty. After all, the Reichmanns, the Belzbergs, the Ghermezians, and others have learned what families like the Siftons and the McConnells have not: united, family fortunes grow. Divided, they fall.

Of course, Conrad Black is hardly the type of tycoon to rest on his laurels. He still singlehandedly controls an important empire, which includes Labrador Mining, 26 per cent of Hanna Mining Co., a sliver of Dominion Stores, and Hees. He also owns a small chain of Canadian newspapers, called Sterling Newspapers, which are money-makers but journalistically mediocre.

Of all the businesses he has bought and sold, newspapers are his favourite. He has dabbled at journalism himself, turning a post-graduate thesis on Duplessis into a book and writing a monthly column for the *Globe and Mail*, at the invitation of Norman Webster, editor-in-chief and first cousin to Black's former business partners Lorne and Ben Webster.

In 1982, Conrad Black put together a group including John Bassett Jr., Fredrik Eaton, and George Gardiner to bid for the former FP chain, which included the *Globe*, against the Websters' uncle, Howard Webster. Both were outbid by the Thomson family. It is ironic that Black's one passion in life — newspapers — is a game that he has been shut out of in Canada. This is not because he is undesirable, but because ownership concentration is so high that there are no newspapers, much less chains, for him to take over.

So it was not surprising that within weeks of buying out his Argus partners, he invested $14 million in one of the world's greatest newspapers, the *Daily Telegraph* in London, England. By December 1985, he had controlling interest, 50.1 per cent.

"I could sell it for more than I paid for it," Black said of his newspaper purchase. "Sure I could flip it, but that's not what I bought it for. As they say over there [in England], it's a magnificent 'title' at a good price, at a period when the industry is in a very swift and positive evolution."

The deal came about when Black was invited by *Telegraph* publisher Lord Hartwell to become an investor in order to help finance two new printing plants. But by the end of 1985, the paper had lost millions and Hartwell's family could not top up the paper's treasury with cash from its own resources. Consequently, control was sold to Black. "The *Telegraph*'s underwriter, Evelyn Rothschild, and Andrew Knight [head of the *Economist* at the time] are friends of mine and brought its problems to my attention," said Black, who appointed Knight editor of the *Telegraph*.

As with his other acquisitions, Black is not wedded to this purchase. He hopes to make money by cutting costs, cashing in on the attempt by Britain's press barons to break their oppressive and extortionist labour unions, and changing slightly the editorial thrust of the stodgy and monarchist *Telegraph*. "A nickel-and-dime store in Parry Sound is run better than this place," Black said of *Telegraph* management before taking over. "The British lack basic administrative standards and are still dealing with a delusional structure based on the envy of other nations."

But the purchase of the *Telegraph* gives Black more than just a shot at some swift capital gains. "Conrad's love is newspapers and he thinks the *Telegraph* gives him cachet," surmises his close friend Jackman. However, when I asked him whether he was casting for a peerage by righting the troubled *Telegraph*, Black remarked: "In my heart, I'm a republican, large and small 'r.'"

Like most of Toronto's WASP establishment, Black acts like gentry, spending hours in stuffy men's clubs, surrounded all his life by duke-chasers like Bud McDougald who enjoy having peers of the realm on their boards of directors. Black's investment in the *Telegraph* is not emotional. His intention is to make money, but along the way he may also find that owning a high-profile English newspaper can get him the one thing that money is not supposed to be able to buy: a peerage.

One day, despite his protestations, there may be a Lord Conrad of Black Ink.

THE BRONFMANS (EDWARD AND PETER)

A WELL-FED, eight-foot-tall brass figure in a greatcoat, hat, and briefcase adorns the reception area of Brascan Ltd. Opposite is a wall of brass hiding a concealed door, which opens mysteriously when the receptionist presses a foot pedal beneath her desk. Beside the sculpture is a brass wall plaque bearing the following tongue-in-cheek inscription: "All great civilizations have had their priestly caste. Our priesthood will be those who occupy positions of great economic power. A well-nourished figure looking up as he is about to enter the Sanctuary of Business, he raises his eyes in pious reverence, seeking the divine inspiration necessary for the consummation of the Big Deal."

Brascan is only part of the financial empire of Edward and Peter Bronfman and Edper Investments Ltd., the family holding company. Trevor Eyton and Jack Cockwell are the two most senior executive officers of Edper Investments; with Tim Price, they have been together since the late 1960s and are, with more than twenty others, the high priests of the Edper group of companies. Trevor Eyton is a former partner of the prestigious Toronto law firm Tory Tory DesLauriers & Binnington; he left the practice in 1979 to work full-time with the Edper companies. Today he is chief spokesman and adviser to the publicity-shy Bronfman brothers as well as a millionaire in his own right. Chartered accountant Jack Cockwell is a South African-born financial whiz and fitness buff who has been the key strategist in forming the complex collection of corporations controlled by Edper.

Edper is an abbreviation taken from Edward's and Peter's given names. It is jointly owned by the PB Family Trust, created for Peter's three children, and the EB Family Trust, for Edward's three. Each trust includes amongst its trustees Peter and Edward plus Cockwell, Eyton, and chartered accountant David Kerr.

Each January, a formal meeting of the trusts is held at Brascan's offices in Toronto's Commerce Court West. The meeting is attended by the family members and the trustees. Edward's oldest son works for a film and entertainment company, his middle son is at a brokerage house, and his youngest son is in his last year at university. Peter's son works for Trizec, and his two daughters continue with their university studies. "They are all unassuming, just like their fathers," says Eyton, who runs interference for the family whenever possible.

Although born into a family of considerable wealth, the two brothers are known for their modest lifestyles. "The success of Edper is due to the constant support of Peter and Edward, and to the unique relationship between them and their key managers, who in practical terms operate as a partnership comprising more than twenty outstanding individuals committed to the Edper business principles," says Eyton. Notwithstanding, it is apparent that Eyton and Cockwell play leadership roles within the group; so much so that Peter once suggested they shouldn't travel together on the same airplane on business trips. "There's no way," Eyton told Bronfman. "If Jack goes down, I want to be with him."

Access to Peter and Edward is carefully guarded by Eyton. He jealously protects their privacy, acting as their spokesman when that is appropriate and always seeking to channel public discussion to the business activities of the group.

In writing this profile I had the benefit of discussion with Eyton and other key group executives, and I was also given access to Edper's own internal chronology, an abbreviated business history of the country's most fascinating financial empire.

While the two Bronfman brothers are not considered as rich as Canadian dynasties like the Thomsons or the Westons, they may well be soon. The Edper empire is one of Canada's most pervasive. The group comprises more than a hundred companies and in excess of 100,000 workers. Edper's non-financial empire is bigger collectively than the country's largest non-financial corporation, Hydro-Québec, with $27 billion in assets, roughly 5 per cent of the country's entire non-financial corporate wealth. In addition, Edper is the major shareholder in several Canadian financial institutions, with some $72 billion in deposits and other financial assets, equivalent in size to Canada's second-largest bank, the Bank of Montreal.

Edper companies specialize in financial services, real estate, beer, milk and food products, and natural resources, where they tend to be dominant players. Edper's financial services companies (Hees International, Trilon Financial, and Great Lakes Group) act as super-brokers and super-bankers. Hees alone has in excess of $1 billion in capital, almost as much capital as is owned by all the brokers on the Toronto Stock Exchange. Edper's natural resource interests include Norcen Energy Resources, Westmin Resources, North Canadian Oils, Merland Exploration, and Canadian Hunter, as well as Canada's largest mining company and its largest forestry company, Noranda Inc. and MacMillan Bloedel. Noranda owns almost 15 per cent of B.C.'s mines, and MacMillan owns about 34 per cent of its overall forestry business.

Edper is equally pervasive in real estate. Through Carena-Bancorp, it controls several of North America's largest public real estate developers with about $7 billion in assets, including Trizec, Bramalea Ltd., Costain Ltd., and U.S. developers Ernest Hahn Inc. and Rouse Co. Last, but far from least, is Edper's major interest in John Labatt, with 40 per cent of Canada's beer market. With almost $3 billion in sales and $1 billion in assets, Labatt is the country's forty-third-largest corporation.

It has been suggested that Edper's sheer size poses problems for Canada's small economy, especially considering the speed of its growth since 1979, when Edper went from minority shareholdings in a few companies to controlling interests in a number of Canada's largest and most important companies. "In the absence of any controls over conglomerate ownership, the financial and non-financial sectors will be dominated by less than a dozen very large groups that could wield enormous economic power," Cadillac Fairview's president Bernie Ghert warned a Parliamentary finance committee in 1985. "Canadians are insufficiently concerned about the darker side of such concentration of power." While Canada's tycoons are all honourable men, their heirs or successors may not be.

Ironically, Ghert works for the equally acquisitive Bronfman cousins, Edgar and Charles. His concerns are shared by his employers and are specifically aimed at all conglomerates like Edper that own both financial and non-financial assets. The concern is that this may lead to self-dealing and other abuses. However, Eyton points out wryly that Edgar and Charles Bronfman companies mixed such investments in the past and sold large stakes that they were accumulating in Royal Trustco and London Life before Edper companies bought control.

Canadians are insufficiently aware of this incredible empire, which has been fashioned on specific business principles. "These business principles have as a basis the concept that Edper should be the largest shareholder in autonomous, widely held public corporations with independent managements and independent directors. In practice, this means that Edper limits its holding to 50 per cent of its key group companies, deals only on a consensual basis through the chief executive officers and their boards, and asserts its rights most especially in the areas of strategic planning, succession, management rewards, and transactions involving the issue of equity shares," says Eyton.

Unlike the Thomsons, who prefer to own about 70 per cent of whatever public companies they have, the Edper empire maximizes leverage by buying the biggest piece of the biggest piece of the biggest piece. That way, returns on investments are enhanced because a small amount of capital can be matched by the public at each level, with control retained by the holder of that big piece at the top. For instance, Edper can control Company C without owning any of its shares by purchasing 50 per cent of Company A, if A owns 50 per cent of Company B, which, in turn, owns 50 per cent of Company C. "The leverage means that an equity investment of $100 million by Edper at the Company A level will, with the public matching all the way, translate into a total equity financing at the Company C level of $800 million," says Eyton.

In this way, Edper is a self-financing money machine. Little wonder that a brass can filled with Monopoly money sits on Eyton's desk in his forty-eighth-floor office in Commerce Court West, in Toronto. It was a gag gift. But the truth is that the Edper team has been busy attracting billions of dollars from the public to buy billions of dollars in assets since 1969, on behalf of Peter and Edward, the so-called "poor Bronfmans."

Brascan and major affiliates such as John Labatt and Royal Trustco attract many of the headlines, but a key Edper company, Hees International, has begun to get the recognition it deserves. The predecessor company bought by Edper in the 1960s had been the family firm of Tory cabinet minister George Hees. Hees International sat on a shelf for a time, but Cockwell and his team began transforming it in the 1980s into a powerful economic force. Now Hees's equity is nearly the size of Bay Street's, with more than $1 billion in capital. Add to that the capital of its sister companies, such as Trilon and Great Lakes Group, and the total combined equity is equivalent to the capitalization of Canada's fifth-largest bank and three times larger than Bay Street.

Little wonder that Hees and the other Edper companies are courted by all the country's shooters and all the country's brokers. Between 1982 and 1985, for instance, Edper affiliates bought nearly one-third of all the preferred shares sold in Canada; Royal Trustco, a key player in the Trilon group, holds about 10 per cent of all securities in the country in its own accounts or trusteed accounts; and members of the Edper group raised $3 billion from the public through share issues in three years, equivalent to one-third of all equity investments made in the country in that period. The result has been that the Edper companies have become ever stronger. Because the Edper group has awesome clout, it is capable of making or breaking public offerings and capitalizing on, or even sparking, takeovers. Member companies of the Edper group, each acting on its own, made it possible for George Mann to pull off his $300-million takeover of Union Enterprises in 1984. In what is called a "junk bond" deal, Mann merely issued paper IOUs, in the form of preferred shares in his own company, Unicorp Canada Ltd., in return for Union stock.

First, Edper's Great Lakes Group swapped its 17-per-cent block of Union for Mann's preferred shares, and then other Edper companies purchased additional preferred shares on the market, ensuring the success of the takeover. "On the face it was a big hit for Unicorp. George's position was junior [in overall business terms]. But Unicorp was his living. And we believe in him," says Eyton.

Edper also encourages interlocking arrangements. In an approach called "synergism," members of the Edper group are known to buy one another's preferred shares and use one another's services whenever possible. Preferred share purchases allow Edper to provide financing to its investee companies in a tax-efficient manner without diluting common equity values for all shareholders. "We never permit group companies to buy common or preferred shares in their parent companies. That would be wrong," says Eyton. Not only would it be wrong, but such interdependence would create a house of cards that could tumble, with devastating results to the entire economy.

While the rest of the investment community scorned Mann's preferred shares because they carried an ambitious dividend, few realized that the whole transaction could prove to be a no-lose situation for the Edper group. After all, if Mann defies disbelievers and pays the handsome dividends on his preferreds, the Edper group will have gotten preferreds at bargain prices. If things don't work out, the group might conceivably take over Union Enterprises itself, sending in Hees to do one of its "work-outs" — a cross between a liquidation and a venture capital deal. "But the Unicorp preferreds are trading a year later for more money," says Eyton. Despite the fact that the Edper group and its allies control virtually all the shares, Eyton contends "you cannot fool the marketplace."

Hees is a brilliant business niche. Its "work-outs" perform a necessary business function, allowing companies to restructure and remain in operation rather than fold. They also give Hees assets at fire-sale prices. As Dylex's Jimmy Kay says: "Hees is a business doctor and a business operator." When Kay's Hatleigh, Foodex, and North Canadian Oils empire hit the skids in

1982, he turned to Hees. Some assets were sold, the rest were reorganized, and Hees pumped in fresh cash. Kay, a close friend of Eyton's who was his lawyer for years, ended up with a much smaller interest, but he considers himself lucky. "Hees can get right in there. It's the last guy in and banks don't want to do that. They cut and run and go on to new business."

Hees is a key member of the Edper group, swapping information about the market and trading preferred shares for the group. "We value our access to Hees people. I'm a relative and can get free advice," explains Paul Marshall, president of Edper's Westmin Resources Ltd.

In 1986, Hees agreed to pay about $300 million in cash and shares to Conrad Black and his Hollinger Inc. for the controlling interest in Norcen Energy, acting in a classic role as merchant banker by giving Brascan an option on the position for two years. Such interdependence could lead to abuses that benefit only Edper's sister companies at the expense of other shareholders. But Marshall maintains this is not so. "If I can do business with one of them, I do it, such as a transfer agent, registrar, insurance, or financing through Great Lakes Group. But I canvass the market when buying trust company services, or whatever. If costs are over the market, I tell them they have to come down or we don't do a deal. It happened once. As for synergism, we share ideas, and the giver never charges. In my case, if I lend my time to help another of the companies, I know this is not unfair to my other shareholders, because I will get free advice back in return."

Hees is also involved in preferred shares in a big way, because Edper companies often "borrow" by issuing preferred shares rather than taking bank loans. This policy was imposed by Cockwell during Hees's first work-out — the restructuring of Trizec in the late 1970s. It saves the group millions; preferred share dividends are at a lower rate than bank interest because the companies buying preferred shares pay no tax on the dividends.

"Brokers ignored the preferred marketplace because they only got 1-percent commissions for preferred shares, and 3 to 4 per cent for common. So Hees got into the middle," explains Bill L'Heureux, another alumnus of the Tory Tory firm, who is now senior vice president at Hees and president of Carena-Bancorp, holding company for the group's real estate empire and its 19-per-cent interest in Continental Bank. "Now we have thirty or forty contacts we buy and sell preferreds to. Treasurers of companies call us, because we keep a close watch on all prefs."

Hees is a key player in the country's preferred share market but doesn't make a commission. Instead, it is rewarded by helping its sister companies sell their preferreds. Besides, Hees has two other core businesses, which group members call "risk arbitrage" and "underwriting support."

"Risk arbitrage is a misnomer. Arbitrage is where a takeover is announced and investors start to accumulate stock to make spreads. Risk arbitrage is when you ferret out companies where you believe a takeover is imminent. Our involvement is not as a player, but we have clients we will finance who are in that investment. It's a conservative way of investing because you can count on two hands how many targets are in the marketplace right now, and they are mostly blue-chip companies and not as risky as the name makes it sound," says L'Heureux.

Tim Price, the president of Hees International and a chartered accountant, runs Hees's arbitrage business. Price also engages in underwriting support. Like a European merchant banker, he bankrolls good trading ideas offered by individuals, brokers, or corporations, within or outside the group. "We will do two things: finance them on the basis of net worth, but also look at the deal, and if we feel it is no good we won't finance them. This function is important, because we provide another set of eyes as to deals out there. This is unlike what a bank does, where a triple-A borrower walks in and a bank lends without looking at the deal. Sometimes we don't have security beyond the stock, sometimes we do. We lend to people and companies we have had relationships with for a long time," says L'Heureux.

Hees gives Edper another element of economic power by being a window on most of the country's deals. For instance, Hees supports five or six brokerage firms regularly. Most publicized is Hees's relationship with the aggressive Gordon Capital, involved in the Union-Unicorp takeover. Gordon Capital is controlled by Neil Baker and Jimmy Connacher. Baker served as president of Edper in the late 1960s, but the arrangement with Gordon is the same as with five other brokers: Hees will provide up to $25 million for market transactions. Profits are shared, but brokers must limit Hees's down side. Some other brokers who deal with Hees are Wood Gundy, Dominion Securities, and Merrill Lynch.

Hees also owns important interests in the empire's two most important holding companies: Brascan, including its Noranda and MacMillan Bloedel assets, and Carena-Bancorp, with its real estate assets. Perhaps a sign of things to come is that astute Toronto tycoons Conrad Black and Chris Ondaatje are major Hees shareholders, with 5 per cent and 11 per cent respectively, for a total of 16 per cent. "This represents a resounding vote of confidence in the management skills and record of the Edper team, who, in effect, have been entrusted with the care of an important part of the net worth of these two investors," says Eyton.

Another Edper merchant bank is Great Lakes Group, with some $450 million in capital; it is partly the electrical utility in Sault Ste. Marie, Ont., and partly a merchant bank. "The utility provides a solid asset base against which to borrow and maximize leverage. Merrill Lynch Canada Inc. and the Canadian Imperial Bank of Commerce are also Great Lakes shareholders," says Eyton.

"It grew out of two needs: to assist in financing both within and outside the group, and to take on undervalued equity positions in the marketplace."

Obviously, Great Lakes could be used to prop up stock prices within the empire, thus weakening its own financial health and misleading the public. This is not the case, but it could be. Besides, there have been concerns raised about using a utility's assets to become a bank. Eyton still visibly tenses when asked about testimony at a 1985 Ontario Energy Board hearing by Brascan's investment banker, McLeod Young Weir president Tom Kierans, who said Great Lakes was a "cash cow" using double leverage, implying that the rates being passed along to its power users were too high. "Kierans's speculation was wrong. Great Lakes' rates are lower than those of Ontario Hydro, and its balance sheet has a fifty-fifty ratio, which is most conservative. Kierans later apologized for using Great Lakes as an example of double leverage. It's a utility, and it has significant and reliable earnings. That gave the Great Lakes Group financial substance to build a strong balance sheet."

Some have discovered that the Edper group does not take kindly to public criticism; they have sustained "direct hits" in the form of lost Edper business, according to a prominent Toronto banker. All press interviews were declined for many months following a series of articles I wrote for the *Toronto Star* because Eyton felt they were sensational.

Trilon is another fascinating appendage. Employing only seven people, Trilon has a kitty in excess of $1 billion and controlling interests in Royal Trustco, London Life, Royal LePage, and Wellington Insurance. Brascan owns 40 per cent of Trilon's shares, and the Reichmanns own 12 per cent. Trilon is a merchant bank and a holding company. "Trilon is greater than the sum of its parts," says its president, Mel Hawkrigg, a chartered accountant and ebullient former head of Fuller Brush in Canada. "We are involved in a 'spread game' and have $250 million worth of commercial paper. We issue paper on the street and accept other people's paper. We also have an investment portfolio of $340 million worth of preferreds, including a few Royal Trustco preferreds. You don't see us borrowing. We issue pref and buy pref and make a positive spread."

Hawkrigg, Eyton, and the rest are sensitive to potential conflicts or self-dealing and have established business conduct review committees within each Trilon company, made up of independent directors. This is to ensure that Royal Trustco does not lend mortgage money at below-market rates on properties owned by sister company London Life, and to avoid the myriad of conflicts that touch all financial services companies.

"We go to great lengths to avoid any [conflict-of-interest] problems by keeping our chief executive officers independent, by setting up committees and by giving shareholders cumulative voting [a technique of allowing minority shareholders to appoint their own director on a board]," says Eyton.

Edper's other Trilon is Carena-Bancorp, currently a passive real estate holding company. But the idea is to turn it into the Hees of the real estate business. It owns 54 per cent of the housebuilder Costain and 37 per cent of Trizec. The Reichmanns also own 37 per cent of Trizec's shares, but Carena runs the show because it controls 62 per cent of Trizec's voting stock. Trizec owns such landmarks as the Forum and Place Ville-Marie in Montreal and Yorkdale shopping mall, Scarborough Town Centre, and Atrium on Bay in Toronto. Edper and its affiliates also have controlling interests in Bramalea Ltd.; Canada's largest realty company, Royal LePage; and U.S. shopping centre giants Rouse Co. and Ernest Hahn Inc., totalling more than $2 billion in assets.

"We will change Carena, but we are not certain just how," says L'Heureux, who is devoting his efforts to that company after years at Hees. "We will do banking-type real estate transactions that will create operating income for us. Two shopping centres, for instance, came out of a Hees work-out, and we spruced them up and refinanced them. It's not our expertise to run them, so we sold them to Trizec. Another possibility will be to buy a wealthy individual's real estate, paying cash and stock or just stock, then restructuring them favourably in order to sell them. We may buy a real operating company too."

Edper also has a major interest in John Labatt, which owns 45 per cent of the Toronto Blue Jays, is Canada's largest dairy company with Dominion and

Silverwood Dairies, and sells Château-Gai wine, Catelli spaghetti, Habitant soups, and Five Roses and Ogilvie flour.

Edper is very much the creation of this team of talented lawyers and accountants. Most are millionaires many times over through the group's stock purchase plans, which were given in lieu of fancy salaries, and through individual purchases they financed themselves. Edper is their creature, an empire of paper whose momentum is fed by those high priests of business who know the nuances and ways of tax and takeover laws. Even though they are handsomely rewarded through their share ownership, and even though the group works like a partnership with Peter and Edward Bronfman, controlling interest is still in the hands of the two brothers who, with their families, are the ultimate beneficiaries of the offerings from these priests. And the Bronfmans have the final say.

"We're to keep them informed, aware, and comfortable. We don't want second-guessing," says Eyton. "They are intuitive businessmen and possess tremendous people 'feel.' Peter and Edward have rarely vetoed projects that go through this process. They place a high priority on the group's special business principles; on planning for succession at the family level and within the core management group; on paying close attention to human aspects; and lastly on being socially responsible. For instance, the Brascan budget for charities doubled in a couple of years."

Noranda's chairman, Alf Powis, hears from them, mostly concerning worker safety or environmental issues. "I hear from Peter more than Edward. He will drop me a note, saying he read something about acid raid and wants to know about it. He's in touch more on social issues than financial. 'I've been reading about this and I want to understand it,' he'll say. 'Obviously, there's a problem here and what's involved?' His concerns are working conditions and product quality."

The Bronfman rise to riches began in 1960, when the brothers sold half of their Seagram stock to their first cousins, Charles, Edgar, Minda, and Phyllis Bronfman. The proceeds were invested in a smattering of ventures and properties. The two brothers, who never worked for the distillery their father helped found, have always worked together, originally operating out of a modest Peel Street office in their home town of Montreal. Peter, who had graduated from Yale, and Edward, a graduate of Babson College, were interested mostly in real estate.

The first entry in Edper's chronology reads: "1960-1968 — sale of more than half of Edper's Seagram shares to CEMP, thereby precluding EB's and PB's families from any direct participation in Seagram." In 1966, Eyton became the Bronfmans' lawyer outside Quebec. "I had a friend who wanted to raise $6 million for a chemical company and we put together a package. Chuck Loewen sold units to Edper, they liked it and asked me to represent them outside Quebec," recalls Eyton. The first transaction he handled for them was their purchase of George Hees & Co. and Great West Saddlery.

In 1969, Jack Cockwell joined Edper and set about reorganizing its operations. "We reduced the $200,000 to $300,000 investments, because you work very hard for a small return, and we went for bigger investments," says Eyton. That year, Edper's first big takeover bid, for Great-West Life Assurance, flopped when it was outmanoeuvred by Paul Desmarais.

In 1971, the brothers' diverse real estate assets were rolled into Great West International Equities, which was, in turn, rolled into Trizec in return for about 10 per cent of Trizec's shares. Trizec was controlled by English Properties Corp. of the U.K., after its original controlling shareholder, U.S. founder William Zeckendorf, had gone bankrupt. In 1971, Edper bought Canadian Arena Co. — forerunner of Carena — and acquired the Montreal Canadiens and the Forum; through Peter Bronfman's close friendship with Jacques Courtois, it put together a partnership with John Bassett and the Bank of Nova Scotia. The Bronfmans bought them out in 1973, and for the next three years raised millions more by selling the rest of their Seagram stock.

By 1976, English Properties invited the Bronfmans to help out troubled Trizec and to buy more Trizec shares. In 1977, Trizec was financially restructured by Cockwell and another South African accountant, Michael Cornelissen, now president of Royal Trustco. Shortly thereafter Peter Bronfman asked Harold Milavsky, the current president of the Canadian Chamber of Commerce, to become Trizec's chief executive officer. In 1978, Edward and Peter moved to Toronto after deciding to buy a widely held public resource company. To raise cash for a big takeover, they sold the Canadiens to Molson Industries, but kept the Forum; they sold their 25 per cent of Canadian Cablesystems to Ted Rogers and 40 per cent of a Mississauga development company, S. B. McLaughlin, which later became Mascan. The target was Brascan.

In 1979, the brothers reinforced their control over Trizec and captured 48 per cent of Brascan. Noranda followed a mere year later. By 1979 Edper held 20 per cent of Trizec, and English Properties held 51 per cent, although the two had a working arrangement that allowed Edper to call the shots at Trizec. But Canadian real estate rival Olympia & York, owned by the Reichmanns, was unaware of the arrangement, and it announced a takeover bid for English Properties on the London Stock Exchange. "It was too late to stop, so we prepared to make our own bid," recalls Eyton. "Jack [Cockwell], Harold Milavsky, Mike Cornelissen, and I went to London, and we saw Paul Reichmann check into a hotel there. It was the wrong hotel. We watched him check out, and as he was getting into a cab we went over to say hello. At Paul's suggestion we sat down inside the hotel on a bench in the vestibule to discuss a compromise arrangement [to share Trizec]. We put our arrangement in writing one week later."

But by far the biggest coup was Brascan, taken over in 1979, just months after the Royal Commission on Corporate Concentration declared that control of Canada's economy was not held in the hands of too few capitalists. The brothers had caught a dose of takeover fever, as had others, but the price tag was too high to go it alone. They decided to find a well-heeled partner, and Eyton set up a meeting between Peter and Edward and one of his clients, wealthy Jaime Ortiz-Patino.

"I was the lawyer for the family and Patino NV, listed on the TSE and MSE," says Eyton. "I asked them if they were interested in helping us acquire control of Brascan. Patino in Spanish means 'tin man,' and Bolivia's tin mines were the basis of the family's wealth. There were three reasons I went to them: they were familiar with South America, they were substantial, and they were trustworthy."

The two families set up Brascan Holdings, in which the Bronfmans held 66 per cent of shares and the Patinos the rest. After many complicated lawyers' games, Edper won the contest by the spring of 1979; spending only $174 million to get access to Brascan's $1 billion worth of cash and assets. It put the brothers into the business big leagues.

"We got Brascan after a well-publicized battle and became the dominant shareholder of a company with lots of cash, shares of London Life, Brascan Resources, and John Labatt, and Brazilian interests we thought were worth $100 million, but ended up worth four times that," says Eyton. In fact, it was so big it needed a business plan to determine what operational changes should be made and how Brascan's wealth should be invested.

"We sat down with Brascan's president and two vice-presidents and worked for three months, visiting people and getting a fix on what we had. I was on leave of absence from Tory Tory. Ultimately, Peter and Edward accepted the plan and our investment recommendations. The only change to our management recommendations requested by Peter and Edward was that I come to Brascan full-time. I left Tory Tory in September 1979 and joined Jack Cockwell. One of the first investments we made was to increase our stake in John Labatt."

During 1980, Edper revamped Brascan completely by selling more Brazilian assets to raise cash and by reorganizing Westmin and Great Lakes Power, the Ontario utility. With so much cash in the kitty, the biggest takeover game in Canada was guessing what Brascan was going to buy next.

"We lived in Canada and were closer to natural resources. We decided to make Brascan into an important resource company. We looked at oil companies, but big oil companies were always very pricey, then as now. We also bought many small stakes in a number of consumer products companies, partly because they represented potential building blocks and partly to provide disinformation," Eyton says.

Edper group executive Paul Marshall, president of Westmin, was asked to consider what oil companies would be interesting. "We looked at Gulf [Canada] before Noranda's present difficulties. I told Trevor I didn't want Gulf in the group. I didn't want Beaufort Sea exposure and the downstream." It was decided that Noranda was the target.

But Noranda had other ideas. It had already tried to merge with Brascan to repel Edper's advances; the merger fell through when the managements of the two companies could not agree on who would run them. So in 1980, Noranda restructured in a complicated way, involving a holding company called Zinor. It was to be a vain attempt. Edper was tenacious, its appetite whetted for a fight in the wake of the successful Brascan battle.

"It started with the acquisition of 10 per cent of Noranda from the Black brothers. We don't stay at 10 per cent. Either we increase our position or blow it. Ten per cent is an unstable percentage. Either an investment is important enough to have a say, or it's not, in which case we get out. We're not a mutual fund," says Eyton.

"We decided to talk to the Caisse de dépôt et placement du Québec, which was Noranda's second-largest shareholder. We met with Caisse chairman Jean Campeau at three different meetings over a month to establish that we could work together. We looked at Noranda as the quintessential Canadian company that was, is now, and ever shall be. Noranda was this, and in spite of recent hard times continues to be a unique treasure trove. Noranda chairman Alf Powis had dinner with Jean Campeau and made a pitch to break our partnership, but Jean rebuffed that. Subsequently, we formed our partnership with the Caisse under Brascade Resources. We owned 70 per cent and the Caisse, 30 per cent." The Caisse went for it because it may not hold more than 30 per cent of any company, and this partnership allowed the Caisse to share control of Noranda with Brascan while remaining within the 30-per-cent limit.

Also in 1981, Brascan bought 20 per cent of the U.S. tissue and paper products giant Scott Paper and 18 per cent of Royal Trust. At about the same time, Trizec obtained 20 per cent of the U.S. real estate giant Rouse Corp. and 100 per cent of Ernest Hahn Inc. in California.

"We bought our stake in Royal Trustco at the invitation of Paul and Albert Reichmann. Paul came over and sat down in my office saying, 'I've got 14 per cent of Royal Trustco and I would like you to acquire a similar stake.' There was no discussion then about the deal or our arrangements, I suppose because we had worked well together in Trizec. Later on, we developed the idea of Trilon," Eyton continues.

In 1982, Brascan increased its share of London Life to 56 per cent and sold its Brazilian bank to the Bank of Montreal. Ironically, Brascan had acted as a safe warehouse for about 30 per cent of London Life for London's old-line Jeffrey family since 1977, when they became worried about a perceived takeover by the other Bronfmans, Charles and Edgar. "London Life was a sleepy company with a good name, great service, and great sales. We were partners with the Jeffrey family prior to that point, and wanted to head in the direction of acquiring other financial services companies compatible with London Life."

Also in 1982, Edper bought out the Patinos' interest in Brascan Holdings, although Jimmy Patino remained vice chairman of Brascan. Born in 1930 and living in a German castle, Patino is a modern-day Renaissance man who was once an outstanding athlete who played tennis at Wimbledon, a scratch golfer, and an expert skier. He is also a linguist and world-class bridge player who now serves as president of the World Bridge Foundation.

Trilon evolved in 1983 when it sold $100 million worth of shares to the public to increase its share of London Life to 98 per cent and to buy, with marketable Trilon shares, the Reichmanns' 18 per cent of Royal Trustco, for a total of 49 per cent in that company. "We had to form Trilon to go into a variety of financial service companies. London Life couldn't buy Royal Trustco, so we needed Trilon in the middle," says Eyton.

For 1985 the Edper chronology reads: "Brascan sells its 25-per-cent interest in Scott Paper for a gain of $170 million, plus four million warrants running for seven years. Labatt purchased Johanna Farms, Omstead Foods, and a division of Henkel Corporation. Trilon acquired CVL Leasing and sells $225 million of Lonvest Corp. Royal Trust issued $100 million in preferred shares. Noranda sells its interest in Placer Development to reduce debt. Carena issued $93 million in common shares; Trizec issued $150 million in preferred shares, and increased its interest in Bramalea to 43 per cent. Hees issued $170 million of preferred shares and arranged for the issue of $110 million of capital by North Canadian Oils and Costain."

In early 1986, Hees acquired Conrad Black's 41-per-cent stake in Norcen Energy Resources, held through Hollinger Inc., and granted a two-year option to Brascan to purchase the position.

Such is life in one of Canada's biggest corporate groups — a head-spinning amount of activity. A legitimate concern is the relationships members of the group have with one another, and their collective ability to virtually create a market. Some also question their control of other people's money in financial services companies such as London Life and Royal Trustco. "There is a new type of money being manufactured today," says former Ontario Securities Commission chairman Henry Knowles, now a lawyer with Woolley Dale & Dingwall in Toronto. "Crap like the Unicorp preferreds, which the Edper group can turn into money by their endorsement." In rebuttal, Eyton points out that the Unicorp paper accepted by Great Lakes Group has consistently traded at or above the attributed face value of the paper.

One astute investor, Stephen Jarislowsky, of investment counsellor Jarislowsky & Fraser in Montreal, says he hasn't seen "a consolidated balance sheet yet from the Brascan bunch"; he adds he doesn't buy "confusion." Ed Waitzer, a lawyer with Stikeman Elliott now based in New York City, says that the sheer size and pervasiveness of the Edper/Brascan group could lead to abuses. Waitzer acknowledges such abuses don't exist now, but they could. In fact, the potential is frightening. While the current members of this gifted management team are ethical and honourable, their replacements may not be. While the brothers are strikingly responsible, it remains to be seen whether their children or grandchildren will be. And under current laws, it would be difficult for this family's fellow-shareholders to force out undesirable management or directors without its blessing.

Another concern involves the support Hees provides to the securities underwriting community. As a merchant bank, it does not disclose its holdings if it unknowingly accumulates shares for a takeover artist. There is also the problem of Hees's role as both an up-front moneylender and a lucrative liquidator in work-outs. Chartered banks are not allowed to own more than 10 per cent of real economy companies, in order to prevent lenders from pulling the plug on a venture merely to get their hands on the company's assets. Hees potentially can do this.

Edper/Brascan may simply be too big for Canada. Given its capital and position, Edper could hurt any bank or broker by red-lining, although there is no evidence of this. In fact, to date the opposite has happened. "The group spreads business around and that way everyone develops dependencies on them," says Waitzer. There is not a major brokerage in Canada that would speak out publicly against the Edper/Brascan group, even if criticism were warranted. In unscrupulous hands, Edper could theoretically blacklist the shares of rivals.

"The concern is these large groups will be able to use their power to advance the interests of some customers or suppliers and/or penalize others," says Cadillac Fairview's Ghert. "Or they could use power to undermine rivals, provide excess rewards, or influence the political process."

Brascan's Noranda and MacMillan Bloedel are so pervasive in B.C., for instance, that they must be dealt with politically. Eyton's political influence is considerable, because of his role in the group as well as his gregarious personality. He, Paul Marshall, and two other Edper associates were recruited by industry minister Sinclair Stevens in 1984 to plan how to privatize federally owned corporations. In 1985, in a whirlwind four weeks, Eyton raised $70 million from two Edper/Brascan companies and twelve others for Toronto's domed stadium. Such good works give him a unique political leverage at all levels.

On the other hand, there is a positive side to Edper/Brascan. The group has dramatically improved companies such as London Life, Royal Trustco, and Trizec. Unlike ugly conglomerates, Edper is not harvesting its companies by extracting large dividends and avoiding reinvestment. Conflicts are closely guarded and independent committees have been established in order to ensure fair and responsible dealing. Hees and Carena, through work-outs, provide a service where banks can refer troublesome situations and companies can be saved from liquidation. And while takeovers don't create jobs or new goods and services, they do provide a market for entrepreneurs. As one of Canada's most remarkable builders, Stephen Roman, points out, "Everyone has his place. Companies that buy someone else's accomplishments provide a market for an entrepreneur who may not have a market otherwise."

Noranda's Powis notes other advantages: "I didn't want to get taken over. But the way the world's turned out, they may regret taking us over at the price, because ever since they came into the thing we've been losing money. Literally the first meeting they turned up at, we started to lose money for the first time, and we have lost $200 million [up to November 1985]. The $500 million they put into it gave us more financial wherewithal to go into a perfectly disastrous situation in better shape. Because they are there, in some people's minds it's a comfort."

To refute the suggestion that groups like Edper do not make new investments or create new jobs, Brascade Resources president Paul Marshall points out that the two major mining projects in Canada in recent years involving more than half a billion dollars were undertaken by Noranda, with its Hemlo development, and by Westmin Resources, with its Vancouver Island project. Marshall commented that neither project would have been undertaken as it was without the encouragement and financial support of the Edper group.

Eyton maintains corporate concentration is unavoidable and beneficial and will not be abused. "Some concentration in a country this size is inevitable. Remember this country came about because of one railway," he says, referring to Canadian Pacific. "The country now nurtures and sustains the railway." As for potential political abuse, he says: "Abuse? Sure, there is a political danger. But being aware, everyone is careful not to abuse."

Besides, there are limits to ambition, even among these high priests. "We once had the fantasy about taking over Canadian Pacific, but decided it was like making a takeover offer for Ottawa."

THE REICHMANNS

BEGINNING AT SUNDOWN every Friday, the elevator in the Forest Hill home of Renée Reichmann mysteriously moves for twenty-four hours from the first to the second floor every ten minutes. This is a "Sabbath" elevator. The Reichmanns are Orthodox Jews and forbidden to work on Sabbaths and holy days; they may not even push an elevator button.

Renée Reichmann's house, with 7,000 square feet of space, looks like a small high school and is nicknamed Third Canadian Place, referring to the two-phase development of the Reichmanns' skyscraper First Canadian Place — the country's tallest building. Renée, born in 1903, is the chairman of the board of Canada's biggest family business, called Olympia & York. Three of her sons have built it in just thirty years, and their story is beyond belief.

Next to New Brunswick's Irvings, the Reichmanns are the richest Canadians in the world. But while it has taken a long lifetime for K. C. Irving to amass a net worth of up to $8 billion, it has taken the Reichmanns merely three decades to parlay millions into billions. At a rough estimate, if their debts were deducted from their assets, they would be left with $5 billion.

The Reichmanns barely escaped the Holocaust, fleeing Europe for Morocco just one step ahead of Hitler's Nazis. They immigrated to Canada in the 1950s and have since built an empire of real estate and resource assets worth a total of $25 billion, nearly twice as much as the $13 billion the province of Alberta has socked away in its Heritage Savings Trust Fund. And every single day, Olympia & York generates $700,000 of cash flow from its vast worldwide network of some 100 skyscrapers and other investments.

The Reichmanns became billionaires because shortly after arriving in Canada they stumbled across the ultimate road to riches: real estate. In Canada the development business is a veritable money machine for those who learn how to play it well. In essence, Canada's strict town-planning traditions create "franchise" areas for development, preventing competitors from nibbling away at the fringes, as happens so often in the U.S. where planning is decentralized.

Franchises and rezonings mean overnight riches for landowners. In addition, when a building is completed, it is instantly worth more than it cost to build, because once tenants sign leases and move in, there is no longer any risk. Then the building can be resold for considerably more money, it can be remortgaged at a higher value to free up cash without selling, or its higher value can be added onto the asset side of the balance sheet, against which more money will be borrowed.

This well-worn path to prosperity has been chosen by the Reichmanns and both branches of the Bronfmans, through their real estate companies Trizec and Cadillac Fairview. In fact, almost all of Canada's "new money" fortunes are real estate fortunes, including those made by the Belzbergs, the Singers, the Jodreys, the Sobeys, Campeau, Mann, Love, the Ghermezians, and, to a lesser extent, the Eatons, the Thomsons, and the Steinbergs.

But the Reichmans are at the very top of Canada's development élite. They are the world's largest office landlords, owning 10 per cent of the office space on the island of Manhattan. They also own, as of mid-1986, Abitibi-Price, the world's largest newsprint producer; large stakes in their main Canadian real estate competitors, Cadillac and Trizec; 80 per cent of Canada's eleventh-largest corporation, Gulf Canada Ltd.; big blocks of the pervasive Trilon Financial, with $77 billion in financial assets (as much as the Bank of Montreal); and 93 per cent of the distillery and oil giant Hiram Walker Resources, Canada's twenty-third-largest corporation. Added together, their holdings are equivalent to Canada's largest corporation, in terms of assets — making the Reichmanns as big as Hydro-Québec, with some $27 billion.

Their real estate holdings give them an unprecedented grip on their rivals. In the absence of any anti-trust proscriptions, the Reichmanns have eliminated any significant competition. Through their share ownership and seats on the boards of companies in which they have major interests, they have a window on all real estate dealings in Canada. Through their interests in Olympia, Trizec, and Cadillac, their indirect interest in Bramalea and housebuilder Costain and in realty giants Royal LePage and Block Bros., and their stake in Trilon, which owns Royal Trustco and London Life, the Reichmanns have a piece of everything: from the brokerage commission paid to buy a home to the insurance, the mortgage, the nearby shopping centre, and the office in which the homeowner works. It is a level of marketplace concentration that would not be tolerated in the U.S., where a company would not be allowed to become a major shareholder in virtually all its competitors.

Albert, born in 1930, is the oldest of the three and president; Paul, two years younger, is senior executive vice president and secretary; and Ralph, born in 1934, is senior vice president and treasurer. The three own 92 per cent of Olympia & York, and the rest is believed to be divided among the other siblings: Edward, who lives in Israel, Louis, of New York, and sister Eva Heller, of London. Olympia's board of directors is headed by their mother, Renée, and comprises the three brothers and their wives, Lea, Ada, and Egasah.

Considering their wealth, the Reichmanns live modestly. Although their mother has her mansion, the three brothers and their families do not live at particularly posh addresses. They own no private jets, vacation homes, or strings of polo ponies. They do not throw frequent and lavish parties, and do not rub elbows with royalty or with prime ministers. "We acknowledge our wealth, but do not feel we are powerful," says Paul Reichmann.

However, in celebrating religious or family events, they spare no expense. In the spring of 1985, one of the brothers spent $1 million to celebrate the marriage of his daughter to a man from Mexico. Guests were flown in from around the world for the occasion, at the expense of the Reichmanns, and an entire hotel — the Inn on the Park in Toronto — was "rented" for the occasion. Only kosher meals were served to guests, complete with two sets of dishes.

In true Orthodox fashion, the marriage was arranged by a broker, and a dowry was exchanged. The young groom did not see his bride until her veil was lifted back during the ceremony, which was — again according to tradition — held under a massive tent outdoors. The tent was imported from Austria for the occasion and covered most of the hotel's parking lot.

The devout Reichmanns live as Orthodox Jews have done for centuries, although in business terms, they are strictly twenty-first century. Each of the brothers speaks eight languages and is a Talmudic scholar, well versed in the ancient commentaries contained in dozens of volumes called the Talmud. Written in ancient Aramaic, these books contain Jewish wisdom over the ages in the form of parables or aphorisms. The Talmud is studied for hours every Sabbath by fathers and sons, who sit in pairs across from each other, taking passages in turns and moving through different courses and arguments. Several more hours per week are devoted to reading portions of the Torah in Hebrew.

Their father, Samuel Reichmann, was a devout man who died in 1975, while carrying a sacred Torah to donate to his Toronto temple, Yeshiva Yesodel Hatorah Synagogue. Paul, credited as the most creative of the three brothers, spent two years as a social worker in Casablanca in his early twenties, working in destitute ghettoes. He is a Hebrew scholar who studied in Belgium, England, and Israel before coming to Canada. The Talmud is his principal avocation today, and it has prepared Paul and his brothers for the business world.

Paul once told a reporter that the study of the Talmud was a better preparation for business than a formal education in law or accounting. "My nine-year-old son can discuss civil and real estate law with me as a result of his Talmudic studies."

The Reichmanns have a holistic approach to life, melding business with religion. As a result they are highly ethical, unusually modest, and surprisingly unaggressive. For instance, the Talmud teaches temperance, not ruthlessness, in business. If your customer has little and you know this, you should make less profit and give a little more to him because he may need the profit. If you are getting the better of a deal, you should warn the other party.

These tenets have led to a unique way of doing business. A Toronto drywall contractor called on the Reichmanns a few years back to bid on the huge First Canadian Place contract. A few days later, he and his estimator were invited to an appointment with Albert Reichmann. They expected to pick up specs about the job and to return with a bid later, hoping to be the lowest tender. Instead, Albert informed them they had been selected to do the job. They were given instructions on how best to tackle the task and told what they would be paid.

"They had come up with the most efficient way to do the job themselves, then figured out costs and built in a profit for us," says the contractor. "We were amazed. Naturally, we did the job and would do anything for them."

The Reichmanns have a reputation for being the nice guys of Canadian business. There is no hardball and no horse-trading. This is also the reason why countless suppliers queue up to do business with them. They get, and keep, good people because they never nickel-and-dime others. They do not make take-it-or-leave-it offers, and once deals are struck, their word is their bond even if they lose money.

As Orthodox Jews, they are also charitable, tithing their enormous income (giving away at least 10 per cent) to worthy causes. An Olympia & York employee reportedly devotes most of his time to this. They are also humble. None of their 100 buildings is called the Reichmann Building, and it is doubtful that any ever will be.

As befits their beliefs, the brothers wear dark suits, skull-caps, and the kind of black shoes postmen wear. The company's female office staff must observe a strict dress code, but it is less severe than that of the Orthodox wives, who wear wigs and long sleeves. Mezuzahs, tiny metal containers with scripture inside, traditional reminders of the faith, adorn the elevator doors on the thirty-second floor of Olympia's offices.

Their devotion means that secular concerns never overshadow spiritual ones. That is why their employees and suppliers, Jewish or not, must not work on Reichmann business on the Sabbath. This meant that when winter darkness fell early, the 10,000 New York City construction workers building Olympia's Battery Park complex left the massive job site at 2:00 P.M. every Friday so they would have sufficient time to get home before Sabbath began at sundown. Work ceases during another fourteen holy days every year, in addition to the traditional holidays all enjoy. Workers are not paid for these holidays, but must make up the time.

The Reichmanns have refused to back off this rule, even when in 1984 they suffered a strike in Boston by construction workers, upset that work was suspended because of a Jewish holy day. This rule also cost them money in the fall of 1984, when brokers secretly accumulating Cadillac Fairview shares for the family suddenly ceased trading during Simchat Torah, a two-day religious holiday. That tipped off traders that the Reichmanns were buying. Others jumped into the fray and prevented the brothers from accumulating the number they wanted at the price they were willing to pay.

While devoted to their religion, they are not intolerant of others. In fact, they recruit their management team from untraditional ranks. Their executives are young and do not fit the stereotype of the Canadian — or, for that matter, American — executive. They are neither Upper Canada College nor Harvard. Examples are senior vice president Kenneth Leung and his U.S. counterpart Patricia Goldstein. Leung immigrated to Canada as a teenager from Hong Kong in 1965, attended Carleton University, and sped rapidly through the ranks. As for Goldstein, she says, "Another woman executive is comparable to me here in the finance area, and there are not that many women in the U.S. at that high a level. It is unusual and it is a very liberal attitude — to get the best people for jobs. The Reichmanns are comfortable with themselves. A lot of men are threatened by women executives."

While much attention is focused on the brothers, they have built a world-beater of a multinational. Leung says turnover among executives is negligible because the brothers are easy to work with. "Over the years, they have told me, 'I want this by a particular day. Do your best.' There are no deadlines put upon us. They want you to take your time and present your proposal succinctly, like all senior executives."

Interactions are mostly verbal and the brothers work closely together. "Paul spends more time in New York, while Albert mostly attends to holdings or projects in other parts of the U.S. Basically, the two brothers are interchange-able. Paul is a little more financially oriented and is very active in New York," Goldstein says.

She notes that the brothers have impressed everyone in her native city of New York because "they build excellent buildings. Others are catching on, but the Reichmanns always understood that. I've worked with a lot of devel-opers, and many are very unsophisticated when it comes to finance. The Reichmanns are not just builders. They are able to sense when to move into a new market. The brothers do it themselves. There are no strategic planning committees that report to the chairman. We do our own homework. This is not like a major corporation with all kinds of teams and task forces. They also think big." A picture of the company's organization would look more like a law firm's, with many executives in parallel positions, rather than the pyramid structure of most other large multinationals.

The story of the Reichmanns is remarkable, but it is not a rags-to-riches tale. Their father, Samuel, was one of Europe's most successful entre-preneurs, building a large produce distribution and export network in Hungary that eventually spread to Austria. Their mother is Renée Gestetner, member of the wealthy family of printing fame, whose first cousin invented the offset press and left Hungary for England.

"My father's main business was the distribution and export of eggs. He had farms all across Hungary and distributed eggs there and in Austria when we moved to Vienna. He exported on a large scale to Britain and kept the money there," Paul once told a reporter. The family fled to France from their Vienna home when the Germans occupied Austria. They stayed there until the Nazis came again.

"We left Paris on foot, thirty-six hours before the Germans came in," Paul said. "We went to Biarritz, near the Spanish border. But as the Germans kept advancing, we crossed the Spanish border illegally and got to Tangier in Morocco. There my father developed a banking business with the money he'd kept in England."

Morocco became unstable, and the post-war rise of pan-Arab nationalism worried Samuel. He could see the future of Jews there would be troubled, so he sent his two youngest sons, Paul and Ralph, to scout North America. Ralph went to Toronto in 1955, and the next year Paul went to New York City. One month later, Paul joined Ralph in Toronto, and found it so attractive he became a landed immigrant immediately. In 1956, Samuel bankrolled Ralph and Paul in their own tile business, which was called Olympia — a sign of Ralph's love of Greek mythology. Paul built another import and distribution business for steel products in a small rented building, called York Steel, named after the county. Olympia & York was born.

"We built a building in 1957. We knew something about construction and learned a lot more about Canadian methods and the attractiveness of the industry, so I handed over my part to Ralph and ended up buying industrial areas [in the suburbs], putting up industrial buildings for lease or sale," said Paul.

In 1958, Albert and the Reichmann parents arrived in Canada with huge amounts of money to invest in Paul's business. In the early 1960s, they were catapulted into Canada's big time when they bought 500 acres of land in the Toronto suburb of Don Mills, for $17.5 million from American developer William Zeckendorf. It was a fire sale because the innovative developer had gone bust, and the family recouped the investment in months, multiplying it many times more as the area was developed into dozens of high-rise and townhouse complexes, known as Flemingdon Park.

In 1977, they added a few more zeroes to the equation, pulling off what rivals call the real estate deal of the century. The Reichmanns bought eight New York skyscrapers for the bargain-basement price of $400 million because other developers, thinking the city was on the skids, had turned to sexier Sun Belt regions. The market turned, and the buildings doubled and redoubled. They were worth about $2 billion by 1984, when the Reichmanns put a $1-billion mortgage on the buildings to raise the cash to undertake the massive $2.2-billion Battery Park project, finished in 1985 — the city's most ambitious since Rockefeller Center in the 1930s.

"Being outsiders, we didn't accept all the depressing news of New York City's financial problems," Paul explained simply.

With real estate bringing home profits, the Reichmanns went shopping for assets. In 1978, they bought Canada's fourth-largest realtor, Block Bros. of Vancouver; England's fourth-largest developer, English Properties; and stakes in Canadian competitors Cadillac Fairview, Trizec, and Bramalea. They also diversified away from real estate, into resources like forestry, mining, and oil, as well as taking a 13-per-cent stake in Trilon Financial, a financial services supermarket that owns Royal Trustco, London Life Insurance, Wellington Casualty, and Royal LePage realty and is controlled by Peter and Edward Bronfman.

Now the brothers have restructured their resource businesses into a gigantic holding company that they control, called Gulf Enterprises. This holding company was a brilliant stroke, allowing the brothers to keep control of Gulf and Abitibi and to recoup nearly half their costs of acquiring the oil company.

In May 1985, the Reichmanns made a stunning bid of $2.8 billion for 60 per cent of Gulf Canada. Then they approached Petro-Canada and others to buy the less profitable portions of the oil company, such as gas stations and refineries. In July, the Reichmanns backed off the bid, shocking everyone by leaving behind a $25-million deposit. "Chevron was so kind to have extended the deadline twice, that we were embarrassed to ask them to do so again," explained Paul Reichmann at the time. "We will only bid again on an unconditional basis."

The Reichmanns regrouped and rebid, getting Gulf for $200 million less than they had originally bid. In August, PetroCan agreed to buy $886 million worth of Gulf gas stations. This cash was in addition to Gulf's $800 million worth of cash in the bank, for a total of $1.68 billion.

That money was used to buy about 40 per cent of the Reichmanns' 92-per-cent interest in Abitibi, and also to buy out unhappy Gulf shareholders who did not want their company to buy Abitibi shares. The Reichmanns were left controlling both companies through their new holding company, and using cash from one to buy them out of another. They also saved $600 million in taxes by setting up a convenient short-term partnership with Conrad Black and his Norcen Energy Resources, using a loophole commonly called the "Little Egypt bump" by tax specialists. It was a uniquely real estate approach to the oil business: you buy land, then subdivide off and sell the bits you don't want, do joint ventures in order to build houses, and then keep the corner lot for yourself. Some corner — some lot.

Their purchase of Gulf brought them into the limelight they have shunned for years. "Being private means we can make better decisions," Albert once said. "There's no need to have shareholders and the press looking over our shoulders."

However, the brothers hired aggressive former deputy minister Mickey Cohen, who steered them into a second, spectacular deal, a $3.3-billion take-over of Hiram Walker Resources Ltd., just six months after gobbling up Gulf. The deal had all the earmarks of the feisty Cohen, who rode shotgun over the controversial National Energy Program as deputy minister of energy during the Trudeau years. The Hiram Walker takeover marked the first unfriendly takeover bid ever made by the Reichmanns. And undoubtedly it was not their last.

In spring 1986, the Reichmanns made their bid, in a tender offer that became a media event as the Hiram board dug in its heels to fend off the family. On Easter Monday in 1986, the directors voted in favour of selling all the pieces of their huge liquor and energy conglomerate rather than have it taken over by the Reichmanns. But some two weeks later, the day before Passover, the Reichmanns won the match, but not before being badly bloodied in the press.

Along the way, Hiram's besieged and unhappy management tried to hold firm, and pulled off a brilliant defence. The distillery alone was sold to Britain's Allied-Lyons food conglomerate for $2.6 billion, and TransCanada PipeLines made an offer for the oil interests. The plans were to eventually sell off Hiram's gas utility, Consumers' Gas. These moves were gutsy and brilliant. They recognized the facts behind the Reichmann takeover: most of Hiram's assets were non-oil, and yet the collapse in oil prices caused its stock to fall to record lows. This afforded the Reichmanns non-oil assets at an oil discount.

Realizing what the Reichmanns had done, and seeing that the parts were worth more than the sum, the Hiram directors decided to fight the bid by courageously agreeing to break up the conglomerate they had created. "It was traumatic," said a Hiram director of the four-hour meeting at which this strategy was decided. And the directors benefited shareholders, because their tactics forced the Reichmanns to more than double their original bid. They began the bidding at $32 for just 38 per cent of the shares and ended up paying $38 for 93 per cent of the shares.

The battle dominated headlines for several weeks and marked a change in the style of the Reichmanns. They hired an expensive public relations firm along the way to polish up their image, and they appeared at the Gulf Canada annual meeting, smiling and triumphant. It was a far cry from past meetings. Paul's hands trembled during his first Abitibi public meeting in 1983. And Albert once walked backwards out of a public function to avoid having his photograph taken. "I prefer to be unnoticed where my notice is of no importance," he said.

Their egos are in the right place, and the brothers are totally devoted to business, family, and beliefs. Albert and Ralph already have sons in the business, and room will be made for more family members. Phone calls made to one brother are often returned by another. A pledge by one binds the entire family. While they play differing roles, all share equally in profits. They take turns hosting one another on weekends at family get-togethers, live within a block of one another, and visit four or five times a week after work hours.

They are devout and admirable workaholics; their lives are spent tending their riches and their souls. A remarkable family that has survived centuries of diaspora and discrimination, they are twentieth-century Jews who behave as their forbears did in the fifteenth. They are Jews who have not only overcome the land ownership restrictions that have plagued their people for generations but have become kings of the world's landlords. They are the new Rothschilds, made in Canada: an empire to last.

THE MANNS

IN THE SPRING of 1985, the venue of one of Toronto's most glittering evenings — the annual fund-raiser for medical research into liver disease — was switched to the Primrose Club from its traditional staid turf, the Toronto Club. It was the idea of long-standing Primrose member George Mann, chairman of Unicorp Canada Corp. To ensure the evening would be unforgettable, Mann personally arranged that as the tuxedoed, prominent guests arrived for the posh stag, car jockeys dressed as Arabs, complete with burnooses and flowing robes, parked their Jags and Caddies. Once inside, guests nibbled on Jewish delicacies such as lox and chopped liver.

Such mischief-making among magnates is a rarity. But George Mann walked tall in those days. He had just beaten the establishment at its own game. Fiercely proud of his Jewish heritage, Mann had beaten off such WASPish adversaries as the Ontario cabinet, the Ontario Securities Commission, the Ontario Energy Board, and countless detractors to capture control of Union Enterprises Ltd., an energy conglomerate four times larger than his own company, with $1.8 billion in assets. Even more significant, the takeover had not cost him a penny.

For three months the battle raged between the courtly Mann and Union's besieged chairman, Darcy McKeough. A former Tory cabinet minister, McKeough called in all his political markers, getting the Ontario government to launch three investigations and two full-scale public hearings in order to impede Mann's takeover attempt. Headlines dragged Mann's name through the proverbial mud, as talk about "grey" markets and shareholders' rights were dredged up by Union's management. All measures failed.

By March 1985, 48 per cent of Union's shareholders had swapped their stock to Mann in return for preferred shares in his company, Unicorp, only one-quarter the size of Union. It was a brilliant "junk bond" deal, meaning no cash was exchanged, only paper IOUs. Mann got Union shares, and those who swapped got Unicorp preferreds, paying a very high rate of dividend for seven years. In truth, the deal was only made possible because companies aligned with the Brascan empire of Peter and Edward Bronfman swapped all their Union shares.

This is what MBA types call an "LBO," or leveraged buy-out. It means that for little or no down payment, a takeover artist uses his prey's assets or future dividends to pay the cost of taking it over. Mann pulled it off thanks to the Brascan bunch, and he maintains he made no special deals with that group in return for its help.

"I don't owe Brascan a thing," he says. Many do not believe this.

Walking tall with good reason, Mann now controls Union, an energy conglomerate with assets such as Union Gas, Ontario's second-largest natural gas distributor; two oil companies, Precambrian Shield Resources and Numac Oil & Gas; and Burns Foods Ltd., an eclectic Calgary-based food conglomerate with $1 billion in revenues. Burns was acquired by McKeough during the height of the fight. He swapped Union shares with Howard Webster and other Burns shareholders. Called a "poison pill," that deal was designed to make Union too big, or too undesirable, for Mann to swallow. Mann bit anyway.

Unfortunately while the Union deal catapulted him into the big leagues, it ended up being somewhat costly. A good portion of the poison pill was sold in 1986 for half of what McKeough had paid for it. Not only that, but a drawn-out Ontario Securities Commission hearing into the trading activity resulted in a temporary ban on takeover activity by Gordon Capital Corp. for its trading activities, as well as an unprecedented order that Unicorp pay smaller share-holders some $7.2 million because they were deprived of an opportunity to sell their Union shares for cash before swapping them to Union, while big institutional shareholders were able to do so.

Mann has been on the fringes of the big leagues for a while. His father, David Mann, went from dry cleaning to real estate riches. Mann & Martel realtors became the largest in Toronto's lucrative market, with dozens of branches around the city. It also became the first to twin the real estate selling business with the real estate mortgage business, through a trust company called United Trust.

David Mann was a self-made millionaire driven to make money, who fought constantly with his wife. In sharp contrast George, the only child of this stormy relationship, has had an idyllic marriage since 1954. "George treats his wife like a queen and she treats him like a king," says his best friend Cassil ("Casey") Sapera, who grew up with him in Toronto. "It's probably because he learned it's more important to get along with each other than to shout and scream like his parents did all the time."

Similarly, the dishes flew during the Union battle as headlines screamed insults about Mann and his allies, causing friends and relatives to feel badly for him. Sapera recalls that during one particular spate of innuendo and looming government inquiries, he dropped by Mann's office. Mann was totally unperturbed, and surrounded on all sides by paintings and sculptures. He was puzzling over which pieces to buy.

"George was totally cool, everybody else was running around and emotional, but not George," says Sapera. "He just said it's a fight and that's what happens in fights. People say things."

At nineteen, George joined his father's real estate business and began buying and selling mortgages. He rose through the ranks quickly. In the 1960s he and his father pioneered one-stop financial shopping when they twinned trust company services to their realty business. They sold out to Royal Trustco in 1978 for $26 million worth of Royal shares. A short while later they sold those shares to Robert Campeau, sparking his unsuccessful takeover bid for Royal. When the dust settled on that one, Campeau was out and Brascan took over.

Unicorp was the holding company that had owned most of United Trust's shares, and Mann used it as his investment vehicle, honing it into a takeover and investment team. He bought oil, insurance, real estate, and banking assets, reaching the financial big leagues in 1982, while checking out a shopping centre in California with an agent. He was told about real estate investment trusts — stock market creatures in the U.S., half real estate fund and half tax shelter. The agent told him about a building that was part of a REIT's portfolio, but was worth a great deal more on its own. Mann quickly realized that REIT shares were trading at a price substantially below the value of the assets they owned. That meant real estate on the floor of stock exchanges was selling at fire-sale prices.

So he and his youthful-looking Unicorp president, Jim Leech, went to work. They began to investigate the real estate values of every REIT listed on the New York and American Stock Exchanges. They divided the country in half and travelled from city to city to do their own evaluations of some forty REIT portfolios. "We were looking for several things. Low share prices, low or negligible mortgages, and fundamentally good properties," says Leech.

The only details they had were the locations of REIT buildings. Like reporters and sleuths combined, the two took along cameras to photograph lobby listings in some office buildings to guesstimate square footages, and then rents. Because rents determine property values, they quizzed local realtors and landlords to determine value. They began snapping up shares in those REITs with undervalued buildings, eventually buying $300 million worth of shares in REITs with property worth $475 million.

Mann operates out of a comfortable penthouse suite of offices in Unicorp's building, across the street from the Weston family's headquarters. This is not Toronto's high-rent district, but it is within walking distance of fashionable Forest Hill, where George Mann lives and where he grew up. He and his wife, Saundra, and their two dogs now live in a mansion, but during his childhood he lived in this neighbourhood with his parents above their dry cleaning store.

"Our parents were friends and used to go to Florida every winter, so we'd bunk in together," says Sapera. "I introduced him to this gal, whom he married, and I lost my best friend. George was always driven to make money. It came from his childhood. His father was driven, an entrepreneur — and he picked it up."

Mann, born in 1933, and his wife of thirty years commute regularly between their Toronto home and a newly renovated 10,000-square-foot Florida mansion, complete with servants. "He doesn't live like a baron, but he lives well," says Sapera. "With all the money he's made, he doesn't act like a big shot."

Mann controls billions, but is personally worth around $100 million. Still, he is as powerful a business player as others who receive more publicity, such as the verbally entertaining Conrad Black. Black is worth about the same and controls an empire of similar size.

Mann's penthouse office suite is as natty as he is. Well groomed and poised, he is hardly Central Casting's idea of the capitalist cowboy who wrested Union away from an unwilling, and feisty, management. He is laid back, charming, and all smiles. But he is also a tenacious trader, who has made money buying and selling things. The name of his game is to hunt for bargains, then move in for the kill. Perhaps symbolically, Inuit and primitive sculptures of hunters dot the lobby in tasteful, back-lit glass cases while inside, the offices are like drawing-rooms with Persian rugs and antique furniture. Coffee is served in expensive china. Good-looking and trim, he is always charming and exceedingly ambitious.

"One of the benefits of buying Union," Mann explains, "is that when you're bigger, deals are safer and fewer risks are necessary — because the bigger you are, the less competition for assets you have. This is a stepping-stone."

Union was invincible until the fall of 1984, when it began to blaze a takeover trail of its own and was reorganized into a holding company to do that. This made Union obtainable because bidders could get around the 20-per-cent ownership restriction for utilities by purchasing the parent company only. This led to Mann's decision to take it over. He also says Union was obtainable because of its track record. Five years of increasing earnings but languishing stock prices can undermine shareholder loyalty, particularly among big institutions, which will turn over their shares in a takeover bid.

Mann moved in for the kill. He originally intended to buy control of Union and "flip" those shares to a bigger entity such as Bell Canada Enterprises. But he says he changed his mind. Weighing options constantly is what Mann and his team do all the time.

"We work until seven most nights, and even then he phones me two or three times a night at home with ideas," says James Leech, Mann's right-hand man. "He phoned me once from a movie theatre lobby — on his way home after seeing '10' — with an idea for a takeover. I said, 'You just watched Bo Derek prancing around on the screen. How can you be thinking about business?' Our vice president of finance says George's idea of a fun weekend is reading A to L in Standard & Poor's. I came in one Sunday and he was doing M to Z; he found a company we made a lot of money on."

Despite the long hours, Mann is considerate. He often sends flowers to Leech's wife to compensate for her husband's absences. Once, after jetting around the country with Peter Pocklington in his Edmonton Oilers airplane, negotiating an artwork purchase, he arrived back exhausted. But he still brought Leech a hockey stick signed by Wayne Gretzky, for his youngsters.

Mann and his wife, Saundra, have two grown children, a son and a daughter. Their son, David, works out west as a labourer and their daughter, Tracy, lives at home and runs a flower shop in Toronto. Mann was not a late bloomer, but certainly he was an indifferent student, who never attended university. "We used to sit around and figure out ways to stay out of school," says Sapera. "George and I spent hours in a walk-up pool hall near St. Clair and Yonge. He's still a fabulous pool player."

George Mann still knows how to sink those shots. And the game is far from over.

THE THOMSONS

CANADA'S MOST GENEROUS one-shot donor to date is Lord Kenneth Thomson, who handed over $4.5 million towards Toronto's new performing arts hall, now called the Roy Thomson Hall in his father's memory. This although his father once told guests at a gala he sponsored years ago: "Thanks for coming, but I have no interest in the performing arts." And on another occasion, the blunt Roy Thomson said, "The most beautiful music to my ears is a spot commercial at ten bucks a whack."

Although Roy Thomson, a Toronto barber's son who dropped out of school at fourteen, was not a patron of the arts, he became an artist of the balance sheet. In 1931, he began blazing a trail to business fame and fortune when, at the age of thirty-seven, he bought a radio station in North Bay and, for a down payment of $200, a local newspaper in Timmins. He soon learned how to turn the sale of advertising time and space into wealth. By 1953, he was a media magnate; after rescuing the venerable *Times* of London some years later, he was awarded one of Britain's last hereditary peerages, becoming Lord Thomson of Fleet.

His son, Kenneth, sits atop the world's biggest publishing fortune, richer by far than the Hearsts. It is an empire with nearly $9 billion in sales and $7 billion in assets. Toronto's Thomsons are among Canada's and the world's wealthiest families, thanks to their acquisitive patriarch, Roy Thomson, a late bloomer of a salesman who did not make his first million until he was fifty-five, then could do nothing wrong. He died in 1976 and left his fortune to his seven grandchildren, with the provision that the empire be run by Kenneth or a male from Kenneth's branch of the family.

A combination of hustler and high-finance genius, the late Lord Thomson was the creator of the "reverse takeover," where a smaller company buys a larger one by borrowing money against the future profits and assets of the takeover target. That allowed him to gobble up companies, with little or no money down. In 1953, at age fifty-nine and on his way to wealth, he trod the well-worn path of other anglophile Canadians and left home for Britain's greener financial pastures. He joined a long, pin-striped line of men such as press baron Lord Beaverbrook (born Max Aitken) and Sir James Dunn, both from New Brunswick. Now ambitious Canadians, including his son, head for the bright financial lights of the United States. He did not, and returned from Britain with staggering riches and a peerage.

Roy Thomson launched his British empire by purchasing *The Scotsman*, Scotland's leading newspaper. In 1957, he obtained Scotland's first commercial television franchise, and two years later, in 1959, he bought an eighteen-paper chain that included *The Times* and *The Sunday Times*, the leading Sunday paper. By 1964, he was Lord Thomson.

Kenneth Thomson has reversed the strategy of his father, who invested profits from Canadian operations in the U.K. Since his father's death, he has been repatriating much of his family's wealth back home to Canada. He sold the prestigious but union-plagued *Times* papers in 1981, to Australian press lord Rupert Murdoch. His three main public vehicles are Thomson Newspapers, with publishing investments in North America; International Thomson Organisation, with worldwide publishing, oil, and travel assets; and Hudson's Bay Co., Canada's largest retailer, a huge real estate developer, and the country's thirteenth-largest corporation, with sales of nearly $5 billion a year and nearly $4 billion in assets. If all three were combined, the Thomsons would own Canada's sixth-largest corporation, slightly smaller than Galen Weston's food empire.

Despite the sell-off of many of Roy Thomson's British interests, such as Scottish Television and the two *Times* papers, the Thomson empire remains international. Born in 1923, the current Lord Thomson runs a staggering empire: shares in North Sea oilfields, which throw off $3.3 million a day, or about $1.2 billion a year, as well as retailing giants The Bay, Simpsons, Zellers, and Fields, with 846 stores, peddling their wares in 30.5 million square feet, equivalent to 1,000 football fields.

In publishing, the Thomsons are without peer, controlling a vast worldwide network of more than 400 publications, including *The Globe and Mail*, thirty-four other daily newspapers, and twelve weeklies in Canada; eighty-five U.S. dailies and four weeklies; and the publishers Thomas Nelson (textbooks) and Dun & Bradstreet. The family's real estate holdings are sizeable through The Bay's subsidiary Markborough Properties Ltd. Markborough owns large chunks of forty-seven of the country's biggest shopping malls, in which The Bay and Simpsons operate, a handful of hotels, seventeen office towers, hundreds of acres of land, and twenty-three industrial buildings.

International Thomson's huge oil revenues have financed Thomson's shopping spree in Canada and elsewhere for publishing and retail companies. Ironically, the investment was made reluctantly in 1971 by Roy Thomson, who had been talked into putting money into a North Sea well by the late American billionaire J. Paul Getty, also an anglophile who preferred Britain to North America.

Roy Thomson thought it was a good idea to get into the oil business with his friend Getty until he was told that the well would cost at least $100 million, and his share would be $20 million. Always short of cash because he borrowed so heavily, Roy Thomson tried to find a way out of his commitment because he suspected it was a silly gamble. He could not get around his promise and did not want to be thought of as a "piker" by Getty and others.

So against his better judgment he hustled up the money, and the well came in. Others followed, with the result that oil has catapulted the Thomsons into the billionaire leagues. More ventures later, the two tycoons were still good friends. When they were both in their eighties, Roy Thomson threw a luncheon in London for Getty, after which he joked: "He's richer than me, but then again he's six months older."

Thomson also has sizeable transportation businesses: trucking, airlines, and travel agencies. Thomson Travel is second only to Thomas Cook in Britain and has 200 outlets. He owns Unitours in the U.S. as well as Britannia Airways, with a fleet of twenty-nine large commercial jets, contracted to fly Britain's servicemen to and from Europe. The family also owns the Scottish & York insurance group, which had some financial difficulty in the early 1980s, along with other casualty insurance companies.

The current Lord Thomson would never fit the popular image of a press lord with awesome power, in both politics and finance. He has the manner of a Sunday-school teacher. For a newspaper publisher and former journalist he is extremely shy; he only talks to the press at annual meetings, where he is an outgoing, but captive, contributor. Always polite, he once declined an interview through an intermediary, saying, "I'd really rather keep a low profile, but thank you anyway."

Like so many of Canada's tycoons, he has a less than extravagant lifestyle.

He does live in a twenty-three-room red-brick Georgian home in Rosedale, but he is often seen grocery shopping on Saturdays with his wife. Marilyn Thomson, an attractive woman who was once Miss Cheerleader of Toronto and a model with Eaton's, is from a modest background. She attended Vaughan Road Collegiate; her husband attended Upper Canada College and then Cambridge University.

They were married in 1956 and have three children. Their son David works for The Bay, Peter is still in school, and their daughter, Lynne, has been a stockbroker and fashion consultant. Thomson has a low-key lifestyle, rarely rubbing elbows with power players. His passion is the arts, and his collection of Krieghoffs is the best in Canada. They are kept near him at work, in a temperature- and light-controlled gallery off his office.

Kenneth Thomson began working in the family business as a teenager and was a part-time disc jockey with one of his father's radio stations near the family cottage up north. He also served briefly as a cub reporter with a Thomson newspaper, where one editor described him as a promising journalist — a dubious distinction, as his father once described news as "what fills the space between the ads."

Friendly at annual meetings or social functions, he has none of the brash turns of phrase his father was famous for. Roy Thomson, as described by former colleagues, was a dishevelled "compulsive expansionist," who once said colourfully, "The difference between rape and rapture is salesmanship."

The aphorisms his father coined sometimes bother the present Lord Thomson, if taken too seriously. "People don't understand that my dad was just a kidder," he told a group of journalists at an annual meeting in 1984.

Kenneth left writing to read balance sheets and became chairman of the board; he became Lord Thomson of Fleet after his father died in 1976. Three years before, in 1973, the family convinced hot-shot Toronto lawyer John Tory, a partner with Tory Tory DesLauriers & Binnington, to become its full-time adviser and a director of the Thomson family companies. He and Thomson have masterminded the family's activities since.

Using profits derived mostly from North Sea oil, they launched a Canadian buying binge in 1979, beginning with what became known as the "store wars," involving an unfriendly bid for The Bay and its subsidiaries such as Zellers and Simpsons. Eventually The Bay was captured for $641 million. In January 1980 Thomson bought FP Publications — which includes the *Globe and Mail,* the Winnipeg *Free Press*, and the Victoria *Times-Colonist* — for

$164.7 million, outbidding two other consortiums, one led by Conrad Black and the other by Howard Webster. In 1981 he bought the worldwide publishing interests of Litton Industries Inc. for $75 million and also bid unsuccessfully for Abitibi-Price Inc., the forestry giant, in partnership with Calgary developer NuWest Ltd.

Thomson bought trouble with some of these investments. The Bay has consistently lost money throughout the recession of the early 1980s and now limps along, carrying the Simpsons chain and some money-losing stores. It expanded too rapidly. And shortly after Thomson bought the FP chain, its flagship, the *Globe*, began to lose readers; its Ottawa newspaper was folded, and the government charged Thomson executives with conspiring to close that paper in order to lessen competition. In 1984, the courts ruled they were innocent of conspiracy.

The Bay's profits were supposed to help defray the massive cost of buying the company, but losses have forced the Thomsons to sell some shares in their two main holding companies — Woodbridge Co. and Thomson Equitable Corp. In 1983, the Thomsons reduced their holdings in International Thomson to 73 per cent from 82 per cent, realizing $76 million to pay off debts but still leaving the family with a staggering $1.2 billion worth of shares. Another 10 per cent of Thomson Newspapers was sold to reduce more debt.

But the family's businesses still make astounding profits overall. Proceeds are shared equally among Roy Thomson's five granddaughters and two grandsons to avoid estate taxes. However, the grandchildren's shares are held in trust until they reach thirty years of age and are controlled by four trustees: Kenneth, his sister Phyllis Campbell, family lawyer John Tory, and an accountant. Because Roy Thomson stipulated that the business could be run only by males from Kenneth's branch of the family, the only heirs apparent are Kenneth's two sons, David and Peter. Ronald Dawick, married to Kenneth's niece Linda, is the only other family member to work in the family business, at Thomson Travel.

Besides Kenneth's three children, his late sister Irma had one daughter, Sherry Brydson, a go-getter who took her initial $4.5-million inheritance from her grandfather and developed the Elmwood, a Toronto women's club; she also has interests in oil and gas and other business interests. Phyllis has three daughters, including Linda Dawick and Susan MacNamara, who owns a 400-acre horse farm in Cheltenham, Ont., where she hosts jumping competitions and breeds horses.

Like his father's, the current Lord Thomson's tastes are neither as far-flung as his empire nor as exotic as his wealth could afford. He has a passion for spumoni ice cream, raspberry pie, and candy, and is often spotted buying jelly beans at lunchtime at the sweets counter of the downtown Toronto Simpsons store. By most descriptions, he is a quiet and gentle patron of the arts. Yet in takeovers, he follows more closely his aggressive father's image. And that is why this dynasty is far from finished.

It may also explain why his office is decorated with a picture of an elephant trampling on a tiger. "To remind me of the cruel law of the jungle," he once said.

THE CAMPEAUS

ROBERT CAMPEAU is one of two French Canadians to make it to Canada's billion-dollar league. The other francophone who controls a few billion in assets is Paul Desmarais. What is remarkable is that they started with nothing: no money, no contacts. Both were born and raised in Sudbury. They were briefly business partners, and each is very well connected to this country's power base. The secret of their success has been their extreme aggressiveness and ability to use francophone political contacts to more than make up for not attending Upper Canada College, Harvard, or the other traditional breeding grounds of Canada's economic élite.

Campeau and Desmarais are close friends of Pierre Elliott Trudeau, whose rise to the prime ministership in 1968 marked a dramatic shift in favour of French Canada and French Canadians. This trend continued more or less smoothly until 1984, and perhaps beyond. Trudeau's legacy — bilingualism — was a policy based on principles of fairness, but in practical terms, it was a policy that paved the way for favouritism and the wholesale takeover of civil service jobs by *les Canadiens*. And it was Canada's francophone decision-makers — minister and mandarin alike — who ran a government that made Robert Campeau an exceedingly rich man.

"I had known Trudeau a long time before politics and we became good friends," says Campeau.

Campeau personally owns 60 per cent of the Campeau Corp., with well over $3 billion in assets, primarily in Ottawa. The skyline of our nation's capital is mostly Campeau's skyline. Its city centre is his in large measure. He is the federal government's biggest landlord, owning up to 40 per cent of the office space it rents in Ottawa. Campeau owns the Journal Towers, Centennial Tower, Place de Ville, Place de Portage, and others. Campeau even houses the civil service; he built one out of every five dwellings in Ottawa. And when the mandarins took to the road during the Trudeau years, he was there. He owns the $500-million Place Guy-Favreau — the federal government's presence in Montreal.

It is interesting that the only two hugely successful French Canadians are Franco-Ontarians. Perhaps it was growing up as aliens in their native land that taught them how to apply political muscle to match the economic might of anglos. Whether making heavy political contributions or entertaining politicians in lavish fashion, both Desmarais and Campeau are in a class by themselves. Both subscribe to the Duplessis school of business.

"We were both born in Sudbury. Maybe sulphur had something to do with it," jokes Campeau. Short, grey, and as active as a healthy eight-year-old, Campeau detests the press and has successfully sued for libel. He rarely grants interviews, and barks answers to questions he dislikes, pointing his finger and raising his voice.

Campeau's chumminess with the prime minister gave him cachet. He certainly landed many government leases, occasionally without competing against others, and — on top of that — charges the government rents that are higher than market rates, in some cases. These deals were documented by Parliament's spending watchdog, Auditor General Kenneth Dye, in his 1983 and 1984 reports. Dye noted that four Campeau Corp. buildings had received special favours and unduly high rents, worth a total of $417.5 million to Campeau over ten years. The last deal, worth $131 million, was signed August 29, 1984 — the last day of the Turner Liberal government.

Dye's accusations were elaborated in Parliament's public accounts committee hearings in 1985. A. D. Wilson, assistant deputy minister, operations, for the Department of Public Works, said: "There is no question that the Campeau Corporation appears to wield a great deal of clout. The department was directed in certain instances — for example, on Centennial Towers [a Campeau building] we were directed by Ministers to rent the building. So perhaps the question should be addressed to those Ministers."

In a section in his report for the fiscal year 1984–85, Dye noted several examples. "Place de Ville Tower C: additional costs to the Crown of $42.7 million over the ten-year term of the lease. Centennial Towers: loss of the opportunity to acquire the building through lease-purchase for only $15 million more than the present value of the total ten-year lease payments. In 1981, the Department estimated the value of this building to be $46.5 million. Journal Towers North and South: leases for the two buildings for a term of 10.5 years for a total cost of $135 million were entered into without public tender."

However, public accounts committee member Michael Cassidy, a New Democratic Party MP, said Campeau is a good developer and may have simply cashed in on the chaos in the Department of Public Works. "The department was clearly out of control, but being chummy with the prime minister didn't hurt," says Cassidy. "He's used connections his entire career and has done well keeping close to the Liberals."

But Campeau has done well across party lines wherever he has developed real estate. Whether Campeau's success is due mostly to his connections or to an ability to outmanoeuvre less savvy civil servants may never be known. But he certainly created a profitable Ottawa base that provided him with the collateral to borrow hundreds of millions of dollars and expand elsewhere.

Because the government was a tenant with a triple-A credit rating, Campeau could easily borrow hundreds of millions on the strength of his leases at a lower interest rate than other developers building on speculation. This meant his Ottawa buildings were cheaper to carry and instantly more valuable when completed. That, in turn, allowed him to borrow against their higher value to buy more land and undertake more developments. His has been an aggressive, highly leveraged path to riches.

"Of course I'm aggressive. It's the only way to be in life," Campeau says.

Beginning in 1981, as the size of the federal government peaked, Campeau began to shift emphasis away from Ottawa. His company moved aggressively into luxury condominiums in Texas and California and into commercial property and land assembly in Florida, Colorado, Texas, California, and Ontario. He stayed away from western Canada, where values have plummeted in the 1980s, "because we are smart," he snaps.

In 1983, Campeau moved his head office and himself to Toronto. He lives in the city's biggest house on the exclusive Bridle Path. It has 11,000 square feet of living space, nearly one acre under a roof, and includes an Olympic-sized, indoor swimming pool. No chemicals are used to keep the pool crystal-clear. Instead it is constantly replenished with drinking water, which is heated and sent out hours later to the sewers. His house-warming was attended by Prime Minister Trudeau and a stellar selection of ministers and mandarins.

"We moved because our business has shifted to here and the U.S.," says Campeau. "Like it or not, Toronto is the financial capital of Canada and that won't change. My family and I were apprehensive, but we love it."

Flamboyance and financial chutzpah are Campeau and Desmarais watchwords. Heaping debts onto gains in order to pile up wealth is the only way Campeau or anyone else can rise above such a humble start in life. Born in 1923, the youngest of seven children, Campeau finished Grade Eight and attended technical school. He became a machinist's apprentice at age fifteen with Sudbury's biggest employer, Inco Ltd. He used to joke about his big family, saying that his struggling father was taxed double because "he was a Roman Catholic."

As a teenager, he worked in war plants and was recognized for his aptitude at reading plans. By nineteen, he was a foreman and went to Quebec to plan an expansion for International Paper Co. at Gatineau. By 1949, he had saved money and was working at a paper mill near Ottawa. He decided to get ahead by investing his savings in a home of his own. He also decided to build it himself to save money. Instead, he made money.

The house cost $5,000 to build, but he was offered $7,300 before it was finished. He sold it and with the profits launched Campeau Construction Co. In a year, he had fifty houses under construction and had branched out into apartment and office towers. By 1969, his company had amassed $80 million worth of properties, and he decided to sell shares in his company and use the proceeds to become even larger.

"I am an entrepreneur, and you are brought into the world with it," he says. "To make it you need that talent and energy, and you must work hard."

In 1969, Campeau joined forces with Desmarais's Power Corp., whose trust company and insurance and mutual fund companies had billions to lend as mortgages. Power bought 54 per cent, in a match made in heaven. But differences in philosophy led Campeau to buy his shares back from Desmarais later that year, for $13.5 million more than he had received for them.

The problem was that Desmarais's Power Corp. "was acting out of abundant caution. Rather than getting the normal treatment, we got the opposite. We were almost cut off," said Campeau Corp. vice chairman Jean Charles Paradis. Campeau himself says simply, "We are still great friends. We made a deal we thought would work and simply unravelled it. That's all."

Instead, Campeau formed a close association with the Bank of Nova Scotia, a link that continues to this day. He has assembled what he calls "the best real estate team in the world," and he encourages them to own shares. "I don't think there is another company in Canada whose management owns 15 per cent of its shares like this one does," he boasts.

But concerns about Campeau's financial wherewithal continued to dog his company's shares in stock markets. His principal problem has been that few investors outside Ottawa knew of him.

His first high-profile project outside Ottawa was the construction of the Harbour Castle Hilton Hotel and Harbour Square condominium complex, the first of many complexes built along Toronto's lakeshore. The project suffered from cost overruns and the hotel struggled for years until he sold it. During those years, he captured unfavourable headlines as his company lost millions, because it had borrowed money in Swiss francs and the currency had risen in value against Canada's, making repayment much more costly. The firm also had problems developing sites around Montreal's Blue Bonnet Raceway and in St-Bruno, Que. There were detractors, and the Campeau stock continued to slump. Campeau dismissed the critics, saying, "It's the story of my life. People said when I built my first ten houses I was going to go broke, and I've built thousands since then."

In 1977, he dropped a bombshell on the establishment with a surprise bid of $413 million for stolid, blueblood Royal Trustco, the country's largest trust company. He obtained very favourable terms from the Bank of Nova Scotia, which agreed to lend him the entire amount over seven years at only one percentage point above prime. His bid rose, but eventually it was foiled as the country's biggest companies ganged up on Campeau by warehousing Royal Trustco stock and not selling it to him. They got their wrists slapped, when all was said and done, but Campeau was left out in the cold.

While some members of the media billed the takeover as the establishment against a francophone, it was not. It was pure hardball competition. Royal Trustco's management wanted to remain in charge of the company, so to fend off Campeau, they enlisted help. Leading the charge among the white knights who shut Campeau out were Oxford Development Co. and its partner, the Toronto-Dominion Bank. Unknown to many, the TD Bank has become one of the world's largest real estate developers by virtue of its 40-per-cent owner-ship of Oxford, and its partnership with Cadillac Fairvew Corp. in two major office-retail complexes in Toronto's downtown — the Toronto-Dominion Centre and the Eaton Centre. The battle was not racial; it was real estate.

"It was the first French-Canadian attack on a major financial institution controlled by Anglo-Saxons. There were two fights: one was because an English Montreal guy [who ran Royal Trustco] didn't want to see a French Canadian own it, and then there was a battle between owners and managers," Campeau says.

Almost all of the trust company's allies were widely held companies controlled by professional managers. They did not want to see an individual buy the company any more than they wanted their own companies sold to individuals, says Campeau. However, belying that theory is the fact that the battle was eventually won by Peter and Edward Bronfman's Brascan group.

In 1984, Campeau squared off against the same set of rivals when he pulled off a coup and got unusually quick permission to build a $400-million headquarters in Toronto for the Scotia Bank. The TD unleashed an uncharacteristic series of newspaper ads attacking the development, angry because it had taken Oxford nearly two years to get a similar development approved. "Dick Thomson [TD chairman] led another dirty fight," says Campeau, who won only after placating anti-development forces on Toronto's city council and giving $2 million towards subsidized housing.

Now he operates on the same Bay Street where he battled over Royal Trustco. His six children are all in Toronto and involved in the business. But he remains the boss in every sense of the word. And whether it is NDPers in Toronto, Republicans in Dallas, or Liberals in Ottawa, Robert Campeau can play them like a fiddle to get his way. The master of the art of compromise, he has turned politics into tremendous profits.

THE WOLFES

THE FOOD BUSINESS has made billions for many of Canada's wealthiest dynasties like the Westons, the Steinbergs, the McCains, the Sobeys, and the Richardsons. But another relatively unknown family has also made a food fortune: the five sons of two Lithuanian immigrants, brothers Max and Maurice Wolfe, who share equally the Oshawa Group, Canada's thirty-third-largest enterprise, with $2.6 billion in sales. The Wolfes went from selling hay to the cavalry in the First World War to the brink of bankruptcy after the Second. By the 1980s, their company was the country's fourth-largest food business.

And they have done it by helping family businesses, as small as they once were, to be as cunning as the big chain-store competitors. The Oshawa Group is a gigantic, private-sector version of the co-operative: it does not own a high-profile chain or name brand, but supplies everything from soup to nuts for some 3,000 independent grocers from Saskatchewan to the Maritimes. It also supplies engineering, real estate, public relations, advertising, insurance, accounting, recruitment, and training advice to its self-employed merchants.

"We are the bank, confessor, lawyer, negotiator, and estate planner for our merchants. We keep fifty stores as our research and development department. That's where we test out gimmicks, techniques from scanning products to new back-door techniques and displays," says Ray Wolfe, oldest of the five Wolfe sons, who has masterminded the company's growth since the late 1940s. "You don't make money unless you help people. The only success we've had is a reflection of our ability to make others successful."

In return, the independents buy all their supplies from the Oshawa Group and pay a royalty on their sales. Some 30 per cent of the nation's food market is held by independents and the rest is carved up by six major chains: Sobeys, Loblaws, Steinbergs, A&P, Canada Safeway, and Provigo. But the independent sector has been growing by one percentage point annually during the 1980s, as the chains suffer sluggishly from too many locations and changing lifestyles. And Oshawa has captured the biggest share of the independent market. Not surprisingly, both Sam Steinberg and Galen Weston's father, Garfield Weston, courted Ray Wolfe and his family — without success.

Besides grocery and convenience stores, Oshawa Group owns and operates the Towers department store chain, sixty-nine Kent drugstores, twenty-nine Drug City stores, seventeen Metro stores, twenty-three pharmacies, five health and beauty aid stores, and sixty restaurants and snack bars in Towers stores. It owns Marchland Holdings Ltd., a real estate arm that owns Sudbury City Centre; four Towers–Food City shopping centres; and nine other shopping centres and land.

In 1960, assets totalled $6 million; they had risen to $436.5 million by 1984. During that time, shareholders' equity went from $3.3 million to $195.2 million. All Oshawa common shares are owned equally by five branches of the Wolfe family: Max's son, Harold Wolfe; the heirs of Maurice's son Leonard Wolfe; and Maurice's three remaining sons, Ray, Jack, and Harvey Wolfe.

Jack is vice president in charge of the perishable business. Leonard died in 1976, and Harvey, the youngest, became president in 1974. He resigned in

1976, following disagreements about how he was running the company. He now operates his own real estate development business, called Harlesk. But his son, Daniel, has just joined Oshawa.

Ray Wolfe controls the voting trust among family members. His son, Jonathan, born in 1953, is heir apparent. He got onto the board in 1984 and runs the distribution unit, Oshawa Foods. Leonard's son, Myron, is in the perishables division; Jack's son, Richard, works for the company in Regina, and his daughter, Rhonda, is a buyer with Towers stores. Harold, Max's only son, is the company's secretary and counsel.

The only other third-generation member is Ray's daughter, Elizabeth, who is a lawyer with McMillan Binch in Toronto. The commitment remains to keep the firm in family hands even though the brothers nearly sold out to Sam Steinberg in the 1970s. "The kids decided to stay with it. We could have sold out and just sent cheques to everyone and said you're on your own, but they decided to stay with it," says Ray.

The driving force of the family has been Ray Wolfe, a smallish, soft-spoken man who has steered the company around various shoals since he returned from the Air Force. He snatched it from bankruptcy and built it into a giant, an achievement he modestly calls "pure serendipity." Born in 1917, he is a shy, socially aware man who has made business history even though he transferred to general arts at the University of Toronto in 1937 after failing his third year of commerce and finance. "I couldn't cut it," he jokes.

Now one of the giants of Canadian business, he usually arrives by seven at his spacious office in suburban Toronto. "I'm up at four, I shower and read for two hours and get into the office around seven. I leave at four," he says. "I grew up working in a fruit market, and we always started work at five in the morning. I never got out of the habit."

It began in 1912 on Toronto's Queen Street West, with a feed store that Max Wolfe set up with $57. His brother, Maurice, joined him in 1914, and they prospered during the First World War by getting the hay and feed contract for Camp Borden. The popularity of the horseless carriage convinced them to get into another line of work, so in 1918 they bought a potato and onion distribution business called Ontario Produce.

By the 1940s, Ontario Produce had become a principal supplier to Loblaws and its arch-rival Dominion Stores. But within two months of each other in 1948, both Loblaws and Dominion announced they were going to buy and import their own produce. Those were black days for the Wolfe family.

"Loblaws and Dominion were half of Oshawa's volume. It was traumatic. My brothers and I returned from the Air Force and suddenly the business couldn't support all of us," says Ray.

Ironically, it was a Loblaws buyer who analysed Oshawa's predicament succinctly for Ray. "We had to broaden our customer base. He pointed out to me that produce only accounted for 8 to 9 per cent of volume, and when there were forty produce guys fighting for only 8 or 9 per cent of what was left, I soon got the picture," he says. "Unfortunately the problem was that the Canadian Wholesale Grocers Association was a tight little combine. They would only deal with certain qualified buyers. We would sell celery and onions to Heinz and Campbell Soup, but they wouldn't sell their products to us."

Ray cast about for a company he could buy that was already in the grocery business and bought a small Toronto trading company called Bakers. It turned out to be a dud. Its previous owner had a poor reputation and the big food processors would not deal with him. But family friend Sam Steinberg of Montreal advised them to hang onto the company, and they took his advice.

In 1949, Wolfe bought Oshawa Wholesale, a well-established supplier that had just gone bust because the teenaged son of its founder had driven it into the ground after his father died. Ironically, even though it was bankrupt, the grocers' cartel would supply it on a cash basis only.

With supply nailed down, Wolfe needed customers. He decided to study the more innovative U.S. grocery business and ended up making a deal in Chicago with a Guelph-born Quaker named Frank Grimes, who pioneered the Independent Grocers Association concept in North America. Called IGA, it allowed independents to combat the growth of huge supermarket chains by pooling resources to match the buying power, advertising clout, financing, and location selection that big chains could afford.

"He sold us the IGA franchise but wouldn't deliver after he came up and looked at our operation and said we didn't have enough experience to handle the program," says Ray. "We went ahead with a program of our own anyway, with his preprinted forms and program. And when he realized we would go ahead without him, he gave us a franchise. Some 49 of our 550 accounts joined the program. And we have never looked back."

Initially, grocers had to pay cost plus 4 per cent, help drivers unload trucks, buy everything from Oshawa, and pay one week's cash in advance for groceries. By comparison, wholesalers were charging independents 18 per cent on top of costs. Oshawa opted for guaranteed high volume and settled for a small margin.

Trouble hit again in 1959, when Oshawa had to go public to raise money. "We ran out of money, we had trouble getting good locations for our merchants, the developers building malls all wanted the chains as anchors. IGA were becoming corner grocers, and a covenant from them was not nearly as financeable for developers as a chain's."

The company bought its way into some good sites, but in fact IGA has good locations in Ontario towns, but not the cities. That is why Oshawa's latest strategy is to pick up stores that the troubled chains are discarding. In the 1980s, it bought several dozen Dominion Stores in Halifax and in the Prairies and two dozen Safeway stores in Toronto.

During the 1960s Ray Wolfe continued making acquisitions and extended the IGA franchise into all provinces except British Columbia and Alberta. In 1972, however, his frenetic lifestyle was interrupted when he was stricken with a heart attack on an airplane. In 1974, the reins were turned over to his youngest brother, Harvey. But in 1976, Ray returned as boss, mostly to stem losses at the Towers stores, in disarray after the chain's president, Stanley Lipson, resigned. Lipson later pleaded guilty to receiving $400,000 in kick-backs in five years from three Oriental suppliers.

"He wasn't really a crook — he had a sense of individual ethics," says Wolfe.

The family also began selling some of its sideline businesses, such as a chain of coin-operated laundromats and half of the Consumers Distributing Co. catalogue store chain, with sales of $108 million a year. Along the way, both the Westons and the Steinbergs approached the Wolfes to sell out, but Ray declined mostly for reasons of personality.

"I spent many hours on Fleet Street in George Metcalfe's [former head of Loblaws, owned by the Westons] turret, drinking tea from Fortnum & Mason in Wedgwood china cups, and I've been with Garfield Weston on his boat in the Aegean Sea. They made us several offers, but the one condition was that I remained to run the company."

But Metcalfe had a way of treating his executives like serfs, so Wolfe politely declined. Similarly, he turned down another generous offer made by his mentor, Sam Steinberg, in the early 1970s, despite pressure among the brothers to cash in the chips.

"There were pressures on me to sell, and finally I made a deal, agreed on a price, and got down to signing contracts. Then several days before the closing, Sam sent his personal assistant to my office. He said, 'Sam's asked me to come and check the equipment in the warehouse. I guess he wants to make sure that after he buys the company the equipment that's there now is still there.'"

Insulted, Ray phoned Sam the next day to tell him the deal was off, and exactly why. Sam never apologized, but said it was normal business practice. Wolfe didn't agree.

Similarly, Wolfe nearly rejected an award given to him in 1968 by the Canadian Council of Christians and Jews, startling the black-tie crowd at the ceremony by saying, "In the light of the failure of this generation to cope with, let alone solve, these [world] problems, are we not guilty of a monumental self-deception? Are we not, each of us, by this huge display of camaraderie, just playing the games people play?"

Wolfe said he accepted the award because he did not want to offend the council. But it shook everyone up. Then again, so has Oshawa.

THE RICHARDSONS

AT THE TURN of the century, Winnipeg boomed as the remarkable Richardsons became the world's biggest wheat merchants, exporting most of Canada's grain along the nation's spanking new railway. The now-minuscule Winnipeg Commodity Exchange was bigger and more important than Chicago's, thanks to the Richardsons. But the Depression changed all that. In fact, the only remnants of Winnipeg's importance are the head office of James Richardson & Sons, Ltd., and the city's world-class ballet company, the Royal Winnipeg Ballet — both there thanks to the Richardsons.

While the Richardson rise to riches was hampered during the 1930s, being a member of this family remains as close to royalty as is possible on the prairies. Fabulously wealthy, the four Richardson heirs run their billion-dollar-a-year grain and investment banking empire out of their Lombard Place complex, at Portage and Main — the tallest building between Toronto and Calgary. During their childhoods they were pampered and protected, entertained by occasional visits from family friend Winston Churchill and members of the British royal family. George is a friend of Queen Elizabeth and Prince Philip. In 1984, the Queen went to Winnipeg on her tour of

Canada, in part to visit her close friends the Richardsons.

But the Depression changed the direction of these prairie princes and princesses. Collapsed prices led to a farmers' revolt, as wheat plummeted to the same price as a bushel of sawdust. The Richardsons were resented, as were the other grain merchants whose mansions along Winnipeg's Assiniboine River were in sharp contrast to prairie poverty. In the 1930s, the federal government established the Canadian Wheat Pool, which propped up prices and bought all of the nation's wheat, eliminating most of the export, handling, and speculative action the Richardsons had monopolized for two generations.

At the same time, the government helped western Canadian farmers establish co-operatives at a local level, again sidestepping the Assiniboine barons. While other merchant families like the Gooderhams (who turned their grain into liquor) cashed in their chips, the Richardsons remained, buying up those who did not choose to sell out to farmers' small wheat pools. The Richardsons compete against the provincial pools, but help the federal wheat board export wheat. As a result, they are still the largest privately owned grain company in Canada, and the largest private corporation in western Canada.

"We were forced to live under strict regulation, but we are the largest Canadian exporter today, working on behalf of the [federal] Wheat Pool," says George, a mountain of a man with a shy manner, who runs the family's business operations.

The Richardsons are among those rare families who wholly own a corporation in the billion-plus league, along with the Irvings, the Reichmanns, the Ghermezians, the Batas, and the Eatons. In 1985, James Richardson & Sons — called "JR" by its employees long before the television series *Dallas* made these initials pejorative — was the country's fifty-sixth-largest enterprise by revenues, which totalled $1.5 billion. Assets were $1.3 billion. And the shareholders' equity, shared equally by the four Richardson siblings, was around $200 million.

JR is the umbrella company under which dozens of companies operate. Its two principal assets are Richardson Greenshields, Canada's second-largest stockbroker and largest commodity broker, and Pioneer Grains, the country's fourth-largest grain merchant by sales (after the Canadian and Saskatchewan Wheat Pools and U.S.-owned Cargill). Pioneer operates 520 grain elevators, three wheat terminals, and a fleet of ships.

It also owns feed and fertilizer plants; 6,000 acres of Manitoba farmland;

livestock breeding operations; 4.5 acres of downtown Winnipeg plus urban real estate in the U.S.; a fuel distribution operation in Kingston, Ont.; Systems Equipment, which manufactures accounting systems; Patricia Contractors, a land-clearing and road-building business; the country's largest oil and gas pipeline company, called Marine Pipeline Construction of Canada, which built two-thirds of the $1.2-billion Alaska pre-build line in the early 1980s; and a business forms printer.

The Richardsons are aloof, patrician, and very Liberal. After all, the posh Manitoba Club has traditionally been a de facto branch of the Liberal Party. In true small-"l" liberal fashion, the Richardsons are socially conscious and never indulge in conspicuous consumption. They live better than most, but they aren't jet-setters, with flashy ways and six wives apiece. The two brothers, James III and George Taylor Richardson, live in the countryside around Winnipeg. They and their three sons go to work at Lombard Place every day, and often eat in the employee cafeteria during lunch hours. All the Richardson heirs are imbued with the Protestant work ethic.

"I grew up to it at the dinner table," says George, who has always run operations. "We started working summers, there was no pressure, and I made my first major investment when I was fifteen — in Alberta oils."

Their great-grandfather, James, was an orphan who came to Canada from Ireland in 1823. He apprenticed with a Kingston tailor and eventually fell into the grain trading business by accident. Some of his customers could not pay cash, so he accepted wheat, barley, or oats as payment.

He soon learned there was more money brokering grains than cutting cloth, and he made his first fortune during the U.S. Civil War, between 1860 and 1864, selling grain to upstate New York granaries. In 1880 — three years before the Canadian Pacific Railway reached Winnipeg — he sent emissaries to sign up farmers. Three years later, Richardson made the first shipment of western Canadian grain to Europe via the Great Lakes and Welland Canal. His firm also threw up a string of grain elevators across the country as the steel ribbon snaked its way to the west coast.

His two sons, also George and James, were presidents from 1906 to 1918 and moved operations to Winnipeg. The biggest push came under George's son, James II, who took over in 1918. In the 1920s Canada became the world's largest grain exporter, and the Richardsons were the country's uncrowned kings and queens of grains. In 1928, the stock and commodity brokerage was launched, as were insurance, airline, and radio businesses.

While expansion was considerable, the Richardsons have not been as acquisitive as others. They never took over the nickel giant Inco Ltd. or the Hudson's Bay Co., even though they were the largest shareholders in both for years. Perhaps, like Charles Bronfman, they grew up with the resentment over their wealth and its roots, choosing to mind their inherited businesses but to maintain as low a profile as possible. Besides that, they certainly did not need money.

In 1939, James II died suddenly at the relatively young age of fifty-four. His sons, James III and George Taylor, were too young to assume the reins of such a huge enterprise. But weeks later their mother, Muriel, suddenly arrived at a meeting and informed all executives she was personally assuming the presidency.

Muriel was a tough-minded Manitoban who had met her husband at teachers' college. For a pampered housewife and mother, she certainly rose to the occasion. She trimmed the ship, selling airline, insurance, and radio assets in order to underwrite the costs of new grain facilities. She also found time to rescue her beloved Royal Winnipeg Ballet. (Her daughter, Kathleen, continues her mother's patronage as the ballet's honorary chairman; she is also chief fund-raiser for many other charities.) For whatever reason, Muriel did not hand over the firm until 1966, when her two sons were over forty, although they had been running it for years.

"We worked well together," recalls George. "I was the operations man by inclination and choice, with an interest in the grain and agricultural side; and Jim liked the external things — he sat on outside boards and enjoyed the brokerage business."

James is the eldest, born in 1922 and heir apparent, but he left the firm's day-to-day operations in 1968 to become a Liberal member of Parliament and a cabinet minister for eight years. His move was hardly surprising: the Richardsons knew only too well that government policies make and break dynasties. In fact, it was their great-grandfather's good friend Sir John A. who built the railway that made Canada a country and the Richardsons rich. And it was Depression politics that established their rivals, the wheat pools.

James Richardson III found it easy to leave his pinnacle of business success. By 1966, while only forty-four, he was in charge of western Canada's biggest corporation, had collected a clutch of directorships on the most high-powered boards of directors in the country, and had just become the youngest director in Canadian Pacific's history. But two years later, in 1968, he left all that and entered the cabinet, which he called "the ultimate board of directors." He is the only member of Canada's wealthiest dynasties to be elected to Parliament.

"There is nothing more exciting or fascinating than a cabinet meeting," says James, who won elections in 1968, 1972, and 1974 without putting a penny of his own considerable fortune into his campaigns (unlike Stephen Roman, who outspent everyone else). "Cabinet is more free-wheeling than any board meeting, and the power really sits with the man in the chair."

Despite a silver-spoon upbringing, he maintained a sensitivity towards his constituents and their needs and problems. But it was not easy. A friend recalls James's first day of campaigning at a bus stop. "It was painful. I don't think Jim had ever been at a bus stop in his life."

James was not a natural politician who could raise compromise to an art and press the flesh readily. As the pampered son of one of the country's richest men, he never learned how to be a team player. He didn't have to, because he never needed to muster support from allies. In 1976, Richardson was labelled a redneck when he resigned as Trudeau's defence minister over the principle of bilingualism and crossed the floor, sitting as an independent until the 1979 election.

Trudeau refused his resignation for twenty-four hours and spent four hours trying to talk him out of leaving. "I told him to his face, I've never known a better man for a worse cause," says Richardson.

His clash with Trudeau over bilingualism was not his only problem. He was called "Jimmy Two-Sticks" for an earlier insensitive remark about Canada's native people: "What did they ever do for Canada? Did they find oil? They didn't even invent the wheel. When we came to this country they were still dragging things around on two sticks."

Since leaving Parliament, he has attempted to influence events behind the scenes, lobbying premiers or MPs in support of unilingualism and free trade and on a variety of agricultural issues. He has a number of private investments, mostly in the Alberta oil patch, including a large stake — about 5 per cent — in Ocelot Industries Ltd.

James, George, and their two sisters, Agnes and Kathleen, are the only directors of JR. They meet once every quarter at a round table in George's thirtieth-floor corner office. Atop that is a heliport with George's chopper, in which he occasionally commutes from home, to the airport, or to his Lake of the Woods weekend home. George is the only family member running the company day by day. He and his wife, Tannis, live on a working farm outside Winnipeg. They have two sons and one daughter. Their daughter, Karen Somers, is not involved in the business, but Hartley heads a real estate development division and David heads Pioneer's research arm.

James mostly looks after his own private financial and political interests. He has an office at home and a courtesy office at the opposite corner of the thirtieth floor from his younger brother. His wife, Shirley, is a member of the wealthy Cunard family of England. They own a rambling grey and green house on thirty acres where the Assiniboine curves. There, they raised their three daughters and two sons, and Shirley breeds rare Sicilian donkeys, Welsh ponies, and Suffolk sheep. Their older son, James Jr., runs a heavy-equipment leasing company called Tundra and a junior oil company with the same name, in partnership with the wealthy Cohen family, which controls Gendis Ltd. (which has the Sony franchise for Canada and several hundred fashion stores). Younger son Royden (named after his mother's uncle, Lord Royden, who ran Cunard for years) is a hard-working vice president of the stock brokerage firm.

Two of James's daughters are in show business. Serena is a talented dancer with the prestigious Bella Lewitsky Dance Troupe in Los Angeles, and Sara is a professional actress. Carolyn is a social worker with two sons.

Like James, Agnes Richardson and her late husband, Senator William Benedickson , were very involved in federal politics. He died in 1984, but she remains in Ottawa with her children. Kathleen Richardson never married and lives in downtown Winnipeg, a few blocks from Lombard Place. She looks after the family's charitable donations, buys Canadian paintings for the firm's collection, which numbers several hundred, and is a director of several companies.

With tens of millions of dollars of profits falling on their heads annually, the four Richardsons are fabulously wealthy in their own right. While George seems to have assumed the largest burden of business, they have all eaten, slept, and breathed JR. Growing up Richardson meant a cloistered life along the Assiniboine, servants, and dinner conversations that always centred on business. As part of their education, the four children were given $2,000 each to invest during the 1930s, when it cost families that much to buy a farm. "I don't know what Jim and Agnes did with their money, but George probably made a fortune," Kathleen told a newspaper once.

Seems he still does.

THE SINGERS

STEPHEN SINGER'S WEDDING in 1984 was pure Hollywood. It was held in the studio where Francis Ford Coppola created the *Godfather* movies. Bride and groom and hundreds of guests shifted scenes, from a lavish Grecian set complete with flora and fauna, where Stephen and his bride exchanged vows, to a high-tech and art deco set complete with neon and lasers, for cocktails and dancing. Motown, Michael Jackson's band, entertained in one room and the famous Four Tops in another. Comedian George Burns was the unofficial emcee, and guests included Calgary's finest, movie stars, and moguls. The whole thing cost $100,000.

Stephen had wanted just a small wedding, but his father — Jack Singer, who helped bankroll one of Coppola's films and now owns his studio — thinks big. Virtually unknown outside Calgary, Jack Singer is nonetheless one of Canada's biggest shooters, and one of its few rags-to-riches success stories. He is also one of Hollywood's biggest studio moguls, and it all happened by accident.

"We get scripts in here every ten minutes," he says in his Calgary office. "But it's not our expertise."

Buying and selling real estate is. Born in 1918, Jack is the son of Polish immigrants. At eleven years of age he was collecting 75 cents weekly rent from his mother's boarding-house roomers in Calgary, mostly drunks and hookers. "I used to go with my briefcase and collect. It was hard to know who the tenants were," he recalls.

As a teenager, he was buying buildings of his own, along with his first cousin, Abraham Belzberg, whose three sons own the First City Financial Corp. empire, with $3 billion in assets. While the Belzberg sons and Jack Singer are not partners, he and Belzberg Sr. made a fortune buying and selling slums on the wrong side of Calgary's tracks. And Jack went on to greater riches as a Canadian developer and land speculator in the U.S.

"I was great at raising money, and he was great at trying to do business every hour," he says. "He would call me to see if I was going downtown and he would want to do a deal. He did deals when he was eighty-four. I loved him, and I miss him."

Operating through twenty companies under the umbrella Alsten Holdings Ltd. (named for his sons Alan and Stephen), Jack Singer has amassed nearly $750 million in assets. His brother, Hymie, and sisters, Rosalie and Diane, are also rich in their own right. Hymie and Rosalie live in Los Angeles and own property there. Diane lives in Vancouver and is married to a shopping centre developer, Jack Aceman. But most successful of the four is Jack, who is, among other things, czar of Calgary's landlords.

He owns 1,500 apartments, thousands of acres of land, and one million square feet of office space in Calgary. His companies are planning subdivisions on both sides of the border, involving thousands of homes. He also owns thousands of undeveloped acres in Vancouver, Edmonton, Regina, and Winnipeg, and in California, Arizona, Oklahoma, and Texas. His biggest single coup was in 1980, when he bought out of bankruptcy 2,500 acres in Dallas for $37.5 million; he sold it just four years later for $125 million, plus 25 per cent of the profits when it is developed.

Likewise, he bought Coppola's studio in 1984 out of bankruptcy for $15.3 million, and a year later was offered $51 million. But there were also losers, like Cornwall Petroleum and a large shareholding in Dome Petroleum. "We blew $75 million drilling in Cornwall. We were drilling like we were Exxon. In Fiji, New Zealand, and all over the place," says Jack.

Singer and the Belzbergs were business partners until 1976, when Abraham's three sons — Sam, Hyman, and William — cashed in their half of the real estate company they shared, Western Realty, and went into the trust company and investment banking business. The two branches of the family have little to do with each other, partly because of their differences in style: Jack Singer is street-wise and Runyonesque, while Sam Belzberg is buttoned-down banking.

The Belzbergs were invited to Stephen Singer's wedding, but did not attend. But as Jack says, "I admire them. Who wouldn't? There's no animosity. Their father was my partner for thirty-five years. We were great partners and had fun doing business."

The partnership began when Jack could not join the armed forces in the Second World War, with his buddies and brother. He was disqualified because of perforated eardrums caused by scarlet fever when he was a child.

"I came to Abraham with a building to buy and said if we do this, we'll be partners forever," recalls Jack. "The main reason we were successful is that we used brokers, and they used to line up. We never bought anything direct, which is why we saw all the deals available. And we still do."

Jack Singer's executive office is in Calgary's low-rent district, above the Danceteria Towne Billiards and Coffee Shop on seedy First Street S.W. It is an area populated by drunks and lined with rooming-houses. But once past the unimpressive foyer and creaky elevator, Singer's offices are strictly top-drawer: an architecturally designed open-plan carpeted oasis amid Skid Row, complete with artwork and European furnishings.

Singer is pure Hollywood: large pinkie rings, shades, open-necked shirt, hairy chest, and gold chains. He has been a boxer, promoted prize fights, backed movies, owned a string of thoroughbred racing horses, tried to buy the Dallas Cowboys, been flat broke, and come back. He has a self-deprecating sense of humour and a zest for living that has taken him on an emotional and financial roller-coaster all his life.

For years, he has commuted between Calgary's Mount Royal area and Palm Springs, near the Eldorado Golf Club. Now when he is in the States, he lives mostly in the same three-bedroom bungalow on his Hollywood studio lot where Howard Hughes lived. His parking space is beside Gene Kelly's, and his next-door neighbour is George Burns, who spends every morning working with his three writers in the bungalow beside Singer's. Some of his best friends are moviedom's greats like Burns, Bob Hope, and movie mogul Jack Warner.

The Singers have always dabbled in showbiz. In 1981, Jack Singer visited Coppola's Zoetrope Studios just to get his hero's autograph. He ended up putting his signature on a $3-million cheque to help bail out the director's troubled extravaganza *One from the Heart*. Singer signed without reading the script. The musical ended up costing $26 million and flopped in 1982, making only $1 million. Singer had a collateral mortgage as security, but a worried first mortgager moved in on the nine-acre studio and foreclosed when payments were in arrears. Singer bought the property for its real estate value.

Jack's older brother, Hymie, was the first Singer involved in the world of entertainment. In 1937, he opened Vancouver's Palomar Burlesque with $3,000, but ran afoul of the law. He was busted in 1946 over an act by a six-foot-four-inch amazon stripper named Lois Roper, billed as the "Eiffel Eyeful — 200 pounds of stripulating delight."

Hymie went into the Air Force during the Second World War, while Jack stayed behind doing deals with Belzberg. For a short time, Jack boxed as a lightweight. "Until I got hit," he recalls. Even when he didn't, he feared for his life. "They used to come to my fights to see the Jew get killed," he says. At one match he made a lucky punch and knocked out his opponent, and there was a riot in the stands. He barely escaped through a side exit.

John Duby, a prominent Calgary oilman, rented space from Jack and Abe in the 1950s and complained during the winter that there was little heat. Abraham Belzberg came to the office and made a great scene, personally scolding some of his workers, brought along for effect. Thermostats were installed immediately. A month later Duby discovered they had been installed, but the wires hung down inside the wall, unconnected to the furnace. It was all for show.

The two cousins were an odd couple: Belzberg was excitable, Singer laidback. The two trusted each other implicitly and rarely quarreled. Their close relationship did not extend to the next generation, and Jack and his sister Rosalie have also had their ups and downs.

"The family's been fighting for years," says Rod Sykes, mayor of Calgary for four terms, who knows the family well. "The Singers are carnival people compared to the Belzbergs. Sam [Belzberg] is building a very solid, longlasting business. He has honesty, patience, smarts. Sam's first-class, building the next Royal Trustco. The Singers are gamblers, their lives are exciting. They're either in the chips or in trouble, but they always win. The Singers are speculators, not developers. In the 1960s, Jack sometimes had no money. He used to take creditors out for a coffee and a sandwich and sweet-talk them. He paid eventually."

As Jack wheeled and dealt with Abraham Belzberg in Calgary, he was also doing deals in the U.S. with his brother and sister. And because speculators are only as successful as their dreams and schemes, the Singers never feared size. Hymie and Jack Singer once proposed to build a $150-billion subway across America; apartments under the Hudson River in New York City; a 123-storey building in Toronto with 4,600 apartments; and a pneumatic tube system for sucking mail from city to city. On a trip around the world, Hymie suggested to Indonesia's finance minister that he convert the country into a corporation and sell shares. In 1980, Hymie wrote Israeli prime minister Menachem Begin and offered to help finance the construction of canals linking the vulnerable port of Eilat and the Dead Sea.

Thinking big helped them make it big too. Jack and Hymie helped expand one of the world's food giants, Safeway. They found good grocery store sites for the gigantic U.S. chain throughout Alberta, B.C., and the U.S. northwest, then built the shopping centres and strip plazas for them. "You cannot manufacture land. I believe in land," Hymie once told a newspaper.

Hymie's main company is Warner Holdings, named for Lita Warner Hiatt, the adopted daughter of film magnate Jack Warner. He had a romance with her in the early 1950s, but never married her. He lives with his second wife in Beverly Hills and has a daughter, now married, by his first wife.

Rosalie has two daughters, one son, and two ex-husbands. Over the years, she has bought and sold houses in partnership with Jack. In fact, during most of the 1970s, they owned the largest home in the United States, a ninety-two-room mansion outside San Francisco, in which she lived.

"At one point she owned part of the companies. She has a flair for making the right buys on houses," says Alan Singer. "She's the Auntie Mame type. A remarkable woman. My father was close to his mother, and the next closest to him has been his sister, but they have had a love-hate relationship. Rosalie sued everyone [for hundreds of millions of dollars] and settled."

The Singers inherited their real estate smarts and ambition from their mother, Bella, a remarkable and tough Polish immigrant. She and her husband, Abraham, drove to Calgary with a horse and cart they had bought in Toronto. He peddled junk, and she bought and sold rooming-houses on Skid Row. He died in 1941 and she died in 1984, at the age of 105.

In 1959, *Time* magazine honoured her as "the woman who cared." She brought hundreds of Jews from her Polish village to Calgary, paying their fares in return for promises from them that if they, too, did well, they must also sponsor others over. She tenaciously badgered prime ministers and civil servants to pull strings to let the rag-tag villagers immigrate, and it is estimated that she personally brought over 800 to 1,000 Jews. Jack Singer worshipped his mother. Her portrait in oils hangs over the fireplace in his Calgary office. He still keeps a loose-leaf binder, with the word BELLA in gold lettering on the cover, containing clippings about her life. It was compiled to commemorate her ninety-fifth birthday. "If you save one life in a lifetime that's incredible, but my mother saved thousands and their children and grandchildren. Her work will go on forever," says Jack.

Bella sponsored Abraham Belzberg, who was her nephew, and his wife to come to Calgary. "I remember when Abraham first came and lived with us," says Jack of his partner. "I turned around at breakfast time and he had swiped my porridge. He loved to do deals."

Jack married Shirley Cohen, whose family owns western Canada's Army and Navy department stores, in 1944. Their two sons, Alan and Stephen Singer, live next door to each other in Calgary and run the empire's day-to-day affairs. Both made it in business on their own before joining the family firm.

On Jack's behalf, they donated $1.5 million towards the Calgary Centre for the Performing Arts, which opened in September 1985. "It's nice to have something named after you before you die," says Singer.

The night the centre's 1,800-seat Jack Singer Theatre opened, Jack and his family arrived in a chauffeur-driven limousine. The $80-million centre is just two blocks away from the city's slums where Jack grew up. And he undoubtedly could not help marvelling that his has been a long, eventful journey since the days when he collected nickels and dimes for his mother from hookers and drunks.

THE MANNIXES

FREDERICK CHARLES MANNIX is one of Alberta's most powerful men. And yet, to all but a handful of execs and relatives, Mannix is a mystery. He could probably walk down a street in his home town of Calgary and remain unrecognized. His passion for privacy extends from his personal to his professional life: the 135 Mannix companies worldwide have more than $1 billion in assets and annual revenues of nearly $1 billion a year. But firm figures are hidden. The companies have provincial charters, which require scant disclosure and only ask corporations to divulge annually the names and addresses of directors and head offices.

"He was like a brother to me, and we travelled the world together," says former Alberta premier Peter Lougheed, who worked as chief counsel to Mannix before his election.

Virtually unknown outside Alberta, Mannix's sheltered existence is all the more unusual considering the types of high-profile projects his companies have cashed in on, such as the Trans-Canada Highway, the Toronto and Montreal subways, Calgary's and Edmonton's light rail systems, the St. Lawrence Seaway, big power dams, and Arctic artificial islands.

"They are simply the world's best dirt-movers," says Bill Peters, a former Mannix executive and Calgary oilman, "and they have done work on megaprojects such as B.C.'s Revelstoke dam, Quebec's James Bay hydro project, and dams, highways, and canals in other countries."

In addition to their huge contracting operations, the Mannixes are the princes of Canada's coal business, owning and selling more than anyone else. Every year, Mannix's Manalta Coal produces 13 million tonnes of thermal coal to generate electricity in Saskatchewan and Alberta — or ten times as much as the next-largest coal miner in Canada, Denison Mines, which ships 1.3 million tonnes to Japan annually. Mannix companies also explore for minerals; own oil, gas, and pipeline companies; repair thousands of miles of railroad track in North America every year; and have broadcasting, real estate, and other investment interests.

His companies' head offices are in a twelve-storey, fortress-like, no-frills office tower in Calgary. The Mannixes employ four full-time public relations officers to keep them and their companies out of print.

"An interview? No way," public relations chief Linda Buckley says. "I've never issued a press release in eight years."

Mannix and his first wife, Margaret, raised their three children on a 326-acre ranch in Calgary. She died in the mid-1970s and Mannix remarried; Janice, a stunning brunette, is thirty years his junior.

For the next few years, they lived on another 300-acre ranch, 40 kilometres southwest of Calgary. Complete with underground car wash and an indoor pool, the 7,000-square-foot house also had several wine cellars kept at differing temperatures and a master bedroom the size of a small high school gymnasium. Like many wealthy Westerners, Mannix is obsessed with security, and the ranch was surrounded by guards and hidden electronic eyes. This was not surprising after an unreported, but genuine, kidnapping attempt in the 1970s, when a member of his family was nearly abducted.

Mannix also has a home in Palm Springs on the Eldorado Golf Course near comedian Bob Hope's mansion, and there are several more thousand-acre spreads in Alberta. According to court documents relating to the city's expropriation of his Calgary ranch, the value of his personal real estate portfolio was $25 million in 1982.

Mannix has suffered two strokes since he remarried. In 1983 the couple moved into two adjoining $500,000 penthouses in the Estates, a high-rise development attached to the exclusive Ranchman's Club in downtown Calgary. There he can travel easily into the office and exercise in the complex's health club.

Like his father, Mannix loves construction; all the family's other lucrative investments — from oil and gas to coal and pipelines — were simply offshoots. His father, Frederick Stephen Mannix, was the son of Irish immigrants, and Fred C., born in 1913, is his only son. Young Fred learned the business at his father's knee — on the road with him at three, travelling from construction camp to camp and supervising construction of a dam at age twenty-one.

His father built many Alberta dams, and in the 1920s he realized the province was running out of hydroelectric sites. So he beat his customer to the punch, snapping up local coal mines, then selling these to the utility in return for contracts to operate them. He also pioneered coal strip mining for his customers.

In the early 1940s, the Mannixes always turned adversity into advantage. Short of capital for expansion, the father and son sold 51 per cent of their operations to Morrison-Knudsen Co. of Boise, Idaho — an arch-rival for lucrative contracts and the world's biggest earth-moving contractor. The proviso was, however, that young Mannix run the operation.

By 1951 — mostly because Mannix companies cashed in handsomely after the discovery of two world-class oilfields in Alberta — Fred C. was able to buy back the family firm. Not only was the parting amicable, but his brief partnership with a world-class contractor catapulted Mannix into the big leagues. From Morrison's executives, he learned techniques that enabled him to bid on the sort of projects that had been engineered in the U.S. until then.

One of the reasons he could afford to buy out the Americans was that in 1947, a massive oilfield at Leduc was discovered near Edmonton, ushering in a new prosperity for Alberta. It also offered new opportunities for capital-rich native sons such as Mannix to become wealthy on a world-class scale.

His company was hired to lay 440 miles of twenty-inch pipe for Interprovincial Pipeline; they became pioneers in the techniques of "big inch" pipe. This led to many more contracts. The boom-and-bust cycle of the construction business means massive payrolls one month and massive pink slips the next. And in a never-ending search for more work to keep key people employed, he cashed in on a second elephant-sized oilfield near Leduc, called Pembina.

Mobil Oil had discovered the field and wanted to build a pipeline to tap its reserves in Pembina. Mobil, now one of the ten largest companies in the world, was short of cash at that time. So to snare the pipeline contract, Mannix offered to put up the cash, turn the pipeline back to its owners for their use, but operate it for a fee and a royalty on the oil production.

Mobil jumped at the chance, and Mannix flew immediately to the Montreal head office of the Royal Bank; he got $14 million in interim bank loans to finance the project within twenty minutes. That formed the basis of $200-

million Pembina Pipelines, now on the Toronto Stock Exchange, in which Mannix still holds controlling interest. It's the only Mannix company listed on a stock exchange.

The 1950s were salad days for construction companies worldwide as governments rebuilt, refitted, or extended their country's roads, hydro facilities, factories, and subway systems. Mannix took advantage of all of it. While the oil boom filled company coffers, expansion back east led Mannix into another business. In 1950, he was one of four contractors to build the 360-mile ore-handling railway for Quebec's Iron Ore Co. From that experience and other railway contracts, he became one of the world's biggest railway construction and repair outfits.

Little known, but vastly profitable, is his U.S.-based Loram Maintenance of Way. The huge Minneapolis operation has patented and designed custom-made machines. These repair-shops-on-wheels slither daily along the continent's roads of steel like gigantic mechanical caterpillars. Pioneers in this technology, Mannix's machines lift old rails off their beds, bolt new ones in place, replace ties, and tidy up the beds beneath — at a mile an hour.

In 1964, Mannix built in Seattle the third underground powerhouse and dam project completed in North America. It won him the lucrative contract to build key portions of Hydro-Québec's $16-billion James Bay hydroelectric mega-project during the 1970s.

Innovations were critical, but so were connections. Like any world-scale engineering and construction firm, Mannix's firm found that political pals became all-important. After all, mega-projects were either financed or blessed by governments. And the men who controlled the purse-strings were courted. Every year, Mannix takes the entire House of Commons out to lunch. The Mannixes are also heavy political contributors and supporters of the Canada West Foundation, a lobbying group.

While other fortunes have sprung up there, Mannix was certainly king for a while in capital-poor Alberta. In fact, it was Mannix's signature, not that of Social Credit premier Ernest Manning, that personally guaranteed to buy the shares of Alberta Gas Trunk, now known as Nova Corp.

Now the Mannixes have holdings around the world. Fred's daughter, Maureen, is in charge of the family's donations through the Carthy Foundation. She has two children and is married to Ed Ebert, a dapper and gregarious public relations man who represents a number of junior oil companies in Calgary.

The older son, Fred P., is in charge. A pilot and a military buff, he was the first in the family to earn a degree, obtaining a bachelor of commerce from the University of Alberta. Like his father, he is reclusive, shunning directorships on any companies other than Mannix ones. Divorced and the father of a daughter, he lives 40 kilometres south of Calgary on his 2,000-acre ranch, called the FM2 Ranch. He is an avid outdoorsman and hunter, and his ranch is a game-bird rearing enclave where he hunts pheasant. He often travels to the United Kingdom for bird shooting and to Africa to hunt big game on safari.

Now an honorary lieutenant-colonel in the Calgary Highlanders reserve regiment, Fred P. Mannix has even set up an obstacle and weapons course for manoeuvres amidst the fields and streams of his ranch. His interest in the military is undoubtedly the reason why the executive ranks of Mannix companies nowadays are peopled by many former military officers, or by weekend soldiers such as himself. A capable administrator, Fred once confided in a rare interview (granted only to publicize the activities of his beloved Highlanders) that heavy lies the mantle of management. "Altogether there are 132 companies. It can drive you out of your mind."

Ronald is two years younger, dark and chunky, and considerably more outgoing than his older brother. He is president and in charge of the family's sizeable coal businesses; he sits on two outside boards of directors, the Bentley family's Canfor, a forestry outfit, and the Bank of Montreal.

The future is in their hands, and while they are undoubtedly capable, there are problems. "There was always a terrific turnover because no matter how good you were, you'd never get a piece of the action," recounts former executive Peters. "But while you were there, you were always well paid, appreciated, and challenged."

Toronto broker William Reidl noted another flaw during his dealings: "This company is exceedingly slow in making any decision because everybody had to 'go upstairs' as they say, to get one of the brothers or the father to approve anything."

THE GHERMEZIANS

THE MYSTERIOUS Ghermezians live in a clapboard commune surrounded by barbed wire in Edmonton. The four brothers, their wives, sixteen children, and parents are among Canada's wealthiest citizens, having built a $2-billion empire through rugs, real estate, and resources in just a little over three decades. A secretive clan of nomadic capitalists, they wandered over three continents — from Europe to Asia to Canada — before finding their billion-dollar pot of gold in Edmonton.

Operating through a corporation with the sphinx-like name of Triple Five Corp., they own the world's biggest shopping mall in Edmonton and hope to build an even bigger one outside Minneapolis at a cost of $1.5 billion. They also own a score of apartment and office buildings and hundreds of town-houses, and they are the largest urban landowners in Alberta, with 15,000 acres outside Edmonton and Calgary.

In addition to all that, they own thousands of acres of phosphate deposits in British Columbia; they have their own trust company, advertising agency, and travel outfit. The Ghermezians spend as much each year to promote their Edmonton mega-mall and its indoor amusement park as the province of Alberta will spend to garner tourists ($5 million).

It all began 250 years ago. For seven generations, the Ghermezians have been rug traders. The patriarch, Jacob ("Poppa") Ghermezian, was born around the turn of the century in Azerbaijan, Russia, near the Turkish and Iranian borders, one of five sons who all eventually landed in Tehran before the Second World War. The family immigrated to Montreal in the early 1950s and set up Ghermezian Bros. on Sherbrooke Street.

Jacob, who goes to the Edmonton mega-mall daily to watch the children play in the amusement park, is still consulted on major family decisions, but his four sons run the show. Eskandar, born in 1940 and the oldest, is the boss. Raphael, who speaks seven languages and is a mathematical whiz, is the land acquisitions person. Nader, the most public of the four, is in charge of the all-important lobbying function, and the youngest, Bahman, born in 1947, looks after property management and construction. The brothers bear little physical resemblance to one another and share few traits, except a passion for business.

"Eskandar is the most serious of the four. He negotiates arrangements with bankers, and also has a good eye for design and colour. Bahman is the most sociable of the four, Raphael is the friendliest in the office, in charge of land acquisitions and new developments, and Nader is the most visible publicly because he handles the press and politicians," says Deane Eldredge, a public relations woman hired away from Los Angeles mayor Tom Bradley in 1985 by the Ghermezians.

In fact, Nader is so tenacious and vocal at Edmonton council meetings that

Mayor Laurence Decore once called him the city's thirteenth alderman, because of his outbursts during debates. Deane does most of the talking for her four bosses, who speak several languages proficiently, but English haltingly. Their everyday working tongue is Farsi, a Persian dialect.

Commune living comes naturally to these four unusual Ghermezians. In Tehran, they grew up sharing a five-storey building with sixty-five uncles, aunts, and cousins. Each family unit had a separate apartment, but there were communal gatherings on special occasions.

Tehran's streets were mean, which undoubtedly led to their departure as well as forged their almost fanatical closeness and concern about security. Life in Iran was so harsh that the only people you could trust were your relatives.

Their Edmonton lawyer, John Butler, once gave the *Toronto Star* an insight into their childhood. "As boys [in Iran] they saw a friend killed before their eyes, simply because while playing a game he had accidentally hit another boy with a rock. They also saw people taken right out of their midst by the police, for no apparent reasons."

In the early 1950s, Jacob sold out and took his wife, Nahenjan, and four young sons to Montreal, where he set up a family store. Raphael and Eskandar majored in commerce at McGill University, but only Raphael finished. The others worked in the family business, which became a great success. There is a surprising amount of money in rugs, because carpet merchants are like merchant bankers. Rugs — like diamonds — are an easily marketable commodity, and for generations, both have provided a way around currency restrictions. Thousands of wealthy Iranians, Arabs, Ugandans, Chinese, and others have gotten money out of their countries this way. And wheeling and dealing in carpets was how Edmonton's richest citizens, the Ghermezians, made their first fortune. The second one, catapulting them into the billion-dollar big leagues, was in real estate — the industry that has created most of Canada's billionaires since the Second World War.

By 1965, Jacob had built Ghermezian Bros. into a sixteen-store chain, which made it the largest importer of Oriental carpets in the U.S., and he headed his nomadic clan of capitalists for oil-rich Alberta. The family wanted to cash in on the new-found prosperity in the province, thanks to the discovery of a second world-class oilfield. Initially, they hunted for oil, snapping up land around Edmonton. They struck out because they knew little about geology or engineering. But their land holdings led them to pay dirt. Like many of

Canada's other wealthiest citizens, they realized the road to riches is through real estate: when politicians agree to rezone land, wealth results.

Jacob also knew something about real estate, having been a fairly large-scale landlord in Tehran. They began operating as Ghermez Developments, later changing the name to Triple Five (555), which "represented the company's original 551 silent shareholders, plus the four brothers," wrote Gary Weiss in the *Toronto Star*.

"They are silent partners who make available to ourselves silent money," Raphael told Weiss in 1978. The need for anonymity explains Triple Five's strange by-law, which states that shares in the company must never be sold to the public. The silent partners are no more, and sources say Triple Five's net worth is about $200 million.

They began this rapid rise to riches by assembling land and selling rezoned lots to builders. Even when zonings worked the opposite way — in the early 1970s, for instance, when the province of Alberta designated thousands of acres around its cities as greenbelt — the Ghermezian brothers made a king-sized fortune. They sold the farmland for hundreds of millions to the province. While such strokes may be luck, the brothers are more than astute at making their own luck.

The lobbying effort for the first phase of the West Edmonton Mall in the mid-1970s was ferocious, recalled a politician. "I couldn't believe the lobbying. They phoned aldermen on weekends and didn't hesitate to almost tackle them in the halls."

In 1985, Premier Peter Lougheed found himself beset constantly by Nader, who would find out the premier's schedule and beseech him for a $20-million government grant at social teas or sporting events.

There is little doubt now that the West Edmonton Mall circumvented the rules of orderly growth, and it now singlehandedly sucks in 25 per cent of the city's entire retail business. It has made a shambles of downtown Edmonton. To critics it may be a planning boondoggle. To anyone else, it is a capitalist coup.

"I fail to see how an independent city council could have approved such a scheme," maintains columnist and former Calgary mayor Rod Sykes.

Similarly, the brothers handily beat out American rivals to build a $1.5-billion mega-mall in Bloomington, outside Minneapolis. The mall is to be a clone of Edmonton's giant, complete with amusement park, hotels, and convention centre. With hard-hatted hoopla and fanfare, the brothers made their announcement that the project was proceeding on July 4, 1985. But a few weeks later, they found some obstacles still in their paths.

A month later, they cunningly used newly elected Ontario premier David Peterson to goad Minnesota officialdom into making a faster, more generous decision. They met with the premier for an hour to discuss the possibility of a gigantic project, somewhere in Ontario. But landless developers don't announce plans because land prices will heat up on them. The real intention of the audience with Peterson was to let Minnesota politicians know they had other fish to fry.

However, such savvy set off a small scandal in 1974 in Edmonton. That year, a report claimed that Raphael had offered $40,000 to bribe an alderman, sparking a judicial inquiry. Weeks later, a judge concluded that Raphael did offer the money to reward the alderman for past service but that the payment wasn't a bribe within the definition of the Criminal Code. "It was a legitimate token of appreciation for past services and did not constitute a bribe."

West Edmonton Mall is the flagship of the Ghermezian empire. Built at a staggering cost of $1.2 billion, it is definitely a creation of this unique family.

The mall was not originally intended to be this ambitious. Landscape architect Ronald McCarthy, with Moorhead Fleming Corban & McCarthy, said the mall was originally an amusement centre, with just three rides. However, Eskandar attended an amusement ride trade show in Kansas City three months after work began, and became so excited that he called architects at six the next morning to tell them to quintuple the space in the mall for rides.

Now, two expansions later, the mall is twenty-eight blocks square. This is not your average shopping centre: it's a zoo, an amusement park, a huge shopping centre, and the Canadian National Exhibition all rolled into one. Baby Siberian tigers in glass cages lounge outside a Suzy Shier fashion outlet. A twelve-storey roller-coaster ride rumbles alongside a women's wear outlet. An indoor car dealer displays his wares beside the mall's ice rink, where Wayne Gretzky and the Edmonton Oilers practise. Three McDonald's Restaurants and everything from tacos to tofu are proffered amid carnival surroundings.

The mall contains the world's largest indoor water park, a ten-acre spread with a vaulted glass ceiling that artificially creates sunlight through the use of low-level infra-red lighting. The 1.5-acre lake has six-foot surfing waves and water-skiing.

While shopping and circuses attract crowds, many shopping centre experts wonder aloud if West Edmonton is really making money in a city too small to support such size. Rumours say it doesn't matter whether West Edmonton makes money: the Ghermezians are a conduit for Middle East money seeking a safe haven.

The "silent partners" no longer exist, says Deane Eldredge, and the mall is very profitable. When asked, astute tenants like Dylex say sales have tipped $1,000 a square foot a year, five times the national average, and they have signed up for twice the space in the final expansion.

The brothers put in twelve-hour days at Triple Five's headquarters overlooking Alberta's legislative buildings. Their offices are decorated with expensive Persian rugs, marble floors and baseboards, blond wood, and plenty of space and light. Eskandar and Nader have an enormous office each; Bahman and Raphael share a long, narrow office with desks thirty feet apart at opposite ends. In the middle is a table, where the four eat lunch together every day, comparing notes and dividing duties. They talk loudly, yelling for people rather than using an intercom or telephone. They devour local publications, such as the *Edmonton Journal* and the *Edmonton Sun* as well as the weekly provincial magazine *Alberta Report*.

"They dislike firing people and will move them around to another position, hoping they'll make it there," says Eldredge. "The pace is frantic, and employees start off at salaries 20 per cent lower than average because they are looking for people with the right attitude. Some people cannot get used to their manner and there are often shouting matches between brothers. They also insist on getting involved in every detail, picking out every piece of building material."

All four brothers have different religions, each having adopted his wife's faith, which explains their confusing contributions to religious sects. One is Roman Catholic, another Jewish, another belongs to a Persian sect, and another is Moslem. They recently donated $450,000 worth of land for construction of a Roman Catholic church and $35,000 towards the construction of the Canadian Islamic Centre in the city. They are particularly generous to Edmonton Children's Hospital and earmark most of their charitable donations to any causes that have to do with children's diseases.

They are devoted family men. Eldredge says whenever Nader calls her from home, she can hear his children playing loudly in the background. "He never tells them to shut up. And I remember once he was walking around for months like a robot because one of his kids had jumped on his back from a landing in his house. He wasn't upset with the kid."

All four marriages were arranged; their mother returned to Iran to hand-pick their wives, who are all Persian, beautiful, and taller than their husbands. "That's because they wanted good-looking, tall sons," says Eldredge.

The family shares its rambling, two-storey white clapboard compound overlooking the North Saskatchewan River Valley. An adjacent home was bought and demolished, and a six-foot chain-link fence topped with barbed wire was erected around the lot. Security is an obsession with the family because of kidnapping threats.

Winters are spent working or at home with their families. They are often seen, with their statuesque wives and children in tow, at the mall, at local restaurants, or at Oilers games. No fancy Palm Springs winter address for them; they aren't jet-setters. In summers they have a small outboard motor-boat for water-skiing. They are just multimillionaires who, like the rest of us, enjoy satisfying careers and a day's shopping away from the elements.

The Ghermezians are truly amazing.

THE SOUTHERNS

THE SOUTHERNS are western Canada's first billionaire industrialists. Father-and-son proprietors of a multinational manufacturing outfit, their success is unusual in a country where political needs and geography have traditionally dictated that Canada's industrial heartland be located in Ontario and Quebec.

Don and Ron Southern started Ron's Trailer Rentals in 1947 in a Calgary backyard with $4,000 savings. Back then, Don was a Calgary firefighter with a Grade Eight education who made $200 a month. His son, Ron, then 17, intended to be a doctor and needed spare cash.

Now, $3 billion in assets later, Don is chairman and Ron president of ATCO Ltd., a mixed bag of manufacturing, resource, oilfield servicing, and real estate assets. Even more significantly, the Southerns are the only individuals in Canada to have controlling interest in an electrical utility, Canadian Utilities Ltd., which supplies 15 per cent of Alberta's power needs and 80 per cent of its natural gas. The family also tried to buy the only other power utility in Alberta, called Transalta Ltd.; they now indirectly own 15.6 per cent of it. The rest of Canada's power utilities have been nationalized over the years and are Crown corporations.

The family also owns one-third of an oil exploration partnership with Sun Life Assurance Co. and Texaco Canada Inc.; a travel agency; a customs brokerage; residential real estate and one million square feet of office space in downtown Calgary; and a world-class equestrian facility called Spruce Meadows, on 295 acres just outside Calgary.

"My father was mustered out of the service with $2,000 in credits. I had saved $2,000 from my summer jobs as a busboy [at Banff Springs Hotel]. And on a family holiday in Vancouver, my father spotted some small trailers, and we decided to try renting them in Calgary," Ron Southern told the *Globe and Mail* in 1983.

From that modest grub-stake, ATCO became a world-beater, its orange and aluminum cubicles home to everyone from scientists in the Antarctic to construction workers in Greece, pipeline welders in Argentina, oil explorers in Sumatra, missile trackers in the Indian Ocean, highway builders in France, miners in Nigeria, and smelter workers in Australia. ATCO is the world's largest manufacturer of construction camp shelters, but it has also shipped schools to Saudi Arabia, entire towns to Algeria, and portable hospitals to Vietnam. ATCO is also the biggest land-contract drilling and well-servicing company in Canada.

It is a uniquely western Canadian business, forged by the needs of Alberta's infant oil industry. ATCO began by building housing for oilmen to use when drilling in empty wasteland where roads, good weather, and accommodation are scarce. That is in part why ATCO became the world's first, and pre-eminent, builder of pre-fab structures that can be disassembled quickly and transported over roadless glaciers, tundra, or deserts.

Back in 1947, father and son pooled their money, bought ten small trailers and set up shop renting through service stations. That was the year Alberta's first world-class oilfield, Leduc, gushed in a new era of prosperity for the province. As a result, the Southerns and many others were also catapulted into the big leagues. In no time flat, they operated the largest trailer dealership in North America. Some time later, acting on a request from an oil industry executive, they built their first industrial trailers in a repair shop. The prototypes were no-frills and ugly, but strong and warm. This was a turning-point.

"Jim Turner at Shell Oil asked us to build heavy, strong, warm mobile bunkhouses for workers up north. That led to our most important decision. We decided to provide the whole thing, to manufacture relocatable industrial housing, structures, and factories that were easily transported to the outback."

One innovation followed another. First it was Canada's oil industry and construction camps, then ATCO began to export, finally expanding into hospitals, schools, and barracks. Its first major contract outside the country totalled $12 million, to build pre-fab housing camps for technicians at Minuteman missile sites in five states. Other new techniques led to more sales, similarly forged from the unique Canadian experience. After all, who else but a Canadian, used to our remote resource lands, would have built and designed a complete village for polar expeditions that could be assembled by ten men in six hours? ATCO did, and the U.S. government bought plenty of them.

Ron Southern dropped out of medical school because the business was doing so well. Don Southern turned out to be a genius at production methods, while Ron combed the world for business. Ron is persuasive, relentless, and sometimes arrogant, an ambitious man who owns 59.6 per cent of ATCO's stock. He and many other successful Albertans lack the timidity that afflicts Canadians, who all too often are inadequately trained branch plant managers. Albertans involved in the rough-and-tumble oil business go for broke — and most of them have gone broke, destroyed by a combination of the recession in the early 1980s, the oil cartel's disarray, and the made-in-Canada catastrophe known as the National Energy Program, with its onerous taxes. By 1984, Calgary fortunes made in the salad days of the 1970s had ebbed or disappeared altogether.

Ron Southern's strategy saved the family from a similar fate. He decided to offset the roller-coaster cycles of oil prices and government tax policies by buying utilities — stable, unspectacular, but always profitable. While Ron's other Petroleum Club friends have swapped their Mercedes for Buicks, Southern still rides high on huge utility profits. The Southerns are economic trailblazers in another sense, too: they are among Canada's few self-made men, unlike most of Canada's dynasties, who inherited fortunes and built upon them.

Southern keeps in touch with politicians, lobbying in both Edmonton and Ottawa to head off problems. It was particularly grating to him when a fellow Albertan, Joe Clark, adopted a Zionist policy of moving Canada's embassy in Israel to Jerusalem — which cost ATCO an $8-million contract in a nearby Arab country.

But for the most part his political contacts have paid off. A confidant to former premier Peter Lougheed, he was asked in 1974 to serve as the first president of Pacific Western Airlines, second-largest in the country, after it was bought by the province. And six years later the province's banking network, called Treasury Branches, loaned Southern 25 per cent of the money he needed to make two gigantic takeover bids for the utilities. While the province lets the branches operate at arm's length, Southern's friends in the legislature turned a deaf ear to concerns about the concentration of power that resulted.

In May 1980, Southern stunned Canada's financial community by paying $317 million for 58 per cent of Canadian Utilities in Edmonton, significantly larger than his own company. Most upset about the takeover was the province's other utility, Transalta, which reacted to the purchase by picking up the remaining 42-per-cent interest. Transalta's management warned of the dangers of having one family controlling all the power and natural utilities in the province.

Southern countered with a $513-million bid for control of Transalta. It failed after two more attempts when another company outbid him, obtaining 15.6 per cent. But two years later Canadian Utilities bought those shares, in return for agreeing not to try a takeover until 1988.

"Ron Southern's family is so nice," says Rod Sykes, former Calgary mayor and unsuccessful Liberal candidate in the 1984 federal election. "He's a friend of mine. He thinks it's macho to win. To him it's no fun if his enemies are not crushed. Alberta contains some of the more destructive forms of capitalism. There's a lack of sympathy, concern. Too many are getting for getting's sake."

Southern spends most weekends at Spruce Meadows, an equestrian centre second only to England's Hickstead. It's the brain-child of his wife, Margaret, a capable businesswoman in her own right, who sits on the high-powered Shell Canada and Woodward Stores boards of directors. The idea sprang from the family's interest in horses. The Southerns' two daughters, Linda and Nancy, have won many ribbons, and they run the centre with their mother.

In 1984, Southern sold some stock in ATCO to pay off the well-manicured horse centre, with miles of white rail fences and Tudor-style stables for 400 steeds, complete with chandelier light fixtures and automatic sprinklers. Opened in 1975, its stands seat 4,000; it hosts championship riding contests every year that draw larger crowds than do the Calgary Stampeders, the Canadian Football League team that Southern and three well-heeled friends rescued from financial difficulties in 1985. In 1983, Spruce Meadows hosted the richest show-jumping competition in the world, called the Masters, with $300,000 in prizes. Southern's father lives on the premises, which includes indoor and outdoor arenas.

The family is flamboyant. In the fall of 1984, one of the Southerns' two daughters was married. The reception for hundreds was held at Calgary's aging Glencoe Club, a favourite recreational haunt of Calgary's oilmen. The entire curved stairway in the club's entrance and the reception areas were festooned with tulips, orchids, and other beautiful flowers, flown in fresh that day from Holland. And the bride and groom drew up in front of the club in a handsome horse-drawn carriage.

Ron Southern has fought, and beaten, the bottle. "I had a drinking problem," he said, adding he is convinced he cannot cope with liquor. He smokes cigars, but he has not had a drink since 1970, and he took up riding with his daughters as "a substitute for drinking. All the extra energy and time went into that."

With his family grown and living away from home, extra energy will be devoted to business interests. ATCO's future rests with the future of the world's economy. It is a manufacturer totally dependent upon mega-projects like dams or drilling programs. It is also dependent on drilling activity in North America. But above all, the future depends on whether Southern's two daughters, still untested in the world of business, will become interested in taking on the reins of more than just the family equestrian centre. At the moment, however, there is little need for successors because their father has no plans to retire. "Once in a while it has crossed my mind that maybe I should slow down and not work so hard. But you talk about executive stress. Well, when I get thinking like that, that's when I feel stress. It's important for me to achieve and to feel that I can go on achieving."

THE BELZBERGS

BROADCASTER LARRY ZOLF will never forget when Abraham Belzberg "babysat" him for a couple of days. It was 1952, and Zolf's family had travelled from Winnipeg to Calgary for his older brother's wedding. His brother worked with Abraham. To kill time, the old man and young Zolf cruised Calgary in the back of the Belzbergs' black Cadillac limo, which Abraham never learned to drive. Talking in Yiddish about baseball, they'd occasionally head into a restaurant — a shy teenager from Winnipeg and an elderly millionaire fishmonger and patriarch of one of Canada's foremost dynasties.

"We'd go into a restaurant and he'd say to me, 'Do you like paying the bill?' He always asked questions like a rabbi. Then he'd say, 'It's lots of money, and I don't like paying it. How are your eggs? Mine are rotten. Should we pay? Look, you go to the bathroom for fifteen minutes and come out casual and I'll meet you in the car.' I'd do as I was told, then we'd drive off without paying the bill," recalls Zolf. "This happened three or four more times, and I told Abraham's sons about it. They said, 'Everybody knows him and they just send us the bill.' He died thinking he got away with it."

The Belzbergs are a Semitic version of the Waltons: forged by tough times, fiercely loyal and close. Even though Abraham's three sons — Hyman, Sam, and William — are now very, very rich, they have never forgotten their humble roots. The brothers and their two sisters were raised in Calgary by parents who left their native village of Radom, Poland, to escape pogroms. Once here, their father peddled second-hand furniture and their mother took in boarders. Abraham and his cousin, Jack Singer, became millionaires, buying and selling seedy buildings. But his sons are now in the billion-dollar leagues, beyond their Runyonesque father's wildest dreams.

Since the Second World War, they have taken a cluster of Calgary slums and converted them into a blue-chip real estate and financial services empire with nearly $3 billion in assets. Their interests straddle both sides of the border and include Canada's fourth-largest trust company, First City Financial Corp.; one of California's five largest savings and loan associations and real estate companies, Far West Financial Corp.; hundreds of millions of dollars worth of real estate in the U.S. and Canada; a New York investment banking house; and controlling interest in Scovill Inc. of Connecticut, maker of Hamilton-Beach appliances and Yale locks. They are also among North America's most aggressive stock market shooters, buying and selling stakes in huge corporations in partnership with colourful Texas oilman T. Boone Pickens and others.

Hyman is the oldest, born in 1927, and the only brother still living in Calgary. His forty-two-acre estate is a far cry from his humble home as a youngster, but he still works as he did as a teenager — serving customers six days a week in his father's store, Cristy's Arcade Furniture. In fact, the day before he was kidnapped in 1982, he stopped by the home of his kidnapper to measure his living-room for a sofa. A day later he would be bound and gagged in the basement, held for a $2-million ransom. But he was freed unharmed, and the bumbling culprits were caught.

Sam is two years younger than Hyman and plays on the world stage. A curly-haired whiz-kid who earned a bachelor's degree at nineteen, he has worked hard to parlay his father's millions into an empire with more than $3 billion in assets. "There's not a day that goes by when I don't think about my father," he told a group of Vancouver businessmen in a touching speech.

By all accounts, Sam is the brightest and most ambitious of the three brothers, dividing his time equally between Vancouver, where he lives, and New York City, where First City Financial Corp.'s acquisitions arm is located. He is chairman of the board.

Youngest is William, or "Billy" — a mercurial magnate who dropped out of high school to run the family's pet food business, Red Top Dog Food. He runs the family's California financial and real estate holdings, as chairman of Far West Financial Corp. He moves in jet-set circles, lives in a Beverly Hills mansion formerly owned by movie star Gene Hackman, and is a hard-driving executive who's gone through six presidents in as many years.

The Belzbergs own 65.4 per cent of First City's shares and divide ownership equally in three portions. Hyman's son, Brent, works for the real estate arm in Vancouver, and Sam's son, Marc, is president of the family's New York-based acquisitions arm, First City Capital Corp. Abraham's two daughters, Fanny and Lil, are not involved in the business now. Despite their wealth, the three brothers work exceedingly hard, but Sam is the driving force.

"My dad said, 'I assume you boys are together,' and I said yes, and it's been that way ever since. In the beginning when money liquidity was a problem, my older brother would advance money from the furniture store to get us over the hump. My dad taught us a lot about solidarity," Sam told the *Vancouver Sun*.

Never forgetting that blood is thicker than the bottom line can be costly. Roots are the reason why the Belzbergs contribute generously to Jewish causes. By some calculations, the family contributes as much as $10 million a year to the Simon Wiesenthal Centre in Los Angeles for Holocaust studies; the money goes towards the cost of hunting Nazi war criminals or on special projects, such as trying to find Swedish diplomat Raoul Wallenberg, who saved the lives of thousands of Jews. They also donate their time. In 1984, Sam Belzberg and Nazi-hunter Simon Wiesenthal met with President Ronald Reagan to get help in finding Walter Rauff, a suspected war criminal living in Chile. Sam explained this commitment: "We lost many relatives in the Holocaust. A few survivors came to Canada and we helped them, but we lost the major portion of our family."

Sam has enormous energy and during tiring trips has the ability to cat-nap on planes and wake up totally refreshed. "He has staying power and energy that are unbelievable," says a business colleague. His workday usually begins at six-thirty in the morning at home, when he talks for an hour or so with executives back east. He then gets into his Vancouver office by seven-thirty, rolls up his shirt-sleeves, loosens his tie, and works until six most nights. Despite such long hours, he keeps in shape by doing daily exercises, swimming, and playing golf and tennis.

The brothers reach decisions through consensus and have never had a vote. Hyman, or "Hy" as he's known to friends, contributes a small-business perspective to decisions; he was key in the decision to take over Scovill, a maker of brand-name consumer products. Billy has a uniquely American slant, as a long-time resident of the U.S. who moves in the sometimes frenzied circles of Hollywood and southern California real estate.

Sam makes decisions quickly and is cool under pressure. Even in the highly charged emotional atmosphere in 1982 during Hyman's kidnapping, Sam kept the ringleader on the telephone for long periods, allowing police to trace the call to a pay telephone.

Perhaps more than many family businessmen, Sam is conscious that opportunities must exist for "outsiders" in order to attract and keep good people. He runs interoffice contests and offers prizes for good ideas. And more than once he has told employees a story about his father's first job in Calgary. A fishmonger by trade, Abraham Belzberg got a job as a buyer for a small produce market. He got a raise after a few months, but the owner's nephew did not. When the relative complained, the owner explained that when he sent Abraham out to buy strawberries, he would buy whatever was the best bargain. But when he sent his nephew out to buy strawberries, he would buy strawberries.

It is with their remarkable father that the Belzbergs' story begins. He immigrated in 1919 to escape Poland's pogroms and poverty, sponsored by his aunt, Bella Singer. The fortunes of these families were intertwined until Abraham's death in 1973, when the Belzbergs and the Singers parted company permanently. Both fabulously wealthy, cousins Jack Singer and Sam Belzberg see each other rarely and have few, if any, business dealings. Singer is colourful and carnival, while Belzberg is strictly blue pin-stripes.

After wheeling and dealing in small-time real estate deals, Abraham had saved enough money by 1932 to open a second-hand furniture store, the forerunner of Cristy's. In the European tradition, he started his eldest son, Hyman, in the family business as a helper; in 1945, he handed him the keys, saying, "You're on your own, Mister."

Sam was the first Belzberg to finish high school, never mind university. He earned his degree in record time and still managed to sell used cars part-time. Until an incident in 1948, after finishing university, Sam intended to be a lawyer. His father summoned a lawyer to notarize some documents for $10.

"My dad said to me, 'What do you want to be in life? Do you want to be the guy who can afford to pay? Or the one who has to take the $10?' That was the end of my law career," says Sam.

Sam sold cars and began buying land, in partnership with his cousins, Jack and Hymie Singer. Their first big score was made by snapping up leases from farmers to the below-surface rights near oil discoveries or on lands with good potential. The first property, for which they paid $2,750, was flipped in months for $27,000. By 1967, they had leases on some forty million acres — an area equivalent to Prince Edward Island, Nova Scotia, and New Brunswick combined.

In 1962, the Belzbergs decided to use $1 million in capital to set up a financial services business to help finance their real estate joint ventures with the Singers. But in 1973, the Belzbergs sold their half of the jointly owned real estate company for $43 million. Sam moved to Vancouver, and a year later Billy bought Far West and moved permanently to California.

In 1979, the Belzbergs began making headlines when they started to invest in high-profile U.S. companies, some of whom regarded them as undesirable intruders. That disdain proved to be the Belzbergs' path to riches. In a practice known as "greenmail," the Belzbergs would buy shares in a company, and the company's directors would buy those shares back for more than the Belzbergs had paid, in order to prevent the family from making a takeover.

There were a string of such deals, but the most controversial came in 1981, when the Belzbergs made $48.7 million on their shares of the Wall Street brokerage firm Bache Halsey, eventually taken over by insurance giant Prudential. This was followed in quick succession by another $22.4 million in profits when they aborted takeover bids for Superior Propane and Pergas, two U.S. gas utilities, and by an $8-million profit after a failed takeover bid for Canada Permanent in Toronto.

The Bache battle bloodied the Belzbergs. Frightened Bache management said the Belzbergs were undesirable because Hyman Belzberg might have ties to organized crime; they cited allegations that FBI agents saw him dining in 1970 with Meyer Lansky and Montreal mobster Benny Kaufman in Acapulco. The matter was simply a tacky defence manoeuvre — the FBI itself said there was no proof of Belzberg links to the mob. Sam was so upset that in a press conference he called the allegation by Bache "circumstantial bullshit."

In 1983, they made headlines again as partners with T. Boone Pickens, bidding to take over gigantic Gulf Oil Corp. Chevron outbid them, and the Belzbergs made $67 million in profit.

More greenmail followed. But Sam rejected the accusation that he was a greenmailer when he told *Maclean's* in 1984: "We never, ever set out to do that. We are not stock players. I do not believe anybody makes money in the long term playing the stock market."

Taken literally, that statement explains the 1985 Belzberg buy that has baffled the marketplace: the $627.6-million acquisition of Scovill for $51 a share, twice the company's book value. One analyst said, "Unless there's an oil well under company headquarters, the Belzbergs may be paying through the nose for it." Another said the price was irrelevant because they bought it "to be taken seriously next time as greenmailers."

Blue-chip, dividend-paying Scovill may simply represent Sam's desire to create a long-lasting dynasty. It may be another cornerstone. But only these three sons of a fishmonger know. It is for the rest of us to watch and wonder.

THE PATTISONS

CANADA'S KING of conglomerates is Jimmy Pattison, a Christian capitalist who is one of the country's few self-made men. He is an expert on both the Bible and balance sheets: a fundamentalist Christian who often goes to church twice on Sunday, but whose companies distribute smutty magazines; a charitable man who gives his time and money freely to good works, but who used to run his car dealership by firing the salesman who sold the fewest cars each month; an avowed free-enterpriser whose company was convicted of conspiracy to lessen competition and received the highest fine in Canadian history — $450,000 — in 1984.

Even more unusual, he is a loving and proud father who not only refuses to hire his children or teach them the ropes, but will leave them with nothing when he dies. His entire conglomerate is already owned by a charitable foundation, "which will go on for sixty years after I'm gone," says Jimmy. "I won't hire my kids or give them anything. Let them do their own thing. If they're any good, they'll get on. If they weren't and I hired them, I couldn't fire them and that wouldn't be fair to the people I employ. I believe in merit and ability as the only reason to rise to a high station in life. If you love your kids, you make them go out and get it. I want every one of my 7,000 employees, even fifteen-year-old drop-outs, to be able to become president of one of my companies, if he or she is capable. I promised my kids two things: no job and no money. I'm doing them a big favour because I've never been impressed with anyone who ever inherited money. I'm giving it all away to charity."

Maclean's columnist Allan Fotheringham wrote insightfully that the five-foot-six-inch, 131-pound Pattison "looks like Mickey Rooney's under-nourished brother, dresses like Nathan Detroit, and thinks like J. Paul Getty." When he asked Pattison why he wanted to make a million before he turned forty, he replied, "Because that's the way they keep score in our materialistic society."

And James Allen Pattison has certainly racked up the points in the game of life. In 1960, he put himself in hock personally to buy a General Motors dealership. Now his relatively small staff of thirteen oversees the operations of dozens of companies with sales of nearly $900 million a year. The group is now one of Canada's ten biggest privately owned companies, with interests in transportation, communications, food products, and financial services — from Orange Crush to a Swiss bank.

Jim Pattison owns more billboards and neon signs than anyone else in the world, sells more Toyotas and recreational vehicles than anyone in Canada, owns Ripley's Believe It Or Not museums and copyrights, and holds the Canadian rights to drinks such as Orange Crush, Hires Root Beer, Wilson's Ginger Ale, and Pure Spring sodas. He owns a Vancouver radio station and magazine; small data processing and real estate companies; the country's fourth-largest airline, AirBC; its largest magazine distributorship operations; two grocery food chains; the Gold Seal label, with 25 per cent of the Canadian canned seafood market; the country's largest canned fruit and vegetable exporter; and his very own Swiss bank and Cayman Islands brokerage firm.

"I prefer to have privately owned companies. It's much more efficient. With other shareholders, the pressure is on share values or profits. Sometimes the best thing for a business is not such short-term concerns like what's it going to do to the stock, price/earnings ratio. I can decide to do anything I want in an elevator. And the cost of informing public shareholders is enormous. The only advantage of having public companies is leverage," says Pattison.

A tiny, ginger-haired man with the quick, jerky movements of a bird and a patter as swift as his best car-lot hustler, Pattison maintains that anyone can be as successful as he was if he has the courage to take risks. Most people do not take risks because of a "lack of courage," he says. "The big companies are full of smart guys. But they're afraid of losing. I took my total life savings of $22,000 and went into the car business for myself. In six years I had $2 million. In four more years I had $8 to $10 million."

The inspiration for his gutsy philosophy is contained in a verse framed and given to him by his mother: "Greatly begin! Though thou have time... Not failure, but low aim, is crime."

Pattison was born in Saskatoon in 1928, an only child. His mother grew up in a sod house and his father, Pat, sold cars. As the Depression worsened they moved to British Columbia. Jimmy was seven; his father eked out an existence and the family lived in an attic. Almost immediately Jimmy began hustling garden seeds and magazines door to door. Whenever Pattison walks past a row of pay phones, he'll flick the coin return looking for quarters — a childhood habit of picking up extra money. At nineteen, he started working for a car dealership at $25 a week, washing cars. Two weeks later, he was selling and pulling in $1,000 a month. He put himself through university by selling at nights and on Saturdays, but quit school in 1950 only three courses shy of a bachelor's degree in commerce.

"The only reason for going to university is that it gives you self-confidence," he says. "I learned more in a used-car lot than I did at university: people, attitudes, integrity. You learn to size up people quickly."

In 1960, ten years later, he bought his first General Motors dealership, borrowing $40,000 against the $15,000 cash surrender value of his life insurance policy and the $7,000 equity in his house, among other things. At the end of the first month, "I sold twenty-five cars and was $13,956.96 in the hole, and that's where I started. That was a turning point in my life," he says.

Pattison implemented a particularly brutal incentive scheme for his salesmen. He would fire the one with the lowest production each month — hardly a management system in accord with Christian charity. But when asked, Pattison shot back at me: "What's charity? Taking care of the sick, the helpless? Or carrying people who aren't very good at what they are doing? I did those guys I fired a favour. They weren't very good at selling cars and were probably better off selling shoes or fixing cars. Letting someone fool themselves or paying them for doing very little is not charity."

Pattison met his wife, Mary, at church camp when he was only thirteen. He married her when he turned twenty-three. Their three children are grown and married. One daughter is a music teacher, another is in the insurance business, and his son works at the Bank of British Columbia. Pattison and his wife still live on the same street in the same modest frame home they bought in 1968. But they also have a home in Palm Springs and a $1.5-million, eighty-five-foot yacht called *Nova Springs*, with four staterooms, three full bathrooms, and a full-scale electric organ.

"I've been on that boat one night in the past eighteen months," says Pattison, who works twelve hours a day, travelling the world in his $2-million Lear jet. He never stops for lunch, and does not drink or smoke. Even though his business affairs take him away constantly from idyllic Vancouver, he is always home on weekends, working on Saturdays and going to church on Sundays.

Because his affairs are scattered everywhere, he has three television screens in his den and watches three channels at once. He also wears three watches on his wrist, set at New York time, Vancouver time, and the time zone of whatever city he's in. He devours business publications, reading at least five newspapers daily and half a dozen magazines a week.

Pattison still looks like the consummate used-car salesman: plenty of checks, stripes, and ultrasuede. His office is decorated in his favorite colours: powder blue, red, and gold. While he pursues worldly wealth, riches have always taken a back seat to Pattison's religion. He usually attends Glad Tidings Temple on Fraser Street, a Pentecostal Assembly in Vancouver's east end, sometimes twice on a Sunday: once to worship and once to perform, playing the trumpet accompanying hymns. He does not belong to a specific church but tithes, giving 10 per cent of his personal income and 10 per cent of his company's profits to various Christian charities. In 1984, he and some others donated $1 million to Glad Tidings. Pattison is probably the most generous supporter of *100 Huntley Street*, Canada's only home-grown evangelical television show. "I believe in God," he says when asked what his religion is.

As a young man Pattison worked as a volunteer in a mission, where goodly doses of food and religion were handed out to Vancouver's down-and-out. Ironically, Pattison was a dyed-in-the-wool socialist, while another contemporary, Dave Barrett, was a free-enterpriser. The tables reversed when Barrett became leader of the New Democratic Party in B.C. and eventually its premier, while Pattison became a ranking member of the right-wing Social Credit government's private-sector shadow cabinet.

Pattison nearly ran for the Socreds in several elections, but has stayed behind the scenes for the most part as a confidant to Premier Bill Bennett. However, he moved front and centre when he accepted the huge job of organizing and promoting Expo 86, the $2.5-billion world trade and entertainment extravaganza — a gigantic mega-project that created 9,250 jobs in B.C.'s depressed economy, employed 90,000 during its six-month run, and was counted on to attract billions to the province in tourist dollars.

Like a car salesman on a gigantic scale, Pattison logged hundreds of thousands of miles, snagging sponsors to build pavilions for the ambitious exposition or to subsidize attractions. One of his first corporate sponsors was General Motors, which gave a record $7.2 million — a company about which he once said, "I owe everything to General Motors." Even more significant, he convinced B.C.'s cranky construction unions to back off requirements that all site work be done by unionized contractors. In a rare instance of unity, the fair was completed on budget and on schedule by union and non-union labourers working side by side.

Pattison has a passion for the car business, and everything else has indeed flowed from that obsession. Moving from selling someone else's cars to peddling his own, in the mid-1960s he acquired more dealerships, a recreational vehicle manufacturing company and its sales outlets, and a car leasing operation in Toronto. Now he is the country's biggest automobile dealer, with five General Motors and Toyota franchises and nine dealerships.

In the 1970s, he bought into another form of transportation: he began accumulating nearly bankrupt bush pilot operations. Out of the ashes of five such organizations, he formed AirBC, now the country's fourth-largest airline, serving the remote forestry and mining communities of the province. From transportation, he parlayed more childhood experiences into the big leagues of high finance.

Before he began selling cars at nineteen, Pattison had applied for a job at Neon Products of Canada, a conservative Vancouver company that sold or leased billboard space. "They told me I was too young and too small," he recalled in an interview. In 1967, he snuck up on the company and took it over — almost twenty years to the day after he had been refused a job.

The sneak attack was orchestrated by a few Toronto brokers and financed by the Royal Bank of Canada. The cash takeover offer succeeded and Pattison

ended up with controlling interest. The chairman of Neon was caught un-
awares, even though he happened to be a director of the Royal Bank. Neon
owned a mixed bag of assets, against which Pattison began to borrow immediately in order to make other acquisitions. He also issued more treasury shares
to pay for new companies. Along the way, the company became Neonex and,
in 1977, the Jim Pattison Group. That was the year he bought out all his other
shareholders.

It was a brilliant manoeuvre. The year before, Neonex had nearly $300 mil-
lion a year in sales and was growing by leaps and bounds. The market for
Neonex's shares had been softened by some Pattison-inspired failures. It had
attempted to buy control of Maple Leaf Mills, in a bold share swap, but failed
when its own shares plummeted. It also lost money on a catalogue store
scheme, a carpeting business, and a WHA hockey franchise. There were far
more successes, but the bad publicity enabled Pattison to pay 75 cents for
every dollar of Neonex's assets.

Neonex's greatest holdings were its sign businesses, with a virtual monopoly in billboards, bulletins, back-lit signs, and bus shelter advertising space
in sixty Canadian cities. In all, it has nearly 70,000 signs leased throughout
North America.

Such a stranglehold on the advertising business landed Pattison companies
in the soup. In 1984, his sign companies were charged with conspiracy to
lessen competition, and in 1985, they pleaded guilty, as did two other
"competitors" who had conspired to carve up the country into unofficial
franchises in order to avoid competing against each other in price. The court
levied a total of $700,000 in fines on Pattison's companies and the others —
an all-time Canadian record under the Combines Investigation Act.

"The charges were against a company, and I bought it after they were laid,"
says Pattison. Less troublesome and more lucrative has been his entry into the
food business. In 1977, he branched out and bought Crush International Ltd.
In 1981, he sold the rights to use and make Orange Crush and other soft drinks
outside Canada for a profit of $53 million, but retained the Canadian rights to
Crush, Hires, and other soft drinks.

The profits from the sale became the grub-stake for sophisticated stock
market transactions, called arbitrage, at a brokerage in the Cayman Islands,
and for starting a Swiss banking operation that deals in Eurobonds. Pattison
has plowed the rest into other parts of the food business, with the biggest stake
in food retailing. He owns a rural discount supermarket chain called

Overwaitea Foods and an urban version called Save-On-Foods — the first chain to break the Sunday-closing tradition.

While he does not flinch when one of his companies breaks with his own religious beliefs, Pattison subscribes to Scripture in his overall strategy. Heeding the Bible, which warns that there are seven bad years for every seven good ones, Pattison has saved during good times and ridden out the bad. During the recession of the early 1980s, he imposed severe restraints on his companies. In 1982, Pattison gave employees at his airline an ultimatum, threatening to shut down service unless employees agreed to a five-year no-strike contract and other concessions. Overall, some 1,000 out of 8,000 workers at Pattison companies were laid off. Those who remained had benefits cut in half, holidays chopped by 25 per cent, and workdays extended by thirty minutes daily. Executives turned in their Cadillacs for Chevrolets, and Pattison sold his corporate jet and flew economy.

This retrenchment enabled him to embark on a shopping spree once things began to turn around in 1983, and the empire is growing once more. But the future is cloudy. He has purposely kept the next generation of Pattisons out of his business affairs because he fears stifling non-family executives. He is building something for others to enjoy. He is not building a dynasty. Serving God and mankind and having a little fun or challenge in the meantime is what Jimmy Pattison is all about. And where the money goes is beside the point: this Bible-thumping businessman may be a self-made man, but he worships everyone's Creator.

THE BENTLEYS

PETER BENTLEY is Central Casting's version of a tycoon: tall, handsome, in fine physical shape, and exceedingly open and engaging. His splendid corner office is decorated in forest-green, with rich wood panelling and moss-green suede couches, overlooking Vancouver's snow-capped and silent sentinels. Beyond the snow-blanketed mountains at the coast is Whistler Mountain, a resort he helped found.

Bentley is a forestry tycoon, heading a family empire called Canfor Ltd., which also includes the country's largest shipyards, an oil company, a chemical firm, and other assets. He is one of the aristocrats of Canadian business and sits on more than a dozen blue-ribbon boards. He's not a part of the flamboyant Vancouver social set, led by stockbroker Peter Brown and former used-car salesman Jimmy Pattison. They do good works for the provincial government in return for healthy influence, functioning as a shadow cabinet from the private sector. Bentley is neither nouveau riche nor provincial.

He and his family are transplanted "old" money, and their business interests are international. When you are in the big leagues and one of the world's biggest exporters of lumber and pulp, events in Washington and Stockholm affect your future more than anything going on in Victoria, B.C. Bentley has had titled Europeans on his board, and has served on theirs. He has entered into countless partnerships with English and German firms, all to grab a bigger slice of the lucrative American pie.

Like so many founders of Canada's dynasties, Bentley's mother and father came from families that were among Europe's most successful industrialists and were forced to flee Hitler's storm-troopers. Jewish at the time, the family left its native Austria the day the Germans invaded it, in the summer of 1938, when Peter was eight years old. With a sizeable grub-stake of $200,000, thanks to Swiss bank accounts, the family eventually immigrated to Vancouver. There, with the blessing and financial support of the city, Peter's father, Leopold Bentley, and uncle, John Prentice, set up shop immediately, opening a veneer factory with twenty-eight employees.

In only four decades, they have created one of Canada's biggest family empires, with well over a billion dollars of assets and 14,000 employees. Canfor is the world's biggest lumber company, exporting nearly 1.3 billion board-feet a year, enough lumber to stretch from here to the moon. Peter, an only child, heads the family firm as its president.

Canfor also produces pulp, and as if running all of that weren't enough, Peter Bentley has "moonlighted" for twenty years by owning the franchise to sell BMWs and Audis in Canada, a sideline that grosses nearly $100 million a year.

Times became tough in the timber business during the early 1980s, because of a glut of lumber on the market and the recession. Canfor, once known in B.C. forestry circles as "the mint," had losses piled as high as a Douglas fir. Between 1982 and 1984 it lost $156.7 million. To stem losses, the family sold one-third of the company to the public in 1983 for $141 million and used the money to pay off huge loans. It also shed its marginally profitable $500-million trust company business and control over Versatile, a Winnipeg manufacturer.

Bentley and his wife, Sheila, raised their five children in a house on a cliff overlooking Howe Sound and the University of British Columbia. They also have a home in Palm Springs, where they enjoy golfing during the winters. Of their four daughters and one son, only the oldest daughter, married with two children, works at Canfor.

Bentley's uncle has two daughters, neither of whom is involved in the forestry business. One is a housewife and the other is a teacher. Shares are divided equally between the Prentices and the Bentleys, with each family owning 32.5 per cent of Canfor's equity.

Bentley took over the reins as Canfor's president in 1975. He is a devoted executive. His workday usually begins at eight in the morning and goes on until six. "I usually take stuff home with me," he says.

The family knew nothing about forestry when it arrived. Leopold's family had dairy and sugar operations in Czechoslovakia and Austria while his wife's family, headed by her brother John, had textile mills. The two founders are very different: Prentice is an avid chess player, who travels extensively to competitions. Leopold Bentley is an outdoorsman, who loves to hunt for big game in Africa or at his hunting estate in Salzburg. He also is as avid a Mozart fan as he is a hockey fan, rarely missing Canucks games when he is in town. The family helped put up some of the millions of dollars that brought the National Hockey League franchise to Vancouver.

Balmy B.C. was a long way from home in 1938, when members of the family were forced to flee for their lives. "We left literally on the night of the day they walked in," Peter recalls. The family went to Zurich, then London, before crossing the Atlantic.

They chose Canada because Peter's father had visited the Rockies on a hunting and climbing trip the year before and had been impressed with the potential and the people. The families changed their names and religions as a way to super-assimilate in their adopted country. The Bentleys' surname was Blochbauer, which means farmer, and Prentice's name was Pick.

"'We have nothing to hide,' said my father, 'but we will anglicize our name because this is now home,'" Peter explains. "We became Anglicans when we came here. We were not particularly religious persons, not practising Jews. We never wore black caps on our heads.

"We were able to escape with some personal furnishings. Dad had problems. I remember him going to the British air ministry to give them plans. We'd bought an old Daimler auto works on the side of an airport. In 1937, we converted it into a textile plant, and it was the first windowless air-conditioned plant in Austria, thanks to U.S. equipment and British engineers. Dad knew the Germans planned to turn it into a Messerschmidt factory. And our factory became the first target attacked after North Africa was liberated. They flattened it."

From London they took a boat to Quebec City, where they rented a car and drove to British Columbia. They came with only two Canadian contacts — Leopold knew the wealthy Rogers family of B.C., through the sugar business, and a British official had given them a name at the Bank of Montreal.

"The Rogerses, in turn, introduced us to John Bene, a Hungarian, and he became a partner in our veneer plant. Once we started to buy timber, Bene wanted out because he wanted to be an industrialist, not a farmer. He began another company, which was the forerunner of Canadian Weldwood."

Like the Irvings on the east coast, Bentley and Prentice landed lucrative defence contracts to aid the war effort and began building airplane parts and wing assemblies at their veneer plant, thanks to short-term loans from the Bank of Montreal. Their first foray into forestry was in 1944, when they bought a logging subsidiary of International Harvester of Chicago. They believed softwood lumber and plywood were the building materials of the future, and the acquisition also assured them of a secure supply of logs for their veneer plant.

Meanwhile, Peter's father decided his son should study forestry. Young Peter was more jock than scholar. His family sent him to the exclusive St. Dredger's, where he met Austin Taylor, now chairman of McLeod Young Weir. In university the two majored in girls, bridge, and trophies. Both left before finishing, at the request of the dean.

Peter began working in a competitor's sawmill and going to night school to study accounting. In 1950, his father sent him to Chicago to learn the ropes by working for a lumber wholesaler. That was where being a jock helped. "I was a scratch golfer and the leading business people liked to play with good golfers, so I was introduced to Phil Swift, chairman of Continental Illinois. I met Chicago's finest and developed a whole bunch of new accounts for the lumberyard."

Also in 1950, the family bought its first pulp mill. "None of us knew anything about the pulp business. I went to New York to work with Perkins Goodwin, who were our worldwide sales agents. I went on calls with them to various people, and I learned what people were looking for," he says.

For the next few years, Bentley lived in Georgia and Texas, learning about paper mills, then in the United Kingdom, where he visited Scandinavian competitors and peddled lumber and pulp for Perkins Goodwin. In 1954, he entered the business full-time with his father and uncle.

That same year, his sports activities led to a lucrative sideline. He had seriously injured his back and had to wear a brace. Because he could not do most sports, he decided to take up trap shooting and car racing, driving a gull-wing 300 SL racer. His love for fast cars took him to a trade show where he fell in love with a BMW, not yet for sale in Canada.

He bought the floor model and also the franchise for Canada. He personally kept most of the three westernmost provinces for himself, but sold portions of the eastern Canadian franchise to Noranda Mines chairman Alf Powis and to Adam Zimmerman, chairman of the rival forestry giant MacMillan Bloedel, among others. In 1985, after twenty years, the franchise was purchased back by BMW. Sales tipped $94.6 million.

Canfor also diversified; in 1974, it bought 51 per cent of Cornat Industries, now known as Versatile, for $17.2 million. The investment was a bid to break away from the boom-and-bust cycles of forestry and own something that would help the family ride out recessions. By 1985, it had sold out for a healthy profit of nearly $100 million, in two lots.

In 1975, Peter Bentley took over as Canfor's president. Ron Longstaffe, four years younger and married to one of Prentice's daughters, became executive vice president. The family prospered until the 1980s; today the lumber and pulp business is plagued worldwide with protectionism, tough competition, and increasing costs.

"We've had a bad earnings record since 1982 because we have grown so rapidly from $200 million in revenues to $1 billion in sales as a result of acquisitions, internal growth, and inflation. High interest rates hurt because we got into debt to modernize our mills."

Canfor is not out of the woods yet, says Montreal investment counsellor Stephen Jarislowsky. "I think they are ruining the company."

Whatever happens, this family's future is firmly rooted in the treed wealth of British Columbia; it needs an end to the vagaries of world economics and a switch to unfettered, free trade. As for the family's influence on events, here or abroad, Peter Bentley is quite philosophical: "Only politicians and policemen have power. The rest of us have responsibilities."

2
PEOPLE'S CAPITALISM

A ROMAN CATHOLIC priest in remote Rouyn, Que., sprinkles holy water, blessing a new automatic teller machine installed by a credit union, known as a caisse populaire. Bob White leads his Canadian auto workers out of the international union. Nearly $1 out of every $2 in Canada is spent by governments or Crown corporations.

Seemingly isolated economic facts, they are all manifestations of Canada's long war against concentration of economic power. It is a war with religious overtones, as priests bless machines and Canadian leaders preach against economic tyrannies such as foreign ownership, foreign-controlled unions, and marketplace bullies in Toronto or New York. The call to arms has led to Canada's unique "mixed" economy, with nearly 1,000 Crown corporations. Besides government policies and huge public enterprises, Canadians have forged other powerful weapons for the fight, such as unions, heritage funds, credit unions, regional banks, ownership curbs, tariffs, pension schemes, marketing boards, and various types of co-operatives.

In essence, Canada's economic history has been a war against economic colonialism and concentration of power. It reflects a relatively small nation's desire to control its own financial destiny, and it has led to populist-inspired intervention. Some call it socialism, but it could also be dubbed people's capitalism.

The enemies have been varied: from Yanks and banks to grain traders, Bay Street, foreign multinationals, or central Canada. The West, Quebec, and Nova Scotia have undertaken a number of ventures to counteract the concentration of financial power in Toronto. The Quiet Revolution was also part of a lengthy battle against the concentration of ownership in Quebec's minority of

198

Westmount Rhodesians, those anglo tycoons who inhabited Montreal's St. James Street and owned most of the province's assets. Ottawa, in turn, has fought to protect Ontario's major industries from concentrations of power outside the country by curbing foreign competition, foreign ownership, and foreign takeovers.

Recent events are simply a repeat of that first skirmish against concentration, when the "enemies" were huge U.S. railways and north–south trading routes that threatened independence. To fight them, the government bought land from the Hudson's Bay Company and guaranteed loans to build the Canadian Pacific Railway, nearly bankrupting the tiny new nation. Next, a battle was joined against the Yankee traders poised to buy out the entire country or flood us with imports. That invasion was fended off with tariffs, ownership barriers like the Foreign Investment Review Agency, and special bilateral deals like the Auto Pact to protect jobs at home.

Some of these skirmishes have had nothing to do with fighting concentration, but have been merely the result of regional rivalry: hinterland versus heartland. However, all too often Canadian leaders have had to take up arms — in the absence of effective combines laws — to curb marketplace bullies or to nurture home-grown enterprise and develop the country when faceless financiers in Toronto, New York, or London were uninterested.

The battle against concentration feeds Canada's growing union movement, putting Canada out of step with its anglo cousins, the United States and the United Kingdom. Because so much is controlled by so few, whether domestic or foreign-owned, large impersonal conglomerates beget large unions. In Canada, membership continues to grow. By 1985, union membership in Canada had swelled to 36 per cent of the workforce while union membership declined slightly in Britain and continued to fall in the U.S., from 36 per cent in 1945 to 18 per cent today. Symptomatic of the fight against concentration of power, in this case against huge foreign unions, was the move by charismatic Canadian labour leader Bob White to pull his flock out of the United Auto Workers in 1985. And everybody thinks God is on his side.

The universal distaste for concentration of power, in all its manifestations, explains why battles have been joined by Canadian leaders of all political stripes, from Tories like Alberta's Peter Lougheed to Liberals like Pierre Trudeau or socialists like Saskatchewan's Allan Blakeney and Parti Québécois architect Jacques Parizeau. Even ultra-conservatives like B.C. premier Bill Bennett have intervened directly in the marketplace. In 1980, he became the

first Canadian leader to scuttle a takeover by declaring "B.C. is not for sale";
he threatened Canadian Pacific into backing off a takeover bid for MacMillan
Bloedel, the Vancouver forestry giant. While that gambit worked, MacMillan
was eventually absorbed into the gigantic Toronto-based Edper empire of
Peter and Edward Bronfman.

Unfortunately, the way in which the war has been waged has created other
problems. Fighting foreign ownership has led to increased concentration at
home. Policies have often been ham-fisted, riding roughshod over the rights
of both Canadian private-sector players and consumers. The playing field is
not level because Crown corporations do not have to play by the same rules.
More importantly, however, the politicians have girded for battle by gaining
access to far too much cash in the form of Canadian savings, invested in
public and private pension schemes. This has meant the savings of ordinary
Canadians have been used too often as open-ended slush funds: money spent
to win votes as well as to create beneficial economic activity.

The result of this warfare is that Canadians have one of the highest per-
capita debt loads in the world: by September 1985, our federal government
owed $213 billion; the provinces, $116 billion; the municipalities, $30
billion; federal enterprises, $30 billion; provincial enterprises, $99 billion
(including hydro utilities); and local enterprises (such as hydro distributors),
$2 billion. That totals a staggering $490 billion, equivalent to $18,845 for
every man, woman, and child in the country.

Every year, all levels of government continue to rack up even more debts,
as does the federal government through hidden liabilities such as civil servant
pensions, soft loans to Third World countries, and loan guarantees. Most
worrisome is the fact that nearly $100 billion of this is owed externally to
foreign investors, an amount equivalent to Mexico's external debt.

By comparison, the U.S. federal debt is only four times higher than
Ottawa's, or $1 trillion, even though its economy is at least twelve times
larger. In addition, U.S. states and municipalities have far more controls on
their spending, and only 40 per cent have run up deficits.

While the fight against concentration may have been beneficial in many
ways, it has often cost the country dearly. Politicians all too frequently think
politically, not economically. The feather-bedding is ferocious, and government enterprises have often thrashed around like marketplace bullies, above
the law and entitled to extra favours from their masters. This, in turn, has
frightened off both foreign and domestic private-sector participants, creating a

vacuum into which even more public enterprise must leap.

While the cost and some tactics of Canada's fight have gotten out of hand, the war has been one of the few means by which Canada has kept from being left behind or left out — or from having to join the United States. It has prevented parts of the country from becoming mere economic colonies, selling raw materials and buying them back from Toronto or New York as finished goods, at vastly higher prices. The battles have been frequent and heated, and they have caused a great deal of pain. But they are the story of Canada.

Fighting the Winnipeg Grain Exchange

One of the first tyrannies against which Canadians struggled was the power of Winnipeg's grain exchange and the muscle of the big-time grain traders like the Gooderhams and the Richardsons, denizens of the handsome mansions along Winnipeg's Assiniboine River. At the turn of the century, the Winnipeg exchange was bigger than the Chicago Board of Trade, now the world's largest. The city and its tycoons thrived as the railway opened up the hinterland to world trade, making Canada the world's biggest exporter of wheat.

At around this time, producer co-operatives sprang up, organized by farmers eager to counteract the concentration of market power held by this handful of grain trading families. These co-ops increased competition — and prices — for farmers' grain and also allowed them to share in the profits of gathering and storage. And the existence of co-ops blunted somewhat the disastrous effects of the Depression.

Wheat became less valuable than sawdust on commodity exchanges in the 1930s, throwing farmers around the world off their land as their banks foreclosed. But by 1934, Canada's organized farmers were able to depose the exchange and the grain traders, which suddenly had to compete with the Canadian Wheat Board, set up by the Tories. As an income support scheme, the Wheat Board would buy wheat at inflated prices in order to prop up Western farmers, then store it until prices improved or sell it at a loss. In the mid-1940s, the Liberals made the Wheat Board a legalized monopoly and the country's sole buyer of wheat.

Income support was not the only reform needed. At the same time, credit unions and government lending agencies grew in response to banks and insurance companies who held farm mortgages.

The legacy is that some of Canada's largest corporations are agri-monoliths. The Wheat Board is Canada's twelfth-biggest corporation, with sales in 1985 of $5 billion. The next-largest agribusiness is the Saskatchewan Wheat Pool, with $2.46 billion in sales; it is followed by Alberta's with $1.5 billion; Federated Co-operatives with $1.359 billion; the United Grain Growers with $1.279 billion; Co-opérative fédérée and Agropur co-opérative agro-alimentaire in Quebec with $1.156 billion; Manitoba Pool Elevators with $617 million; and the United Co-operatives of Ontario with $537 million.

Collectively, these agricultural forms of people's capitalism sold roughly $14.5 billion in products in 1985, making them Canada's third-largest private-sector company, just a notch in sales below Canadian Pacific and General Motors of Canada Ltd. Collectively, they are nearly as large as the world's biggest grain trader, Cargill of Minneapolis, and they would rank as the twenty-fifth-largest company in the United States.

Another latter-day manifestation of farm power is Canada's marketing boards, the so-called "four feathers" of eggs, milk, turkeys, and chickens. Set up by the Liberals in the 1960s and 1970s, these boards are also income stabilization schemes, designed to moderate the boom-and-bust nature of these four commodities. However, they have created a marketplace tyranny of their own, says Consumers' Association of Canada spokesman Bob Kerton, an economics professor at Waterloo University. He says marketing boards subsidize inefficient producers and cost consumers hundreds of millions of dollars each year as a result. His association wants them dismantled.

Canadian farmers also flexed their financial muscles against big marketplace bullies when their producer co-ops led to the country's first retail co-operative, called Federated Co-operatives, in Regina. It was begun in the 1920s to counter oil company concentration. "It started as a reply to Imperial Oil and British American [which became Gulf Canada], which had refineries here. It was an oil cartel and farmers felt gouged. The co-op began as an oil supplier and then moved into groceries," says former Saskatchewan premier Allan Blakeney.

By 1928, Federated had spread to all four Western provinces, where it has taken root to various degrees. In Alberta, for instance, the only competitor against the American-owned Safeway grocery chain has been the Calgary Co-op. A remarkable chain only three decades old, it is five times larger than any other non-profit retailer in North America and is Canada's fourth-largest grocery store chain, with $350 million in annual sales.

"We started in 1956 by taking over a losing store, because we thought the farmers were still consumers when it came to buying foodstuffs," says Gordon

Barker, its chairman and founder. By 1986, it owned twelve shopping malls in the city and seventeen stores selling food, including meat and produce, its own no-name brands, hardware, feed, and dry goods. In most malls, the co-op leases space to its own chain of thirteen drugstores, to affiliated credit unions, and to its own chain of co-op gasoline stations.

Co-op families are almost religious about patronizing the chain; they shop there for everything from soup to gasoline to drugs, dungarees, and dimmer switches. Its spotless, spartan stores hum with success, and square footage sales are so impressive that the Japanese have made a number of recent missions to study its techniques.

"They come here to see what we have done. Our stores are considerably more efficient. We have sales of $800 per square foot, compared with the average of $400 per square foot. We have 40 per cent of the city's food business, while in Japan, co-ops are huge with sales of $30 billion a year, but they only account for 2 per cent of the total business. They are interested in how we distribute petroleum, how we package our co-op food label," says Barker.

Members join for $1 and earn dividends thereafter. In 1985, a family that spent $6,000 on groceries, clothing, hardware, drugs, and gasoline would have gotten a $200 rebate, nearly two weeks' expenditure. In the first year, the family would get a cheque for about one-third of the amount and the rest would be applied as "equity ownership" until $400 was accumulated. After that, full cash rebates are handed out annually and equity, plus interest, accumulates.

Battling the Big Banks

As producer and consumer co-ops spread throughout the country, Canada's credit union movement spread rapidly to counteract the power of the Montreal and Toronto banks, foreclosing on farmers. Banking is very concentrated in Canada, and the big five have evolved into enormous branch operations, protected from foreign rivals and foreign takeovers. The result is few choices as well as abuses, both real and imagined.

By far the biggest credit union movement began at the turn of the century in rural Quebec with the help of the Roman Catholic church. Few realize that caisses populaires have quietly grown to become the country's eighth-largest financial institution, with some $20 billion in assets. The Quebec network, called the Fédération de Québec des unions régionales de caisses populaires Desjardins, was started in January 1901 by Alphonse Desjardins in Quebec City.

In all, some fourteen large credit union chains, mostly in Quebec and western Canada, are among the country's 100 largest financial institutions. Their combined assets total $28 billion, equivalent to the sixth-largest financial institution in Canada.

The Desjardins empire is housed in a $250-million Montreal headquarters, called Place Desjardins, owned jointly with the province. The sprawling financial network also includes a life insurance company, a general insurance company, a trust company called Fiducie de Québec, a hotel, other real estate, and an investment portfolio that controls Vachon Cakes and SICO Paint Co., among others.

Caisses are generally named after the local Catholic parishes where they were nurtured. There are about 2,400, ranging in size from $3 million in assets to one in Hull, with $130 million. By 1985, the caisses had captured half of Quebec's residential mortgage market and about 40 per cent of its personal loans business.

Like the Calgary Co-op, the movement has an almost socio-religious meaning for its members. "We are not political, not péquistes, not Liberal. We are Desjardins," says Gaeton Couture, vice president of the Caisses populaires Desjardins in Montreal, one of eleven federations representing the 2,400 caisses. "The Desjardins movement started because the banks were thieves. Our customers own the caisses, and it costs $5 to join. When they leave, they get interest on the $5, the $5 back, and profits. It is up to each caisse to share its yearly profits. Some have paid dividends of up to two months' reimbursement on a mortgage. Others have added 5 per cent more interest payable on term deposits. The church has a great deal to do with it. Look at the twenty-five founding members of most caisses and the priest will be on the list."

Each caisse has its own board of unpaid directors. Every year, all customer-owners are invited to an annual general meeting, often held in the caisse's basement, to elect their board. Unlike credit unions elsewhere, each caisse has to join the Desjardins umbrella group, giving them access to expertise the big banks enjoy, combined with discipline. Every Friday, the confederation's eleven federations recommend interest rates to their caisses. Since 1984, a local branch has had to seek its federation's approval to make a loan exceeding $175,000. Federations recommend asset mixes: how many longer-term loans or mortgages should be made in proportion to the length of term deposits. Federations must approve managers and can step in if there are problems.

Such rules explain why Quebec's caisse movement is unique. Its centralized system of controls, also called unit banking, has prevented the types of abuses found elsewhere in North America. It has also allowed these caisses to grow and be more innovative than others. Customers enjoy the same economies of scale and convenience they realize when dealing with huge chartered banks, because deposits and withdrawals can be made at any one of the caisses in the province. As for innovations, these caisses introduced the first computerized automatic teller machines in Canada as well as the first weekly mortgage payment scheme, allowing homeowners to pay off their mortgages in two-thirds the time it takes through conventional, monthly mortgages.

The centralized nature of the caisse also prevented some of the other problems facing smaller, regional financial institutions. In 1981, because of the recession and the collapse in house prices in Quebec, nearly 200 caisses were in trouble. They not only were losing money, but were suffering from a mismatch of assets, meaning that the amounts lent out as loans or mortgages were for longer terms at lower interest rates than the money "borrowed" by the caisse from depositors. However, management controls were imposed and the units did not fail because the system as a whole was strong.

While the caisses populaires fought one of the first battles against the big banks in Canada, governments over the years have also moved directly to control or create lending institutions, the economy's crucial levers. By 1982, the Economic Council of Canada estimated, governments ranked second to the chartered banks among financial entities, with 18.1 per cent of all assets, compared with the banks' 50 per cent. That calculation included enterprises such as the Canada Mortgage and Housing Corp., the Export Development Corp., the Farm Credit Corp., Alberta's Treasury Branches and Home Mortgage Corp., the Federal Business Development Bank, the Province of Ontario Savings Office, and others.

Control by politicians over such a huge amount of capital is worrisome if it is used for strictly political ends or to run up reckless deficits that would not otherwise be possible. A good example of political persuasion without financial expertise was the fate of the Northland Bank and the Canadian Commercial Bank, which went bust in 1985, costing taxpayers $3 billion.

The banks were established because the Alberta government wished to cultivate home-grown financial institutions, in order to balance the power of Eastern banks. The two were born during the heady days of the oil boom in the late 1970s. Alberta and Ottawa encouraged pensions and co-ops to contribute tens of millions of dollars to give them a start. Among initial shareholders and depositors were the Alberta teachers' superannuation funds, Alberta and federal civil service pension funds, a number of Western co-ops, as well as the funds of employees working for federal Crown corporations such as Canadian National Railways, Air Canada, and others.

The result was a collection of passive investors, some totally naive about running banks. They exercised little control over the two banks' runaway managements, who used questionable accounting principles to inflate profits quickly and questionable lending practices to boost assets quickly. Directors' attendance records for the Canadian Commercial Bank show that elderly teachers, politicians, and political hacks were on the boards, but attendance was poor.

The banks were a case of political push without follow-through. Years before their bankruptcies, the two banks were in trouble. Astute directors such as oilmen Bill Siebens and Jack Pierce resigned in disgust from the Northland and Canadian Commercial boards respectively. Siebens wrote a detailed, five-page letter of resignation from the Northland board outlining serious concerns that had been ignored by the board, its auditors, and federal regulators.

Even more seriously, Pierce says that in 1979 he took his concerns about the Canadian Commercial Bank and its absentee chairman Howard Eaton directly to Chip Collins, Peter Lougheed's right-hand man and top civil servant. Pierce says he told Collins he was concerned that fees due to the bank were possibly being skimmed in Europe. Pierce does not believe his allegations were ever checked. Collins, under questioning in the legislature, was reported to have said he could not remember the conversation.

Added to the recipe for disaster were individuals like Howard Eaton who ran the banks into the proverbial ground through shoddy management practices. When all was said and done, nearly one-third of the Canadian Commercial Bank's loans were bad, according to former inspector of banks William Kennett, compared with a more tolerable bad loan average of 1 or 2 per cent for the other Canadian banks. Eaton left the CCB after he became involved in deals with Leonard Rosenberg, who intended to take it over and combine it with Crown Trust and Greymac Trust, later seized, along with Seaway Trust, by the province of Ontario over alleged wrongdoings.

In March 1985, at the insistence of Alberta, Ottawa agreed to bail out the banks, but by September they were both beyond hope and the plug was pulled. At the same time, Ottawa announced it would cover all deposits, even those exceeding the Canada Deposit Insurance Corp. ceiling of $60,000.

Once again, this was smart politics but dumb economics, designed as it was to "repay" the co-ops, municipalities, and pension funds that had been almost pushed into investing in the banks and keeping deposits there. The country's first bank failures in more than sixty years were the direct result of misguided people's capitalism. The entire affair was political from its auspicious beginning to its tawdry end.

That battle ended in defeat, and others may follow. Equally fragile are a handful of other regional banks, such as the Bank of British Columbia, whose existence has been promoted by that province. A number of small credit unions, fostered by provinces, have also been suffering from regional economic downturns. In 1985, Alberta had to bail out its credit unions by lending them about $150 million.

Apart from Quebec's caisses populaires, where strict controls are in place, the majority of credit unions are poorly managed and dependent upon a few eggs in a few baskets. But they persist, fighting the good fight against the big banks.

Battling the Brokers

Like Desjardins supporters, Jacques Parizeau grew up distrusting big banks and investment bankers — perhaps for good reason. He remembers Rue St-Jacques when it was St. James Street, and its bankers and brokers were bullies. "It was amazing the power those guys had," mused Parizeau, who quit in 1984 after eight years as finance minister for the Parti Québécois. "The usual practice was to dump $50 million worth of Quebec bonds onto markets after a provincial election and frighten stiff new governments. They would be in a panic, in 1962, 1966, and 1970. In the first few months of any new provincial government, the spreads between Ontario and Quebec bonds would be usually 35 to 40 basis points [a difference in interest rates of 3.5 to 4 per cent]. The record was 120 basis points with Bourassa in early 1970, even before the trouble [the FLQ crisis in October 1970]. I saw ministers of finance enter the boardrooms of these guys and come out mesmerized."

Whether Quebec's banking enemies were real or imagined is no longer important. Parizeau's first order of business was to rid the government of the bullies of St. James Street. In the 1960s, as financial adviser to provincial premiers, Parizeau had pushed to create one of the cornerstones of Quebec's strategy, its closeted bid for independence: the Caisse de dépôt et placement du Québec. With $20 billion by 1985, it is a heritage fund for francophones and North America's fifth-largest pool of capital, only slightly behind the first-place California teachers' pension fund.

Naturally, its creation was bitterly fought. The creation of the Caisse de dépôt began in the early 1960s in Ottawa, with the desire to create the Canada Pension Plan to supplement old age pensions, administered by governments but paid for by workers and their employers. But the debate centred on whether the plan should be a pay-as-you-go plan, as exists in the U.S., or a "fully funded" plan. Pay-as-you-go plans are designed so that contributions coming in match benefits going out. Fully funded plans operate as do private-sector plans, creating giant pools of capital, invested to pay future benefits and create some economic spin-off benefits in the meantime.

As a master economist — with a PhD from the London School of Economics — Parizeau could foresee the economic power of the fund. He convinced Quebec premier Jean Lesage that the fund was a valuable instrument, and Lesage pushed the federal government for acceptance. "We were refused for four years by the federal government. The unofficial representatives of St. James Street in the government fought tooth and nail against a fully funded plan. Realizing the money involved, Lesage put his fist on the table, and said we would go for it. We ended up with a typical Canadian compromise — a partly capitalized fund [after negotiating this with Ottawa and the other provinces]."

Thus were born the Canada and Quebec pension plans, which would become principal weapons in the war against foreign and domestic concentrations of power. The government required employers to match employees' contributions dollar for dollar, then all proceeds would be lent to provinces, in proportion to contributions, to finance schools, hospitals, and roads. Unlike the others, Quebec would collect Quebec Pension Plan contributions and manage the funds itself, investing them in stock markets as well as lending them to the province to build schools, hospitals, and roads.

"This was a Quebec fund administered in Quebec by a plan we could control, to use as one of the levers [of public policy]. At the outset, the Caisse was the way to assure financing automatically for Quebec government bonds and the way to finance private business. Twenty years later, with all these levers, a peculiar kind of economic strategy has appeared. Most Quebec Crown corporations are not against working with private interests — and are involved in joint ventures. There's a hell of a lot of mixed enterprise, and there's nothing like it in North America."

The Caisse de dépôt was established in 1966 with its first chairman, Claude Prieur, former assistant treasurer of Sun Life Assurance and a former brigadier general in the Canadian Forces. Initially, the Caisse was created to buy Quebec's bonds and liberate its politicians from the whims of Westmount bankers. "That saved us from securities markets," says Parizeau. Now it's an awesome player. Every day, about $5 million of pension contributions, automobile insurance premiums, and workers' compensation premiums fall into the Caisse's massive treasury. It is the largest stock market player in Canada, with stakes in more than 100 of Canada's largest corporations, worth $6 billion. It also holds another $14 billion in provincial bonds and real estate.

Prieur established the Caisse's unique role, of facilitating and enhancing the concentration of wealth in the hands of Quebeckers, with the creation of Provigo. "Provigo is the largest food retailer in Canada, a merger of three small operations. The Caisse became the largest shareholder in each, and the chairman had three-cornered lunches for quite a while. The Caisse talked them into merging," says Parizeau.

Since then, the Caisse has facilitated the repatriation of many Quebec industries from Ontario, or "foreign" hands, and has also swung some trading to the Montreal Stock Exchange and away from Toronto's Bay Street. However, in 1980, the first trouble sign surfaced. Former federal and Quebec cabinet minister Eric Kierans quit the Caisse as a director because he said Quebeckers' savings were being improperly siphoned off to finance Quebec's deficits.

"The only power Quebec's minister of finance has is to ask questions," maintains Parizeau. "Of course, that also means the minister has the right to enter into any conversation. That is true. I often lunched with the Caisse's chairman, but I could not order that chap around. He is the only one of Quebec's civil servants who can only be thrown out by the vote of the House. And to remove him would trigger a Coyne affair." (The firing of James Coyne as governor of the Bank of Canada triggered a currency and political crisis in the 1960s.)

But even Parizeau began to see problems, and before leaving office he had drafted legislation to divide the Caisse into two separate funds. "It is too big," he said. "The City of Quebec tried to sell bonds to the Caisse and it said no. The bonds had to be withdrawn from the market. That's why I would have split it. It's too powerful. Everyone must do business with it. Even [Paul] Desmarais."

Others see the Caisse as economically inefficient. "The Caisse de dépôt is run poorly," says Stephen Jarislowsky, owner of Jarislowsky Fraser & Co. in Montreal, Canada's largest investment counsellor. "It holds too many Quebec bonds, doesn't sell during bad cycles, and has very little invested in U.S. securities, where the returns are greater. Most private portfolios have 10 per cent abroad."

Of all forms of people's capitalism, the Caisse de dépôt has been the most creative, influential, and fearsome. It propped up Quebec bonds even after the election of the Parti Québécois might have caused a panic in money markets over the province's paper markers. It helped to finance the $16-billion James Bay hydroelectric development in Northern Quebec during the 1970s. But it is also a good example of some of the abuses.

"Crown corporations are not efficient. Appointments to boards are so political that these directors of government enterprises are not the best brains, but politically important. Look at the head of CN, Air Canada, the Caisse de dépôt," says Bell Canada chairman Jean de Grandpré. "Do you think Mr. [Louis] Laberge [head of Quebec construction unions] ever managed $20 billion in pension funds before? It seems to me they could have had better representatives than the head of a labour union."

Headed by its $81,000-a-year chairman, Jean Campeau, the Caisse de dépôt has engineered corporate raids of questionable ethics and has the power to make or break businesses. It flaunted Ontario securities laws in the 1981 takeover of Domtar by the Quebec Crown corporation Société de financement by refusing to file insider trading reports. It was forbidden to trade in Ontario, but won a subsequent court case when it was found that the Caisse enjoyed special status and was exempted from Ontario securities laws.

In 1982, the Caisse similarly trampled over Montreal's Lorne Webster in a boardroom squeeze play to return Trust générale to francophone financier André Simard (a relative of Robert Bourassa), even though Webster had 51 per cent and Simard only 4 per cent of its shares. In essence, Simard had asked Webster to buy his majority interest years before and Webster kept him on as chairman of the board. They were still friends, or so Webster thought, but Simard discovered that the capital of the company had fallen below a certain amount, which suspended Webster's right to any votes.

Webster was voted out even though he owned the majority of shares. "I could have written a cheque right then and there for the capital that needed topping up, but they wouldn't let me," said Webster. Simard lobbied the board and enticed the Caisse to buy shares. Webster sold his shares two years later, refusing to be pressured into divesting just because he had lost control of the board.

The Caisse also helped engineer the capture of Noranda, with Peter and Edward Bronfman. While trampling over the wishes of some companies, it suddenly became a champion of minority shareholders' rights in 1985 by frustrating plans by Peter and Edward's cousins, Charles and Edgar Bronfman, to create restricted shares to protect their distillery giant, Seagram, from takeover. Similar plans by Southam in 1985 were scuppered by the Caisse and others, leading to a share swap deal with Torstar.

The Caisse need never fear unfriendly takeovers. Its potential power is so fearsome that in 1982 Pierre Trudeau's finance minister, Marc Lalonde, threatened Dome Petroleum's former chairman Jack Gallagher that if he accepted a penny of help from the Caisse, Ottawa would back out of its participation in Dome's initial bail-out proposal. This was followed a year later by proposed bill S-31, which was intended to limit individual ownership in transportation companies, amid concerns by CP over a possible takeover by a Desmarais-Caisse partnership. The bill was never passed, and Desmarais sold his CP shares in 1985.

Similarly, bad feelings have resulted within International Paper of New York City over a muscular manoeuvre by the Caisse that led to the sale of its Canadian subsidiary, Canadian International Paper, to CP. The subsidiary had "its financial problems so they went to see the Caisse de dépôt. It bought some stock in the parent company in the U.S. and forced it to build a plant in Sept-Îles," recalls an insider. The embittered company sold out to CP in 1981, and it has led the battle in the U.S. against Canadian lumber and forestry exports with uncharacteristic exuberance.

Forging the Financial Weapons

Canada did not industrialize until the Second World War. In order to catch up, the country needed capital, quickly. So Ottawa encouraged foreign investment and decided to encourage Canadian ownership, too, by restricting the investment activity of the country's pools of capital, such as insurance companies, pension funds, and banks, to keep the money here at home. Pensions were exempted from taxes, to enhance their accumulation of wealth, but they were not allowed to take over companies or to invest more than 10 per cent of their money outside Canada.

Those strictures provided huge amounts of capital with which to fuel solid, home-grown enterprise, and government enterprise, too. But because of a number of factors unique to Canada, the rule restricting pension investments in Canada has greatly enhanced concentration of power. It has given tycoons a chance to play takeover games with a vengeance, an economic activity that contributes nothing to the nation's wealth.

Decades later, the arsenal of takeover tools in the form of capital is indeed awesome. By 1985, public pension plans such as the Quebec and Canada pension plans and Alberta's Heritage Fund as well as private pension schemes totalled $238 billion, enough to buy 50 per cent of the shares of every company on the Toronto Stock Exchange. Pensions and insurance companies now dominate stock market activity. In 1985, such institutional investors bought or sold 55.6 per cent of all securities on the TSE, compared with 43.9 per cent in 1975 and 27.3 per cent in 1965. This will increase exponentially, as both public and private pensions grow at the rate of around $19 billion a year, nearly $60 million a day.

Pension power has increased as employees are forced to save for their old age. Because so much of Canada's workforce is unionized or employed by governments, the country's private pension plans are enormous. About 60 per cent of the workforce, or six million Canadians, contribute to private pension plans sponsored by their employers. The value of these reached $100 billion in 1985 for the first time in Canada's history. Pensions sold by insurance companies total another $21 billion.

The twenty largest private pensions had assets of $33 billion in 1985, equivalent in size to the country's largest corporation, Hydro-Québec, or three Imperial Oils. In all, there are some 16,000 private pension plans in Canada, but the biggest fifty hold two-thirds of the assets. The Ontario Municipal Employees Retirement System is the largest, with $4.3 billion in 1985; the funds of Canadian National Railways, Bell Canada, Canadian Pacific, Ontario Hydro, Hydro-Québec, Air Canada, Alcan, General Motors of Canada, Imperial Oil, Royal Bank, and the CBC, and the Hospitals of Ontario Pension Fund are each worth more than $1 billion. Soon there will be other billion-dollar players.

In addition, another $46 billion in "ghost" benefits is owed to civil servants working for the federal and Quebec governments and some other provincial governments. In these cases, employee contributions have never actually been set aside for investment, but have been automatically loaned to the governments involved — an open-ended and vast slush fund for politicians.

For those who do not work for governments or companies with private pension schemes, the government created registered retirement savings plans (RRSPs). By 1985, these totalled roughly $30 billion; they should grow spectacularly during this decade, by as much as 20 per cent annually, according to some estimates. Growth will soar because of revisions to tax policies in 1985, allowing considerably higher tax-free contributions.

These private savings are mostly invested in banks or trust companies, which often lend money to federal and provincial governments to finance their overweening appetites for capital. Similarly, the institutions finance governments in a big way.

The rule forbidding pensions to invest more than 10 per cent outside Canada has artificially inflated prices for securities, other assets, and real estate. They can afford to overpay and outbid everyone else for Canadian assets, and often do. "There has been a serious distortion, and Canadian equities are overpriced on a worldwide scale," says Stikeman Elliott lawyer Ed Waitzer, former vice president of the Toronto Stock Exchange. "Pensions are bidding against one another for a limited supply of companies, real estate, and other assets."

Most unfortunately, the 90-per-cent rule has fuelled the takeover game in the country. Instead of building factories, pipelines, dams, real estate projects, oilsands plants, and other massive schemes, pension money is often handed over to Canada's paper entrepreneurs who make takeover bids with it to buy common shares held by these same institutions in other companies.

To cap it all off, after a takeover, the takeover artists sell common or preferred shares in their own companies to these same institutions in order to pay for the transaction. In effect, Canadian institutions stuck in Canada are selling their stock in takeovers, then financing the takeovers by taking back what amounts to a mortgage. Not only is this an empty exercise in economic terms — costing jobs, not creating them — but it means that Canada's pensions are getting increasingly stuck with shares at inflated prices or shares in highly indebted takeover artists.

In Japan, by contrast, similar limits to pension or other investments outside the country have provided cheap financing to thousands of hard-working entrepreneurs with spectacular results. Canada, with a considerably smaller population, different cultural traditions, and few entrepreneurs, has allowed all this money to flow into the hands of paper entrepreneurs, not the real kind who build factories and economic wealth.

The restriction has also led pensions interested in U.S. assets to invest heavily in those conglomerates, such as Genstar, Imasco, Trizec, and scores of others, that have large holdings in the U.S., where opportunities are greater.

Indeed, the pension community is aware of this problem and has been pressing Ottawa for some time to make changes. The pension restrictions should be relaxed before the paper entrepreneurs buy everything, putting a bigger mortgage on corporate Canada. If it takes years, the price Canadians will have paid will be dear indeed. Restrictions on the flow of Canadian savings may have encouraged Canadian ownership, but they have also created an inordinate amount of paper entrepreneurship and concentration from which we suffer.

On another level, pension power concerns Winnipeg financier James Richardson, a former Liberal cabinet minister. "I think pension funds, and the fact that they don't pay taxes, are a form of concentration of ownership that poses some important questions for Canada. Who are the men running them? As long as the guys running them don't get too powerful in their own eyes, then they're good. Anything that gets too big has to be watched. Pensions could take over everything."

The Battle of Quebec

Thanks in part to the banking bullies, Parizeau says Quebeckers inherited a legacy of severe self-restraint from Maurice Duplessis. "After Duplessis was re-elected, he swore never to borrow from these guys again, and he devoted himself towards paying off the provincial debts. The result was few roads, few schools, few hospitals, but no debt." There was little in the way of a provincial economy. "A smatter of small business, and the rest was public-sector, inherited from Duplessis. It was tiny: a piece of Hydro-Québec, a sugar refinery, and the liquor board. That was that."

After the Second World War, Quebec's pre-eminence as the financial and industrial capital of Canada began to slip because of other unavoidable trends, which simultaneously reduced the economic power of New England south of the border. "The opening of the St. Lawrence Seaway made a profound difference to Montreal," says Parizeau. "It opened up the interior of the continent."

At the same time, Quebec's industries were aging and massive new reinvestment was needed to keep up with newer industries in Ontario and the U.S. The province did not cash in on the jobs and investment of the auto industry. Ontario did.

Ontario's "golden triangle" manufacturing base is merely the result of a three-cornered steelmakers' cartel bordered by Oshawa, Windsor, and Sault Ste. Marie, says Parizeau. Transportation costs within the triangle for minerals or flat steel were at a single, fixed rate. Transport costs for anything that left the triangle were 15 per cent higher. This was designed to even out the transportation costs among the three primary steelmakers: Stelco and Dofasco in Hamilton, removed from the iron ore fields in the north, and Algoma, north of Lake Superior.

This cost advantage landed Ontario the lion's share of the lucrative auto assembly plant locations. But it forced other provinces to create steel operations or to subsidize existing ones. To combat that marketplace concentration in Ontario, Quebec supported Sidbec, while Saskatchewan and Alberta supported Interprovincial Steel and Pipe Corp., and Nova Scotia supported Sysco.

In the 1950s, utilities were nationalized into Hydro-Québec. By the 1960s, almost 100 Crown corporations were established in Quebec, designed to buy back or provide capital — which had left for Toronto's Bay Street and other regions — to resource industries such as forestry, mining, asbestos, fishing, agriculture, and oil and gas.

In the early 1970s, after Parizeau and Quebec's politicians harnessed the savings of Quebeckers with the creation of the Caisse de dépôt, the province's hydro utility became a cornerstone of industrial strategy. Ready, willing, and able to buy bonds, the Caisse de dépôt provided funding for Robert Bourassa to embark on his ambitious $16-billion James Bay hydroelectric project. The massive development created tens of thousands of jobs in the province during its construction in the 1970s, and it also fostered new enterprises in Quebec.

"Hydro-Québec had procurement policies that singlehandedly produced a number of establishments in Quebec. For one thing, it would give suppliers five-year contracts, which would allow them to go to the bank and borrow the money to gear up," says Parizeau.

Of course, Bourassa's hydro scheme would have been a boondoggle if it had not been for the twelvefold increases during the 1970s in the price of oil, an alternative energy source. The high cost of the project, plus the expense of transmission across thousands of miles to southern markets, would have back-fired if the price of oil had been lower. However, the power ended up being cheaper than rival fuels, and Hydro's energy has been used to subsidize existing industries or attract new ones, such as the $200-million Pechiney aluminum smelter. "They are giving it away," says Manitoba premier Howard Pawley.

In 1976, the Parti Québécois was elected. What followed, thanks again in part to the constant capitalization of the Caisse de dépôt, was a tightrope act involving international financial markets. Undoubtedly, the province would not have kept its double-A credit rating without the type of self-financing scheme that had been set up. After all, financiers would have raised the ante, considering Parizeau's goal of breaking up the country.

During his time as Quebec finance minister, Parizeau also decided to take on Bay Street, embarking on a number of reforms of provincial financial institutions. He instituted the Quebec Savings Plan and generous tax write-offs for Quebec-based companies; he removed foreign ownership restrictions on brokers and let insurance and trust companies trade in stocks. Such reforms swelled the volume of trading on the Montreal Stock Exchange, as did the decision of the Caisse de dépôt to trade there, more or less exclusively.

Parizeau planned to let mutual insurance companies, owned by their policy-holders, become stock and bond brokers in Quebec securities. He was also going to let Quebec insurers take deposits and lend money to the public, act as trust companies, sell financial vehicles, buy subsidiaries in any type of business, and be foreign-owned. "The Toronto financial community was up in arms, accusing me of balkanizing. It was a bombshell," he admits. "Then I was ready with a similar bill for trust companies and revisions for caisses populaires. Let them get into everything. Then let the chartered banks get into everything later."

In fact, most of Parizeau's ideas were incorporated into a Green Paper on the reform of financial institutions in Canada, proposed by minister of state for finance Barbara McDougall in 1985. "I was glad of the moves I provoked. The money game for the first time will be open. The third step is to open up everything to the chartered banks," Parizeau says.

While he was tilting at other forms of concentration, Parizeau's biggest problem was to stem the outflow of economic power from his own province. Between 1976 and 1980, some 130,000 Quebeckers left, mostly anglophones disgusted with unilingualism and the goal of separation from Canada. This brain-drain robbed Quebec of both business talent and head offices, and culminated with the departure of gigantic Sun Life Assurance to Toronto. That move and hundreds more like it undoubtedly led Parizeau to shore up economic activity through stock market write-off schemes as well as by encouraging the Caisse de dépôt to buy large portions of every public corpora-tion with a Quebec head office and use moral suasion to keep them there.

Some of Parizeau's regional development schemes were duds, such as the takeover of the province's asbestos industry before lawsuits all but ruined that business. Another flop was the massive tax breaks given to Quebec's big textile industry to modernize operations. "We gave them eight years to modernize," he says. "They didn't, and the days are probably numbered for most of them."

Parizeau met financial force, no matter how concentrated, with political power. Faced with a collapsed housing industry because of high interest rates in 1981 and 1982, Parizeau used a French tradition of community involvement in rural Quebec to get things going again. "We asked construction unions to contribute 12.5 cents an hour and employers to match that for each hour worked. Then we called on financial institutions to shave off part of the cost, and municipalities, which have a direct interest in residential construction, for contributions," he says.

"Everyone pitched in: the National Bank and the Desjardins group. But the Bank of Montreal and other large chartered banks rebuffed the scheme and sent us to hell. They said, 'What will happen if all the provinces ask us to contribute to a similar scheme?' So we put a tax on their capital, and we raised a few million dollars from the big five banks towards it." That subsidized thousands of mortgages and resulted in Quebec leading the nation in housing starts. Taxes and schemes were eventually cancelled once they were no longer needed in 1984.

Playing hardball or running up massive deficits never worried Parizeau or his party. His goal was to rid Quebec of external economic concentrations and forge a truly independent marketplace there. "I remember what de Gaulle said about France's expensive nuclear program. 'I do not care if I throw every single weapon or reactor into the ocean after we are done. We will have modernized French industry.' Here in Canada, for instance, the Avro Arrow should never have been cancelled. We lost 5,000 engineers because of that. Unfortunately, Canadians too often have the mentality of shopkeepers."

Skirmishes in Saskatchewan

While Parizeau created Crown corporations and blessed procurement restrictions to offset Ontario's dominance, his Western counterparts were also combatting concentration and their own business bogeymen.

Soon after leaving Nova Scotia in the 1950s as a young lawyer, Allan Blakeney became convinced something had to be done about the fact that Saskatchewan was captive to cartels, Bay Street, and ugly foreign-owned

multinationals. "There were not three employers of more than 100 persons
outside the provincial government or co-ops." To reverse this, Blakeney, both
as a civil servant and as a politician, took some dramatic steps.

Saskatchewan's first move into industrial activity was in 1955, to combat a
cement monopoly controlled by Eastern interests. Blakeney recalls: "We were
upset about the monopoly of Canada Cement, its high prices in the West
compared with the East, because there was virtually no competition." So
Blakeney, then an adviser to the premier, bankrolled two entrepreneurs,
providing a provincial loan guarantee against a $7.5-million plant.

In 1960, Blakeney was elected to the legislature. Tommy Douglas was premier, and the two set up Interprovincial Steel and Pipe Corp., known as Ipsco.
Ipsco was designed to counteract marketplace concentration by Ontario's
three steelmakers, who charged identical prices for steel used in building
Canada's first natural gas pipeline during the 1950s as well as the country's
first oil pipeline. "We paid a great deal for steel, and prices were the same no
matter whether it was Dofasco, Algoma, or Stelco. However, rates to transport steel from Ontario to Vancouver were considerably less than to Regina
and Calgary. This was because transportation rates were adjusted to Vancouver, out of fears that water-borne steel transportation would allow the Japanese
to undercut. We were shafted because we were interprovincial captives."

The plan was to use the same two entrepreneurs who had started the cement
business to build a $16-million steel mill, with $10 million funded by provincially guaranteed bonds raised on Bay Street. However, the steelmakers held
sway on Bay Street and lobbying was intense. "It was difficult to sell. No big
houses would sell them. Even government-guaranteed bonds and the fact that
Saskatchewan had virtually no debts at that point didn't sell the bonds —
because Stelco must have told the big brokers not to touch it. Charles Gundy
of Wood Gundy would not touch it. Nobody would. Finally a small company,
no longer in existence, called Annett & Co. sold them. That made us decide to
hire some big Bay Street houses in 1962 and form a syndicate for future bond
sales in order to get some Bay Street clout," Blakeney recalled.

The cement and steel mills were run by the entrepreneurs — William Sharp
and Jack Nelles Turvey; they made fortunes, but hit some heavy weather even
after the financing was done for the steel mill. "Stelco tried to bust that plant
with price-cutting. It never cut its prices on lines Ipsco didn't produce, but
only on lines Ipsco produced. In 1961, when Ipsco needed more money, it

went to the Royal Bank. We were willing to guarantee the operation, but the bank was reluctant to lend anyway. I had to go to Toronto and talk to Earle McLaughlin, who was its chairman."

(Similarly, Nova Scotia bailed out Sydney Steel — Sysco — after its closing was announced in 1968, and the feds nationalized almost all of Cape Breton's industry, from coal to fisheries to heavy-water plants.)

Fresh from Ipsco's success, Saskatchewan then gave an American group a $50-million guarantee to build a $60-million pulp mill at Prince Albert. In 1971, Blakeney became premier and stepped up efforts to get Saskatchewan citizens an even bigger piece of the economic pie, particularly in the oil, uranium, and potash industries. Altogether he reinvested about $1 billion worth of the province's royalties from resources into Crown corporations, which have explored for new sources of supply or bought existing mines or oilfields.

The Saskatchewan Minerals Development Corp. discovered and now owns half of Key Lake, the world's largest and richest uranium mine, as well as half of Cigar Lake's uranium deposits, believed to be ten times richer. In 1974, Blakeney created Saskoil, forerunner of Ottawa's Petro-Canada, created in 1976. While creating Crown corporations to compete in the private sector, Blakeney also increased royalties and taxes to recapture some of his rivals' profits. Sometimes he was too heavy-handed in his approach, and in 1973 a windfall profits tax virtually drove away oil drilling for years.

In the case of potash, his heavy-handedness resulted in an official nationalization of much of the industry. When Blakeney took over, 85 per cent of the potash mines were foreign-owned and 15 per cent domestic. What began as a tax dispute ended up in massive public ownership. At the time, Noranda owned half a mine and Cominco one mine. "We had a spat. Potash prices went up spectacularly and they said the tax was too high. They sued us with success and we got together for a settlement. They reacted not only by litigating — which is fair ball — but by doing it in a way that was to be as provocative as possible.

"They started to impose production quotas and minimum prices and pro-rationing between 1969 and 1972 to save the industry from competition. We decided we were going to have to own a piece. The idea of a capital strike is silly. It's never justified. People get angry and that's the fertile ground: the idea of resource companies trying to defeat a government. We had a June election in 1975; we won and had another round of legal action. The war was still on. Then one day they all came in and sat down in the cabinet room and said, 'This is our position,' including Noranda and Cominco, who should have known better.

"In January 1976 we formed Potash Corp. of Saskatchewan in an attempt to get 50 per cent of the industry through joint ventures. We also had powers of expropriation in the legislation. Owners included Esmark [Swift meats, Chicago], Borax, the gigantic South African mining interests through Hudson Bay Mining and Smelting, and a French group called Duvall. Duvall and Swift offered to sell immediately." Prices paid were more than fair. Duvall had paid $70 million two and a half years before for its potash operation, and Saskatchewan bought these for $120 million. Now the province owns about 40 per cent of the potash industry and is the monopoly buyer, selling all local production worldwide through the Crown agency Canpotex.

All the while, Blakeney remained aware of the ultimate power of the private sector. "New Democrats don't want balanced budgets in order to be proper capitalists. It is so nobody can dictate your policies. Lévesque lost support because he had to back off contracts with the public service, because he was under pressure from financial organizations for his deficits. That is why in the case of potash we have been very careful financiers and careful to avoid huge debts." Most other Canadian governments have not been so careful.

Oil Wars in Alberta

While politics have encouraged governments to take economic excursions into inappropriate and unprofitable areas, very often interventionist actions have been more than called for. When Peter Lougheed became Alberta's premier in 1971, the province had a wealth of resources but was struggling financially, thanks to the lowest royalties in North America. Concentration of power among foreign-owned multinational oil companies was a problem, too: they had snapped up and were sitting smugly on all the best leases to drill on Crown lands, which constitute 80 per cent of Alberta's lands.

Their dominance slowed the development of the oil patch, not to mention virtually eliminating Canadians from the action. Lougheed reversed all that with a number of dramatic moves, culminating in the creation of Alberta's awesome Heritage Fund, which had about $13 billion by 1986, $7,000 for every person in the province. That wealth has been, and will be, invested in many more enterprises. Some will be economically beneficial and some not. But all will be politically beneficial.

Premier Lougheed took steps to grab some of the resource action for his constituents and in addition took serious steps to bust up concentrations of ownership. A Calgary lawyer, Lougheed ran for office after working for one of the province's most powerful men, Fred Mannix, who dominated the province's coal, construction, and pipeline businesses.

"The oil and gas men were happy with the 16.66-per-cent maximum royalty rates that had been in effect. When I took office I made a series of decisions," Lougheed recalls. "Resources were owned by the citizens and I wanted to increase the revenues to them. I also wanted to create a balance between smaller and larger companies. The most major decision was to create the Alberta Petroleum Marketing Commission, which took away control over oil pricing and distribution. This was to reverse the situation in effect when I took over. Industry told government what to do. Government was captive attitudinally. I would have to get on the telephone to Mr. Twaits [chairman of Imperial Oil], when we inherited the royalty system, asking him as a premier to please raise his prices."

The new commission was a monopoly buyer, establishing prices, taking oil from large and small companies on a pro rata basis, and selling all the oil; it gave smaller companies the same marketing advantages enjoyed by large, foreign-owned, integrated companies. Then royalties were doubled overnight in 1973, in order to cash in on OPEC's windfall profits. Those royalties, in turn, were placed in the Alberta Heritage Fund, a rainy-day nest egg in case the oil runs out. "The oilmen were upset with us. We also gave royalty tax credit to little guys."

Next, Lougheed brought in measures to stop big companies from just sitting on big land spreads. (About 80 per cent of sub-surface mineral rights are owned by Alberta. The rest are freehold lands, acquired before the province joined Confederation and mostly owned by the two railways.) "In 1974, we shortened terms on new leases and increased drilling requirements. In 1976, deeper rights reverted to the Crown if a company had no drilling program. Small companies wildcatted the land."

"Small outfits" like Turbo Resources were nurtured along by the Lougheed regime. In 1983, when the company faced bankruptcy, Alberta's commission made its one and only exception by waiving a requirement that Turbo's Calgary refinery pay cash on delivery for oil it bought. The province lost about $40 million on the deal and ended up getting Turbo shares as payment in 1985.

In the 1970s, Lougheed also seized the financial reins of power, strengthening Alberta's Treasury Branches, subsidizing mortgages through the Alberta Home Mortgage Corp., and siphoning royalties into the Heritage Fund. The three now have combined assets of $21.4 billion, equivalent to the Caisse de dépôt.

"We had two strings to our bow — the Heritage Fund and the Treasury Branches, which were even more important and were stronger rurally in mortgages and farm loans. We decided to keep its profile low so it wouldn't be chartered as a federal institution. Its policy guidelines have been to support small business, to keep interest rates competitive or slightly lower, and to emphasize loans in rural Alberta. It wasn't a dislike of banks but a counterbalance. The big banks responded to our pressure to put more Western directors on their boards, and they became more sensitive to rural needs. As for the Heritage Fund, we invested in the bonds of other provinces, limited stock market investments, and imposed a 5-per-cent ceiling for each company [compared with the Caisse de dépôt's 30-per-cent ceiling]."

Alberta also pioneered hybrids, launching, subsidizing, and partially privatizing "Crowns" like Nova, Alberta Energy Corp., and Vencap, a new venture capital outfit where the Heritage Fund matches shareholders' investments dollar for dollar. However, buy-Alberta procurement policies were never instituted. "We thought it would penalize our entrepreneurs. If we started to erect a provincial border, we would lose more than gain."

Lougheed also tackled the transportation troubles traditionally faced by his province. The oddly socialistic takeover of Pacific Western Airlines was undertaken because "we thought PWA would end up being a B.C. and Yukon operation, and we wanted to be the gateway to the North and the Mackenzie Valley with our land-locked province." In 1985, Lougheed's government bankrolled new grain handling facilities in Prince Rupert to relieve the bottleneck at Vancouver that was costing prairie grain farmers millions in unnecessary storage fees. Lougheed's government also invested in a new container facility on the border at Coutts, Alta., using competing U.S. railway rates to force Canadian rates down for the first time in history.

Lougheed's battles against big oil were unappreciated in the East in the light of huge price hikes by OPEC. Despite royalty benefits to Albertans, Eastern politicians had another concentration of power to fight, namely Alberta's oil industry. Eastern consumers felt gouged by increases as oil companies continued to break profit records. In fact, by the time the Shah of Iran fell — and the writing was on the wall for oil — Ottawa was getting worried. Federal forecasts frightened Ottawa, showing that the economic power of Alberta, predicated on $50-a-barrel oil by 1987, would be mightier than Ottawa's and would cause a massive shift of wealth to the province and the mostly foreign-owned oil companies.

This anxiety led to Ottawa's hated National Energy Program of 1980 — a thinly disguised tax grab. Billed as a Canadianization and consumer program, the NEP infuriated Lougheed because new federal royalties and falling oil prices brought many of his home-grown favourites to their knees. It also unleashed Petro-Canada and other Canadian oil companies onto takeover trails, a chain of events that eventually backfired for economic nationalists. The end result of all that encouragement of Canadianization is that Lougheed's Canadian-owned contingent will reel for years under the burden of costly takeovers, lower prices, and federal royalties, while the big foreign-controlled multinationals, banned from takeovers by Ottawa's FIRA, have weathered the recession without so much as a scratch.

The battle between Alberta and Ottawa over the NEP represented the best example of how Canada's warriors against concentration are often at odds. The difference between the ways Lougheed and Trudeau fought Big Oil showed that one politician's enemy is not necessarily another's. And caught in the crossfire were mega-projects denied building permits by Lougheed. Such strong-arm intervention held Imperial Oil's $11-billion project to ransom, doing as much harm to Canada's reputation around the world as Trudeau's Foreign Investment Review Agency ever did.

Other Clashes

Most provincial politicians, no matter how capitalistic, have dabbled in public enterprise every bit as interventionist and socialistic as the endeavours of Parizeau, Blakeney, and Lougheed. Free-enterpriser and underwear heir Robert Stanfield appointed Nova Scotia tycoon Frank Sobey to set up Industrial Estates Ltd. to entice manufacturers away from traditional locales in Ontario by offering huge subsidies. Unfortunately, Nova Scotia snared big money-losers like Clairtone Sound Corp. and Bricklin, but it also wooed winners like Michelin Tire, which still employs some 3,000 workers.

True-blue Tory Ontario also dabbled in public enterprise, putting up about $100 million towards the construction of the Syncrude oilsands plant in Alberta; some $625 million to buy 25 per cent of Suncor through the Ontario Energy Corp., which is now worth considerably less; and millions of dollars worth of research into the Urban Transportation Development Corp. and

IDEA Corp. Besides providing such grub-stakes to encourage economic activity when the private sector will not, Ontario has also bailed out businesses such as Massey-Ferguson, Harding Carpets, and McClelland & Stewart. In addition, loan guarantees were extended to Chrysler (they were never used), and numerous incentives and grants were made to encourage other businesses.

Ontario has also pushed Ottawa into making a number of bail-outs, notably Massey and de Havilland. The province has also benefited the most from Ottawa's petrochemical investments in Sarnia through Polysar and Petrosar; from Atomic Energy of Canada Ltd.'s massive nuclear program; and from the construction of two uranium refineries by Eldorado Nuclear, both of which have always lost money.

British Columbia has as many Crown corporations as does Saskatchewan, mostly the legacy of its former New Democratic Party regime. While the Social Credit Party does not subscribe to socialism, it certainly has been as enthusiastic to intervene as its rivals: there was the $1-billion provincial investment in northeast coal projects with the Japanese, and the huge make-work project Expo 86, which could cost federal and B.C. taxpayers hundreds of millions of dollars if it doesn't recoup its long-term costs.

Many other such adventures have riddled Canada's economic history, in virtually every province: more make-work projects such as Quebec's Expo and Olympics extravaganzas, the $1-billion Winter Olympics in Alberta. Newfoundland's Joey Smallwood made a number of eyebrow-raising deals, as did Manitoba and New Brunswick leaders.

The result is nearly 1,000 Crown corporations, which fall into four categories: monopolies, such as utilities; bail-outs, such as the Cape Breton Development Corp., Canadair, de Havilland, Canadian National, and Sydney Steel Corp.; research ventures such as Atomic Energy and Ontario's Urban Transportation Development Corp.; and Canadianizations, such as Petro-Canada, the British Columbia Resources Development Corp., and the Canada Development Corp.

Some have been misguided ventures, concerned mostly with politics rather than economics. Both Ontario's purchase of Suncor and PetroCan's purchase of BP Canada and Petrofina were too costly. Then there was Ottawa's $3-billion investment in de Havilland Aircraft and Canadair, after foreign parent companies decided to manufacture in their own countries instead. Frankly, that money might have been better spent buying controlling interest in the world's biggest aerospace manufacturer, Boeing of Seattle, then "persuading" it to create jobs here, as Parizeau used the Caisse de dépôt to keep head offices in Quebec.

Some ventures — in the name of development or to counteract concentration elsewhere — have been downright unjustifiable, such as the Liberals' subsidy for several years of two heavy-water plants in Senator Allan MacEachen's province of Nova Scotia, at a staggering cost of around $1 billion — all to keep about 500 Cape Bretoners busy for five years making a substance for which there may never be a demand. By the same token, Tory deputy prime minister Erik Nielsen pushed through subsidy of Cyprus Anvil Mines in the Yukon. When the 1985 deal was announced, international zinc prices tumbled because of the huge glut that would be created by the reopening of that mine. All in the name of giving zinc miners jobs in the Yukon instead of in Ontario, Quebec, or Africa.

With its arsenal of impressive weapons and wily leaders capable of tough-nosed decisions, people's capitalism has become the single most important actor in the Canadian economy. Designed to counteract concentration of ownership by foreigners or central Canadians, to Canadianize industries, or merely to give leaders control over economic destinies, it has problems. Because it awards advantages to government enterprises, it hurts our reputation as a safe place for the private sector to do business.

Government "pets," such as PetroCan and Alberta's Nova Corp., annoy oil-men like Gus Van Wielingen, chairman of Sulpetro Ltd. of Calgary. The same applies in other industries in which public enterprises compete. "With government credit behind them, they didn't have to hustle and could pay 7 or 8 per cent less to raise money in the form of preferreds, allowing them to bid on land and acquisitions in an unfair way," says Van Wielingen. Any business with government loan guarantees can borrow money at half the rates paid by private-sector companies, under a little-known amendment to the Bank Act.

William Stinson, president of Canadian Pacific, says Canada's mixed economy fosters both feather-bedding and favouritism. "We compete against a government railway, government airline, and government trucking company. Nowhere else in the world is this the case. It's always a worry. Canadian National Railways has been recapitalized three times since it was taken over in the 1930s, once in the 1950s and twice in the 1970s. The government pumped money in to reduce debt. Of course, they say if they were a private-sector company, they would be able to raise equity on public markets and the government's infusion is the same thing. But we haven't had an equity issue in a zillion years. We have grown from internal profits and conservative debts."

In 1985, for instance, a Canadian National official admitted that despite massive investments, the company is virtually insolvent and should be permitted to withdraw completely from Newfoundland, among other areas. In the early 1970s, Stinson says, when airline route allocations were being handed out by the federal government, the government's own airline, Air Canada, got twenty-two cross-border routes to the U.S. while CP Air got only one. "The problem is that the people deciding who gets what are the shareholders of our biggest competitors."

Other such conflicts can occur at the Canadian Radio-television and Telecommunications Commission, concerning the CBC, or at the Canadian Transport Commission. As for feather-bedding, Stinson says, "We have one-third too much railway in this country. Governments poured a lot of money into highways, and trucks can go anywhere now. But if you want to abandon a branch rail line, there's a big hue and cry. You have to apply to government, there's a hearing, and if you can prove the line should close, the government usually pays you a subsidy to keep it open."

Resentment of public enterprises is widespread. William Hagen, a thirty-six-year-old native entrepreneur from Inuvik, says his "blood boils" every time he sees one of PetroCan's fleet of planes load up with freight in one of the North's remote locations. Co-owner of Aklak Air Ltd., in partnership with the Inuvialuit Development Corp., Hagen says, "Guys like me have stuck it out here in the North for years building businesses. While my planes sometimes sit empty, there's PetroCan, shipping PetroCan goods and passengers, thanks to my tax dollars. It makes me mad."

Another harmful effect of Canada's battle against concentration is that it has led governments to adopt non-tariff barriers such as procurement restrictions or massive subsidies of industries that compete with other Canadian industries. Alberta, for instance, launched an entire petrochemical industry in the 1980s to compete against aging ones in Ontario and Quebec by subsidizing it with half-priced natural gas.

Beer companies cannot transport their products across provincial boundaries because each province wants its very own brewery. The result is many inefficient breweries, which threatens our competitiveness, whether or not we negotiate a special free trade pact with the United States. Other means by which inefficiency is subsidized are policies in most provinces that give local companies a 10-per-cent advantage in tendering for government contracts.

Canada is an economy engaged in both world war and civil wars. Financed by politicians' open-ended access to far too much capital, this warfare has sometimes been necessary and all too often misguided. The result is a country hobbled with a huge mortgage and an economy increasingly dominated by civil servants, not entrepreneurs. But the call to arms will continue, an adolescent nation's sometimes naive desire to control its own destiny, embracing the fanaticism of the picket line and the near-religious quality of priests anointing automatic teller machines. As Allan Blakeney explains, "Concentration of power in Canada will be a significant problem until there is more distribution of wealth. Until then, you will see more interventionist governments trying to even the scale. Public ownership is an instrument of policy, not only for ideological reasons, but for regulatory control over our own destiny. To not intervene means economic decisions are made in Toronto or New York. We want to be masters of our own destinies."

The next generation of Canadians must decide, however, who are its real enemies and what are the tolerable wages of war.

3

PAPER ENTREPRENEURSHIP

IN THE 1970s, Canada lost its three traditional economic advantages: proximity to the biggest, most lucrative marketplace in the world; an abundance of resources, mostly owned by the Crown, for which the world hungered; and a reputation as a safe, hospitable haven for foreign investors who wished to help us exploit those resources. Then along came the Vietnam war, OPEC's meteoric price hikes, and Canada's most costly indulgence — the Foreign Investment Review Agency.

Vietnam financially impaired our principal customer — the United States — and diverted massive amounts of capital towards the creation of weapons and the care and feeding of troops, money that would otherwise have been invested in Canada and elsewhere or used to buy more imports. Vietnam also, along with OPEC's twelvefold price hikes, caused worldwide inflation. The oil cartel gave Canadian oilmen and producing provinces billions of dollars in windfall profits, but the world's banks recycled OPEC's petrodollars to developing countries who used them to build agricultural, mining, and oil facilities in competition with commodity-based Canada. The result has been a glut of almost everything Canada produces. Since the 1970s, prices for many of our commodities have been equivalent, in real terms, to Depression prices. Besides collapsing commodity prices, the high inflation era of the 1970s also fostered the takeover game here and abroad, culminating in Canada with the nearly catastrophic events of 1981.

Last, but far from least, the creation of FIRA in 1974 hobbled the country's economic growth, costing opportunities and jobs. It also enhanced the type of concentration of ownership we now have, with thirty-two families and a few oversized management-run conglomerates and Crown corporations dominating our economy. Their grip increased mightily, mostly because Canadian assets became cheaper when foreign rivals were forbidden to bid. Their grip also increased greatly in the light of favourable tax laws and public policies encouraging "Canadianization." Harmful foreign investment curbs cost Canada the advantage of proximity to the U.S., as American companies turned elsewhere to create subsidiaries or build projects. Some even developed competing facilities at home.

For all these reasons — misplaced economic nationalism, harmful economic trends, and tax changes — Canada's private sector has turned to paper entrepreneurship. This country's best and brightest have been preoccupied with fancy financial footwork rather than the type of technological innovation that contributes to a nation's wealth. Far too many of Canada's thirty-two wealthiest families act merely as private mutual funds, hiring lawyers and accountants to buy, strip, combine, or sell assets in businesses about which they sometimes understand nothing. And because of tax wrinkles and regressive innovations such as restricted, or non-voting, shares, these paper entrepreneurs have become a permanent oligarchy that will grasp increasing control over our economic and political lives. Unlike any other developed country, Canada has paved the way for a handful of dynasties and management fiefdoms to last — hypothetically — forever.

Paul Desmarais, Conrad Black, Peter and Edward Bronfman, Sam Belzberg, Howard Webster, George Mann, Jimmy Pattison, and Ken Thomson may have started off by running companies, but they have turned into paper entrepreneurs. They are far from alone. On a smaller scale, there are the Atkinsons, with controlling interest in Torstar and now about 30 per cent of Southam; the McCutcheon brothers and their Traders Group financial empire; Leonard Ellen and Reuben Cohen and their Exco financial group; and Michael DeGroote and his conglomerate called Laidlaw Transportation.

Other paper entrepreneurs are big, widely owned conglomerates like Canadian Pacific, Imasco, Nova and Husky Oil, the Dome Petroleum–Dome Mines empire, and Bell Canada Enterprises, as well as government enterprises like the Canada Development Corp. and Petro-Canada. For the most part, these have not been builders. They have turned to paper chases, mastering the ability to borrow huge sums of money for acquisitions, to manipulate accounting principles, play legal takeover games, or avoid taxes. Such paper entrepreneurs do not contribute to Canada's wealth: the pie remains the same size, but the pieces are cut differently.

Corporate Canada for the past few years has been (and will be for years to come) a Monopoly game gone wild, and players have snapped up just about all the squares. By 1986, among Canada's 400 largest non-financial corporations, only 20 were widely held, lacking a dominant shareholder with 15 per cent of the stock or more. By 1985, the last of Canada's trust companies became controlled when the San Francisco-based conglomerate Genstar bought the country's largest trust, Canada Trustco. Genstar, in turn, was gobbled by Imasco. The wholesale takeover of financial institutions such as trust companies is a particularly worrisome development, because some past incidents of conflicts and self-dealing resulted in the government takeover of several trust companies to protect billions of dollars worth of government-insured savings.

By 1983, according to federal figures, fifteen corporate groups controlled 21 per cent of the country's entire store of non-financial assets, $130 billion out of $618 billion: the Belzbergs' First City Financial; Bell Canada Enterprises; Conrad Black's Argus; Edgar and Charles Bronfman's CEMP; Canadian Pacific; Paul Desmarais's Power Corp.; Peter and Edward Bronfman's Edper; Genstar (now owned by Imasco); Hiram Walker (now owned by Gulf, which is owned by Olympia & York); Imasco; Nova/Husky; the Reichmanns' Olympia & York; the Southerns' ATCO; the Thomson family, with news-papers and The Bay; and Galen Weston, with George Weston and Loblaws.

Since 1983, the value of assets has grown in total, but very large takeovers have exceeded the overall growth. Bell Canada bought Daon, TransCanada PipeLines, and British American Bank Note, with $7.3 billion in assets; the Reichmanns took over Gulf Canada with $5.6 billion in assets and Hiram Walker with $5.3 billion; Genstar took over Canada Trustco (with $11 billion in financial assets), and Imasco took over both, a total of $17 billion in assets. Smaller takeovers included Stephen Roman's purchase of Seagull Petroleum and Lawson Mardon, Weston's takeover of several large food processing companies, and Kenneth Thomson's continuing acquisitions in the newspaper business. When these, plus the assets of all of Canada's thirty-two wealthiest families, are tallied, they add up to roughly $210 billion, or nearly one-third of all Canada's non-financial assets. By contrast in the United States, it takes the 100 largest firms, few of which are controlled by individuals, to reach the 30-per-cent level.

Such figures make it obvious that our private sector is already an economic oligarchy and may be hurtling towards a form of economic feudalism such as existed in Sweden before socialism took root. It is a twentieth-century version of Upper Canada's Family Compact of the 1800s, when agrarian Ontario was politically and financially controlled by the few. Indeed, Canada's pervasive people's capitalism, and the inordinately high proportion of public enterprise and intervention, have been backlashes against concentration of ownership. And these activities will continue unimpeded unless changes occur.

Open foreign investment and freer trade with the U.S. are answers. Tragically, foreign investment fears were unfounded in regard to our bread-and-butter industries. In the forestry, mining, and oil businesses, foreign investment is never exploitation; it is always a partnership with the people of Canada. That is because some 90 per cent of Canada's land mass is Crown-owned, so foreign investors exploiting our resources must lease lands and pay royalties to governments. As for manufacturing, the biggest industry by far is automobiles, and its suppliers are the steel companies. Steelmakers are Canadian-owned, and American automakers are bound to invest here, and protect Canadian jobs, by the special bilateral treaty with the U.S. known as the Auto Pact. The rest of Canada's manufacturing base has been steadily declining, mostly because of high taxes, high labour costs, and a tiny domestic marketplace too small to act as a springboard for export.

FIRA was unnecessary because there were more subtle means already in place to help home-grown proprietors, the most powerful being the 1972 change in tax law concerning dividends. The law made dividends tax-free when paid to Canadians or Canadian corporations, but imposed a 10-per-cent tax on dividends paid to foreigners or foreign companies. This was discriminatory, but surprisingly it was never the subject of a formal complaint under the General Agreement on Tariffs and Trade. However, it quietly and singlehandedly facilitated a massive transfer of wealth into Canadian private-sector hands.

In addition, foreign investment was held at bay as a result of the remarkable rise of people's capitalism in Canada, which has repatriated or created many gigantic home-grown pools of capital. With such policies in motion, we need not have made such a public relations blunder by hanging out an "unwelcome" sign to all the world. Unfortunately, the Liberals felt FIRA was popular back here at home. Unfortunately, it was.

"We must grapple with the problems of concentration of substantial economic power in Canada in the hands of a new aristocracy consisting of twenty or thirty powerful families and the Canadian banks," says Henry Knowles, a Toronto lawyer and former chairman of the Ontario Securities Commission.

Reforms must be done with a scalpel, not an axe, and by people who understand that the problem is not all forms of concentration, some of which may be inevitable in a country this size. The challenge is to discourage paper entrepreneurship and to encourage our most enterprising citizens to engage in other, more nationally beneficial money-making ventures, without driving them and their capital out of the country. Canada also needs to revamp laws to protect the rest of us from the bullying and abuses that can occur, and are occurring, as a result of inordinate concentration.

Bankers' rivals like Hal Jackman, a Toronto insurance and trust company tycoon, also worry about concentration, but Jackman blames it on banks like the Toronto-Dominion and their cosy relationships with their biggest customers. "Concentration of all kinds, including management-run conglomerates like banks and monopolies, has to be one of the most serious problems we have in this country," says Jackman. "Think about the enormous power these people have. The present generation is okay and does not abuse. But what about the future? The story of Canada is that the banking system means the big guys get bigger and the little guys wait to get taken over by a big guy. I don't worry about family concentrations because the children lose interest, blow the money, or pay estate duties."

However, taxes on wealth — such as estate and gift taxes or annual wealth taxes — are virtually non-existent in Canada except, ironically, for those who can least afford them. In the past, wealth ebbed and flowed as heirs were taxed or lost interest and managements lost their momentum. Now they need never lose their grip, thanks to a tax-free ride combined with some more fancy footwork by these paper entrepreneurs, such as restricted shares or other anti-takeover measures. What is under way, for the first time in Canada, is the creation of a handful of management fiefdoms and dynasties — an economic aristocracy that will survive even if it is incompetent.

Traditionally, families lost control when they had to sell shares in public markets to raise capital. This is no longer the case. "Effective control decades ago used to be 5 to 17 per cent. Then it became 51 per cent, as more pools of capital began to compete for assets. Now all you need is 50.1 per cent of voting and nothing of Class Bs," says Henry Knowles. "How can anybody ever buy a company controlled through voting shares if it is not for sale? If they need to raise capital, they can sell non-voting stock. These family-controlled companies can all end up as passive portfolios. And absenteeism never worked. The fact they cannot be bought out reduces opportunities and means a heritage for Canadians of nothing other than serfdom, working for the lord of the manor or Becker's, owned by the lord."

The TD's Richard Thomson agrees that voting shares are a bigger problem than most people realize. Between 1979 and 1985, the number of companies on the Toronto Stock Exchange with non-voting shares jumped to 130 from 64. "Voting stock worries me. Ultimately, an individual could own one share and control a huge empire. We let it go too far and should have stopped it a long time ago."

Corporate acquisitor Alf Powis, chairman of Edper's Noranda Mines, says fears about concentration are unfounded. "When I was growing up, the concern was that E. P. Taylor would end up owning Canada. Look at the rump of what's left of Argus. CP as a percentage of GNP between 1925 and 1975 was cut in half. Companies like Noranda are responsible for that by competing for assets. Ain't nobody ever going to buy all of Canada."

Powis's point is interesting. While Canada's economic élite increasingly protects itself from forced sales, or takeovers, many families will in fact surrender control, for a variety of personal reasons. Take the case of Edgar and Charles Bronfman, whose two sisters — Phyllis and Minda — steadily sold out their shares in Seagram's, bringing the family's holdings down to a potentially perilous 41 per cent. Then there was squabbling among members of the Woodward family, which led to sale of their controlling interest in 1985.

Philanthropy saps fortunes; Montreal's McConnells sold their sugar and newspaper businesses because of lack of interest, gave away half their $400-million fortune to a non-profit foundation, and now thrive as private, passive investors. Next to charity, nothing saps economic power faster than mistakes. Conrad Black, Canadian Pacific, Hiram Walker, the Thomsons, the Bentleys, and even Peter and Edward Bronfman, who borrowed mightily to buy financially troubled Noranda and MacMillan Bloedel, have sustained setbacks that undoubtedly have affected their personal net worths.

But although Powis may be right in practical terms, theoretically Canada could be taken over by a few aggressive families and conglomerates under current tax, securities, and competitions policies. Those who remain in the game are able to play it more aggressively than before. The fifteen conglomerates with 21 per cent of non-financial assets grew by 86 per cent between 1980 and 1983, according to combines officials. Without brakes, they will continue to outpace economic growth — not by coming up with new goods and services, but just through takeovers.

Of course, paper entrepreneurs serve a purpose, if only to provide a ready market for the accomplishments of entrepreneurs who want out. And Canada is not the only place where this is happening. Paper entrepreneurship is on the rise in the U.S. and elsewhere — a symptom of the fact that it is cheaper to buy than to build. But nowhere is it as aggressive or as pervasive as it is here. And there is something drastically wrong with an economy like Canada's that is overwhelmingly devoted to parting entrepreneurs from their enterprises. There is something drastically wrong with a system where Conrad Black and his fellow-shareholders can clean up on the Argus stable of companies, even though Dominion Stores and Massey-Ferguson fall by the wayside as casualties.

There is also something drastically wrong with our tax system. Most of these families and conglomerates pay virtually no income taxes and may never pay any. The Reichmanns, for instance, took over Gulf Canada in 1985 thanks in great part to a $600-million tax savings pulled off in partnership with Black's Norcen Energy Resources. Called the "Little Egypt bump," the complicated tax loophole that produced the savings was sewn up after negative publicity. But civil servants face a constant battle to stem the tax avoidance tricks of the country's most highly paid tax lawyers and accountants. All too often, as with the Reichmanns and Black, they shut the door after the horse has bolted.

"So much of the takeover activity is a parasitical game — finding tax avoidance tricks. Morally it is tax evasion. Legally it's called avoidance," says Stephen Jarislowsky, whose firm Jarislowsky Fraser & Co. manages some $4 billion worth of Canadian savings for clients, some of whom have benefited from the takeover game as shareholders. "Fixed assets should only be depreciated once, and that's it. There should be a 20-per-cent flat corporate tax to avoid subsidies, avoidances, and exemptions. Resource and research-development exemptions are all crap. Corporations pay no income tax. Tax losses should not be carried over by someone in a different business. Accounting procedures should be standardized to end numbers games. And there are securities and competitions laws violations all the time. Like policemen everywhere, regulators do a good job of catching small fry, but the big whites are swimming freely."

As a result of Canada's paper entrepreneurship, there are no Lee Iacoccas among Canada's corporate élite, much less technological geniuses like

Stephen Jobs, who started Apple Computers. Most chief executive officers are lawyers, accountants, or stock market jockeys. Those heading huge public enterprises, like Petro-Canada or Canadian National Railways, are all too often more politically astute than bright in business. None of Canada's richest citizens has concentrated on inventing a better mousetrap.

Our best and brightest are not — as Iacocca is — truly wedded to the products they make, with the exception of takeover-innovators like the Ivaniers, the Poslunses, and Michael DeGroote or venture capitalists like Ben Webster. Most do not eat, sleep, or breathe technological innovations. They do not slug away trying to invent a better compact or a cheaper carburetor. They eat, sleep, and breathe ways to buy someone else's technologies and then hang on to them. Small wonder that less money is spent on research and development here than is spent in Egypt. While foreign-owned enterprises are often blamed for doing insufficient research, the facts are that Canadian-owned firms are not doing much either.

With foolish foreign investment curbs and a private sector so devoted to acquisitions, the job of developing Canada has been left to a handful of entrepreneurs, to public enterprises, led by governments and their Crown corporations, and, ironically, to foreign investors. Among the thirty-two most successful families, only a few are builders who rely greatly on internal growth rather than on takeovers: the Richardsons, Stephen Roman, the McCains, Thomas Bata, the Irvings, the Eatons, the Mannixes, Ray Wolfe, the Bentleys, and Canada's most successful "manufacturers" such as real estate developers Donald Love, Robert Campeau, and the Ghermezians.

(It should be noted, however, that Campeau wanted to take over Royal Trustco, and the Ghermezians tried for Crown Trust, but both were foiled. Others like the Bentleys, the Irvings, and the McCains are also astute paper entrepreneurs but have been stopped for financial or other reasons from successful takeovers.)

Since the unfortunate creation of FIRA in 1974, the lion's share of meaningful mega-projects developing Canada have been government-sponsored. The paper entrepreneurs have been busy buying and paying for their purchases. Since 1974, all that they have built have been some urban development schemes, Ocelot Industries' methane plant, and a handful of gold mines. Most projects were built in part by government or foreigners, like Syncrude, Alberta's subsidized petrochemical industries, Ontario Hydro's massive nuclear program, Hydro-Québec's James Bay, Stephen Roman's Quintette coal mine (with Japanese partners) and his potash mine (with European partners), other B.C. coal projects (with Japanese help), the Alaska Gas Pipeline pre-build, Ottawa's $1-billion gas pipeline to Quebec City from Montreal, B.C. Hydro's Revelstoke dam, Saskatchewan's Key Lake uranium mine (with a German partner), two uranium refineries built in Ontario by Ottawa's Eldorado Nuclear, nearly $10 billion in frontier drilling with government grants covering up to 80 per cent of costs, and transportation schemes like double-tracking or Prince Rupert's grain and coal handling facilities.

Since takeover fever began heating up in 1979, the only two scheduled mega-projects have been cancelled — the Cold Lake and Alsands oilsands projects. Ironically, both were to be built by multinationals with government assistance. Only a few more are on the books for the foreseeable future, either foreign or government projects: three Japanese car plants; two heavy-oil up-graders in Saskatchewan needing government help; Hibernia, which needs massive royalty concessions; Manitoba's $3.2-billion dam project; Imperial Oil's scaled-down Cold Lake project; and expansions of James Bay and Syn-crude, which both involve governments. The country remains afflicted with a Canadian economic élite that is devoted to paper entrepreneurship — taking over wealth and not creating it — and governments that have been hostile to foreign investors.

Apart from civil servants, the only Canadians taking real risks to build the country are the country's farmers, who "build" a mega-project every spring when they spend billions planting. The farmers in their Caterpillar hats and jeans are Canada's real entrepreneurs, not the killer bees in three-piece suits on Bay Street.

Tall, gangly George Richardson of Winnipeg may be the only stock market broker in Canada upset by the takeover game. The rest revel in it. Richardson sits in his Winnipeg office penthouse, surrounded by photographs of grain elevators and other projects his family firm, James Richardson & Sons, has built. He has everything: thousands of acres of farmland, his own helicopter, a Lake of the Woods retreat, access to the world's most important people, power to run a billion-dollar empire, a sense of pride and *noblesse oblige*. "My dad built those elevators," he says pointing to some of the 300 elevators located at his grain company's Lake Superior facility, "and I did that." The Richardsons sell $1.5 billion worth of grains around the world each year and are the only family in the country allowed to own 100 per cent of their own brokerage firm, Richardson Greenshields, because it was founded decades ago, before ownership restrictions were imposed. Now individuals cannot own more than 25 per cent of a brokerage.

"Takeovers have never entered our thoughts," he says. "We own 100 per cent of everything. We don't attempt to buy control of public companies and exert an influence on the board. What is business but people and capital? Unfriendly takeovers are not good unless you know all about the business. It is upsetting. It upsets the people you want to keep. We are happy doing what we're doing. We stick with things we know how to do, and that takeover type of operation doesn't have any appeal."

As for the "cascade effect" used by family conglomerates like Argus and Brascan to capitalize on tax avoidance by sending dividends, which are tax-free, from operating companies up through a series of holding companies and ultimately to proprietors, Richardson says bluntly, "It's a fiddle. It all boils down to what you are trying to get out of life, your motivation. Are you trying to build successful Canadian companies and make a contribution to the country or line your pockets by taking over someone else's accomplishments? Serving the country is the most important thing any of us can do. Our construction company cleared a town site for Inco in Thompson, Manitoba, and cut the right of way for Manitoba Hydro, [projects] that were not highly profitable and in fact cost us money. But they are important because they develop Canada. I don't think people involved in paper games are motivated to build and lead. They are into stripping and shifting and moving. We have everything we started with and rely on our internal growth rate rather than acquisition."

Richardson earmarks a great deal of money for agricultural research, investigating problems of soil salination, creating better grains and hybrids, and improving fertilizers and chemicals to enhance growth. But the Richardson type of enterprise is rare. Paper entrepreneurship is the name of the game and has spawned wasteful counter-takeover measures, the growth of conglomerates, which are often inefficient, and the reduction of competition in the marketplace, robbing consumers of bargains and throwing Canadians out of work.

One of the best examples of the negative effects of takeovers can be seen in Petro-Canada's $886-million purchase in 1985 of 2,400 Gulf Canada gas stations in Ontario and the West. The Reichmanns sold the stations after taking control of Gulf. The takeover will mean a loss of up to 2,000 jobs. Dozens of stations will close, throwing more out of work. With control over one out of every three stations in Ontario and the West since the fall of 1985, PetroCan singlehandedly imposed a truce on gasoline price wars — to the detriment of consumers. Such a huge market concentration would not have been allowed in the U.S., under anti-trust laws. Worse yet, PetroCan will be hobbled for years with an additional $886 million in debt for stations that make minimal profits. That means cutbacks in drilling, research, or other capital projects where rewards can be huge. It may also mean that the company will find it hard to come up with its portion of the cash needed to develop Hibernia, off Newfoundland's coast. In this case, by enlarging its piece, PetroCan has shrunk the pie.

Other People's Money

The most damaging aspects of paper entrepreneurship are the questionable forms of financial footwork that have resulted in the huge mortgage on our nation: debts accumulated merely to change ownership, and debts that add to companies' costs, reducing their competitiveness abroad and here at home. On average, Canada's Canadian-owned enterprises are carrying 70 cents of debt for every dollar of assets they own, compared with the American average debt of only 45 cents per dollar of assets, according to the Bank of Nova Scotia's economist, William Mackness.

"I have made my calculations by avoiding the gimmick of preferred shares. Here prefs are counted as equity, but for my purposes, and in practice, prefs are really debts," says Mackness.

Many of our industries traditionally carry higher debts because of the huge amounts of capital involved in exploiting resources. But the resource companies operating in Canada that are controlled by foreigners have much lower debts than the Canadian firms, an average of 45 cents per dollar. Ironically, foreign investment restrictions might have prevented some of Canada's foreign-controlled companies from getting caught up in the highly leveraged takeover game that has destroyed many Canadian firms. No matter what the excuses, the result is that Canadians are at a huge competitive disadvantage, both at home and abroad.

Such high debt rates are even more worrisome considering how many high-flying Canadian speculators are moving into the lending business themselves by taking over financial institutions. The growth of family-owned financial conglomerates is a concern because of the possibility of reckless management or self-dealing, as occurred with the Ontario trust companies affair, involving

Leonard Rosenberg. And in a country where individuals cannot own more than 10 per cent of the shares in a bank or brokerage firm because of these dangers, it is unjustifiable that the wholesale takeover of virtually every trust company in the country by individuals or holding companies has been allowed. Even more dangerous is to allow conglomerates or individuals to be both lenders and borrowers.

"The easiest way to steal from a bank is to own one," maintains Toronto-Dominion Bank president Robin Korthals. In 1985, a brief by the Canadian Bankers' Association warned about the dangers of a handful of families controlling huge amounts of financial assets. So did Bernie Ghert, in a brief submitted to a parliamentary committee in 1985. His remarks were surprising because he works for Edgar and Charles Bronfman as president of Cadillac Fairview Corp., one of the largest concentrations of family power in Canada.

"Canadians have been insufficiently concerned about the 'darker side' of the concentration of economic power," said Ghert, whose company has $3 billion in assets and is 51-per-cent owned by CEMP, the Bronfman family holding company. "In the absence of any controls over conglomerate ownership, within a decade or so both the financial and non-financial sectors will be dominated by less than a dozen very large 'groups,' [which could] wield enormous economic power. We believe that the current level of concentration of economic power is both undesirable and greater than necessary for Canada, and further concentration should not be encouraged by public policy.

"The concern is that these large groups will be able to use their power to advance the interests of some customers or suppliers and/or penalize others; undermine the position of rivals; provide excess rewards and use economic power to influence public policy via the political process, i.e., expenditures on lobbying, advocacy advertising, public relations, campaign contributions and the ability to redirect corporate locational decisions," Ghert's brief continued.

CEMP controls Cadillac, Seagram Co., and Warrington (which makes Greb boots and Bauer skates). With combined assets of $10 billion, these three companies are already equivalent to Canada's fifth-largest corporation. However, this branch of the Bronfmans has never owned financial assets. And Ghert maintained that those who do own such assets wield considerably more economic power, and eventually political power, than those who do not. He believes that those who own lending businesses should not own businesses that borrow because of the obvious conflicts of interest.

Ghert also took direct aim at the Bronfmans' cousins, Peter and Edward Bronfman, owners of the gigantic Edper/Brascan empire, which includes Trilon Financial Corp., one of the country's largest financial conglomerates, and resource conglomerate Noranda.

"His remarks amused me," said a piqued Trevor Eyton, spokesman for Peter and Edward Bronfman and president of Brascan. "CEMP tried to get into the financial assets business themselves and attempted to take over London Life and Royal Trustco, which are now owned by Trilon. We were invited to take more shares in London Life because of fears about CEMP."

Bitchiness aside, Ghert is right in saying that those who own financial assets should not own companies that borrow money. It remains inarguable that potential conflicts can undermine the entire financial system if these conglomerates use their deposit-taking companies to bail out other companies they own.

Such favouritism will undermine the system, and financial power is too important to let individuals control it; individuals can use this power to hurt others. "Let us consider the case of a large financial organization which, for reasons of spite, calls the loans of a large, previously reliable customer," said Ghert. "The customer will be hurt in a number of ways. He will have to find a new lender, and may have to liquidate other assets to cover loans. He becomes a 'marked man.'"

In fact, Ghert knows of one such abuse already, where a financial institution controlled by a non-financial conglomerate was told not to lend money to another corporation because it was a competitor. Ghert did not reveal identities because that could have cost someone his job. Hypothetically, the conglomerate could be Genstar instructing Canada Permanent Trust or Canada Trustco not to lend money to Cadillac, because it is in the real estate business, as is Genstar. Or Edper companies like Continental Bank or Royal Trustco or London Life might be told not to lend money to Cadillac, which is in competition with Edper's Trizec. Conversely, another abuse would be if a Genstar or an Edper told its financial institutions to lend money to Cadillac at favourable rates because Cadillac had agreed to buy a Genstar or Trizec property.

When a company is refused a loan, it suffers other repercussions, whether deserving or not, said Ghert. "Another problem is that financial intermediaries are necessarily privy to a great deal of confidential information about their customers. Even though nothing is wrong, people whose opinion counts — including those of other financial institutions — may alter their behaviour towards the firm that the financial institution has 'abandoned.'"

Such situations not only are immoral, they are bad economics and an abuse of shareholder responsibility. Financial institutions that turn away lending business on the basis of vindictiveness forfeit profits; so do those who give favourable rates to friends.

"No family or conglomerate in the business of 'real economy' [non-financial] assets should be allowed to keep financial assets. They should be forced to divest immediately," says TD's Thomson. "They should not be allowed to control companies in the business of taking deposits from the public, which are covered by government insurance. It is wrong. An intolerable amount of leverage."

While Thomson's talk is tough, it must be remembered that his own bank owns 40 per cent of the equity of Oxford Development Ltd., with $3 billion of non-financial assets. This would ordinarily be contrary to the Bank Act, which allows banks to own only 10 per cent of a real economy company. But the TD has gotten around the letter of the law by having 40 per cent of non-voting shares, and only 5 per cent of votes.

Not all conglomerates are as enamoured as most with the financial asset game. "At one time, CP had a 'grandfather' position of well over 10 per cent in a bank that eventually joined National Bank, and we backed off. We were also the largest shareholders in Montreal Trust and Canada Trust, and we moved out of these areas some time ago," says Senator Ian Sinclair, who ran Canadian Pacific for twenty years. "A mistake? I'm not sure. People tended to overlook the sensitivity of handling other people's money. The managers of Pioneer Trust, Northland, and Canadian Commercial Bank [all three went bust in 1985] thought they were proprietors. We decided financial assets were not the way we should go. Financial intermediaries are a different kind of business than mining or oil. All those businesses are our traditional businesses, and they are borrowers, not lenders. We didn't feel we belonged there."

The handling of other people's money is the principal problem of allowing individuals to control financial institutions. It is the same problem that plagues the control of financial institutions by politicians — a form of misguided people's capitalism that led to the poor management practices at the Northland Bank and Canadian Commercial Bank. Governments encouraged pensions and co-operatives to bankroll the two, then encouraged their growth by depositing funds there. These shareholders were passive and naive, allowing questionable accounting and lending practices to go on for years until the banks became insolvent.

"Banks should be widely held. Banks have a different role than industries," says Rowland Frazee, chairman of the Royal Bank of Canada. "They are instruments of government policy through the Bank of Canada governor. Concentration of family ownership is a concern. There's the possibility of self-dealing and of conflicts of interest. I worry about the lack of rules. I don't sit on top of this bank in the same way one of these families sits at the top of its organization. We have a review process. I don't make loan decisions in this office. I always say I must know more about it and refer big loans to the board's loan policy committee."

TD Bank chairman Dick Thomson provides this insight into the lending business: "When we are going to lend someone's competitor money, we get calls from rival customers. They tell me all the dirt they can, what problems the other guy has and so on in the hopes of scuttling the loan. We simply listen."

The concerns of the bankers are obviously valid, but they are the views of interested parties. Our banks have been more concentrated and have enjoyed more anti-competitive advantages than most Canadian businesses: they have been allowed exclusive access to the lucrative big-ticket corporate lending business (loans over $7 million). And they have been protected from foreign competition. Nonetheless, the bankers' concerns are right, but for the wrong reasons.

Figures used in the Canadian Bankers' Association's 1985 brief on concentration grabbed headlines, but they are misleading. They say that family conglomerates are already as big as the five largest chartered banks, if the bankers' assets (after deducting foreign assets) are compared with trust company assets, such as estates and trust funds. By the CBA measurements, the Edper empire is larger than the Royal Bank of Canada, the country's largest. The association says Hal Jackman's financial empire is bigger than that of the Bank of Nova Scotia or the Toronto-Dominion Bank.

Of course, such comparisons are specious because trust companies do not have discretion to invest all the trust and estate money within their care. Far from it — they often have "control" over less than 10 per cent of such funds. The owners are not supposed to play fast and loose with that 10 per cent any more than banks can play with funds they hold in trust for life or casualty insurance companies. Such assets do not belong to the banks in the same sense as a bank's own capital belongs to it. All that being said, however, some of Canada's most prominent trust company proprietors have pulled off a few eyebrow-raising manoeuvres.

At an Ontario Securities Commission hearing in 1982 into the takeover of Domtar by the Caisse de dépôt et placement du Québec, it was revealed that trusteed accounts in Desmarais-controlled companies sold all their Domtar stock to the Caisse in 1981 when he decided to help the Caisse take over the forestry company. Perhaps unconnected was the subsequent sale by the Caisse of Canadian Pacific stock to Desmarais, who wanted to take over the railway. If it was connected by some binding agreement, such an arrangement would have been illegal, because Desmarais would have been receiving more than just money in return for his shares — a sweetener that should have been offered to other shareholders.

Similarly, on a Sunday night in 1985, Hal Jackman decided to sell his 5 per cent of Union Enterprises stock during a takeover by Unicorp's George Mann, but he also ordered the sale of another 1.5 per cent of Union stock in trusteed accounts managed by National Victoria Trustco (of which he controls 40 per cent). "When Union bought Burns Foods, we wanted out, and we heard every other major shareholder was getting out. [As for the trusteed accounts] if it's not me [who makes the decision to buy or sell], it's some investment officer. Usually such things go to the investment committee [of National Victoria] but this didn't because the time frame was so short."

Jackman's short cut in procedure may have been prudent considering the rapidity with which events unfolded. However, the incident proved that proprietors do have control over trust accounts in their care, which tends to discredit arguments made by some acquisitors that they have little, or no, say over other people's money in their care. That is certainly how Toronto-Dominion chairman Dick Thomson interprets the incident. "It would prove he runs those trusteed accounts as though that was his money. That would mean arguments about the way trust companies are operated are no longer credible."

Similarly, the fact that so many Edper-controlled financial institutions swapped Union Enterprises stock for George Mann's Unicorp preferred shares in 1985 raised concerns that they were operating not independently, but in concert. Edper companies such as Royal Trustco, Continental Bank, and London Life were joined by Edper's partners, the Reichmanns and Jimmy Kay of Dylex, in making Mann's swap scheme work. While Edper spokesman Trevor Eyton maintains that each of the companies is autonomous, the facts are that an empire that vast is capable of making or breaking stock issues — using both its own capital as well as other people's money in trusteed accounts — if its members choose to act in concert. Whether in unison or independently, the decision of the Edper group allowed George Mann to buy Union without putting up any cash.

While enough to raise eyebrows, these transactions are tame compared with the immoral manoeuvres involving Leonard Rosenberg and Seaway, Greymac, and Crown Trusts, as well as Peter Pocklington's Fidelity Trust. All four have been seized and are being wound up by the federal government.

In 1982, Rosenberg, using various companies, sold to Saudi Arabian interests an option to buy 11,000 apartments in Toronto for $500 million in ten years, even though Rosenberg paid only $270 million for them. It was a scheme to get around rent controls: the only way rents could be hiked beyond 6 per cent a year in Ontario was if a landlord remortgaged and therefore had to pass along the new financing costs. So two trust companies controlled by Rosenberg, Crown Trust and Greymac Trust, and a third, called Seaway Trust, advanced him $152 million in third mortgages on the apartments, bringing total mortgages to $422 million, even though the apartments were not worth more than the $270 million he had paid. His plans were to use the refinancing to get the rents up, thereby increasing the value of the buildings so that the Arabs would be willing to pay $500 million by the time they could exercise their option.

While Rosenberg has not been charged by police regarding the apartment deal, he and six others face fraud charges concerning other trust company transactions, involving more than $100 million. Even so, after that gigantic flip occurred, the Ontario government moved in, for good reason. After all, Rosenberg had asked the trust companies to recklessly lend deposits taken from the public and insured by Ottawa to unverified parties in order to circumvent public policy.

Another high-flying paper entrepreneur who fell from grace was Peter Pocklington, owner of the Edmonton Oilers hockey team and Gainers Meats. He bought control of Fidelity Trust, then sold to it millions of dollars worth of highly speculative properties that he owned. The trust company's losses on the land and buildings were so severe that about two years later Fidelity's entire equity was wiped out and it went into receivership. In one case, he sold Fidelity an empty Gainers building in Edmonton for $10 million, over which he is now being sued because his board of directors made him sign a buy-back arrangement.

As such examples illustrate, there are potential problems with individuals controlling financial assets that belong to the public. And if it is wise policy that ownership in chartered banks must be limited to no more than 10 per cent per owner, it follows that the same policy should apply to trust companies and other financial intermediaries who handle other people's money. This makes sense not only because of what has happened, but because of what may happen.

Of course, such problems can also occur in widely held financial institutions; they happened at the Canadian Commercial Bank, the Northland Bank, and Pioneer Trust. But the biggest factor in those collapses was the fact that the institutions were launched by politicians who encouraged non-profit co-ops to invest and keep deposits there, in order to nurture home-grown banking enterprise. And the principal shareholders did not know, or did not want to know, what was going on. The result was that the professional managers behaved like proprietors, giving loan officers commissions, giving directors or managers special terms, and lending money in non-arm's-length transactions. That is why solutions do not lie strictly in ownership strictures. But there must be laws requiring more disclosure and shareholder approval of any non-arm's-length transaction. Leaving ethics up to the players involved has invited the problems that have occurred.

"Are Chinese walls ever going to be that thick? There's an assumption that a lot of people haven't got larceny in their soul," says Senator Sinclair. "Players I know tend to be proprietors, and a proprietor looks at his job in a different way than a professional manager. A manager operates a company on behalf of others. A proprietor looks upon things as his, even though they belong to others. Ask Paul Desmarais how many CP shares he owned and he'd say 12 per cent. But he's including shares owned by Great-West Life, trusteed accounts in Montreal Trust, and others. These never belonged to him."

Funny Money

Besides the potential for self-dealing and destructive conflicts, unbridled control over financial assets by paper entrepreneurs has other dangers: it creates self-financing circles, which can accelerate concentration dramatically or create shaky paper pyramids that cannot fail without harming the entire economy. In a sense, powerful groups can buy and sell to one another shares in their companies, making an artificial market for the shares in order to prop up otherwise sick companies. Self-financing circles can virtually manufacture money, swapping their own paper for stock in a desired takeover target, whose assets are the underlying security for their paper.

Also called junk bond deals, these transactions are widespread — Dome and Turbo were examples — and are reminiscent of scams gone by. Several decades ago, an insincere takeover bid would be made, the stock would go up, the takeover bidders would sell out and run with their profits, and the take-over bid would be abandoned. "That led to a rule in Ontario that the takeover company had to provide to the director of the commission proof it had the economic wherewithal to do the takeover," says Henry Knowles, former chairman of the Ontario Securities Commission. "Even Dome or Turbo showed us a letter from a bank saying their deals had financial backing. Can you imagine that?"

Neither Dome nor Turbo had the financial backing they promised. They could not peddle their paper to the public to pay off minority shareholders in companies in which they had obtained controlling interest. This pushed both — and some of their lenders and suppliers — to the brink of bankruptcy.

Such speculative shenanigans cost consumers money, because interest rates in Canada have been higher than they would have been without them. Takeovers also hurt Canada's medium-sized and smaller enterprises indi-rectly. "All these takeovers and problems have hurt small entrepreneurs. While banks hold the bag for huge loans to huge companies, they are chasing individuals for $300,000 [loans]," says Ross Curtis, former senior vice president of the Bank of Montreal.

As small borrowers struggled during the recession to repay debts or face loan demands by banks, one oilman who had an insolvent company told me in 1982, "I have $35 million in debts, which we cannot repay. Now I am going to borrow another $15 million, because when you owe a bank $50 million you get a special work-out." The "special work-out" teams of experts from banks work to "restructure" troubled companies, by stretching out loan payments or swapping loans for stock to save them.

This is done to avoid messy bankruptcies and to spare bankers embarrass-ment. And when it comes to the Domes and Turbos, even more generous rules apply: Dome did not repay any principal for two years while a restructuring was worked out among its dozens of lenders, and Turbo paid no interest or principal for nearly three years. And it never will. It remains an unfair fact of life that when you owe the bank a million dollars and cannot repay, you are in trouble. But when you owe a billion and cannot repay, the *bank* is in trouble.

Paper entrepreneurs are very good at playing the debt game. They also use leverage, the art of buying as much as possible for as little cash as possible. The result is that many empires are owned by families with mere toe-holds, in comparison with the rest of shareholders. Some use the Argus formula — "to own the biggest piece of the biggest piece of the biggest piece" — or they create special classes of shares with votes, denying votes to the rest. For example, Laidlaw's chairman and founder Michael DeGroote sold all of his common stock in 1985, worth about $36 million, but kept total control because he still owns 50.4 per cent of voting shares. Another example, one of the most glaring, is Fred and Jim McCutcheon's control of their $7.7-billion financial empire through a $20-million shareholding in Canadian General Securities Ltd., which owns Traders Group and Guaranty Trust.

"We have let the use of restricted shares get too out of hand to force divestiture now," says the TD's Thomson. "It's gone too far, but something should be done."

Other examples include Dylex's Posluns family, with 51 per cent of voting shares, or Magna's talented Frank Stronach, who personally put up very little cash, but controls his corporation because each one of his shares has 500 votes. Similarly, the Billes family of Canadian Tire fame and the Atkinsons of Torstar control their billion-dollar corporate empires with voting share majorities. All of these are gifted business people who are running prosperous conglomerates, but restricted shares give them power enough to ride roughshod over their partners, who happen to own the majority of shares. It is simply unfair and has led to injustices.

"Voting and non-voting shares are like being indentured for twenty years," says Hal Jackman, who does not believe in them. "You shouldn't sell your right to a vote. You can't do that in politics. It's illegal." Significantly, the Eaton family scrapped its voting share control in Baton Broadcasting in 1985 for philosophical reasons, by eliminating all voting shares and converting them into non-voting shares. The Eatons still own 51 per cent. Also in 1985, Edgar and Charles Bronfman backed off a proposal to create a special class of voting shares in Seagram amid criticisms by Stephen Jarislowsky and pension funds like the Caisse de dépôt.

Such measures are often justified as "shark repellents," needed to fend off predatory takeover artists. But they are simply more "funny money" methods employed by Canada's paper entrepreneurs and their hired hands.

Shark Repellents

Rampant paper entrepreneurship has resulted in a raft of defence tactics, called "shark repellents," that have a number of negative side effects. They entrench managements unduly, including some who should get the shove; they are anti-competitive because they present obstacles that impede the competition for assets; and they often trample the rights of shareholders.

By far the most common shark repellent is to attract white knights to fend off attack; this happened with the Canada Development Corp. and Falconbridge share swap in 1985. In this case, the companies were white knights to each other: Canada Development replaced Dome Mines as Falconbridge's largest shareholder, and Falconbridge nudged aside Noranda as Canada Development's largest shareholder. Hiram Walker did a similar swap with Interprovincial Pipeline to frustrate the Reichmanns, who were Walker's largest shareholders, nibbling away at its stock with 15 per cent. It didn't work, and the Reichmanns ended up with 93 per cent of Walker shares.

Another deal occurred between Southam and Torstar in 1985, but Torstar's controlling shareholders — a voting trust comprising the Atkinson family and a handful of individuals — maintained the upper hand. The Atkinsons swapped non-voting Torstar stock for Southam shares, which all have votes. They kept intact their controlling interest, which greatly increases the concentration of ownership in the newspaper business.

In another case, Canada Malting's management feared a takeover bid and asked the two main shareholders — brewery giants John Labatt and Molson — to ante up more money in order to raise their joint stake from 28 per cent to 39.7 per cent, just a nudge below 20 per cent apiece. (The two took marginally less than 20 per cent because once a shareholder reaches that level, takeover rules are triggered, requiring them to make a bid for all the other shares.)

"This is offensive," said Bill Allen, president of Allenvest Securities, a small Toronto broker. "It is taking money away from shareholders. The book value [of Canada Malting] is $30 a share, break-up value $40, and the company sold these shares for $24 a share." The $24 represents a premium over the price the shares had been trading at for some months, but such companies with dominant shareholders — who are also the company's principal customers — often trade low. This is because the company is not getting a premium price for the malt it sells to its two major shareholder-customers.

The Ontario Securities Commission held hearings into both these cosy transactions to determine whether minority shareholders' interests had been trampled. The commission need not have done so. It is obvious that all such swap deals are so far-reaching and so beneficial to the dominant shareholder that other shareholders should have a say and be protected.

In 1977, the first attack on the problem came when the Ontario Securities Commission imposed certain requirements in a case where a dominant shareholder had made an offer to buy out all the other shares. Securities officials required the company to commission and publish an independent evaluation of the offer's value and required approval of the buy-out by a majority of the minority shareholders at a special meeting. Most large companies have abided by these procedures, called "majority of the minority" rules, many times since, but they are not, in fact, legally required to do so, and they should be.

"Anglo-American corporate law has developed on the premise that ordinarily the majority is entitled to rule. Nevertheless, the courts have recognized the dangers in permitting tyranny by the majority and have given relief in cases where they believed the majority was clearly abusing its powers," wrote Alex MacIntosh in the *Dalhousie Law Journal* in 1983, in an article entitled "Corporate Governance and Minority Rights." MacIntosh is one of Canada's most prominent corporate lawyers, a senior partner in the country's largest law firm, Blake Cassels & Graydon, and a director of a dozen major corporations. "As more and more public corporations become controlled by a dominant shareholder, who either holds a majority of the shares or sufficient shares to control the proxy machinery [votes], the relations of majorities and minorities become increasingly important both for the corporations and society."

He suggests a number of solutions: forbidding directors with conflicts from voting on those transactions (most do not vote, as a matter of practice, but it is not illegal to do so); stripping shareholders of votes at annual or special meetings if they are directly involved in the matter at hand; requiring full disclosure and approval by outside directors of any deals between a corporation and its directors or dominant shareholders; and requiring court or shareholder approval of any transaction between a shareholder and the corporation that is out of the corporation's ordinary course of business.

"In developing such rules, it must be recognized that there is a danger of the tyranny of the minority, as it would be most unfortunate to have a system in which a small group could effectively stalemate a corporation and 'blackmail' the other shareholders. The objective is to ensure fair treatment while not stalemating the corporation. Such a goal could be attained by making the court the final arbiter when a majority has an interest extraneous to its shareholder interest," MacIntosh concluded.

Another harmful shark repellent is the poison pill. Recent examples were Union Enterprises' purchase of Burns Foods to frustrate George Mann's takeover, and Noranda's takeover of MacMillan Bloedel to frustrate Brascan and the Caisse de dépôt. Poison pills are swallowed during a takeover in the hope that they will be too unpalatable or too large for the takeover artist to digest. Unfortunately, the poison pill is sometimes too unpalatable or too large for the takeover target's other shareholders to digest.

Sometimes the management fiefdoms enlist trading help to fend off paper entrepreneurs, as occurred in 1980 when Robert Campeau attacked Royal Trustco, an establishment bastion run by a Montreal anglophone. It was to be a battle between proprietor and professional manager. "I will not work for Robert Campeau," Royal's chairman Kenneth White said in a press conference, after Campeau's takeover bid was announced. "Campeau, constantly in search of risk capital, would be an unsuitable owner with little or no experience in the trust business."

Rather than let shareholders decide Campeau's desirability, White called other professional managers who, like white knights, snapped up $200 million in Royal Trustco stock. The group included Sun Life Assurance Co. of Canada, Bank of Montreal, TD and Oxford Development Group, Commercial Union Assurance Co., National Trust (now National Victoria), Noranda Mines, Canadian Pacific, Canadian Imperial Bank of Commerce, Olympia & York Investments, and three foreign banks. TD's Thomson calls his bank's participation "strictly an arbitrage opportunity." By the time it was over, White's white knights had effectively warehoused 55 per cent of the stock, which they did not sell to Campeau.

Before Campeau's bid, the stock had been trading at $16 a share. He bid $20, then increased it to $23 "to break up the club." After Campeau gave up, shares fell to $17.63; it had cost the white knights $30 million to keep him out. Campeau then bought 8 per cent of Royal's shares for $19 apiece. Later he sold them to the Reichmanns in March 1981 for $22 a share — making the family Royal Trust's largest shareholder. The Ontario Securities Commission held a hearing and found rules had been violated because Royal's management encouraged its friends to buy the shares and not turn them in under Campeau bids. Trading bans were imposed on White and his executive vice president, John Scholes. Some white knights had to pay their share of hearing costs. Ironically, the Reichmanns, in their turn, joined forces with Peter and Edward Bronfman and obtained controlling interest from the white knights in March 1981.

In 1985, a sneaky new shark repellent came into being: quota by-laws. Created by Genstar, then followed by Fleet Aerospace and Lac Minerals, quota rules state that shareholders cannot change directors without the consent of all the directors or without the approval of 75 per cent of all shareholders. This virtually disenfranchises most shareholders because of the practical difficulty of reaching them all. Not only do these measures achieve the desired result — and keep away would-be takeover artists who cannot remove a board of directors even if they gain controlling interest — but they guarantee the most mediocre director a job for life. In the case of Lac, the quota by-law also allows president Peter Allen, with a toe-hold of just 4 per cent, to control the company as though he had the majority of its shares.

Sometimes shark repellents involve cabinet-level lobbying, as was the case in 1983 when Canadian Pacific faced a potential takeover threat from Paul Desmarais in partnership with the Caisse de dépôt. CP's Ian Sinclair and others made their concerns known to Ottawa, and the Liberal cabinet proposed Bill S-31, limiting ownership in any national transportation company like CP to 10 per cent. Sinclair pooh-poohs the need for the bill (which did not pass) and says there were other strategies up his management's sleeve, should a takeover have been attempted.

"If Paul Desmarais controlled it, he wouldn't know what to do with it. There are ways of working for someone, but giving him no help, in fact hindering him. S-31 was a reaction to statements by Parizeau that positions would be taken and used for the advantage of Quebec. Now that Parizeau and Desmarais are gone, I can't see the Caisse controlling CP or wanting to."

The question raised by all these energy-sapping shark repellents is that while it may be desirable to stem concentration or the takeover by individuals of Royal Trustco or CP, it may be undesirable to have an élite of professional managers who can protect themselves even if they are doing a poor job. Increasingly — and often because of shark repellents — mediocre managements remain ensconced within a corporation, leaving shareholders completely out in the cold. This can also lead to exorbitant salaries, lucrative stock options, or golden parachute arrangements. In the cases of Genstar and Dome Petroleum, their directors voted themselves stock options and then, when stock prices fell and options would have caused losses, not profits, they altered the plans with more favourable terms. Golden parachutes are arrangements that make executives rich if takeovers are successful. Again Dome Petroleum leads the pack; its chairman, Howard Macdonald, is automatically entitled to about $2 million if the company is taken over or if its principal shareholder, Dome Mines, sells its 27 per cent of Dome Pete.

The Casualties

The paths of paper entrepreneurs are often strewn with the corpses of minority shareholders who, among other problems that Alex MacIntosh points out, are insufficiently protected against self-dealing or management manipulation. While this goes on in many countries, new laws are needed here because of Canada's unusually high degree of concentration. As mentioned before, only 20 of Canada's 400 largest non-financial corporations are widely held, without a large shareholder who owns 15 per cent or more: Canadian Pacific, Bell Canada Enterprises, Alcan Aluminium, Moore Corp., CAE Industries, Stelco, Dofasco, Massey-Ferguson, Bow Valley Industries, Inco, British Columbia Resources Investment Corp., Innopac, Drug Trading Co., Westburne Industries, Inland Natural Gas, Nova, Newfoundland Light & Power, Asamera, Ranger Oil, and B.C. Sugar Refinery.

Because of the unique nature of Canadian public companies, new protections are needed. Some are already in place, such as the dissident shareholder provisions of the Canada Business Corporations Act, but they are inadequate. Unfortunately dissidents can only protest if a special shareholders' meeting is called to vote on a transaction, which does not always happen. Secondly, the law is inadequate when it comes to the definition of a shareholder. One case involved a Calgary investor, named John Duby, and Aberford Resources. In 1985, Duby lodged his dissent, but his broker had failed to tell him that his stock was kept in a "street" name, technically in the possession of the broker. Therefore, his own name did not appear on the shareholders' registry. An Alberta court would not let him dissent even though he was the beneficial owner because the deadline to dissent — at or before the special shareholders' meeting — had transpired. "It's a sham," says Duby. "When is an owner an owner?"

Those who do dissent are entitled to an offer from the company to buy their shares at fair market value. There is often a dispute over fair market value, and then the "remedy" costs a bundle in legal fees. The venue for the court case is sometimes inconvenient to the shareholders or their lawyers. "We are looking at $250,000 for our dissent," says Allan Aitken of Montreal broker Lafferty Harwood & Partners, who became upset about Noranda's buy-out of the minority shareholders of New Brunswick's Fraser Inc. in 1985.

However, where there have been cases in Canada, the courts have been sympathetic. A litigious Stephen Jarislowsky took Paul Desmarais to court over a buy-out in which Domglas shareholders were offered the market price for their shares, as part of an amalgamation. In 1980, a Quebec court ordered Domglas to pay Jarislowsky's shareholders about 25 per cent more for their shares than it had first offered. The judge concluded that because the buy-out was equivalent to an expropriation, the shareholders were entitled to a premium for forceable taking.

In 1985, dissidents led by Aitken sued Noranda over its "buy-out" of minority shareholders in the New Brunswick forestry company Fraser Inc. That case points out the gaps in the current laws. In May 1985, Noranda bought out the 37 per cent of Fraser it did not already own, although the Fraser board of directors was not interested in selling. Neither were some shareholders. "Noranda offered us a rotten price in crummy paper," says former Fraser shareholder and professional investor A. Scott Fraser, president of Montreal's IFL Investment Foundation Canada Ltd., a $10-million closed-end investment trust listed on the Montreal Stock Exchange.

Noranda wanted to take over Fraser to avoid up to $20 million a year in U.S. income taxes. (Noranda would avoid taxes by writing off its U.S. losses against Fraser's U.S. profits.) Despite their disdain for the deal, Fraser's directors were unable to communicate this disdain, much less deflect the wishes of the controlling shareholder. "It's fair to say Fraser wasn't particularly interested in a merger. It does minimal for Fraser, but Noranda basically had control of the company," says former Fraser chairman John Fisher, a Southam heir and now chairman of that media giant. "But shareholders got a fair price."

Fraser's board appointed two outside directors to negotiate the price with Noranda before it was publicly announced. However, one of the two "outside" directors was a Noranda appointee, as were the majority of the Fraser board. Then the agreed-upon price was independently appraised by Burns Fry, a brokerage firm for whom one of Fraser's directors and shareholders — David Hennigar, a Jodrey heir — works. Burns felt the price was fair, and the Jodreys as well as their partners the Sobeys were among those who agreed to sell.

Finally, the board decided to hold a special shareholders' meeting and to allow the transaction only if the majority of the minority shareholders approved it. The problem was that the announcement was sent out only three weeks ahead of time, as required by law. That was insufficient time for many to mount an offence or make arrangements to get to the inconvenient location of the meeting (in tiny Edmundston, N.B.). Some shareholders did not even receive notice of the buy-out in time because of the slowness of the mail or because their brokers were slow to forward the information. It was also insufficient time to get an exhaustive appraisal of the offer's value, which is what Burns Fry mentioned in its appraisal letter presented to shareholders in the documents distributed about the buy-out. The brokerage firm said it thought the offer was fair, but it also said it did not have sufficient time to evaluate in great depth the value of Noranda's preferred share offer in exchange for Fraser stock.

The upshot was that Fraser disappeared into the Noranda maw without much of a whimper, although management felt it was not best for the company. And it is doubtful that minority shareholders were fairly treated.

The courts are far from an adequate remedy even in clear-cut cases of "oppression." However, those who risk a court battle usually find sympathy. In a 1979 Quebec decision, the directors of Sabex Internationale Ltée were not allowed to issue new shares to dilute the holdings of existing shareholders unless they personally bought some. In a case against Jackets Enterprises Ltd., Hal Jackman, the majority shareholder, was forced by the court to personally guarantee a loan to the company and to pay for what the court felt were excessive interest obligations. In *Redekop v. Robco Construction Ltd.*, the majority shareholder of Robco received shares in another company. As a director and shareholder of both, he caused Robco to agree to carry on its construction business for the other company at a fixed price. The court decided Redekop was using Robco to advance his own personal interest in the other company.

Even when abuses can be proven, in some cases damages are difficult to obtain. Financiers Leonard Ellen and Reuben Cohen convinced Ontario Supreme Court Justice David Griffiths that the Canadian Imperial Bank of Commerce had treated them shabbily, but they failed to win damages. The bank knew the two men wanted to take over Crown Trust throughout the 1970s, and had lent them millions to do so. However, another Commerce customer and director, Bud McDougald of Argus fame, did not want them to get it. So the bank itself accumulated Crown shares, then sold them to a third party in Winnipeg, in concert with Conrad Black, who had taken up where McDougald left off in 1979.

Griffiths said in his reasons: "I have had considerable sympathy for the plaintiffs in this matter, although I have been unable to find any legal basis upon which they would be entitled to recover. With regard to the policy of the bank in this case to secretly purchase shares in an effort to thwart the efforts of one of its customers in favour of another, although not illegal, I find that policy morally offensive. In the circumstances, the action will be dismissed without costs."

Stephen Jarislowsky cites other abuses by controlling shareholders. "One company with 25 per cent of shares owned by a majority shareholder decided to issue shares. The company's underwriters offered few of the rights to the public. After the issue the stock split and dividends increased. The stock went from $24 to $40 a share and the public, plus minority shareholders, had little opportunity to take advantage of the additional shares." To avoid such games, rights should be offered on a pro rata basis to all shareholders.

"There should be cumulative voting" — where shareholders can vote for a dissident director and not have to put up an entire dissident slate of directors — "and a code of ethics for outside directors. There should be no directors' insurance, indemnification, or golden parachutes. And bank boards are a joke," adds Jarislowsky.

Minority shareholders also suffer because the very mechanics of paper entrepreneurship create enormous opportunities for self-dealing. Corporate officers, lawyers, accountants, and bankers, or their relatives, can obtain insider information that their company is about to be acquired or to make a takeover. Undoubtedly many have reaped enormous profits as a result, as witnessed by the feverish trading activity that precedes almost every major takeover in Canada. Meanwhile the owners of the companies involved are kept in the dark.

The most obvious examples of leaks involved PetroCan's two takeovers — $1.6 billion for Petrofina in 1981 and $700 million for BP Canada in 1982. Trading went wild in the weeks leading up to the lucrative takeover bids amid rumours they were going to occur. Because of such leaks, both deals were investigated by securities officials, but the trails evaporated into Swiss banking accounts, bearer stock (bearing no beneficial owner's name), or thin air. "It was obvious that there were leaks, but we just couldn't catch anyone," recalls Henry Knowles, who was chairman of the securities commission at the time. In fact, there has been only one minor conviction under insider-trading rules in Canada since they were implemented in 1978.

Minority shareholders are also in the dark because of inadequate disclosure requirements. "If we allow concentration, there should be very tough disclosure rules," says current OSC chairman Stanley Beck. "And we should require managements every year to publish more information on where their corporations have been in the past year and good information from independent analysts on where they are going and what conditions in their markets are expected to be like."

Current requirements are lax. Ownership links are supposed to be disclosed to Ottawa under the Canada Labour Relations Act. However, subsidiaries are sometimes missing from the list of holdings if, as is often the case, they are provincially rather than federally chartered. In one glaring incident, it was impossible for trade unions to determine which Irving company owned a ship they were attempting to organize. Unable to find the owner with whom to negotiate a contract, they gave up in frustration. Companies can also trade subsidiaries back and forth in order to hide one of them, usually for competitive reasons. All that shows on the list is the subsidiary that did the buying. The one that was purchased is only mentioned as a "note payable" on the balance sheet.

Similarly, companies often bury important information in footnotes at the back of their annual reports, rather than at the bottom of balance sheets and income statements. Another technique was used by Denison Mines in 1985 when it sold $150 million worth of preferred shares to replace bank loans against its troubled Quintette coal mining operation. Denison divided information into two documents concerning the terms of the loans with its banks. One part was in the prospectus sent to those interested in the new preferred shares and the other part was contained in a separate document. It was essential to read both in order to realize that until Quintette ran at an operating profit, all the bank loans were secured against Denison's other assets, not Quintette's. Once profits were achieved for a number of months, the loans became "non-recourse," which means that in case of default, only project assets could be seized by lenders, not Denison assets.

Another confusing area is the use and misuse of creative accounting. Coseka Resources is the best example in Canada of financial make-believe, says Burns Fry oil analyst Paul Joseph. Coseka is controlled by Bramalea, which is in turn controlled by Trizec, which is controlled by Carena-Bancorp of the Edper empire. In 1984, Coseka's calculations showed a "positive cash flow" of $1.36 a share, or $24.4 million in total. But boosting the figure was the fact that some $14.7 million in "capitalized" interest costs were not deducted. Also missing was another $5.3 million worth of expenses in "capitalized" overheads, such as salaries or office expenses, and another $1.4 million in preferred share dividends. "If you deduct these expenses, Coseka's actual cash flow was really $3 million, or 18 cents a share, compared with $1.36 a share," says Joseph.

Capitalizing overhead in a small production company such as Coseka is unusual. More typically, oil companies involved in long-term projects in the Arctic or on the east cost capitalize interest, and justifiably so. Similarly, it is unusual for any company to fail to deduct expenses equivalent to nearly 90 per cent of cash flows.

This is important because oil company shares in stock markets trade in relation to cash flow figures. Using the company's figures, Coseka should have traded at around $5.44 a share, but using Joseph's figures, the stock was worth 72 cents apiece. For most of 1984 and well into 1985, it traded at around $4 a share. "Coseka is the worst example, but there are others," Joseph says. "And there is some justification for capitalizing some interest, such as work on long-term major projects where there won't be any revenue for years. But in this case, there's no justification."

The worst examples outside the oil industry were the Northland Bank and the Canadian Commercial Bank. By 1985, about 20 per cent of their customers were not paying interest on loans, mostly mortgages, in part because of the collapse of property values in Alberta. Normally, the banks should have written down these loan-assets, depending upon how much less than the mortgage the properties were worth. In most cases, the shortfall was quite severe. In addition, they should also have written off the missing interest from their profits over five years. Amazingly, these two banks, with the blessing of their blue-ribbon auditors, did neither.

Instead, they used "baseline" accounting — mathematical mumbo-jumbo that should be illegal. According to testimony before the Estey inquiry, they took the appraised value of the property at the time of the loan, which had dropped severely, took a guesstimate of what the property would be worth in two years, and computed the average, which became the new appraised value — even though, in many cases, the property had taken a dive in price. To make matters worse, they allowed unpaid interest to be added onto the loan, to the limit of whatever the "increased" artificial value was. They not only escaped the requirement to post losses, but added this unpaid interest as profit. The Northland showed a healthy profit from such tricks on the eve of its insolvency, the inquiry was told. Despite the questionable nature of such practices, the banks' managements, boards of directors, and auditors and Ottawa's regulators did not quarrel with them. All banks are allowed to average loan losses over five years, meaning they only write off 20 per cent of the losses each year. This is done to smooth out the peaks and valleys, but it also artificially inflates profit figures. Other financial institutions such as credit unions or trust companies are not allowed to do the same. "Banks use flim-flam bookkeeping," says Hal Jackman. "Trust companies and credit unions cannot."

The banks pointed out that such accounting practices were in fact quite legal; they are used throughout the industry to this day. Auditors told the inquiry that baseline accounting avoids the problem of writing down and writing up bank assets during periods when prices are volatile.

Between creative accounting, disclosure tricks, and bullying, shareholders in Canada often get the shaft. And having disenchanted minority shareholders means less risk capital for the economy.

Corporate Gamesmanship

Paper entrepreneurship has created a Canada full of large, impersonal corporations. All too often their decision-making process is out of touch, non-existent, or unaccountable. Much of Canadian business is characterized by cosy, interlocking directorates where nepotism, schoolboy friendships, or vested interests have replaced achievement as the prime prerequisites. This makes it impossible to remove and replace some less-than-competent directors or managers.

The questionable way in which boards are assembled not only fails to protect shareholders but has a negative impact on our economy as a whole. It is remarkable, for instance, that the management of the Canadian Imperial Bank of Commerce was not reorganized from top to bottom after a string of dreadful mistakes in lending to such shaky operations as Dome, Turbo, Massey-Ferguson, Maislin Industries, Chrysler, and International Harvester. Such errors affect us all, because we pay for them through lower interest on savings accounts and higher loan charges, as bankers scramble to earn more profits, to make up for slim pickings from flagging companies.

Under the law, directors appoint management and supervise its activities. Some are "inside" directors, members of management itself, needed on a board because they have intimate knowledge of their industry and its operations. To counterbalance their obvious vested interests, boards of publicly owned companies also have "outside" directors, who are not employed by the firm and who theoretically serve as ombudsmen on behalf of shareholders.

The importance of their independent scrutiny is partially recognized in the Bank Act, which dictates that banks, for example, must have a majority of outside directors on their all-important audit committees. In non-bank corporations, the appointment of outside directors is not a requirement even in companies whose shares are widely owned by the public. But in partial recognition of shareholders' rights, changes began in the 1970s, when firms such as the American oil giant Exxon abandoned their decade-old practice of totally excluding outside directors from their boards.

However, the rules for outside directorships do not go far enough. In fact, the independence of most outside directors is highly questionable. By definition, an outside director is engaged in another occupation. All too often, however, that other pursuit involves selling services back to the same company he is supposed to be watching. The management he should occasionally shake up as a director may be the same management that signs his cheques as a consultant or lawyer.

Another potential conflict of interest arises when bankers are appointed to boards. This practice is tightly restricted in Britain, where bankers feel that a distance should be maintained from clients, so that both sides can judge situations impartially. The Dome fiasco reinforced the wisdom of this rule: five of Dome's twelve directors sat on the boards of banks or trust companies to which Dome owed money at one time or another. The biggest lender was the Commerce, owed a staggering $1.3 billion out of the $6.5-billion total; Dome chairman Jack Gallagher and Dome director Maclean Jones sat on the Commerce board.

There is no question that such cosy arrangements can lead directors to plunge their enterprises into risky ventures without traditional caution. The shareholders in Dome and the banks have every reason to ask what their directors were doing as the company slid towards the brink with a debt load equivalent to one-quarter of Poland's debt to the West. The answer is: probably very little, because the boards of the big five chartered banks are a manipulative management's dream. They are the size of small parliaments, often including a staggering forty or fifty directors. (The Bank of Montreal, for example, has forty-nine members.) If each director spoke for just fifteen minutes, a board meeting would run for twelve hours. In fact, they generally last two to three hours.

Besides their bias towards appointing customers, banks are also partial to nominating peers of the realm, former cabinet ministers, and the occasional celebrity. Toronto broadcaster Betty Kennedy is on the Bank of Montreal board. Interestingly enough, her husband, Allan Burton, is on the Royal Bank of Canada board. Bank directors also happen to be the most popular board choices in the country. "It is the equivalent of a PhD in business," says Westmin's Paul Marshall.

Bank directors hold an average of eight directorships. Such popularity makes it virtually impossible to devote anywhere near the amount of time to the task that one would expect of directors. From management's point of view, if not the shareholders', this is fine. Directors who are preoccupied with their other business affairs must be spoon-fed a great deal of information at meetings, and agendas must be raced through. Busy bees are not busybodies.

Former Bank of Montreal senior vice president Ross Curtis says the Bank Act stipulates that any loan higher than $1.2 million must go to the board. "And that's a rubber stamp. The morning before a meeting, directors get a package eight inches high. I'd have to attend in case of questions. There weren't any. Dome sparked a lot of discussion after the fact. And during meetings people are flipping in and out constantly because of conflicts. Sometimes there are only six directors sitting there because they must excuse themselves."

Bank-bashers like Hal Jackman, who owns rival trust company assets, say boards should be smaller. "Banks should not be allowed to make loans to their directors or companies with which they are affiliated," says Jackman. "Bank boards now are a joke: fifty guys sitting around a table with an overhead projector. They have not turned down a loan in six to ten years."

Consider John Hewson Coleman of Toronto, president of his own consulting firm, J.H.C. Associates, and a Royal Bank director until 1983. The Royal holds board meetings twelve to fifteen times a year, and most directors also sit on board committees, which meet up to five times annually. When travel and preparation time are factored in, it would be logical to calculate that bank business could occupy a board member up to twenty-five days a year — not an unreasonable commitment, considering the awesome responsibility involved. In actual fact, Coleman estimated his duties as a director of the Royal required forty-eight *hours* a year.

Of course, he could not have done it any other way. In 1982, he was a member of twenty boards, including giants such as Colgate Palmolive, Imasco, Roman Corp., and Thomson Newspapers, as well as the Royal. The year before, the tally was two dozen, including one of the world's largest corporations, Detroit-based Chrysler. If Coleman had spent forty-eight working hours a year, or roughly seven days, on the business of each of the twenty-four companies, he would not have had time for much else. That would have added up to 168 days — two-thirds of the regular working days in a year.

"We've reviewed the issue of board size," says Royal's chairman, Rowland Frazee. "Our boards are not too big. If my directors are not speaking at a meeting, I make sure I ask each one a question. The only benefit of smaller boards would be shorter meetings."

Another practice of questionable value to shareholders is "double-dipping," whereby an executive sits on the board of a parent company as well as on that of its subsidiary, collecting fees from both, a widespread practice here in the land of the branch plant. Of 354 companies surveyed by the Conference Board of Canada in 1983, 45 per cent had one so-called outside director who was employed by a parent or controlling firm; another 14 per cent had one employed by a subsidiary. The problem with such outside directors is that their loyalties lie with management.

While double-dipping can be profitable, being a director is not exactly the path to riches — unless, of course, you are also the firm's lawyer, a consultant, or a celebrity like Gerald Ford, who collects $400,000 a year in director's fees. In 1982, the highest fee paid a director was $40,000, and average retainers are usually as low as $4,600. However, there are often lucrative stock options, such as those created by Dome Petroleum and Genstar — options to buy stock at an agreed price. When the prices of the stocks fell, the options were revised by the board to ensure that the directors still made money.

While most directors do not get rich in a hurry through such immoral means, they are increasingly wriggling out of taking any responsibility for their actions. The lack of risks is probably the single biggest reason why so many directors remain placid even if management should be taken to task on behalf of shareholders. In one Conference Board survey, 90 per cent of companies said they completely indemnify their board members against losses sustained as a result of legal actions arising from their activities as directors, and another 59 per cent indicated that they buy liability insurance for directors as protection against shareholder lawsuits and related matters. But most importantly, the law itself protects outside directors: they are not liable if they "acted in good faith," even if more investigation or common sense on their part might have averted a costly mistake.

Obviously, the law should change to require the appointment of truly independent outside directors, in proportion to the number of outside shareholders. This can be done through cumulative voting, where minority shareholders can cast all their votes for one director, rather than for an entire slate. This allows them to elect a director to look after their interests. Few companies now allow cumulative voting, so unhappy shareholders are powerless to secure representation on a board unless they put up a complete slate of their own and undertake a costly proxy fight.

And the definition of "outside" should change. It is silly to suggest that a Jack Gallagher is an outside director of a bank to which his company owed a billion bucks that it could not pay. Shareholders should kick up a fuss over appointments such as Bruce McLaughlin's nomination several years ago of his twenty-one-year-old daughter to serve as an "outside" director of his development firm, Mascan.

Some companies, such as Canadian Pacific, have bent over backwards to look after shareholders. At CP, widely held by the public, only two of the twenty-six directors are "insiders." "We are great believers in few inside directors. This means management runs scared, there are more viewpoints, and ultimately the responsibility of a board is to change management," explains CP president William Stinson. "Ian Sinclair was a powerful chairman of CP, but he was very respectful of the board. We have many committees with all outsiders.

"Another difference is that our outside directors must have 2,000 shares to get on our board, which before the split [in 1985] meant an investment of $120,000. We want our directors to have something at risk," says Stinson. In 1985, when CP and CP Enterprises merged, the company went beyond legal requirements by insisting that 50-per-cent approval of all CP shareholders be obtained for the deal, and that majority-of-the-minority approval be obtained among CP Enterprises shareholders, whose dominant shareholder was CP itself.

As CP shows, it is inappropriate for directorships to be handed out to suit entrenched managers, for promotional purposes, or as commerce's equivalent of the honorary doctorate. Directors and their corporations have a great responsibility to shareholders and to the entire economy. Both are entitled to accountability from directors, as well as the ruthless elimination of incompetence and the pursuit of efficiency.

Paper entrepreneurs not only play games with the directors, they also have an upper hand because they have spawned enormous concentrations within the brokerage, legal, and accounting fraternities, as their hired hands earn huge fees and commissions for their help. Protected from foreign investment, the country's ten biggest legal, accounting, and brokerage firms dominate their marketplaces and act as the knights errant for the dynasties and management fiefdoms. Among brokers, Richardson Greenshields, Dominion, Wood Gundy, McLeod, and Gordon have 50 per cent of all the brokers' capital, and the top ten have 72.8 per cent.

"The concentration means the owners have inordinate influence, and it makes it difficult for people in service industries — like brokers, lawyers, or accountants — to speak out on the issues or the abuses," says TD's Thomson.

Such concentration means that honesty can be equivalent to committing economic suicide, and blacklisting can be brutally easy to accomplish. Such cosiness means the suspension of free speech in share sales — a conspiracy of silence that makes stooges of small investors. Unmitigated, it can also mean that when ranks are closed, "outsiders" can be shut out of services. Bill Richards, former president of Dome Petroleum, found that after he left the firm — after the company nearly went bankrupt and his services were no longer required — there was no large Bay Street law firm with whom he had relations that would help him negotiate a severance package. In New Brunswick, there is only one law firm that does not work for the Irving empire and that will take on lawsuits against its companies.

Anachronisms

The new paper entrepreneurship has also made an anachronism out of the current mechanisms of shareholders' democracy. With the new fancy footwork and overwhelming vested interests of managers or controlling shareholders, the shareholders' meetings are as modern as four-legged transportation, corsets, or Canada Post. In the summer of 1985, when Noranda squeezed out Fraser's minority shareholders, the meeting was held inconveniently in Edmundston, New Brunswick. When Lac Minerals decided to ask shareholders to approve its new quota rules, which eliminated their voting rights, only a handful attended because many shareholders lived away from Toronto and because Lac is a company where shares often trade hands. Far worse are American examples: American Maize Products shifted its meeting in 1985 to a tiny Texas town, called Dimmick, so remote that most members of the board did not get there in time. And even if they had arrived, there was not a hotel for hundreds of miles. Another company controlled by a wily New York financier has not held an annual meeting in years, somehow seducing securities officials into granting stays of execution.

Here such ruses are rare, but in fact many annual meetings are considered to be necessary nuisances. Conrad Black once prided himself on the fact that one of his meetings took a mere fifteen minutes. Even those that are successes underline the impracticality of the tradition. Bell Canada's Toronto meeting was staged in Roy Thomson Hall, with a capacity audience of more than 2,700. But if every one of Bell's 175,000 shareholders had wanted to attend, facilities would have had to be on a papal scale, with an airport leased for the occasion.

Annual meetings are not the only problem plaguing corporate democracy. Another is that the process of notification, with balloting for those who cannot attend a meeting, is primitive or non-existent. In politics, voters are notified by mail and reminded in person by canvassers. On election day, polls are placed for the convenience of voters. Ask yourself how many people would vote in parliamentary elections if they were only told about it once, by mail, three weeks ahead of time, and had to mail in their ballots — or, if they didn't do that, had to appear personally at a meeting in Ottawa.

It remains a paradox that you can pick up a phone and make a multimillion-dollar stock market transaction, but such modern telecommunications are not permitted when it comes to canvassing shareholders for their opinions — or votes — on key issues. Instead, corporate democracy focuses on the good old annual meeting, even though it is a throwback to the nineteenth century, when the Industrial Revolution made some family businesses so successful that they had to go public and sell shares to partners in order to raise capital for expansion.

The annual meeting was a great way for everybody to meet, face to face, to discuss the year's financial results and swap ideas. It was great when firms were no bigger than the present-day corporation's smallest profit centre. And it was simply dandy when shareholders all lived so close together that they bumped into one another at church. Times have changed. The money business is international now, with shareholders in Canadian companies scattered around the world, only a telex or phone call away. Despite this, companies rely on the primitive mail service. Notices of meetings must be sent three weeks before a meeting, but in a country with a mail service that is occasionally no better than Wells Fargo, company–shareholder communications remain very much in the nineteenth century.

It is not unusual for shareholders to receive a meeting notice after the event has taken place; nor is it rare for shareholders not even to be contacted. Our mail service is not the only culprit. The biggest problem is that the system has not realized that the holders of millions of shares are not contacted at all, because their stock is in "street" names — names of brokers — or registered with the Canadian Securities Deposit Corp. This means there are several layers of intermediaries between a company and its shareholders. Also, there is no law ordering the broker to forward the material to shareholders in time.

The Ontario Securities Commission has been looking at changes to force intermediaries to pass along information and to force companies to reimburse intermediaries for their costs. "Companies probably don't know who their shareholders are. Even if brokers get the stuff, there's a question as to whether they forward it on to the beneficial owners. The big guys get it, but the small guys probably don't," says Allan Aitken of Lafferty Harwood.

What is interesting is that when a management team has an axe to grind, it spares no expense in getting to its known shareholders. Take the case of Southam, which paid Dominion Securities Pitfield 10 cents a share to "solicit proxies" and gain support for its controversial quorum rule, which it eventually backed away from after severe criticism.

Stikeman Elliott lawyer Ed Waitzer says the system should change and should go even a step further than bringing typical decisions to shareholders. "For instance, depending upon how much chance you want to give them to participate, you could decide whether a corporation should give more charitable donations. There's no reason why you can't pass that through the proxy machinery."

Shareholders could phone a certain number to cast their ballot, and some kind of identification could ensure that counterfeit votes would not be counted. As for annual meetings, however, many — like American corporate gadfly Lewis Gilbert of New York — maintain they are an important forum for shareholders. "It's a chance to state your views and coalesce. We fight for post-meeting reports for shareholders who could not attend."

That may be so, but annual meetings could not accommodate questions from all shareholders. Taking the case of Bell again, if the company granted every shareholder a few minutes to have his say or ask a question, the meeting would last a month. All too often, the freedom to speak at an annual meeting is seized by a person with an axe to grind, a pest with little to offer, or questionable-cause champions like the United Church of Canada, which supported the greedy claim of the Lubicon Indian band to lands the size of Nova Scotia plus $250 million, a million dollars for each member of the tiny band of 250.

The rise of paper entrepreneurship and subsequent trampling of shareholders' rights begs for change in the mechanisms of corporate democracy. Without it, shareholders will remain disenfranchised, paper entrepreneurs will always get their way, and confrontations — or, worse yet, indifference — may result.

The Tax-Takers

Donald Harvie's father was one of Canada's richest men, but he gave it all away. And Don, a successful oilman in his own right, has absolutely no regrets. "Not a bit," he says. "I don't believe in free rides between generations. It doesn't do kids much good and often ruins them." Jimmy Pattison feels the same way and has already put in place charitable foundations that will be the beneficiaries of his billion-dollar conglomerate in perpetuity. Their generosity is even more remarkable in light of the fact that they are not bequeathing their fortunes to escape punitive estate taxes. The rich get a free ride in Canada.

Donald's father, Eric Harvie, was a lawyer from Orillia, Ont., who struck it really big in Alberta in 1947. He accumulated land where Imperial Oil eventually found two of North America's biggest oilfields. "Dad had dabbled in Turner Valley, but without much success. He got that package of land in the early 1940s from estates and receivers of a bankrupt land company, paid $10,000 or $12,000, and took it as is. He looked after unpaid property taxes, which was why nobody else would touch it. It was 1,000 separate parcels of land. In 1947, Leduc came in. Then came Redwater in 1948. And both are still producing," says Donald.

Eric died in 1976, but he had already enticed his son away from his own successful oil career, as a chemical engineer for Petrofina, to give away the family jewels. His Glenbow Foundation was set up in 1955, as was the Devonian Foundation, named after the geological formation where oil was found beneath Harvie's lands. Among Devonian projects is the Niagara Institute in Ontario, beautiful indoor and outdoor parks in cities across Canada, and the famous Devonian Gardens in Calgary, a mile-long atrium greenhouse that is copied by architects all over the world.

"Dad wanted to return the money to the people," says Don. "He asked me to take over charitable activities. His idea was to completely liquidate it all, and I am nearly finished now, having given away $75 million," says Don. "My dad also felt that if he did nothing, most of his fortune would go to the government in estate and succession duties, and he felt he could do better than that. The money would have been dropped into general revenues and lost forever. I agree that we should have succession duties, if only to get people with money to set up foundations and do something useful."

Of course, Harvie was not just getting around taxes. He only needed to give away a portion of his estate in those days, as did Montreal philanthropist J. B. McConnell, who put half of his $400-million newspaper and sugar fortune into the Griffith Foundation, Canada's largest. It gives away $11 million a year without even touching its capital base. The other half went into trusts for his eleven heirs.

But since the 1970s, "generosity" has not been necessary for tax purposes, because at that time Canada became one of the few developed countries in the world without wealth, estate, or gift taxes. And that fact has contributed greatly towards further concentration of family wealth. Estate taxes used to amount to 30 per cent on estates worth $250,000 or more. There were also gift taxes to prevent heirs from receiving assets tax-free before the donor's death.

But Alberta's huge oil and gas wealth ended all this. With the Leduc discovery, the province ushered in an era of amazing prosperity. Flush with royalties, Alberta was so rich that it began shedding normal tax takes, such as sales and gasoline taxes. Then it dropped estate taxes, because in 1972 the federal government introduced capital gains taxes assessed on a realization basis (when assets changed hands, such as at death). Because Alberta's ranching and oil communities were concerned that both a capital gains and an estate duty would afflict their heirs at the same time, the estate taxes in Alberta were scrapped. Neighbouring provinces felt forced to shed theirs, too, because their well-heeled residents were migrating to Alberta to take advantage of the tax break. The abandonment of estate taxes spread westward and eastward until the last province — Quebec — gave them up in 1985.

In essence, estate taxes are a toll on wealth once a generation; they are one way a society can break up pools of capital. They are also a way to funnel wealth into socially useful purposes, by allowing rich families to put some or all of their wealth into non-profit and non-taxable foundations that distribute the funds to charities. Either way, private wealth is tapped and recycled to the public.

Charitable foundations are commonplace in Europe and the United States, where estate taxes are as high as 50 per cent in some cases. And never has serious consideration been given to letting the richest in those countries off the hook, as has happened in Canada — no matter the distress such taxes can cause. For instance, U.S. chewing gum heir William Wrigley of Chicago was faced with enormous taxes after both his parents died within months of each other; he had to come up with tens of millions immediately. Fortunately, it only took him a few weeks to sell his family's precious Chicago Cubs baseball team and its valuable ball park in downtown Chicago. The alternative was to sell shares in his family's private company.

Virtually all our trading partners impose estate taxes, gift taxes, or annual taxes on wealth of half a percent or so. We do not. In Canada the system is grossly unfair — only the un-wealthy pay a wealth tax. In a sense, the lower and middle classes pay an annual "wealth" tax in the form of real estate taxes. For most families, a home of their own is the only nest egg they have, yet every year they must pay property taxes based on its appreciated value. As for those not wealthy enough to buy their own homes, they pay their landlords' "wealth" or real estate taxes indirectly, through their rents. The rich pay property tax on their mansions, but that is a drop in the bucket.

Estate taxes break up concentrations of wealth because very often — when they are set at 35 to 40 per cent — they force the sale of assets to outsiders. Of course, those taxes are not really onerous if money is invested properly. The difficulty comes when families have not done careful estate planning, setting aside insufficient money for the eventual tax — like Bill Wrigley.

"The capital gains taxes are onerous enough," says Donald Sobey, of the wealthy Nova Scotia clan. "They have replaced estate taxes, and they will mean that a great many Canadian family businesses will be sold in the next few years, sometimes at distress prices."

Capital gains came into effect as of January 1, 1972, and that is the "valuation date" by which gains are computed. Whatever value has been added to an asset since then becomes the capital gain, and 25 per cent of that gain is handed over to Revenue Canada when its owner and the owner's spouse die. Within days after the law came into effect, K. C. Irving became a permanent resident of Bermuda to avoid the taxes. When he dies, his heirs will pay a capital gains tax of 25 per cent on whatever value was added for those few days in 1972 before K. C. moved. Likewise, Calgary oilman Harold Siebens sold his 34 per cent of Siebens Oil to Dome for $120 million in 1978 and immediately became a permanent resident of the Bahamas. Income taxes and estate taxes are non-existent in both Bermuda and the Bahamas.

While they have escaped taxes, if not death, the rest of Canada's wealthiest have been allowed to defer their capital gains until 1993 by setting up twenty-one-year trusts for their heirs. And there are indications they may be able to defer tax payments indefinitely.

There have been a few precedent-setting decisions that may allow postponements, and possibly avoidance. One 1985 case allowed a change in beneficiary of one of these trusts, allowing a new trust to own the assets and to postpone taxes for another twenty-one years, until 2014. In addition, the wealthy are busy lobbying Ottawa to remove the tax altogether. While current laws stipulate eventual payment, the ability to transfer and roll over to another trust will enhance the concentration of wealth in Canada.

The capital gains taxes were recommended by the Carter commission on taxation during the 1960s. However, it also recommended an "accession" tax, taxing beneficiaries, not estates as a whole. Naturally, it also recommended gift taxes to prevent beneficiaries from avoiding the tax by getting gifts from relatives before they died.

"The establishment detested the recommendation and many of the others," recalls John Tinker, a tax lawyer with Blake Cassels & Graydon who served on the commission. "Kenneth Carter was a partner with Fraser & Beatty, who did work with many of these wealthy families, and you had to admire him. His was an exercise in courageous integrity."

As recommendations curbing concentration went by the wayside, sweeping ones facilitating it became law. Two of the most profound allowed interest on loans made for takeovers to be deducted from income for tax purposes, and allowed Canadian individuals and companies to receive dividends tax-free. "I was riding an airplane with Paul Desmarais when this came into effect, and he said to me after learning about interest deductibility, 'Here come the takeovers,'" recalls corporate lawyer Alex MacIntosh.

But it was the combination of the two that made paper entrepreneurship really pay. Interest deductions made it cheaper to buy assets, but tax-free dividends allowed takeover artists to get cash out of their partially owned companies, tax-free.

The reason for these changes was that interest deductions were allowed south of the border, and that fact was causing Canadian capital to flow south. But the difference in the U.S. system is important to note here. American banks were severely limited in the amount of loans for takeovers or any purpose that they could make to any single customer. This put a lid on paper entrepreneurs. Besides, American takeover artists had to put out a "down payment" of at least 25 per cent in cash when buying shares.

Meanwhile, in Canada, we encouraged takeovers with interest deductibility, then made them far too easy by failing to restrict the size of bank loans or to require down payments. In a sense, we allowed gigantic corporations to be bought with the business equivalent of a Visa card, then wondered why we ended up with a Dome Petroleum and an overly indebted corporate sector.

The goal of tax-free dividends was to discriminate against foreigners in favour of Canadians, contrary to the General Agreement on Tariffs and Trade signed by Canada and its trading partners. This provision is discriminatory because dividends paid to Canadians are tax-free while those leaving the country are charged a 10-per-cent tax.

While tax-free dividends have transferred untold millions into Canada's private sector, this bonus has also encouraged paper entrepreneurship and the creation of highly leveraged holding companies like Brascan and Argus. That is because tax-free dividends allow paper entrepreneurs to buy only part of a company in order to get their hands on its cash flow. Instead of buying all of a company, they can buy control by getting as little as 20 per cent, or a block of voting shares; they take control of the board of directors and harvest the company's earnings by declaring regular dividends tax-free to another one of their companies. This is why Conrad Black has made so much money out of his Argus companies, despite some operating problems at Standard Broadcasting, Massey-Ferguson, and Dominion Stores.

What Black did was a series of paper restructurings, swapping shares in one company within his empire for shares in another company. Dividends were declared regularly, and buy-back offers were made when companies had spare cash. Buy-backs are another technique of increasing the value of a dominant shareholder's position: shareholders can sell shares back to the company at a certain price, allowing the company's coffers to be used to reduce the number of shares overall, thus making the dominant shareholder's position more valuable.

According to Black's own internal figures, anyone buying Argus common shares in 1979, when he did, has made a profit of 43 per cent (including share price increases by 1986, plus the value of share swaps in other Argus companies, another form of dividend that is tax-free). Dominion's shareholders have made 31 per cent, Standard's, 44 per cent, and Hollinger's, 71 per cent — all of which are understated, considering that dividends are more valuable than capital gains because companies pay no tax on them and individuals pay virtually none.

While perfectly legal, and astonishingly smart, Conrad Black's activities serve no socio-economic purpose except to make himself, and his shareholders, exceedingly rich. Such harvesting also results in fiascos such as the decline of Dominion Stores. Operational problems there were not perceived for years, and when discovered, they were not tackled, but merely sold to someone else.

Tax-free dividends also mean paper entrepreneurs can raise more cash, more cheaply. They "lend" one another money by purchasing one another's preferred shares. Because the dividends from these preferreds are also tax-free, they can pay a lower interest rate to their preferred shareholders than they would pay to a bank. In Edper's case, this is called the "cascade effect" — dividends flow from the lowest operating entity up through several layers of operating and holding companies back to Edper, all tax-free.

This has encouraged highly leveraged pyramids such as the Edper, Argus, and Power empires. In the U.S., 15 per cent of dividends are taxed by the same rules as any other form of income and are fully taxed if they are from a personal holding company. Tax-free dividends and interest deductibility have given paper entrepreneurs here a field day and have contributed to concentration. But there are other negatives, too. For instance, holding companies like Argus and Brascan have no assets, except for shareholdings in various companies. So if they want to provide capital to their underlying operating companies, they must borrow or sell shares to others and therefore be diluted. This is what sank Massey, because Argus was unwilling to borrow or sell shares, and the company lacked capital for research, improvements, or expansions.

There is another tax rule affecting the structure of corporate Canada. Unlike

U.S. corporations, a Canadian corporation cannot roll together all the losses or profits of its companies and pay an average tax rate. Here each company is free-standing for tax purposes, despite its links. This has resulted in more leveraging, as a profitable company can load up with preferred shares sold to affiliates, then transfer what might have otherwise been profit to its affiliates in the form of tax-free dividends on those preferreds. This is a widespread practice among Edper companies, but it makes for an expansionary and highly leveraged paper empire.

Another wrinkle in our tax system encouraged the invasion of the U.S. by Canadian real estate development companies. It, too, is a questionable give-away. Companies are allowed to depreciate their assets and use those "deferred income taxes" resulting from depreciation to invest outside the country. "If they are successful, dividends come back tax-free through the Netherlands Antilles [to avoid taxes in the country where the money was made]," says Stikeman's Ed Waitzer. "If they incur losses outside the country, these can be written off against Canadian income. What this means is that Canadian taxpayers are financing Canada's offshore real estate companies. The point is, why allow deferred income taxes to go offshore? All we get back are the losses."

Another concern is that even when some deals appear to be contrived merely to avoid tax, civil servants do not rule out the transactions. This appeared to be the gambit in the case of the Reichmanns' "Little Egypt bump" where assets were valued higher so that depreciation could start all over again for bigger amounts, thus saving $600 million in taxes (this was accomplished by creating a temporary partnership with Conrad Black's Norcen Energy Resources). "The major income for a takeover is simply taxes and account-ing," says Waitzer. "A takeover allows you to bump up the value of assets in a way that the target companies themselves cannot do." Rules have apparently been changed after the adverse publicity about the Reichmann "Little Egypt bump" ruling, but that family and the others can afford to pay tax experts to find new holes in the Income Tax Act.

Meanwhile, as tax reforms spark new activity among those who play the paper entrepreneurship game, higher and more taxes continue to hobble the country's traditional builders and biggest employers — mostly resource companies and manufacturers. They have borne huge tax tabs in the form of taxes both on their income and on their products, in the form of sales taxes.

Currently, Canada's hidden and enormous federal manufacturing tax is 12

per cent — an anomaly in a country that professes to encourage manufacturing and job creation. Few Canadians know of its existence, but it is the reason
why a Buick made at General Motors in Oshawa, for instance, sells for less
money in Tulsa, Oklahoma, than it does at a dealer in Oshawa — despite
transportation costs and the fact that the Canadian dollar is about 30 per cent
cheaper. The difference is that the Canadian federal manufacturing tax and
provincial sales taxes on vehicles are higher than in most states. As for oil,
nearly two-thirds of the cost of gasoline consists of taxes levied by both levels
of government.

If it is wise policy to encourage investors by special tax treatment of paper
capital gains and dividends, it may be even wiser to encourage manufacturers
and resource companies by cutting in half the corporate income taxes they
must pay. As for takeovers, there are some mergers that benefit a company's
international chances or rescue a company from outright bankruptcy, just as
there are others that just encourage paper entrepreneurship. There is no reason
why Ottawa's department of finance cannot withdraw interest deductibility for
those takeovers it deems unbeneficial and allow it for those that it deems in the
nation's or the economy's interest. Likewise, it is unfair that rich individuals
get off so lightly, escaping estate and gift taxes and deferring capital gains,
while the poorest citizens pay what amounts to an annual wealth tax.

As the charitable Jimmy Pattison says: "I believe in merit and ability as the
only reason to rise to a high station in life. I have never been impressed with
people who have been given money. If you love your kids, you make them go
out and get it. I'm giving it all away."

Power Brokers

All this paper entrepreneurship has resulted in a level of concentration so
severe that it has spilled over into the political arena. Both Prime Minister
Mulroney and Liberal leader John Turner have socialized with Argus Corp.'s
Conrad Black, worked and played in Palm Beach with Power Corp.'s Paul
Desmarais, and watched the Montreal Expos play at the personal invitation of
Charles Bronfman, the billionaire distiller who runs Seagram's. This is not to
say that either Turner or Mulroney is tainted, but it does underscore the
concentration and the fact that no matter who is elected, a handful of the
powerful have their ears. And what is good for Conrad Black is not necessarily good for Canada.

"There's too cosy a relationship between economics and politics," says

David McQueen, economics professor at York University. "Canada's biggest businessmen have entry to the highest policy-making circles, and this means a secrecy and centralizing of decision-making and fixing things up between the old boys."

Even Edper's Trevor Eyton admits there is a potential for abuse because of Canada's small size. "Abuse? Sure, certainly there is a political danger. But everybody's being careful not to abuse."

Despite such boasts, the power is very much on the political foot, not the financial, maintains Hal Jackman. Mulroney went to the Palm Beach, Florida, home of his former "employer," Conrad Black, whose companies are the largest shareholders of the Iron Ore Co., where Mulroney was president. The purpose of the 1983 visit was to garner Black's blessing for an inevitable leadership test of former prime minister Joe Clark, whose support was beginning to crumble. "Black asked him, 'Why do you want to run?'" says Jackman, a Clark supporter. "'The prime minister is not that powerful. The job doesn't pay that much and there's no security. You're not interested in country-governing, are you? I guess it's because you don't want to kiss ass, you want other people to kiss your ass.' Brian agreed."

Canadian Bankers' Association head Robert MacIntosh says economic concentration definitely undermines democracy. "When you get a country where Desmarais entertains past, present, and future prime ministers all at once, you've got a problem," he says, alluding to a 1984 New Year's Eve party at Desmarais's Florida mansion attended by tycoons as well as Mulroney, Trudeau, Bill Davis, Jean Chrétien, and John Turner. Prime Minister Mulroney was the guest of Ted Rogers, Toronto cable-TV mogul, when he attended the 1985 Commonwealth leaders' conference in the Bahamas. Not surprisingly, the oil patch's best lobbyist — Smilin' Jack Gallagher — cultivated close personal friendships with Lougheed, René Amyot, a Quebec City lawyer and ski buddy of Trudeau, as well as former energy minister Marc Lalonde. Trudeau's friends included Desmarais, Charles Bronfman, and Robert Campeau. Campeau became rich in great part because of government contracts.

A feather bed for fallen Liberals, the Senate is also populated by some of business's most powerful friends. It is not uncommon for senators to hold a dozen directorships. Among the most prominent senators are Leo Kolber, who runs the CEMP Bronfman empire and is on the board of the TD Bank and many others; Ian Sinclair, who is on the Sun Life, Canadian Marconi, and

Union Carbide boards, among others; Michael Pitfield, on the Cadillac Fairview and Power Corp. boards; Jack Austin, president of a division of the Bank of British Columbia; and others like Duff Roblin, Sidney Buckwold, Bill Kelly, David Walker, and Hartland Molson, with clutches of corporate connections.

"The Senate is business's second chamber. It is, and has been, dominated by business interests," says author-broadcaster Larry Zolf. "The Senate speaks for business and has a great deal of influence. The Senate disallows any bill it wants, sits in caucus, and lobbies the House. And in the case of Opposition parties, the Senators very often outnumber the elected members in caucus. Like the Liberals do right now, for instance."

Similarly, politics and business bed down together when former premiers, prime ministers, and cabinet ministers clean up on directorships, too. In 1985, political retirees like Peter Lougheed, Bill Davis, Marc Lalonde, and Donald Macdonald have followed a well-worn path to riches by collecting fistfuls of legal partnerships or directorships — a path trod by John Turner, current Liberal leader. Even socialist Dave Barrett of B.C. did not return to social work after his political career ended, but began a new and lucrative career as a well-paid broadcaster working for Jimmy Pattison.

Even members of Parliament in opposition have cottoned on to new, lucrative sidelines — like Jean Chrétien's $800-a-day arrangement with the Toronto law firm Lang Michener, his connection to Gordon Capital Securities, and Donald Johnston's affiliation with a Montreal law firm.

While it would be wrong to forbid politicians, past or present, to earn livings, the cosiness is a cause for concern. Many reforms to safeguard against abuse of influence are already in place, such as conflict-of-interest guidelines, disclosure requirements, and contribution ceilings. But there are gaps.

The Sinclair Stevens controversy in the spring of 1986 was a perfect illustration of the inadequacy of conflict-of-interest and disclosure requirements. Stevens put his many corporate holdings into a "blind trust." In the spring of 1985, his wife, Noreen, called upon many members of the corporate community to get them to invest in the troubled ventures, or to lend money against their assets. Among those tapped for money were many who were later hired by her husband or awarded grants by him: Frank Stronach at the auto parts manufacturer Magna was approached; he declined to lend her mortgage money. But eventually a Magna consultant and shareholder, Anton Czapka, lent her $2.6 million, with one year interest-free; Trevor Eyton, president of

Brascan, was approached to arrange a $5-million private placement (a share purchase), and he, in turn, asked three blue-ribbon Bay Street brokers to examine the deal. These were Burns Fry, Dominion Securities Pitfield, and Gordon Capital Corp.; all were later hired to evaluate and sell Crown corporation assets. They did not buy any shares.

Both Stronach and the brokers refused to participate, but the dealings raised eyebrows within the business community and hackles in Parliament. Those approached were under pressure, because the wife of one of the country's most powerful ministers was calling. In the case of Eyton and his brokers, the facts are that Stevens's company — York Centre Corp. — is a penny stock listed on the Vancouver Stock Exchange and would not normally have been given any consideration at all by the heavyweights from such large, blue-ribbon investment houses or by Eyton's Brascan. Approaching them was inappropriate on two levels: not only were Noreen Stevens and York Centre not in their league, but she should not have placed her husband in such a position. Toronto MP Bob Kaplan, leading the charge in the House of Commons, said, "What we have here is a minister's wife shaking down our business community. This is intolerable."

Stevens said in his defence that his wife, who is also a lawyer and businesswoman, acted on her own and never discussed business matters with him after he became minister. The point is that Stevens's wife was placed in an impossible situation, as was Stevens himself. Clearly he should not have been in a portfolio that is so important in the business community, handling grants and other sensitive decisions, such as those relating to Investment Canada.

North America's toughest disclosure requirements for politicians were imposed by the Parti Québécois, undoubtedly to clean up the kind of patronage that had characterized politics in Quebec. The PQ required all elected members to disclose their assets and those of their immediate families and, in an unusual move, required them to reveal to whom they owed money and how much. Not only that, but PQ finance minister Jacques Parizeau personally went a step further. "Politicians are absolutely foolish to socialize with these businessmen or with these families. It is asking for trouble because friendship can impede decision-making. It is dangerous to go fishing with Paul Desmarais."

British Columbia is the only province that does not require candidates to disclose a list of their campaign contributors or the amounts of contributions. Federally, there are limits and disclosure rules for elections, but not — significantly — for leadership campaigns. Theoretically, a well-heeled family could bankroll a prime minister's entire leadership campaign and no one would be the wiser.

It would be naive to suggest that money guarantees success in politics, although candidates who outspend opponents nearly always win, with few exceptions. For instance, wealthy Stephen Roman and Hal Jackman both ran several times federally, spent record amounts, and failed to be elected. However, Roman's nephew, Tony Roman, defied usually insurmountable odds by becoming the only independent elected in the 1984 Tory sweep; he spent almost $11,000 more than was allowed, according to the Royal Canadian Mounted Police, who laid charges against him in 1985. Tony Roman is the first person ever to be charged under federal rules imposing a ceiling of $53,287 per riding, and if he is found guilty he could face a $1,000 fine, one year in jail, or both.

Most of Canada's largest players stay away from contributing to individual campaigns. "When it comes to contributions, we give equally to Liberals and Tories, $60,000. We don't give to leadership campaigns. We may give to the parties or the convention itself, but not to individuals," says Canadian Pacific's president, William Stinson. "That figure is published, and every year Ed Broadbent gets up and screams about it. But that's not enough to keep the PCs in coffee. We don't give to the NDP."

Media magnate and Tory fund-raiser Douglas Bassett thinks it is naive to assume that economic power can "buy" political power even when contributions get the chosen candidate elected. "The real power is in government, from the prime minister on down. Money is given with no strings attached," says Bassett, president of Baton Broadcasting and son of media entrepreneur John Bassett Sr. "The limit in Ontario for elections is $2,500. If during a leadership campaign I gave you $50,000, it would be because I believed in you and your policies, and the organization would think it's only logical that we get to know each other. It gets you an introduction, but that's not why you do it.

"If I want to be in the Senate or get on a Crown corporation board as a director, I wouldn't ask, and if I was dumb enough to ask I'd think a politician would tell me to piss off," adds Bassett. "The perception of power is not the same as the reality. And when it comes to politicians strong-arming business for contributions, I don't have to give to any or all candidates. I'm a big boy and I'm not going to be bullied."

William Stinson, whose Canadian Pacific is Canada's second-largest
company by sales — with 20 per cent of the revenue of the federal government, or nearly $15 billion — says being big is just the opposite of being
powerful. "For political influence, being big is worse. In western Canada,
running against CP was the key to getting elected. Sometimes we were heavy-
handed in our actions."

Despite their disclaimers, wealthy individuals or companies are so important because of concentration in Canada that it may not be necessary to "buy"
them anyway. Canada's economic élite is so small and so powerful that it
must be listened to.

"Go back in our economic history. Concentration has always been an
important element of the scene. Five big banks are a terrific concentration of
power, and that led to the 10-per-cent rule. I'm not sure I'm economically
concerned, but I do have social and political concerns," says Ontario Securities Commission chairman and law professor Stanley Beck. "To the extent
that that kind of power is in fewer hands, it means business has a dispropor-
tionate say in political terms. Then there's media concentration. The fate of
two royal commissions on media concentration, Kent and Davey, their
modest recommendations, and the fact they weren't implemented is a demon-
stration of the power of the press. It's not a case of orders, but second-
guessing. Tax reform, competition bills, securities laws also reflect dominant
interests. In the U.S. system, business is against business. Small and
medium-sized firms use anti-trust mechanisms."

Canada has some of the most concentrated media in the world. The Thomson, Atkinson, Southam, Irving, Sifton, and Black families dominate the
world of print, while the Eaton, Irving, Sifton, and Slaight families control
large portions of Canada's broadcast business. This not only reduces the
number of available viewpoints, but causes a deterioration in quality and
coverage. A chain of weekly suburban newspapers bought by Torstar in 1983
for $17 million from the Bassett family is a case in point. That purchase was a
complete duplication of the weekly chain Torstar already owned, and in each
community only one weekly remains. In Canada's tenth-largest city, Mississauga, with nearly 400,000 persons, the Torstar-owned *Mississauga Times*
was shut down and the Bassett-owned *Mississauga News* retained. Before the
buy, the two papers employed at least eight reporters each covering local
events, city hall, and news. Now the *News* employs only eight reporters.

In Lethbridge, Alta., some readers were so incensed by the mediocrity in their only newspaper, Thomson-owned, that they picketed, wrote their members of Parliament, and grabbed headlines in protest. Winnipeg tycoon George Richardson has felt the same way. "I've called Ken [Thomson] and told him that his two papers [the *Globe and Mail* and the *Winnipeg Free Press*] in my city are so poor that they aren't even worth lighting my fires with. The *Free Press* used to be a great newspaper. Its editorials were quoted around the world. Now we're captives to mediocrity."

"The media magnates are powerful and are independent, which is important to our democratic society," says Bassett. "The weakness of some persons is not the weakness of the institutions. You've got to stand up for people. Some advertisers have called me, upset about some story, and they say, 'We've given you $250,000 worth of advertising.' I say, 'Are you threatening me?' It's been tried. Then I say to them all, 'Well, let's just pretend this phone call didn't happen.' They wanted us to tamper with the news. The stupid bastards."

Even so, the fact remains that it is being tried, and it would not take very many phone calls to muster public opinion in an entire city in favour of, or against, an issue or a politician. And as media concentration continues unmitigated, the danger of such an encroachment of money into the political process increases. Eventually, the fourth estate could be owned by a handful of like-minded individuals who could make or break our elected leaders.

Besides the government's continuous failure to curb media concentration — perhaps due to fear of the fourth estate's reaction — government attempts to trim takeovers have failed miserably. For fifteen years, successive governments have attempted to come up with a new Combines Investigation Act to replace the current toothless one. "The lobbying against it has been phenomenal," says University of British Columbia economics professor William Stanbury. "You would not believe the pressure they can bring to bear, sometimes even the implied threat of a 'capital strike' or a stoppage of certain economic activities." As for concentration of ownership, the 1978 Royal Commission on Corporate Concentration concluded that concentration was not a problem, triggering a spate of takeovers that were unprecedented. Nonetheless, no one revived the debate.

In the mid-1970s, the Restrictive Trade Practices Commission conducted a five-year inquiry into whether Bell Canada and other telephone companies should continue to hold a monopoly on equipment, as well as service. The day before the announcement of a hearing, consumer and corporate affairs minister Tony Abbott made a courtesy call to Bell and others to tell them that a hearing would be launched.

"Jean de Grandpré [chairman of Bell] pulled out the stops and in twenty-four hours was able to see fourteen cabinet ministers and deputy ministers," says a federal government source. "In fact, by the time he got around to Abbott, he was downright abusive. It surprised the minister the way he was talked to. I think de Grandpré's access must be a free-world record. In no other country could that many cabinet ministers be seen in that period of time." While the blitz was impressive, the hearings were in fact held, and Bell lost its mighty monopoly grip on telephone and telecommunications equipment.

One of the biggest gaps in disclosure requirements concerns politicians' debts, despite several high-profile incidents that have made headlines. "Do you put a politician into bankruptcy? No way. Pressure exists in any country. It's not unique to Canada," says Jackman. Robert Harrison, former Montreal Board of Trade president, partner with Touche Ross, and financial adviser of former federal cabinet minister Bryce Mackasey, lined up $625,000 in loans for Mackasey's highly speculative stock market portfolio from the Bank of Montreal, a Quebec court was told. Mackasey lost his shirt, and Harrison was discredited.

Harrison was convicted of eight counts of fraud and conspiracy by a Quebec sessions court in October 1985, stemming from these loan deals made on Mackasey's behalf. Some $400,000 of Mackasey's $625,000 of loans with the Bank of Montreal were rolled into and eventually paid off by a numbered company, 109609 Canada Ltd. That $400,000 was guaranteed by the Ateliers d'usinage HAL Ltée, a manufacturing company in Montreal that had been seeking federal government contracts and went bankrupt. The numbered company was "a fiction created to make that transaction [the loan transfer] happen," Harrison testified at his preliminary hearing in October 1984.

The Mackasey-Harrison affair underscores the concern that banks can be forced into making risky loans to people with political power or influence. It also underscores the concern that politicians can be exploited by banks willing to extend overly generous loans in return for implied favours.

A similar incident involved two of Lougheed's aides in Alberta, says former Bank of Montreal executive Ross Curtis. "Two bright young men closely associated with Lougheed borrowed from a bank. Named Dutton and Richardson, they were bright, impressive. They borrowed money to margin stock. Usually brokerages handle that kind of loan, because they will sell you out if the stock falls in price. Banks don't like margined business. Two managers broke the rules to lend to them, and they are no longer working in the bank. If a stock drops, a broker can call a guy and say he's undermargined, but it's hard if the guy is assistant to Lougheed. It ended up that the stock fell and there was nothing left of the $100,000, so the bank had to go to court. Then it hit the papers.

"A lot of stuff doesn't hit the press. In the early 1970s, an Albertan had financial problems on his big cattle ranch and got his MLA to intercede. He went to the Bank of Montreal chairman, who told others to go easy. But all it did was give the guy time to divest assets belonging to the banks, so we moved in," says Curtis.

The CBA's Bob MacIntosh recalled an instance during the Diefenbaker era when he financed a deal at the Bank of Nova Scotia with some cabinet ministers. "We financed it on the grounds that there were lots of Diefenbaker people involved. We bought some of the bond issue and learned a lesson once and for all — to never do that again. The bonds were badly managed, to put a flattering description to it. We were hung out to dry and had to eat it. There was no way senior colleagues felt we could collect our losses because of the pressures on us. It was a lesson to me. We steered clear.

"Another time, in 1980 — after the last Bank Act revision — we were having a cocktail party to celebrate the end of it, all the bankers, and one guy said, 'That fellow [an MP on the House banking committee] owes us a lot of money on his boat.' Another banker said, 'We have a loan on the same boat,'" said MacIntosh. "He'd given us a whole lot of trouble on the committee. Lending money to politicians is like making loans for a church where the ten most prominent parishioners have guaranteed the loan. That's the sort of loan you never collect and try to avoid."

Those and other incidents point out that disclosure laws do not go far enough because they exclude all-important lending transactions, where some of the biggest advantages lie. Other gaps include the lack of disclosure and ceiling requirements on leadership campaigns, both federally and provincially.

As for socializing, it may be a Canadian fact of life that our biggest tycoons are on a first-name basis with our biggest politicians. Says Royal Bank chairman Rowland Frazee: "I have access to the prime ministers in areas in which I have interest. I'm not suggesting they listen to me. I know the current prime minister quite well. We are on a first-name basis and I have no difficulty phoning him."

Sometimes the pressure on politicians from the business sector is social and subtle, says Jackman, who has worked for the Tories for years as a fund-raiser. "Very few people in main parties are genuine reformers. They want to get along with constituents or big guys. Take Barbara McDougall [minister of state for finance]. She doesn't want the chairman of a bank saying to Mulroney at a dinner party, 'That's a crappy policy that minister of yours has come up with.' So she is careful to second-guess."

Epilogue

There are no villains in this piece. But ours is an economy increasingly characterized by takeover binges and little real growth. Paper entrepreneurship has allowed a handful of Canadian businessmen to slice off hefty pieces of the pie, but they have added little to its size and, in some well-publicized cases, have even reduced it. Only the taxpayers, through our governments, have been building anything of importance in this country. And it is those very governments that have brought the tasks upon themselves by freezing out foreign investment. The only other builders are a handful of Canadian entrepreneurs and their foreign partners. Foreign investment curbs have cost jobs and damaged our reputation as a country of opportunities. It is an image that will not change overnight. And those curbs have contributed to the highly concentrated tier of tycoons in this country.

Even though huge debts and lower inflation have slowed the takeover game, the sad fact is that the majority of Canada's economic élite specialize in paper entrepreneurship. They don't build, they buy. And their appetites for acquisitions have left the rest of us with some expensive legacies: several costly bank and trust company failures to pay for; an arsenal of energy-sapping defence tactics for worried managements, which are disrupting capital markets; some serious casualties among minority shareholders; tax inequality; and an economy so concentrated that a handful of tycoons have amassed an inordinate amount of political influence.

The moves to open up foreign investment, negotiate free trade with the all-important United States, and remove taxes from oil and gas companies are all steps in the right direction. But some serious decisions must be taken to address the problems resulting from concentration.

Without changes, the increasing grip of a handful of gigantic conglomerates and thirty-two families will remain so pervasive and permanent that Canadians may have to determine their future on the basis of what the next generation of this economic aristocracy will be like. In ten years, it may suffice to publish their children's report cards on business pages because corporate Canada's prospects will depend on the abilities of their heirs. Besides the political and economic questions this raises, there are the social ones. Between family empires, management fiefdoms, and governments, there is not a great deal of room — or opportunity — left for real entrepreneurs.

Obviously, answers lie in tax reforms that will reward true entrepreneurs, rather than paper ones. Canada also needs new laws and mechanisms to protect shareholders from bullying tactics, to make corporate Canada more accountable, and to protect the savings of Canadians in financial institutions where they may be manipulated by paper entrepreneurs for their own ends. The key is to establish a new economic order that encourages Canada's best and brightest to concentrate on making the nation's pie grow, not on merely grabbing someone else's piece. But the new order must not discourage them to the point where they leave the country — with their capital.

Without rules to rein in free enterprise, smaller, less powerful companies will be squeezed out of markets and new, young enterprises will not have money, or space, with which to grow. Even some of the most aggressive paper entrepreneurs agree their game should end, such as Canadian Pacific's Stinson. This attitude may not be surprising considering that Canadian Pacific's last three major takeovers — Great Lakes Forest in 1971, Algoma Steel in 1974, and Canadian International Paper for $1.1 billion in 1981 — have been less than roaring successes, particularly CIP, which had lost $223 million by 1985. "We paid several hundred millions too much," admits Stinson.

"Shuffling around paper doesn't do much for the country. I'd like to see our growth from within the group. I'm not interested in another acquisition," he says. "I have concerns about family ownership. Shareholders don't have much say, and it is not healthy to have a country controlled by a group of families."

4

OF CATS AND MICE

FOR SEVERAL YEARS, lawyers for oil companies and various government agencies regularly took their seats in a modest hearing room on the third floor of an Ottawa Legion headquarters. They were attending hearings by the Restrictive Trade Practices Commission on allegations that the petroleum industry was highly concentrated and had conspired to take Canadian consumers to the cleaners, overcharging them for home heating oil and gasoline to the tune of $12.1 billion between 1958 and 1973. The whole process dragged on for 200 days of hearings over five years, with 50,000 pages of testimony and 100,000 exhibits, costing taxpayers and oil company shareholders an estimated $80 million by the time it ended in 1985.

The hearings resulted in a report that contained recommendations for revamping the oil industry and limiting concentration levels and accompanying evils. The report was ignored, for the most part, as were six royal commissions and other government studies that also put the oil industry under a microscope. "It has been a scandalous waste of money," Shell Canada lawyer Mac Austin, of Weir & Foulds, said of the commission's marathon oil inquiry. "It's like spending years and millions of dollars to determine the song played on the *Titanic* when it sank. And who cares?"

The five-year oil inquiry is the best example of the country's inability to come to terms with concentration or with its stepchild, lessened competition. A desirable socio-economic goal, competition means successful sellers operate fairly and efficiently; buyers benefit from reduced costs for products and services; more persons are employed; and industries at home are lean and mean when competing abroad for exports.

The laws designed to enshrine competition are contained in the Combines

Investigation Act. Offences, known in law as restraint of trade, have been punished for centuries because they strike at the very heart of personal freedoms: in 1414, a case was heard in England regarding attempts to force down the prices of English dyers or run them out of business. The bullying tactics were proscribed, because courts ruled that individuals could not be deprived of the right to ply their trade.

But this infringement can and does happen in Canada, thanks to the toothlessness of our laws. In 1982, the Law Society of British Columbia was about to suspend an enterprising young lawyer named D. E. Jabour for six months "for conduct unbecoming a member of the Society" because he undercut rates and advertised for business. Federal combines officials went to bat for him on the grounds that the law society's fee-setting and its other rules were anti-competitive. But they lost, in a precedent-setting court case that upheld the right of provincially regulated societies to ignore federal combines laws.

Even when combines laws apply, the legislation has been inadequate to obtain convictions. The result is that inordinate economic power has accumulated among a few conglomerates, families, and public enterprises. Not only do these enterprises own huge chunks of the economy — a form of concentration economists call aggregate concentration — but they have strangleholds on certain industries or specific products or services, called industry or product concentrations. Even more worrisome, the degrees of concentration that we know about are only the tip of the iceberg. That is because disclosure rules and tools of measurement used by the Restrictive Trade Practices Commission and its combines investigators (who work out of the Department of Consumer and Corporate Affairs) are totally inadequate; they perpetuate economic concentration in this country.

Unfortunately, for nearly two decades Canadian lawmakers have attempted, without success, to reform the Combines Investigation Act. Their legacy is an economy that sometimes resembles our national sport of hockey, but without referees. There is high-sticking everywhere and elbowing in the corners, and even when the whistle blows, penalties are less than adequate.

Under the combines law, marketplace offences include everything from misleading advertising, predatory pricing (selling below cost to drive a rival out of business), and tied selling (forcing a customer to buy something he does not want in addition to what he has bought), as well as criminal conspiracies such as bid-rigging or price-fixing. A new combines law, proposed in December 1985 by Tory minister Michel Côté, may improve competition in

Canada by making it easier to get convictions, by decriminalizing many sections of the law, by extending laws to include banks and Crown corporations, and by creating a merger tribunal to decide whether takeovers or mergers are in the public interest. But the virtues of competition must be understood by lawmakers, judges, and the public before any meaningful changes will restore competition in many Canadian sectors.

Competition and the related issue of concentration have been all but ignored. This is because they are little understood in a country where one out of every three workers is employed by a non-profit, government, or monopoly enterprise. Many more work for large, impersonal multinationals. We are a nation of civil servants, cops, and manual labourers who elect leaders who do not understand that the structure of an economy affects everyone's lives, both economically and politically.

The Americans, on the other hand, understand that free enterprise, unbridled, eats its young. Stern U.S. anti-trust laws allow small and medium-sized enterprises to blow the whistle on big marketplace bullies, thus protecting the most vibrant, talented, and fast-growing segment of the economy. U.S. consumers and workers are also steeped in their legal and economic rights. It is all part and parcel of the American dream. There has never been a romantic Canadian dream, in great part because there are no rules protecting the little guys from the big guys. In Canada, Horatio Alger's heroes would probably have worked for Ontario Hydro or been driven out of business by it.

Another marathon inquiry by the Restrictive Trade Practices Commission was its five-year probe into Bell Canada's monopoly on making telephone equipment. And Bell's chairman Jean de Grandpré describes that one as "absolutely useless and a waste of money and time.

"We were investigated for sixteen years before our hearings. Officials seized documents in 1966 and the judgment came down in 1982. We spent millions on this mess. It was stupidity. I saw many cabinet ministers to try to stop the hearing. I was so mad I said I'd never read that crap, and I never have," recalls de Grandpré. What was ironic was that before the combines and commission officials finished their massive task, another government agency, the Canadian Radio-television and Telecommunications Commission, ordered Bell to relinquish its monopoly on equipment to open up competition to others.

De Grandpré is right about the stupidity, but wrong about the reasons. Canada's combines officials and their commission have wasted time and money, but not because their efforts are misguided. They have been held back from guaranteeing competition by uninformed politicians who have not amended laws, hard-nosed business lobbyists who have derailed any attempts at reform, and a naive judiciary, usually drawn from the ranks of the country's best criminal lawyers but typically lacking the business smarts to judge business cases.

"It has been very frustrating," says Ian Nielsen-Jones, a combines investigator and director of manufacturing matters. "The law is difficult to prove, compared with the U.S. laws. In Canada there is a lack of appreciation for white-collar crime and what that means." In four decades, the Crown has not obtained one conviction under its merger provisions and only one in the case of a monopoly. This is primarily because in Canada, it is not adequate merely to prove that a merger is anti-competitive or that a monopoly has been created. It must be proven that the parties involved intended to "unduly lessen competition to the detriment of the public."

Even in an apparently clear-cut case, such as the one involving Thomson and Southam newspaper executives, conviction may elude the Crown. The case, in 1982, concerned an agreement between the two companies that created daily newspaper monopolies in four cities. "That case was outrageous," says Robert Kerton, economics professor at the University of Waterloo and spokesman for the Consumers' Association of Canada. "There was a piece of paper in sixteen pieces in a garbage pail when combines officials arrived. When they entered, an executive attempted to burn the paper with his cigarette lighter. It gave expected profits after closing Winnipeg and Ottawa newspapers. In the end, the court didn't consider it as evidence because of the way in which it was gathered. The warrants issued to combines officials were issued by the Restrictive Trade Practices Commission, and courts ruled warrants were only legitimate if issued by a judge."

Other cases, against Canadian Breweries (now Carling O'Keefe), B.C. Sugar Refining Co., and K. C. Irving, were also difficult to prosecute. Over the years, the courts have interpreted public detriment under the Combines Investigation Act as a situation where conspirators have eliminated all competitors and intended to do so. Even in a case when this was proven, the 1975 Irving case where it was shown that K. C. Irving had stalked and bought all five English-language dailies in New Brunswick, the court said this was not a detriment to the public. The court cited the fact that the Irving papers were the last in Canada to increase circulation rates from 8 cents to 10 cents and also had the lowest advertising rates in the country.

(It is doubtful that the court knew beyond a doubt whether the price hikes were delayed because the papers were already making inordinately high profits or whether managers were simply slow to react. Similarly, the court did not determine whether the low rates were due to the poor economic conditions in New Brunswick or to the fact that many of the Irving advertisers are also Irving companies or suppliers, who would enjoy artificially low advertising rates.)

The Irving case established that, under current laws, an individual could hypothetically own all the newspapers in Canada. In fact, the only way in which Canada's unusual media concentration has ever been abated — albeit temporarily — was by a 1982 order-in-council directing the Canadian Radio-television and Telecommunications Commission to refuse licence renewals to TV stations owned by newspaper companies in the same market. The Irving family began a long, expensive fight all the way to the Supreme Court of Canada against this, but that became unnecessary in June 1985, when the federal Tories rolled back the order.

In the U.S., prosecutors can obtain convictions much more easily because they only have to prove that parties lessened competition unduly. Intent is irrelevant. There are parallel differences between the two countries in the laws relating to bad cheques. In Canada, a cheque writer can be prosecuted if it is proven that he knowingly kited his cheque. In the U.S., it is illegal merely to have the cheque bounce, intentionally or not; in some states, such as Minnesota, five bounced cheques put the cheque writer on a blacklist, and he loses his banking privileges for up to five years.

It is not insignificant that the only conspiracy conviction in Canada involved three American-owned subsidiaries whose parent companies were undoubtedly subjected to anti-trust pressure for these actions. General Electric, Westinghouse, and Sylvania were fined $545,000 in September 1976 for agreeing to eliminate any price competition in the sale of large lamps in Canada. The court said, "Between 1959 and 1965 the three companies sold $238.5 million worth of large lamps, and there is no room for doubt that all three defendants increased profits as a result of the conspiracy."

The "large lamps" case aside, intent has been impossible to prove and easy to avoid in Canada. Robert Kerton points out a technique sometimes used by the country's pulp and paper producers, another cosy group dominated by a few families such as Peter and Edward Bronfman, Paul Desmarais, the

Bentleys, the Reichmanns, the Krugers, and the Rollands, and by smaller, foreign-owned players. "The president of one company will make a public speech somewhere about needing more money for his paper. This is a smoke signal to the others. Sometimes they even state a percentage increase publicly."

"In the U.S. this would be called inferential conspiracy or conscious parallelism, and it's far easier to prove there than here," says Ian Nielsen-Jones. "In Canada, we had a case close to parallelism involving fertilizer companies in 1980, but we lost it. Now we watch for such public statements."

Although such difficulties have frequently been brought to the attention of politicians, combines law reforms have been bungled. Several revisions and reforms have been attempted unsuccessfully since 1959. In fact, the huge services sector did not even fall under the combines act's purview until 1976, leaving those players completely to their own devices. Similarly, banks and most federal Crown corporations have been exempted. It is hardly any wonder that lawmakers have been frozen at the switch: successive regimes persist in consulting too often with business groups in trying to come up with new competition rules — a practice that is equivalent to asking crooks their opinions about amendments to the Criminal Code.

"We have allowed businesses to earn monopoly profits with which to lobby for monopoly power," says University of British Columbia economics professor William Stanbury. "Then there are the examples of lack of economic understanding by the judges. If they understood business and profits, they would recognize that current fines are trivial costs of doing business." In 1984, an Ontario Supreme Court judge threw the book at huge Imperial Oil for driving a small rural independent gasoline retailer out of business. It received a record fine of $75,000 and some stern words from the judge, but the award was only equivalent to two hours' profit for Imperial. The small independent received nothing.

In the U.S., anti-trust traditions run strong and deep. The guardian for economic underdogs is the Federal Trade Commission, which sits in Washington as a severe sentinel over that country's markets. It metes out severe punishments, such as treble damages for bid-rigging or predatory pricing. And it can also unravel huge mergers with a stroke of the pen. In 1985, Chevron was ordered to sell 2,000 gas stations acquired when it bought Gulf, because the purchase lessened competition in certain regions in the U.S. Sometimes the FTC can stop mergers just because they are not perceived to be in the interest of the public; it barred a proposed merger between General Motors and Westinghouse several years ago for such reasons. Its powers are so pervasive and fearsome that executives with rival firms avoid socializing together to avoid suspicion.

By contrast, Canadian combines officials were powerless to do anything about Petro-Canada's 1985 takeover of Gulf Canada's 2,400 gasoline stations even though the deal was intended to lessen competition. It gave the national oil company control over one of every three gasoline stations in Ontario and an overall national market share of 33 per cent, concentration levels that would be intolerable in the U.S. Not coincidentally, years of price wars at the gas pumps ended in a truce after the takeover, depriving consumers of the fruits of competition.

The PetroCan takeover also underscored another advantage to out-and-out competition: it creates employment for more people. While exact figures are not available, up to 2,000 Canadians lost their jobs as a result of the PetroCan takeover, as duplication of services was slashed. Unable to do anything, the combines investigations director in December 1985 tabled a report to the equally toothless Restrictive Trade Practices Commission, recommending that the commission ask the federal government to unravel the deal and force PetroCan to sell all its Gulf stations to independents or competitors.

Not only are rules inadequate in Canada, so are the tools by which combines officials measure and monitor marketplace activity. Economists measure three types of concentration: "aggregate concentration," the degree of ownership by individuals or companies in an economy; "industry concentration," or the relative position of large firms in specific industries, such as steel or meat-packing; and "product concentration," the relative position of large firms in the manufacture and sale of specific products, such as passenger cars or canned soups. Industry and product concentration are separate because a steelmaker may dominate the overall steel industry, but have little or no market share in steel pipes for the oil business.

Canada has some of the highest levels of all three kinds of concentration in the world, far higher than those in the U.S. "Between 1980 and 1981, aggregate concentration [the share of all non-financial assets held by the twenty-five largest corporations], where changes are normally glacial, increased very dramatically to 32.1 per cent from 30.2 per cent. This is nearly quadruple the annual rate of increase in concentration since 1965, when it was 23 per cent. In the U.S., you would have to include the 100 largest corporations to get to a figure of even 30 per cent," says combines branch economist R. S. Khemani.

Regarding industry concentration, Khemani says, "In 1977, the fifty largest banks in the U.S. accounted for 35.5 per cent of total assets; the forty largest electric and gas utilities, 59.8 per cent; the fifty largest retail trade corporations, 20.5 per cent; and the fifty largest transportation companies, 61.6 per cent."

In Canada, his figures show the four largest firms had 76.6 per cent of the air transportation business; banks, 74.6 per cent; trust companies, 51.7 per cent; mutual funds, 61.3 per cent; electric utilities, 77.7 per cent; food stores, 54.8; department stores, 85.2; and variety stores, 87.8. Khemani estimates that "nearly four-fifths of the U.S. economy is essentially competitive, but in Canada the estimate is two-fifths. This is mostly due to weaker anti-trust laws."

As bad as these figures are, they are not the full story. Aggregate concentration figures do not show businesses that are controlled with less than 50 per cent of shares or those that have provincial charters. Industry and product figures are similarly misleading.

The most common measuring stick of industry and product concentrations is the "four-firm concentration ratio." This figure is the percentage of sales accounted for by the four largest firms in an industry or the four largest selling a specific product. Ideally, those four share less than half the marketplace.

In the U.S., when four companies have a combined market share of 55 per cent, they are automatically investigated by the combines officials' counterparts, justice department officials. The rationale behind this policy is that the fewer firms there are dominating a marketplace, the easier it is for them to get together and artificially charge higher prices. If these investigations determine that the big four are abusing their marketplace dominance, they may be asked to desist from certain activities, fined, or forced to divest.

In Canada the tools have not been up to the job, although new legislation passed in June 1986 represents an important step towards protecting competition. In the U.S., justice department officials know, for instance, who are the four largest sellers of canned peas in Chicago. Here, Statistics Canada has a category called "miscellaneous food" that is a grab-bag, including everything from soup to nuts. Equally meaningless are its "major appliances" category, which lumps together stoves, refrigerators, washers, and dryers; "small appliances," which includes everything from vacuums to fans, toasters, irons, and water heaters; and "wood products," which includes almost everything made from trees.

Another misleading category is "pharmaceuticals and medicines." Figures show that four firms have only 37 per cent of the market, but this badly understates the situation because the category includes items like condoms as pharmaceuticals, and as medicines, everything from pills for cattle to those used by humans. This overlooks the reality that there are only two firms in Canada that sell tranquillizers, for instance. Likewise, petroleum and coal are considered as one category, which cuts in half the otherwise highly concentrated ratios in both those industries.

Other faulty tools are Canadian figures that are neither timely nor broken down by regions, or "natural" markets. Figures come out at intervals as large as five years, compared with U.S. figures, which are published annually. Regional representation is also essential to valid measurements, as was shown in the case of Canada Safeway, unsuccessfully prosecuted as a monopolist in Alberta. The grocery chain has a potentially troublesome 60-per-cent market share in that province, but the defence convinced the Crown this was not a problem because it had less than 10 per cent of the national market.

The new combines law may help, but referees must be very well trained and equipped to understand the nuances of the world of business, cautions David McQueen, economics professor at York University. "How to judge competition? Most people feel that a wide variety of brands and prices indicates a healthy, competitive situation. However, prices for products may be near enough the same, but there may be non-price competition, such as advertising, product differentiation, or loss-leaders, like free glasses when you fill up with gasoline.

"Lack of competition is often due to other factors: extreme transportation costs create natural monopolies, as in the case of aggregates, because others farther away cannot compete; unionization and very high wages remove certain players from some markets, lessening competition; extremely capital-intensive industries such as petrochemicals impede most from getting involved; severe price competition; prohibitive advertising expenses may remove some competitors as well as import barriers, tariffs, or ownership requirements, as is the case in Canada's financial institutions and media," says McQueen.

Competition exists when there are no obstacles to entry or exit, no tariffs keeping out imports, and an adequate number of firms involved in production. But most of Canada's economy is carved up into tidy little franchises or money machines. This has allowed a handful of conglomerates or family-owned companies to dominate. In fact, most parts of our economy are oligopolies. Ours is a hockey game that rewards brawn, not brains, and sidelines, perhaps forever, smaller and more talented players.

A major problem is that Canada has never come to grips with concentration, thanks to the successful efforts of the big business lobbies in two principal areas: the imposition of tariffs to keep out foreign competitors, and the imposition of ownership restrictions at home to keep down the number of domestically based foreign competitors.

This has cost the country opportunities as our industry is increasingly characterized as concentrated, coddled, and uncompetitive; this hampers our chances to export internationally. It has cost the consumer billions, shifting massive amounts of wealth from individual hands into the hands of decreasingly efficient enterprises.

"Tariffs and foreign ownership restrictions are key elements in causing high concentration. Studies show if four firms have 50 per cent of a market where there is a high tariff of, say, 15 per cent [which will keep out imports], it will result in 116 per cent higher prices in Canada than in the U.S.," says Stan Kardasz, economics professor at Waterloo. "The problem is a combination of concentration, barriers to entry, and tariffs."

Another factor working against competition has been governments themselves, who create money machines through regulation and red tape. "Governments are barriers to competition," says UBC's Stanbury. "In Canada, provinces do not allow interprovincial transport of beer. We're not a common market. We have regulated airlines. Ontario has cartelized beer for the big three breweries. Before anyone blames private power, how much state power is used to aid accumulation? The state is the enormous engine of monopoly."

The country's financial industries, bankers and brokers, who talk an impressive free-enterprise philosophy, practise just the opposite. On Bay Street, the so-called bastion of free enterprise, the brokers are highly concentrated and fiercely anti-competitive. In 1983, they virtually drove out of the province Charles Schwab Inc., the largest discount broker in the U.S., by placing foreign ownership obstacles in its path. The result is few brokers to choose from, little commission competitiveness, and too much concentration: by 1985 five firms controlled half the capital of the three dozen brokers on the TSE: Richardson Greenshields, Wood Gundy, Dominion Securities Pitfield, McLeod Young Weir, and Gordon Capital. The ten largest had 72.8 per cent of the industry's capital.

Official red tape seriously erodes competition, creating monopolies for those big enough and rich enough to cut through the bureaucratic maze. "Take the case of a farmer who wants to start a gravel pit operation on his land," says Toronto urban economist Garry Stamm, president of Stamm Economic Research. "New zoning has to be obtained, a hearing held under the Pits and Quarries Act showing a plan for thirty years; the area must be turned into a park. The up-front costs alone are $250,000 to $700,000, just to get approval, which means a farmer cannot get into the business any more. And a routine rezoning in Ontario will cost a developer $1 million and a year or two, if there are any objections to it from the public."

Zoning hassles and the strict town planning traditions that Canada inherited from Britain have created Canada's biggest, most spectacular fortunes in real estate. By restricting the game to only the biggest, the rich get richer as rezoning becomes a patented money machine that town planners and local politicians will protect forever if they refuse or limit other rezonings nearby.

Red tape also affords those working against competition time to muster their forces. "All regulatory businesses that are not monopolies, such as trucking firms, act as intervenors in rate or access hearings, which gives [trucking rivals] a chance to set up obstacles," says Garry Stamm. "In Ontario, for instance, because of the red tape, only five firms are allowed to carry all those new cars by truck."

Waterloo's Kerton concurs: "Truckers are nothing more than point-to-point monopolies. Regulated freight rates are so high that a large number of trucks run empty at least one way. They are paid to do so. That is why the price of shipping in Canada is much higher than in the U.S., and it is why we must have deregulation." In Canada, many rates set by provincial or federal regulators are as high as a return fare. This is because truckers argue that they would not take freight from point A to B for any less when there is nothing to bring back from B to A. And these costs are passed along to consumers.

Consumers are not the only victims of concentration. Taxpayers have paid through the nose for the lack of protection from abuses. Former combines investigations director Lawson Hunter pointed out that bid-rigging has probably cost taxpayers billions. "Bid-rigging is a serious and costly crime. In the U.S., it is estimated that bid-rigging has increased the cost of U.S. highway construction by $750 million a year," he said in a speech in 1985. Also affected are schools, hospitals, and billions of dollars' worth of other projects — from dams to nuclear reactors to oil wells — that are procured by governments. "In the U.S. in the five years ending in 1984, 527 companies were convicted and $100 million in fines were assessed."

Meanwhile, in Canada, Hunter pointed out, "the Beamish case arose out of an inquiry in the 1960s into alleged price collusion and bid-rigging on tenders for the surface treatment of roads and highways in Ontario. Charges were laid against twelve companies. Evidence showed by agreement, the contractors determined who would get a particular contract and the others would bid lower. Although the judge found that the agreement was proved, he concluded it was not an agreement to lessen competition unduly, largely because the companies did not have a virtual monopoly over the supply of asphalt, stone, chips, sand, and gravel. However, the judge found it was completely devoid of business ethics."

One successful case involved the supply of school bus services by Travelways School Transit, Lorne Wilson Transportation, and Charterways Co. to the Peel Board of Education in Ontario during the 1977-78 school year. The three submitted identical bids and were convicted for doing so. But another case involved supply and installation of glass for a number of large public and private buildings in British Columbia. Says Hunter, "This case is of particular interest because the court found the accused firms not guilty, even though it found that the firms had arranged their prices. The court found such conduct to be reprehensible and that bids were a fraud and unnecessarily and dishonestly increase the costs to an owner.

"Sometimes the firms agree not to bid at all and sometimes they agree to take turns at being the low bidder. In a recent case involving the supply and installation of reinforcing rods in Montreal, we found that the conspirators played cards to decide who would submit the lowest bid. In an electrical equipment case in the U.S., the bidding rotation was tied to the phases of the moon."

Another major problem lessening competition and resulting in added costs to taxpayers is the complicated interprovincial barriers in Canada, which exist even though Section 121 of the British North America Act specifically forbids tariffs on goods shipped across provincial borders. But governments at all levels resort to a host of non-tariff barriers, such as preferential purchasing policies, regulatory restrictions, and packaging requirements (ranging from mandatory foil wrapping for butter in Quebec to a one-litre maximum for bottles of imported wine in B.C.), that effectively handicap outsiders.

An example of discriminatory practice is found in the East. Newfoundland pays 10 per cent more for locally produced goods, and a procurement agreement among the other three Atlantic provinces gives the suppliers of each province first crack at the market, suppliers elsewhere in the region second, and the rest of Canada third, if local suppliers cannot be found.

Nova Scotia will not entertain tenders from outsiders if there are enough firms bidding already, and New Brunswick will not if three local firms bid. In Quebec, the lowest-bidding Quebec firm always wins. On large contracts, the province pays 10 per cent more to local suppliers. In Ontario and B.C., Canadian bids receive a 10-per-cent advantage over non-Canadian ones, but in Quebec the advantage goes to Quebec firms only. In other words, these provinces have enshrined the practice that their taxpayers will pay 10 per cent more for services or goods than they might otherwise have to.

While the U.S. seems to have taken on cartels with more gusto and success, the situation there is far from perfect. And in the private sector, the cosy U.S. automakers' cartel has resulted in near-catastrophe for huge portions of North American business. The manufacturing of cars is the best example of the dangers of allowing concentration to continue unrestrained. Until the 1970s, North America's four major automakers had 80 per cent of the market. Prices rarely varied, apart from the costs of fancy options, which enabled the automakers to pass along to consumers higher labour costs due to excessive labour demands and shoddy workmanship. Ralph Nader exposed planned obsolescence and poor manufacturing techniques while the Japanese steadily made inroads with their fuel-efficient cars.

By the end of the decade, they had slowly established a huge, reliable dealer network and Detroit was plunged into a depression. Once the automakers were toppled because of the success of cheaper, better Japanese cars, the disruption was enormous. Chrysler had to be propped up, and hundreds and thousands of auto workers, parts-makers, and steelworkers lost their jobs to poor sales or robots. Entire cities in Michigan and Ohio shrank, and trade deficits swelled to dangerous levels.

Says UBC's Stanbury: "If we had had twenty automakers in North America instead of three, one of the twenty would probably have produced an appropriate car, instead of going along merrily producing the high-priced cars we ended up with. This was a good example of the lack of imaginative thinking among a comfortable oligopoly. Not just price competition, but product innovation. Then we wouldn't have needed quotas." According to a Washington think tank, the Brookings Institute, it costs $160,000 per year in subsidies to save just one U.S. auto worker's job. The same holds true in Canada, where quotas exist on an informal basis.

The competition from abroad and the liberalization of world trade since the Second World War has helped to offset some of Canada's concentrations. Restrictions on a number of imports have been removed since the post-war series of GATT rounds. Unfortunately, the exceptions hurt those on the lower end of the scale.

"Generally, Canadian trade policy [which has resulted in a liberalizing or freer flow] in recent years has increased the exposure of domestic industry to import competition. However, there are exceptions in primary textiles, knitting, clothing, footwear, and some agricultural products such as cheese, turkeys, chickens, beef, and eggs," says Lawson Hunter. "One estimate is that the cost to consumers of tariffs and quotas on clothing was $467 million in 1979; moreover, the cost of protectionism was being borne disproportionately by low-income consumers. Another estimate was that removal of tariffs on textiles would alone increase welfare [payments] by $150 million a year."

Waterloo's Kerton says of marketing boards: "Dairies are legally established cartels and we are paying the price, $800 million per year extra for milk products, which is the estimate by the Economic Council of Canada. Introduced in the 1970s were marketing boards for four commodities: eggs, chickens, turkeys, and milk. These people have been exempted to set up a monopoly, costing consumers billions more per year. Most of this was done to protect the family farm, but there has been a massive reduction in the family farm since the legislation."

Such massive subsidies increasingly shift wealth from the more efficient, high-taxpaying individual to less efficient and marginal forms of economic enterprise on the farms. In a country faced with huge debts, choices have to be made as to how best to organize our economy to compete worldwide. It would be wiser to let farmland lie fallow than to prop up the planting of crops or production of commodities if imports are markedly cheaper. By scrapping such cartels, billions of consumer dollars are freed up to spend or invest elsewhere. It also shifts economic activity to other, more lucrative areas.

The steady, unimpeded progress of all forms of concentration has led some politicians to take the law into their own hands. Saskatchewan's Allan Blakeney broke up his province's cement and steel cartels by getting into competition with them. Similarly, Peter Lougheed and Jacques Parizeau brought in policies designed to fight the trusts that plagued their provincial economies.

With few exceptions, however, concentration continues quietly, sometimes through the use of clever techniques that lull consumers into thinking there is competition when there is none. For example, no-frills Brewers Retail stores in Ontario are designed to make consumers think they are government-owned, as are the liquor stores. They are not: they are owned by the big three breweries, whose 93-per-cent stranglehold on the Ontario market guarantees them the kinds of profits that monopoly utilities make. Other examples of concentration disguised as competition are the Dylex and Imperial Optical conglomerates, which sell their goods under a chain of retail outlets under many different names.

To be fair, it would be impractical and foolish to make all oligopolies illegal. Sweeping legislation would break up good as well as bad oligopolies. And no legislation can be all things to all people. But very often solutions are around, although they are almost always overlooked. Take the case of Canada's overly concentrated oil industry, which sparked many controversies and led to the mammoth oil inquiry that dogged the steps of the biggest players — Shell, Gulf, Texaco, and Imperial.

Since the Second World War, the Canadian oil industry has been a good political scapegoat, because every voter buys its products; and for the past decade, it has racked up one out of every four dollars earned by all non-financial corporations in Canada. This has fuelled the complaints of socialist critics. But the result is that the industry has been royal commissioned and inquiried to death. And when it is not under a microscope, it has been repeatedly attacked in a misguided and devastating way. More astute analysis and sensible public policies would have cost less and done more.

The first thing to note is that the big four only dominate the downstream — refining and marketing — portions of the industry. The money is not in downstream, but in exploration and production, and the companies' share of this has been decreasing dramatically. The decrease is mostly due to Alberta's royalty increases, which have affected the big four more than smaller companies, and to drilling requirements that stopped them from straddling all the best lands. So the overall portion of oil company profits pocketed by the big four companies began to decline slightly during the 1970s.

In gasoline selling, the big four have had many other competitors, independents or smaller regional competitors such as BP Canada, Petrofina, Ultramar, Irving, Chevron, Turbo, Mohawk, Suncor, and others. In many regions, there was a lively market with price fights and non-price gimmicks like free glasses, providing consumers with many choices and bargains.

The real problem was neither aggregate concentration nor product concentration levels, but industry concentration in the area of refining. The major companies owned virtually all the refineries, which meant they were in a potential conflict of interest at all times because they supplied on a wholesale basis their own retail competitors. Naturally, this arrangement allowed the big oil companies to become bullies, on occasion cutting off independents, jacking up wholesale prices to them unfairly, or undercutting them severely to drive them out of business. And that sparked all the controversy.

The real solution was to attack the stranglehold on refineries by imposing "divorcement" — the sale of refineries to independents or the sale of the majority of their gas stations to independents. That would have ensured arm's-length transactions and healthy competition. Ottawa should have had PetroCan buy all the country's refineries. Instead, PetroCan became the biggest gasoline seller in Canada, surpassing all others with a whopping 33 per cent of the entire market — a level of concentration that would not be allowed in the U.S.

"PetroCan is just as much of a marketplace bully towards independents as the others. It has absolutely nothing to do with nationality," says Jim Conrad, executive director of the fifty-member Canadian Federation of Independent Petroleum Marketers.

PetroCan's $4-billion takeover spree, undertaken since the National Energy Program began in 1980, eliminated three players from the marketplace: Gulf, BP, and Petrofina. The result has been that industry concentration has increased in refining and gasoline, with PetroCan the biggest culprit, and the profits of the four biggest multinational companies have grown, not shrunk, as a proportion of the oil business. In the name of increasing Canadian ownership, the NEP lessened competition.

Apart from insufficient analysis and weak regulations, another problem facing combines officials in Canada is the lack of vocal consumerism, such as exists in the U.S., led by Ralph Nader and others. Here, the Consumers' Association of Canada operates on a shoestring and with volunteers. Located in Ottawa, it publishes *Canadian Consumer*, a magazine that contains the results of product testing. Costing $26 a year, it is lucky if it breaks even with a tiny circulation of 160,000. Similarly, small-business spokesmen have not made concentration issues the priority that they should because they don't realize that anti-trust laws are designed to protect small business from big bullies.

In the absence of intelligent debate about the issues involved, the big danger is that even if Michel Côté's new laws are more effective, the level of concentration may have gotten out of hand already. Robert Kerton of the Consumers' Association, who took an interest in the Thomson-Southam case, recalls a telling incident.

As a volunteer spokesman for the group, he has found it increasingly difficult over the years to spend the amounts of time required to do the job as concentration critic properly. "Before the trial, I got a phone call from Tory Tory DesLauriers & Binnington [law firm for Thomson]. They offered me a retainer to become a professional witness on their behalf. Retainers would have made me rich. I didn't take it, but this meant by the time the Crown came around for witnesses, the market [for economics experts] had been pretty well shopped."

On the other hand, such anecdotes may jar influential Canadians into realizing that concentration policies must become a higher priority before it is too late. The new laws will help, but only if supported by regulators and investigators who have sufficient tools and staff to do the job and a judiciary that understands the business world.

Canada's marketplace has seen four decades of bloody hockey without referees. Many players have been bruised and battered or, worse yet, have left the game forever, knocked out by rival teams. It may have left our industries weakened and protected with little to offer in a freer trade environment. Tragically, ours has been a game gone wild, robbing many talented Canadians of the chance to participate. And until politicians and our courts realize the importance of anti-trust rules, the game will continue in earnest, with no referees in sight.

5

THE MONEY MACHINES

CANADA'S ECONOMY has become a collection of lucrative franchises, or money machines. Protected by tariffs, restrictive regulations, or subtle business barriers unique to Canada, the country's business life has become profoundly concentrated. Ours is an economy characterized by oligopolies, small groups of sellers, and by oligopsonies, small groups of buyers. This chapter profiles a handful of the country's money machines, industries where concentration levels are high and potential abuses considerable. Far from complete, the sampling shows the lack of competition in some sectors, because of barriers to entry, certain practices bordering on restraint of trade, and other anti-competitive conditions. All are forms of marketplace concentration that rob consumers of choices or bargains and also rob would-be rivals of opportunities. Many are degrees of concentration that would not be tolerated elsewhere.

Shopping Centres

Canada's first shopping centre was built in Toronto in the 1950s, a twenty-store, L-shaped strip plaza called Sunnybrook. Soon such plazas sprang up everywhere, offering better parking than the shoppers could find on main streets. A seemingly innocuous innovation, the shopping centre has led to the most massive concentration of wealth in Canada since the country was a franchise awarded by the Crown to the Hudson's Bay Co.

Instead of main streets populated by dozens of retailer-landlords, the shopping plaza meant there was only one, richer landlord. Then along came the mega-mall, farther out of town, with parking lots as vast as ten football fields. These were, in turn, followed by huge urban malls like the Eaton Centre, now

301

Canada's number one tourist attraction. And these mall monsters are clearly where the retail action is; it is estimated that they capture more than half of all retail dollars spent in Canada.

The shopping centre is Canada's single most significant money machine, but large office projects have also created some of the most impressive fortunes in Canada's post-war era. The mega-malls are owned by a handful of Canada's wealthiest families and conglomerates, and they have already sewn up the best shopping centre sites well into the next generation. The profits from these cash cows will continue to be invested in more properties as well as in other enterprises: the Belzbergs bought financial assets with theirs; Peter and Edward Bronfman have built a resource empire from such proceeds; and the Reichmanns bought Gulf Canada in 1985 with money from office buildings.

Few examples of marketplace concentration have been as profound as the way in which shopping centres have evolved in this country: they impose a form of marketplace tyranny that is perfectly legal, but they have radically altered both retailing and real estate. Malls shut out small, independent retailers and operate on a reverse Robin Hood principle: they take from the poor and give to the rich. Some small retailers do get in, but they must scrap to get space and then pay significantly higher rent than the large, established retailers, presumably for the privilege of sharing the same mall.

Tenants pay three rents: a minimum rent based on square footage or usage, another based on gross sales, and a common-area charge to pay for parking and maintenance. This system allows landlords to skim up to 10 per cent off retail sales, and stores pass along these costs to consumers in the form of higher prices. In effect shopping centre owners impose a private-sector surcharge on half the retail business done in this country — a form of financial feudalism, in which Canadian consumers are serfs.

This system evolved because in order to get big malls off the ground, developers had to entice big department stores with cheap rents. Even years later, no department store in this country pays its way. Typically, in 1985, hardware stores paid $5.50 per square foot as a basic rent, drugstores, $12.50, and department stores, only $4.50.

Add to that the fact that most of the largest retailers are also part-owners of malls, along with their bankers in some cases. This means they make money no matter what is bought in a mall, because they have a piece of their competitors' action by collecting a percentage of their sales. These retailer-landlords are also in a position to make or break competitors by denying them entry into a mall as tenants, by charging them too much, or by charging their competitors too little.

"The result is that the merchant no longer has that opportunity to buy his own real estate, and he is stuck subsidizing the big corporate retailers," says shopping centre expert and urban economist Garry Stamm of Stamm Economic Research Ltd. in Toronto. "When bigger malls came along, the big banks were needed. And they imposed certain rules that shut out even more mom-and-pop operations. Banks would not count a lease from a small guy as security towards construction, but they would count leasing guarantees to chains like Dylex. And Dylex gets first pick. You get two anchors [major stores at ends of malls] together, build the whole thing, and soak the tenants in between to your heart's content. It's legal. Shopping centres are gigantic franchises."

The principal shopping centre landlords in Canada are Bronfman-owned Cadillac Fairview, Thomson-owned Markborough, Bronfman-owned Trizec and Bramalea, Donald Love's Oxford Developments, Cambridge Shopping Centres, Canadian Pacific's Marathon, JDS Developments, owned by Israeli immigrant Jack Israeli, a few life insurance companies, the Singers and the Belzbergs, the Ghermezians, and the Sobeys and the Jodreys. On the retail side, the Eatons, the Thomsons, the Steinbergs, the Poslunses, and Jimmy Kay have profited handsomely from real estate, as both tenants and landlords; they can pick prime mall locations, bargain lower rents, and get extra leasehold improvements.

Retailing is already heavily concentrated. Dylex makes $1 out of every $10 spent on fashion in Canada through its many chains operating under different names. In the world of department stores there are only three players: Eaton's, with 110 stores; the Bay and Simpsons, with 302; and Sears, with 74 stores. The only other player is Woodward's, with 25 stores in Alberta and B.C. And only Sears and Woodward's (which sold its property holdings in 1985) are not landlords.

"These developers and retailers have sewn up the shopping centre business for another generation. They pick up lands nowadays thinking twenty-five years ahead. They are large enough to know where expressways are going. They don't have to squeeze, cajole, or gouge," says Stamm.

In the U.S., the same real estate concentration has been occurring, but the big difference is that there are dozens of department store chains. In Canada, the large operations can extract subsidies out of developers, who pass these costs along to ancillaries. In the U.S., department stores own the property they sit on themselves and are charged for the privilege of hooking up. They pay their own way, just as everybody else must.

Most importantly, however, Americans believe in home rule. They have spent the post-war years fleeing their crowded, crime-ridden cities for fiercely autonomous white suburbs. Unlike Canadian municipalities, whose property taxes are topped up by the provinces through equalization payments, the U.S. bedroom communities rely on their own tax bases to build schools and other amenities. So towns compete heatedly for shopping mall or office developments in order to relieve the tax burdens on home owners. Sometimes two malls are built in neighbouring municipalities where only one is justified by potential sales.

But such duplication means more competition among retailers and lower prices to consumers. Very often malls go bankrupt in the U.S. because of the lack of centralized planning constraints. When this happens, they are bought by others for bargain-basement prices, enabling landlords to lower rents and retailers to lower prices even more.

In Canada, malls rarely, if ever, go under. That is because municipalities are limited in their planning freedom by provinces, who are often their financial benefactors. In Ontario, for instance, local official plans must conform to provincial official plans. Neighbouring municipalities typically protest against development nearby in order to protect their local merchants. But they are not doing their constituents who shop there any favours. Mall monopolies can charge high rents and retailers pass these costs along to shoppers.

Another difference is that Americans do not embrace the same English traditions of strict town planning as Canadians do. In England, to this day, store property deeds include usages. A butcher shop or a fabric shop must be bought and sold as such unless special permission is granted. This helps shopkeepers make money because the less mobile British public has fewer shops from which to choose. But in the U.S., city and suburban landscapes are often a blighted hodge-podge of McDonald's Restaurants, unattractive strip plazas, and relatively unplanned subdivisions. In Canada, all-powerful planners have imposed tough requirements that have eliminated small or impatient developers. The result is that rezonings are expensive because delays ring up huge carrying costs on lands.

Real Estate

It is ironic that the politicians and red tape that Canadian developers moan about so often have forged their fortunes. Canadian developers are the biggest and best in the world, not because they are smarter than their U.S. counterparts, but because they have been saved from competing against one another by our orderly planning system.

Canada's developers have also been able to build their money machines because of the concentration in our banking system. Big projects mean big financings, and each time all the five largest banks are approached. "Everybody sees all the deals and so there is not a chance of duplication," says a top Canadian banker. The banks have also contributed towards the concentration of retailing because, as has been stated, they will not accept as security leases signed with small independents. They want leases from large national chains as security.

Another major money machine is downtown Toronto office space; ironically, its value can be credited in great part to emotional planning debates that ended with the imposition of a forty-foot height limit for several years while new official plans were drawn up. Canada's most valuable turf is Toronto's 200-acre core, bordered by University, Front, Bloor, and Church Streets. The value of this land increases faster than the rate of inflation and always will, because the city is the most important economic region in the country, generating as much as 15 per cent of the nation's entire gross national product.

Although there has been some shifting of office activity to suburban areas, where in 1985 nearly as much office square footage existed as in the core, Toronto's downtown remains the primest of prime property in Canada. And this reality is the basis for Canada's most spectacular family fortune, that of the Reichmanns, who own 17 per cent of downtown Toronto's prime office space.

With profits from this holding, they have invested heavily in the U.S. and in all of their major Canadian competitors: Cadillac Fairview, Trizec, and Bramalea, plus half of the country's largest realtor with half the entire market — Royal LePage — by virtue of their share in Royal Trustco with Peter and Edward Bronfman. If real estate in Canada were a game of Monopoly, the Reichmanns would own Boardwalk and Park Place.

Naturally, the suppliers that feed off real estate are also mini-money machines, such as realtors and lawyers. They engage in legalized price-fixing, setting brokerage fees among themselves, or, in the case of lawyers, establishing fixed fees for closing property deals. Combines officials have been unable to break up such agreements because realtors and lawyers are under provincial jurisdiction as self-governing professionals.

Another form of real estate concentration is the hotel business, where, once more, permits are granted sparingly in prime locations. This explains why room rates are so much higher in Canada than in the U.S., and it has led to potential abuses. In 1985, six Ottawa hotels, for instance, were charged with bid-rigging and conspiracy to lessen competition in bids to provide rooms to federal and provincial government officials. Charged were the Château Laurier, owned by Crown corporation Canadian National Railways; the Holiday Inn; the Delta Ottawa; the Four Seasons Hotel; the Skyline Hotel; and the Hotel Plaza de la Chaudière in Hull.

While real estate is the basis of most of Canada's greatest fortunes, the biggest money machine of all is the shopping centre. The extent of its importance is unknown to most and not easily quantifiable; Statistics Canada stopped collecting data on shopping centres in 1975. But firm facts aside, the shopping centre has squeezed Canada's independents out of the real retail action. Even huge chains like the Wolfe family's Oshawa Wholesale and its IGA stores cannot crack many mall markets without buying existing leases.

Garry Stamm says there is a small comeback on Main Street as people tire of chains and lose interest in department stores. But real property remains the most enduring form of wealth in Canada, given our strict controls on its use. Canada's prime office and shopping centre franchises are the ultimate patents. So are their prime retail tenants: both are money machines that will spew out cash for their owners forever.

Banks

U.S. president Andrew Jackson broke up the banks south of the border in the 1830s — a primitive attempt at economic nationalism designed to keep out the big British banks. What evolved from this action were laws that forbade branch banking throughout the U.S. in most states except California. While branch banking proscriptions are now breaking down, America's disdain for big banks has created an economy vastly different from ours. For more than a century, Americans were served by small unit banks that catered to small individual investors. Very often they took too many chances, sometimes because of sheer stupidity. Very often they failed.

Here in Canada, the skyline of every major Canadian city is dominated by the towers of our five largest chartered banks, as is our commercial life. Even in small towns the main intersection is typically populated by four bank branches. These gigantic banks are actually an amalgam of hundreds of smaller banks, many of which were gobbled up just before going under. Now vigorous and huge, they dominate the country's financial sweepstakes, with the big five alone netting about 80 per cent of all deposits taken from the public.

Big banks are not all bad. Canada's financial sector has not been plagued by the thousands of bank failures that have occurred in the U.S. And big banks have been able to provide more at a lower cost to smaller customers than the U.S. banks; their size provides them with economies of scale in providing services such as automatic tellers, foreign exchange facilities, and other benefits.

However, our banking oligopoly is unduly protected from foreign rivals and combines laws. It has also created another type of marketplace abuse, which has hurt small and medium-sized business, as the events of 1981 illustrated. Big banks shower favourable terms on their biggest customers. And when the going gets rough, they are prepared to hold the bag for these companies, sometimes for years, in order to avoid bankruptcies and embarrassment. While Dome, Turbo, and Sulpetro negotiated new loan terms and missed deadlines for payments, the big banks made up for lost revenues by charging the rest of us higher interest rates and also by pulling the plug on small enterprises and individuals.

The banks enjoy a monopoly on certain lucrative niches such as large loans of $7 million or more. This is where they make their biggest spreads, because they have the big loan business all to themselves; at the same time they do not pay any interest on current, or company, accounts. This means they get corporate money for nothing, then lend it out to others at significantly higher interest rates.

Another golden egg they share with insurance and trust companies is the mortgage business. But the banks have another angle to this, which few people realize. Mortgagers like banks and trust companies can collect property taxes each month, along with monthly mortgage payments of principal and interest. But those taxes are not remitted to municipalities immediately; instead, they are lent out.

While most banks pay mortgagees interest earned on these tax funds, some do not. When they do, the interest is not added onto T5s given to customers,

and therefore no taxes are paid on that income. While taxpayers lose, some
customers win. So do banks whose practice of using this money causes cash
flow problems for some municipalities, allowing the banks to turn around and
lend the municipalities their own money to help them out of their own financial fixes.

This little manoeuvre may seem minuscule, but Kenneth Strang, a retired
business consultant, studied its impact on his community of Cranbrook, B.C.
He calculated that withheld prepayments tallied $534,480 in one year; since
Cranbrook's population of 18,000 is about 1 per cent of British Columbia's,
some $53.448 million in payments are held up in his province alone. Nation-
ally, that amounts to $534 million — a cash flow shortfall that undoubtedly
leads many municipalities to their banks for a few millions.

Another questionable banking manoeuvre involves credit card service
charges. Most cards charge a near-usurious 1.5 per cent per month, or 18 per
cent. But the 11.4 million Canadians who have Visa or MasterCard are paying
up to 609 per cent in certain circumstances. Credit card users who don't pay
their balances in full each month are charged interest on new purchases. The
twenty-one-day interest-free period applies only to balances paid in full. Take,
for instance, a $1,000 purchase made in December, which was added to your
statement January 3. Assume it was the only item on your January 10 statement, due to be paid by January 31. If you pay in full, but are one day late,
you will be charged interest from January 3 to February 1, or $16.68 for that
day, which is equivalent to 609 per cent on an annual basis. They have gotten
away with this for years, even though 60-per-cent interest is illegal under the
Criminal Code.

Canada's deposit-taking institutions are among our most concentrated
businesses. In 1985 alone, the Mercantile and National Banks merged, creating our sixth-largest bank, and Canada Permanent Trust's parent company,
Genstar, bought Canada Trustco, the country's largest trust company and the
last widely owned financial institution of any size in this country. Now the ten
largest deposit-taking institutions have captured 90 per cent of all deposits.
And that means abuses such as price-fixing, conscious parallelism, or other
anti-competitive practices can more easily occur. It is about time to open up
competition to foreign banks.

Food and Beverages

Another cause for concern is the food business, where many of the country's
largest family fortunes have been made, in part or in whole. The Steinbergs,

the Wolfes, the Westons, the Sobeys, the Jodreys, the McCains, the Molsons, Jim Pattison, Paul Phelan and his Cara Foods, and the Woodwards of B.C. have found their riches at various points along the food chain.

The final link in the chain is the highly concentrated grocery business. In Ontario, for instance, grocery chains garner 76 per cent of food dollars, although IGA, bulk food stores, and ethnic delicatessens have made small inroads. At the beginning of the chain are monopolistic marketing boards such as the Canadian Wheat Board and Egg Marketing Board. In between there is plenty of concentration, too, and it costs consumers billions more than they might otherwise pay in a freer marketplace.

Of course, it is hard to complain too vehemently. Canada has the world's second-lowest per-capita food bill. The lowest bills are in the U.S., which is blessed with better soils and more moderate climates. But lower American prices are also the result of a highly competitive food chain.

The domination of grocery chains in western Canada has been painful for consumers. In 1985, the Consumers' Association of Canada published survey results showing that sixty grocery items were 19 per cent cheaper in Saskatoon than in Regina even though Safeway dominates the food business in both cities, with at least 50 per cent of the market. The difference was that Saskatoon also had a new, aggressive store in town called Super Valu, owned by Kelly Douglas of Loblaws. And prices fell in that prairie city because, for the first time in decades, competition had broken out.

In the Atlantic provinces, the principal chains are IGA (the stores are all independently owned, however) and Sobeys; in Quebec, Métro Richelieu, Steinberg, and Provigo; and in Ontario, Loblaws, A&P, Food City, IGA, and Steinberg. Out west, Safeway dominates in all four provinces but faces increasing competition from Loblaws, Pattison's Overwaitea, and the retail co-operatives.

Sometimes the courts have helped fight concentration in the food business. In 1973, an Alberta court imposed certain prohibitions against Canada Safeway in Calgary and Edmonton. It was prohibited from subletting or letting property with restrictive clauses or covenants designed to "prevent competitors from opening stores in the vicinity." The court banned Safeway from selectively undercutting prices of the same item in all its stores at once and from increasing its square footage for three and a half years. It also said the chain could open only one store in both cities within five years and could not saturate either market with advertising blitzes for five years.

The newest concentration wrinkle concerns the formation among competitors of buying groups to get higher rebates and better prices out of suppliers. "There are a few major buying groups, about four, in the food industry and they have served a useful purpose," says combines official John Barker, investigations chief in the retailing field. "However, we would not want to see more of these buying groups disappear or merge."

The suppliers, on the other hand, have not stood still either. They have created marketing boards for some commodities, gotten together to fix prices in other areas, or gone on acquisition sprees. McCain's, for instance, owns 12 per cent of its major competitor, York Farms, and until 1985, it owned 12 per cent of another, Canada Packers. While combines cops have not stepped into these transactions, sometimes provinces have. In 1982, Prince Edward Island passed a law limiting corporate farms to 3,000 acres, amid fears that the Irving conglomerate could turn the entire island into a potato farm after it bought McLean's Farms.

In 1986, a six-month trial was held into price-fixing charges against two of the country's largest meat-packers, Canada Packers and Intercontinental Packers of Saskatoon. They were charged with conspiring to fix prices when buying hogs from the Alberta Pork Producers Marketing Board and when selling pork cuts to retailers. Three others, Burns Foods, Eschem Canada (formerly Swift), and Gainers, pleaded guilty to fixing prices in 1983 and were fined $125,000.

Most concentrated are the bread, dairy, and brewery businesses, controlled by a handful of families and their companies. Two conglomerates — George Weston and Maple Leaf Mills (owned by Canadian Pacific) — sell half of Ontario's bread. In Toronto, there are five dairies: Peter and Edward Bronfman's Labatt, which owns Silverwood and Sealtest; the Weston family's Neilson Dairy, which also makes chocolates; Conrad Black's Eplett Dairies; the Wolfes' Oshawa Group; and Beatrice Foods. There is only one small independent, called Sun Rise Dairy, in rural Wingham but with a Toronto licence. But it has been unable to compete inside the city. The largest and most profitable dairy in the country is Palm Dairy, operating in all four Western provinces. It was taken over in 1985 by George Mann along with Union Enterprises.

With few competitors and licences protecting them from many more, dairies function like utilities, money machines that can pass along cost increases and make profits that sometimes surpass the rate of inflation. So do the breweries.

Beer is a money machine in Canada, dominated as it is by Labatt's, Molson, and Carling O'Keefe, with 93 per cent of the market. Sweetest is their stranglehold in Ontario, where they own the retail outlets, the trucks that ship the beer, and the breweries. Two of them, Labatt's and Molson, have controlling interest in the country's only significant malt supplier, Canada Malting Co.

The system in Ontario — Canada's single most lucrative market, with 40 per cent of sales — is legalized price-fixing. Breweries charge the same amount for similar quantities of beer. They must allow others to sell their beer in their retail outlets, but only at the same price or higher, which excludes the possibility of cheaper, generic beers gaining a foothold. When selling beer made by others, they mark up imports by 80 per cent and domestic beer by 21 per cent.

Combines officials have been unable to do anything about Ontario's beer cartel, even though it is run like a gigantic liquid utility, where increases and mediocre service are poured down our throats. Beer is a provincial matter, and it cannot be transported across provincial boundaries. Restrictions are worst, and most profitable, in Ontario, but they also exist elsewhere. Beer is sold in government stores in Nova Scotia, New Brunswick, and Prince Edward Island, without price competition. Out west, brewers' prices are identical, but at least beer can be bought in hotels and taverns at varying prices. In Quebec, it is available through 10,000 corner stores at various prices, seven days a week.

In the U.S., the beer business is closely watched by anti-trust officials. In 1965, Molson's could not buy Hamm's of Milwaukee because it would result in too big a market share in several states. It is ironic, therefore, that controlling interest in Labatt's was bought by Joseph Schlitz Co. in 1964, but the U.S. justice department forced divestiture because the purchase would give Schlitz 30 per cent of the market. Brascan bought Hamm's, and Labatt's now has 40 per cent of the Canadian market.

The lack of anti-trust policies cost 700 Canadians their jobs in 1985. Seven-Up Canada Inc. and Pepsi-Cola Canada agreed to bottle each other's products, with Pepsi assuming Montreal operations and Seven-Up taking Toronto. This meant that each could close one plant in each city. It was a deal that would not have been allowed in the U.S., where their two parent companies compete.

Ma Bell

Bell Canada Enterprises is another awesome money machine, by virtue of its monopoly over Ontario's and Quebec's telephone systems. Every single day,

some $10 million in cash falls into Bell's coffers from operations, invest-
ments, tax benefits, and shareholders. While most of the money is reinvested
or handed out as dividends ($3.2 billion, more than flows each year into the
Quebec Pension Plan or the Canada Pension Plan), no other private-sector entity generates that kind of wealth. Within ten years' time, Bell could buy
controlling interest in the country's ten largest corporations.

In 1985, Bell made a profit of $940 million and saved another $1.52 billion
in depreciation and deferred income taxes. It also borrowed $400 million and
received another $405 million from its dividend reinvestment scheme for
shareholders. That $405 million worth of "free" money flows into Bell every
year; it would be enough to buy control of Moore Corp., Stelco, or Canada
Packers. It all comes to $3.2 billion, which is sufficient, says Bell's chairman
Jean de Grandpré, "to have bought Gulf Canada with one year's cash flow."

"Bell is monstrous concentration," says Toronto financier Hal Jackman.
"Once a year they get $400 million in free venture capital from dividend
reinvestment schemes, and they could buy a major company every single
February."

De Grandpré counters: "What's wrong with that? Our shareholders get to
own more shares and we get more cash to make investments with. Jackman
could do the same in his companies by offering dividends and reinvestment
programs to his shareholders, but he won't do either because it will reduce his
ownership in his companies. Tough luck to him."

Besides, that $3.2 billion is not cash in the bank. The depreciation and
deferred income are paper entries; some $500 million is paid out in dividends;
$1.1 billion is reinvested in facilities; some $80 million, in dividends from
other companies in which it has controlling interest, is reinvested in those
companies; and finally, there are interest payments to make on debts. "At the
end of the year we are short $115 million in cash," says de Grandpré.

But Bell can borrow against such cash flow and runs no risk of it ever dry-
ing up. The Canadian Radio-television and Telecommunications Commission
holds regular rate hearings for all telephone monopolies to ensure that they
make enough money to deliver the service and reward shareholders ade-
quately as well as to ensure that telephone users are not gouged. Profits are
assured.

Bell was a sleepy phone utility until 1983, apart from its controlling interest
in Canada's greatest corporation, Northern Telecom. That year it reorganized
into Bell Canada Enterprises and went on an aggressive shopping spree. This

was necessary, it argued before its regulator, the CRTC, because it had lost its monopoly on supplying telephone equipment.

Now it faces the possibility of losing its long-distance monopoly to rivals, something that UBC's William Stanbury feels should happen. "We should go for it because huge efficiency gains in telecommunications costs are becoming more important." Bell argues against this, saying that it will mean consumers will see sudden price jumps in their bills for local calls. It says for every $1 worth of long-distance calls, costs are 38 cents, but for every $1 in local calls, costs are $2.

While Bell is subsidizing local calls with its long-distance monopoly, something has to give. Without competition in markets Bell can gobble up the world. In just three years it has bought three major corporations — Trans-Canada PipeLines, Daon Developments, and British-American Bank Note — plus 25 per cent of the country's personal computer retail market through the purchase of Computerland in 1986, and several smaller acquisitions. More frightening is the fact that someone could buy Bell Enterprises itself.

De Grandpré argues against constraints, saying it would be impractical for anyone to buy Bell. Its telephone rates are carefully regulated by the CRTC and its size is necessary because it is small in comparison with U.S. telecommunications companies like the dozen companies formed out of AT&T. That argument is irrelevant, however, because Bell and the AT&T companies do not compete directly. They are separate, regional monopolies.

More compelling is the fact that the Bell empire already represents 9 per cent of the entire Toronto Stock Exchange float. Someone could, hypothetically, take over Bell. To think it is not possible is to misunderstand how leveraged past buy-outs have been in this country. And that, by anyone's definition, would be an unconscionable concentration of ownership. Even for Canada.

Media

The only major newspapers to have developed in Canada since the Second World War have been the *Toronto Sun* and its sister papers in Alberta. But the *Sun* would never have made it without the financial assistance of the city's largest retailer-landlords, such as the Eatons and the Bronfmans, who were angry at a *Toronto Star* anti-development crusade. They backed the fledgling paper because they hoped to divert the lucrative real estate advertising lineage away from the *Star*. But the strategy did not work, because the *Sun* catered to downscale, low-income readers who were not buying real estate. Both the *Sun* and the *Star* thrived, and now Toronto is one of the two cities in North America with three successful daily newspapers.

Elsewhere in Canada the name of the game in newspapers has been to acquire existing papers and shut them down. It is sad but true that most of Canada's major cities are served by only one daily newspaper. Somewhat easing the adverse effects of this has been the national distribution of the *Globe and Mail*, which provides an alternative. But in many cases it is only an alternative to another Thomson-owned newspaper. Excluding the *Globe*, major cities such as Vancouver, the national capital, Ottawa, Halifax, Winnipeg, and Montreal have only one English-language daily. Calgary and Edmonton have small tabloids that were launched by the *Toronto Sun* and are now owned by Maclean Hunter.

Although its importance should not be overstated, as it is often inaccurate or sensational, the daily newspaper is an essential ingredient of any healthy democracy, much more vital than television or radio. Even though broadcasters are more timely and more powerful, newspapers do the sort of digging and detail that broadcasters do not and often cannot do. If sources won't go on air, their stories cannot be told. For those that do, a brilliant idea can be erased instantly if its creator delivers a poor broadcasting performance.

"Owning all five newspapers in a province is quite a different matter than owning all five shoe factories," says UBC's William Stanbury. "We're talking about democracy when we're talking about the media. And what if Irving's sons are congenital idiots with Hitlerian tendencies? This stuff is too important to allow it to get concentrated."

In essence, Canada's media is carved up into three financial franchises: Thomson, Maclean Hunter with its *Sun* chain, and the Torstar-Southam partnership. Holders of regional monopolies include Michael Sifton, with Saskatchewan's only two dailies and several television and radio stations; Graham Dennis, with Nova Scotia's only daily, the Halifax *Chronicle-Herald*; the Irvings, who own all the media in New Brunswick; and the Blackburns, with their television, radio, and newspaper interests in London, Ont. The lion's share of Canadian magazine business is in the hands of Southam and Maclean Hunter, while national television is divided between the Eaton family's Baton Broadcasting, which owns CTV, and Ottawa's CBC.

Magazines, radio, and television are a slightly different matter, however, because they are pummelled by foreign competitors constantly. In television's most lucrative market, Toronto, many regional competitors have sprung up, such as Global, City, MTV, and TVOntario. But newspapers, or newspapers in partnership with broadcasting interests, are a special problem. And it remains the misfortune of most Canadian readers that they are served by fat, lazy, or one-sided media monopolies and that two royal commissions making modest recommendations to correct this were totally ignored.

In 1981, after the controversial closings of the *Ottawa Journal* and *Winnipeg Tribune*, the Kent commission was formed. It studied the concentration in the newspaper business and made several recommendations: that large chains be frozen; that Ken Thomson sell either the *Globe* or the rest of his newspapers in Canada; that individual newspapers with 50 per cent of a market area's circulation not be allowed to buy another newspaper; and that cross-ownership be banned, with those owning print and broadcasting assets in the same market divesting one or the other.

These recommendations were framed into legislation, but that same year Torstar bought from John Bassett all the suburban weeklies ringing Toronto, for $17 million. Undoubtedly the *Star* moved before the barn door was closed, but the law never passed. Called Inland Publishing, the chain included a lucrative printing subsidiary that had competed against Torstar. As Bassett has told a number of friends, he did not really want to sell the chain, which was started, ironically, with the money he had made by closing the *Telegram* years before. He plucked a $17-million figure out of the air, Torstar publisher Beland Honderich did not flinch, and the deal was done. It was a purely defensive move by Torstar and resulted in the closing of one of two weeklies in virtually every suburb around the city.

By far the most significant concentration occurred in 1985 with a deal between the *Toronto Star* and Southam. Although the share swap was somewhat benign — inasmuch as it never resulted in the closing of any newspapers — it means that the two will never start newspapers in each other's current marketplaces. The partnership happened in the fall of 1985 when Torstar was approached by members of the Southam family to be their "white knight" in order to fend off a perceived takeover by George Mann. The Southams had been diluted down to a collective shareholding of only 40 per cent and felt vulnerable. Through a complicated share swap, Torstar gave Southam 30 per cent of the non-voting shares from its treasury in return for 20 per cent of Southam shares, all of which have votes.

While not an out-and-out takeover, the deal certainly gives Torstar the upper hand, especially considering its own restricted share structure. Since 1968, about 55 per cent of Torstar voting shares have been divided between Holy Joe Atkinson's daughter, Ruth Atkinson Hindmarsh, and her nineteen heirs and his late son's daughter, Catharine (Betsy) Crang. Non-family members have another 45 per cent, divided evenly between William Campbell, Beland Honderich, and Burnett Thall. Effectively, this gives the Atkinsons and their partners a major foothold, if not eventual control, over the largest media empire in Canada. Combined, the two own seven of the country's ten largest-circulation dailies, dozens of Southam magazines, the world's largest book publisher, Harlequin Romances, and controlling interest in Selkirk Communications, which owns television and radio interests.

Such a truce between potential competitors is unfortunate, but the degree to which it reduces competition is hard to quantify. Southam has never had a daily newspaper in Toronto, nor wanted one, while Torstar has no newspapers outside that city and its suburbs. As for combined influence, editorial policies could not be more opposed, if you consider the stand of the Liberal *Star* on oil prices compared with the Tory position taken by Southam's *Calgary Herald*. Besides, press councils and powerful editorial unions keep politics on editorial pages and off news pages for the most part.

Far easier to quantify, however, is the sort of damage to democracy caused when out-and-out monopolies exist. "There is an undesirable degree of media concentration in Saskatchewan," says former premier Allan Blakeney. "Of the four dailies, two are owned by the Sifton family and two by the Thomsons. You can imagine the nice breadth of view we get here. The two Thomson papers are in Prince Albert and Moose Jaw, and they are shocking. The major radio station in Regina is owned by Sifton, and Baton [the Eatons] owns six out of seven television stations. Two other local families own several more radio stations."

The concentration affects the political process, says Blakeney, because owners' politics result in newsroom censorship. "I can remember raising problems over a Prince Albert pulp mill and its financing, and I was interviewed by a television reporter. He got around the controversy by saying, 'I'm not authorized to ask you any questions about the Prince Albert pulp mill.' So much for the fourth estate."

The Siftons were one of Canada's biggest newspaper families until disagreements divided the fortune into two profitable pieces in 1953. With Irish tempers, Victor and Clifford Sifton could not get along. Victor kept the

Winnipeg Free Press and Clifford, the Saskatchewan assets. Victor parlayed his paper into a stake in the huge FP chain, in partnership with the McConnells, Max Bell, and Howard Webster. The chain was sold to Thomson in 1981.

Clifford's son, Michael Sifton, still owns his Saskatchewan media interests through Armadale Enterprises Ltd. His empire, estimated to be worth about $50 million in assets, thanks mostly to media profits, now includes five radio stations, the two dailies, a car dealership, real estate, and oil and gas reserves. He also owns one of Canada's busiest airports, Toronto's Buttonville, as well as Torontair Commuter Air Service and North America's largest indoor polo rink, north of Toronto.

Other media moguls in Canada on a smaller scale are Allan Slaight, with Standard Broadcasting; Paul Desmarais, with the prestigious French-language daily *La Presse* and Telemedia; and Conrad Black with his tiny Sterling chain and Britain's *Daily Telegraph*.

No matter how many newspapers in a chain, each link is a media money machine in Canada. It is little wonder that media stocks have outperformed all others in earnings since the Second World War. After all, they have carved the country into profit-making pieces, serving their readers and viewers poorly in the meantime. While politicians fail to come to grips with this problem on the grounds of anti-trust principles, there are other concerns unique to the issue of media concentration.

Because most Canadians live in one-newspaper towns, they can be intellectually impaired unless they seek out other sources of news. Otherwise, their window on the world is narrow; their information fed through a biased, cost-effective focus. The national edition of the *Globe* has helped open up the marketplace, but only where it does not compete against other Thomson papers. And that eliminates forty communities. Apart from Toronto, the iron grip held by a handful of magnates is a problem in a country where balance, impartiality, and independence from other tycoons such as big, powerful advertisers is sorely needed. Without forced divestiture or more competition, Canada runs big political risks in future: in the land of the blind, the one-eyed man will be king.

Eyeglasses and Lenses

Syd Hermant's father, Percy Hermant, founded Imperial Optical in 1900. A poor Russian orphan, who escaped to New Brunswick at the age of fourteen to avoid being drafted into the Czar's army, he started his own business, after taking a six-week course in optics in Boston. It expanded across Canada, manufacturing lenses and wholesaling. Sydney took the business a step further by flouting the convention that wholesalers should not also be allowed to act as retailers. By 1985, Imperial employed 3,000 workers and had $180 million in sales.

Outside Canada, it operates a number of other companies under the holding company called PAJA — for Syd Hermant's four sons, Peter, Adam, John, and Andrew. Peter and John run Imperial, Adam heads Safety Supply Canada, which makes a range of products from protective eyegear to mine detection devices and distributes Bausch and Lomb optical equipment. Andrew runs Manta Sound, one of the world's most sophisticated recording studios, where "Tears Are Not Enough" was recorded.

A series of articles in the 1970s exposed Imperial's stranglehold on the entire Canadian eyeglass and lens market. This led to a lengthy hearing by the Restrictive Trade Practices Commission. In 1979, the commission made recommendations that were ignored, for the most part. It suggested that Imperial advertise eyeglass and lens prices, diversify, and divest itself of many of its retail and laboratory assets. Imperial advertised prices, but did not divest.

"Informed sources put Imperial's market share as high as 90 per cent," said the *Globe*. It also maintained that Imperial was charging $46 to $152 for the exact same frames, depending upon the Imperial outlet, and between $31 and $42 for identical lens prescriptions.

The principal operating companies are Imperial and Standard Optical Co. Ltd., and they are the supreme money machines. In 1979, Imperial's empire operated 129 wholesale and prescription labs and 400 retail outlets, under various names. It had at least 50 per cent of lab sales in six provinces, a large share in three others, and more than 50 per cent of retail sales in twenty-one of the country's thirty-two population centres.

"It is too large to be in the public interest," stated the commission's report. The consumer and corporate affairs minister at the time, Warren Allmand, said the report underscored the need for tougher competition laws. Without them, it was impossible for the government to order divestiture.

At that time, there were some 1,500 independent optometrists in Canada with their own businesses, but Imperial sold prescription lenses to the vast majority. Imperial paid eye doctors and optometrists "commissions" to send their patients to Imperial outlets, and the company also lent money to medical students destined to be eye specialists. Once their education was complete, Imperial lent them up to $30,000 to set up an office in return for written contracts giving them $6 for every prescription they sent to Imperial. As far as is known, the Imperial formula for success has not changed. There is no reason for it to change. Unfortunately, it is perfectly legal.

In testimony before the commission, Syd Hermant said that in retail outlets, his company was often in a fifty-fifty partnership with its optometrist. Each one operated under a different name, for a reason. "If we put the Imperial Optical name on every [retail] building, two-thirds of them would go out of business. People like to have a choice," he was quoted as saying in the *Globe* on June 23, 1976.

Hermant was also a Canadian Imperial Bank of Commerce director at the time, and his "temper flared when [Bruce] McDonald, lawyer for consumer and commercial relations, asked about his position as a director of the Commerce. Hermant cut the lawyer off when he started to inquire into the cancellation of a line of credit extended by the bank to a competitor in Quebec City, Robert Laforce. 'This implication I very much resent,' he said," according to the *Globe*.

Imperial is a royal money machine whose only competitors have been a trickle of foreign outfits that combines officials have urged the Foreign Investment Review Agency to allow in whenever they have applied. But FIRA, Canada's reputation as a country hostile to foreign investment of any kind, and tariffs blocking imports have undoubtedly daunted others who might have entered Canada's marketplaces. Without competition, goodness knows how much more the unsuspecting Canadian consumer will have to overpay.

By no means a definitive list, these are merely a few of Canada's more lucrative cash cows. Others include garbage collection, oil marketing, waste disposal, pharmaceutical manufacturing, movie theatres, certain specialties in film development, and many more. Then there are the cartels such as legal, dental, and other professional associations.

While there are times when competition does not exist because a market cannot support many competitors, this is rarely the case in Canada. Competition is minimal in many markets because there are restraints to trade, barriers to entry, or other marketplace abuses. The new Combines Investigation Act is needed, as is enhanced vigilance on the part of combines cops, courts, and consumers. Without laws and articulate critics, the concentration of power will proceed as the money machines throw off increasing amounts of cash. The end, alas, is nowhere in sight.

6

SOLUTIONS

BY FAILING to address concentration and its problems, Canada has become less competitive internationally and less efficient domestically. Unarrested, concentration has destroyed opportunities, cost jobs, trampled the rights of many individuals or corporate competitors, hurt small investors, and fostered the growth of highly mortgaged monoliths, and it may even lead to even greater socialism. Apart from anything else, it has been reckless public policy to allow more and more important economic decisions to be made by fewer and fewer persons. Public policy nearly brought the country to its knees in 1981; it has handed over far too much power to an unelected élite of economic masters.

Reforms are imperative, but they must be executed with a scalpel, not an axe. There are those who would merely nationalize certain industries or companies to counteract concentration, create more Crown corporations to restore competition, or impose enormous taxes that would drive capital and expertise out of the country. Concentration itself is not intrinsically the problem. After all, bags of gold dust are valuable and can be used to buy goods or to finance the finding of more gold. But, scattered all over a field, that gold is valueless. Canada must cultivate the collection of as many bags as possible, but must also ensure that they are invested both wisely and fairly.

The first priority in Canada's concentration agenda must be to move towards an American-style anti-trust system. Revisions to the Combines Investigation Act proposed by Progressive Conservative consumer minister Michel Côté in December 1985 and passed in June 1986 will repair many of the gaps that have made it virtually impossible for combines investigators to obtain convictions. The most important change is removing the necessity to prove that marketplace abusers "intended to lessen competition unduly to the detriment of the public" and replacing it with a need to prove merely that "competition was unduly lessened." This approach will allow regulators to cast their nets wider and bring in a handsome haul. Côté's laws are improvements because they also decriminalize most charges (except for conspiracies), require prenotification of mergers, create a merger tribunal to evaluate troublesome deals, and include banks and all Crown corporations in the legislation.

However, the act is only as good as those charged with upholding it. The country must make a greater commitment towards the goal of competition. Judges are all too often unschooled in the ways of business. The government should take pains to educate them, or it should create tribunals similar to Washington's Federal Trade Commission to deal with complicated disputes involving business.

Combines officials also need better weapons by which to measure and monitor both competition and concentration. Data on market shares in hundreds of specific areas or involving specific products are non-existent. Information collected now is out of date or incomplete. As the Federal Trade Commission does, we should collect and publish data semi-annually on specific markets and products. Companies should be forced to report details on a timely basis or face fines. A takeover registry should be established, where all companies will be required to report any mergers or acquisitions, to end the educated guesswork that characterizes current combines research in Canada.

A directors' registry should also be established, where directors would be required to disclose all their worldwide directorships, as they are in Britain. Provincially chartered corporations now reveal only directors' names, often merely a lawyer and his secretary, and the address of the head office, often merely the lawyer's office.

A comprehensive guide to ownership is necessary for a number of reasons. Kept by federal authorities on a confidential basis, an ownership registry would be helpful to civil servants who wish to check out the corporate connections of those making representations, and to tax and securities regulators. In addition, it should be available to labour unions who find they cannot negotiate collective agreements with companies because the beneficial owners cannot be traced.

Combines officials should also be empowered to end discriminatory, anti-competitive interprovincial barriers created by provincial governments. Practices ranging from preferential bidding for local firms to residency requirements for employees or employers as well as the ban on the transport of beer across provincial boundaries reward inefficient activity. Combines officials should be able to penetrate other provincial domains in order to crack down on anti-competitive practices by liquor boards, which permit price-fixing, or by provincially chartered realtors, brokers, or professional groups like lawyers and doctors.

Powerful competition laws are more necessary than ever in the light of changes concerning foreign ownership curbs and free trade. Loosening of ownership restrictions as well as the special bilateral trade deal to be negotiated with our largest trading partner, the United States, will increase competition here at home.

However, competition laws must be toughened in order to ensure that the removal of ownership curbs does not lead to an eventual reduction in competition through a new round of takeovers, as well-financed foreign conglomerates become free to snap up smaller Canadian conglomerates. Likewise, tariff barriers should not be peeled away if this means that large American companies can flood the Canadian market with goods or services, unduly lessening competition in our already uncompetitive marketplace.

Specifically, Imperial Optical should be forced to divest some of its holdings unless it can prove that it does not have an inordinate share of the eyeglass frame and lens market in Canada. The four major oil companies, which own everything from oilfields to refineries, portions of pipelines, and gasoline stations, should be forced to sell at least half their stations to independent businesses and to sell all their refineries, as a means of restoring competition in that overly concentrated market. Anyone with 40 per cent or more of a natural market (national, local, or provincial) must defend that amount of concentration or sell out and make room for others.

The entire shopping centre area must be studied; leases must be abrogated that discriminate unfairly against small independent retailers. Large department store chains should not be allowed to own shopping malls, any more than oil companies should be allowed to own pipelines carrying the oil of competitors.

In the concentrated food business, chains with inordinately high market shares, such as Safeway in Alberta, should be frozen; and buying groups as well as marketing boards should be banned because they are marketplace bullies, or have the potential to be.

Similarly, the Reichmann family should not be allowed to own large portions of rival real estate companies, such as Trizec, Bramalea, and Cadillac Fairview — not because these companies have an inordinate marketplace share, but because they often compete against one another for land, suppliers, and services such as banking. They should be completely separate.

On the other hand, the combines investigations director and a merger tribunal should allow companies engaged in competition in Canada to join forces, if certain conditions are met. In the U.S. and Japan, for instance, exporters normally in competition at home are allowed to join forces to sell abroad, sharing research and development, distribution, transportation, sales costs, or other overheads. For instance, American anti-trust officials broke up the gigantic American Telephone and Telegraph Corp. into a dozen entities in the early 1980s, resulting in higher phone bills for all Americans; but they have allowed those same companies to join forces with computer giants such as IBM, Honeywell, and Wang to study the so-called fifth-generation computer. In the past, concerns that tough anti-trust rules in Canada would hamper those companies that must attain huge, international economies of scale have led us to overlook a policy that would, in effect, license cartels for export.

While changes to the Combines Investigation Act will improve marketplace conditions here at home, they do not address the problems associated with concentration of ownership, or aggregate concentration. The new act allows the combines investigations director and merger tribunal to review takeovers from the point of view of their effects on competition. However, the act will not examine these transactions from the point of view of overall concentration. That is why Investment Canada's role should be broadened to examine all mergers, regardless of whether they involve foreign or domestic players. As it did for years (when it was called the Foreign Investment Review Agency), Investment Canada should examine transactions involving both foreign and domestic companies to determine answers to important national questions such as these: What will this deal do to the nation's currency? To bank rates? To employees of the companies involved? To research and development investments? To trade with other countries? To the companies' financial well-being? To communities, suppliers, and customers? And will the transaction increase the potential for self-dealing?

It should also invite intervenors to submit their concerns and even, in some cases, hold public hearings, as does the Canadian Radio-television and

Telecommunications Commission. Examining the evidence of these submissions or hearings, Investment Canada should decide whether the deal should proceed as proposed. It should have the power to recommend to cabinet that a deal be scuttled, it should be able to extract certain pledges from the new owners, and it should be able to impose changes to the deal if its effects would be harmful. Such powers may seem sweeping and interventionist, but they are not more so than those that Canada has imposed on foreign owners. In fact, the level of concentration is already so severe and has caused so much socio-economic pain that mergers must become a privilege, not a right. The onus should be on the takeover players to prove that a given transaction is in the nation's interest.

Besides reforms to competition laws, concentration's adverse effects should be arrested through a number of revisions to securities, banking, and tax laws. In the past, small shareholders have been left out in the cold, often losing everything because of the selfish actions of dominant shareholders. Depositors have been insufficiently protected from the owners of lending institutions who have engaged in self-dealing transactions, and taxpayers have also fallen victim to policies that do not force the rich to pay their fair share.

In Canada, the rules governing securities industries have been left up to provinces. Most follow Ontario's lead, where laws are the most stringent and the industry is the largest. Many companies are interlisted, on the Alberta, Montreal, or Vancouver stock exchange as well as in Toronto, and Ontario's more extensive disclosure and other requirements are the standard to which these companies adhere. Likewise, many of those on the Toronto Stock exchange are listed on the New York, American, or NASDAQ over-the-counter exchange in the U.S. and submit to the stricter rules of Washington's Securities and Exchange Commission.

However, a new level of super-laws is needed in Canada to offset the fact that the vast majority of corporations are controlled by dominant shareholders. Because this has led to abuses in the past and may create problems in future, regulations must enshrine minority shareholders' rights, in order to protect the integrity of the system. These must embrace a number of problem areas, from the way in which boards of directors are organized, to accounting practices, to conflict-of-interest rules. In addition, the mechanics of corporate democracy must be modernized to ensure the full participation of all players, no matter how small.

Currently, corporations rely on the mail, or on the good will of brokers, to transmit information or announcements to shareholders. This method is sorely inadequate. Legally required notification periods are too short, and share-holders' meetings are often held in out-of-the-way places. All too often share-holders never even receive notices because their stock is held in the name of a brokerage firm or with a clearing-house such as the Canadian Depository.

The result is that brokers often do not bother to pass along information sent to them on behalf of shareholders. Little wonder: passing along information is expensive, which is why public corporations should be obliged to compensate brokers for doing so. Such rules are necessary to ensure that shareholders are informed and have sufficient time to attend meetings and vote. The Ontario Securities Commission is studying the implications of forcing this responsibil-ity on corporations.

In addition, however, shareholders should be able to cast their ballots more conveniently than is now the case. The old proxy system — whereby management mails out notices but is not responsible for reaching shareholders and can automatically vote those proxies returned unaltered — should be swapped for one using modern-day technology. It remains a paradox that multimillion-dollar trades can be arranged over the telephone, but a system allowing shareholders to vote by phone on important issues has not been imposed. Code numbers or special credit cards could be used to avoid counterfeit balloting. We can have corporate democracy by referendum.

With 374 out of Canada's 400 largest public companies controlled by a dominant shareholder, protections are needed for minority shareholders on boards of directors. It should be a legal requirement that boards reflect, proportionately, the ownership of the company. If 40 per cent of a company is controlled by a single shareholder, then that owner should be able to control 40 per cent of the seats. Likewise, the other 60 per cent of the board seats should be outside directors, independent representatives of minority share-holders, without any financial connection to the company or the dominant shareholder as advisers, suppliers, or customers. These outside directors should also have a sizeable stake in the company; Canadian Pacific directors, for instance, must own at least 2,000 shares.

Cumulative voting should be required because it allows minority share-holders to cast all their votes for one director, rather than for an entire slate. This means they can elect individuals to look after their interests. Currently, dissatisfied shareholders are powerless to secure representation on a board unless they put up a complete slate of their own and undertake an expensive proxy fight.

In addition, companies should not be permitted to indemnify directors against responsibility for their actions, nor should they purchase directors' liability insurance for them, a commonplace practice. As for other perquisites, public companies should be forced to disclose the individual compensation of each of the five highest-paid executives; current rules require disclosure of the collective salaries of the highest-paid executives only as a group. One Canadian company pulled a fast one by publishing the combined salaries of the twenty highest-paid in one year and of the twenty-five highest-paid the following year, so that it was impossible to determine even a percentage increase on an aggregate basis.

Bank boards should be smaller and should not include the bank's largest customers. Officers of one company should not be allowed to sit on the boards of more than one lending institution. For instance, the Noranda Mines chairman, president, and vice president of finance should not be directors at three competing Canadian chartered banks, as they are now. Likewise, bank officers should not act as directors of companies to which they lend money, or of companies that compete against the bank's other customers.

A directors' code of ethics should require directors and dominant shareholders to disclose to one another and to shareholders "conflicts of interest," any transactions involving the company in which they have an interest. Although most directors now do this, it is not a legal requirement, but it should be.

Once conflicts have been declared by a dominant shareholder with controlling interest, a transaction should be allowed to proceed to a vote only if it is approved first by an "ethics" committee comprising outside directors, representing minority shareholders' interests. If a majority of the members of the ethics committee approve the deal, it must then be approved by a majority of the minority shareholders. Directors with conflicts should automatically forfeit their votes at directors' meetings, annual meetings, or special shareholders' meetings involving these troublesome transactions.

Similarly, a company — with or without a dominant shareholder — offering to buy back part or all of its outstanding shares using corporate funds should commission an independent evaluation of its offer and not proceed until a majority of outside directors agree with the price. Then the company should obtain shareholder approval.

Laws should force companies selling new shares or warrants to offer them to all shareholders on a pro rata basis. In one case, rights were issued to a handful of shareholders and management friends on the eve of an announcement of huge profits, higher dividends, and a stock split. Small investors were completely left out of a chance to increase their stakes.

Securities requirements must protect shareholders from shark repellents, which deny them the opportunity to make money from takeover bids. Poison pill or white knight arrangements should be banned unless approved by shareholders. More permanent shark repellents, such as special quorum arrangements that can give directors jobs for life, should be tested in the courts by securities officials, because they are probably illegal. If they are not illegal, they should be.

Another disturbing trend in Canadian business is the increasing use of restricted or non-voting shares and shares that carry more votes than others. Restricted shares should be banned because shareholders should have a right to vote. They are also damaging because they permit families or conglomerates to control corporations with mere toe-holds. Depending upon how by-laws are worded, a single shareholder could control General Motors with one share, if it is the only one with a vote. The number of companies on the Toronto Stock Exchange with restricted shares doubled in just six years, from 64 in 1979 to 130 companies in 1985. Restricted shares are banned in New York and should be banned here.

Changes are needed to the dissenting shareholder provisions under the Canada Business Corporations Act. Currently, dissent can sometimes be waged only by the well-heeled, because an action costs a minimum of $250,000 in legal fees. Moreover, the money can be tied up for five or six years, and occasionally judges have not awarded costs to winners. Some form of less expensive tribunal, or the creation of a shareholder ombudsman, may remedy this injustice.

Another problem area concerns the preparation of financial statements by public companies. Canada's corporate world is filled with examples of managements that have had fun with figures. Capitalizing interest to hide it from expenses, baseline accounting — used by the Canadian Commercial Bank and the Northland Bank to effectively disguise massive loan losses by calling them assets — and other controversial accounting practices have plagued the investment game in Canada. The principles applied to one company may be valid in one case, but not in another.

Securities officials should standardize the principles that are allowed, on an industry-by-industry basis. Or, failing agreement, they should adopt U.S. Securities and Exchange Commission requirements that a company produce two sets of financial statements annually: one based on accounting principles the company has chosen for itself, and a second using principles the SEC has endorsed as its standard. This allows companies to choose different accounting approaches, but also gives investors a common yardstick against which to measure various company claims.

Another area of serious concern is self-dealing, in which principals of an institution or company — such as officers, a dominant shareholder, or a group of shareholders — unjustifiably engage in transactions for their personal benefit, directly or through affiliated companies and against the interests of clients, the company, or shareholders. Self-dealing must be combatted in different ways, depending upon whether companies have dominant shareholders and on whether companies are lending or borrowing entities.

The easiest way to prevent self-dealing is to impose ownership limits on any lending institution taking deposits from the public and insured under the Canada Deposit Insurance Corp. Federal laws now limit bank ownership to 10 per cent, and this limit should also apply to provincially chartered trust companies. Unfortunately, controlling interest in all trust companies is already held by individuals or conglomerates. Even so, they should be forced to divest over a ten- to fifteen-year period.

However, in the interests of increasing competition, trust companies should also be allowed to gradually become chartered banks and get into the more lucrative aspects of the lending business, particularly large commercial loans. Likewise, banks should be allowed to get into the trust companies' most lucrative niche, as financial intermediaries managing trust funds, once trust companies have become widely held banks.

Before commercial lending is opened up to trust companies, changes should be made in the way banking operates in Canada. As stated before, boards should not include any customers or affiliates; but, most importantly, banks must be prevented from putting all their eggs into one basket. There must be limits on the size of individual loans, and limits on the total amount a bank can lend to any individual client. In the U.S., for instance, loans to a particular client cannot total more than 10 per cent of a bank's capital.

The lack of such limits in Canada allowed the Toronto-Dominion and the Commerce to get in over their heads in 1981 with Dome Petroleum. The two banks were owed $1.1 billion and $1.3 billion respectively by Dome by the fall of 1982, when the government moved in. The government's presence was absolutely necessary to avert what could have been a collapse in the Canadian banking system. In the case of the TD, the amount owing matched the bank's entire capital (and was rapidly reduced), and in the case of the Commerce, it was an inordinate 60 per cent of capital. In either case, a drawn-out bankruptcy or receivership would have threatened the bank's viability.

Since the nearly devastating events of 1981, Canada's largest chartered banks have voluntarily imposed limits on individual loans. "Syndication [sharing loans] is here now," says TD chairman Dick Thomson. "We certainly did learn a lesson in 1981. The number of syndicated loans is increasing dramatically. This was done voluntarily. Internally, we have a limit of $500 million to any one customer." While bankers have learned, memories may be short. To avoid a recurrence of the situation, the Bank Act should be amended to impose lending limits.

In addition, borrowers must not be allowed to make cashless takeovers. Both securities laws and banking laws should require down payments of at least 25 per cent in cash, to eliminate reckless borrowing as well as questionable junk bond deals, like the share swaps proposed by Dome, Unicorp, and Turbo Resources. In the U.S., securities laws require large cash down payments of at least 25 per cent when shares are bought. Here, we allowed Dome to pay $4 billion for an oil company it could not afford with what amounted to a Visa card.

Self-dealing curbs should also be imposed on near-banks, such as merchant or investment banks, which raise their capital through stock markets, not deposits. Like real banks and trust companies, they should have a majority of outside directors on their boards, and they should not be permitted to make loans to affiliates or to a company over which they can exercise control. Most importantly, the definition of loans should also include debt instruments, such as preferred shares. The practice of lending money to affiliates is widespread in the Edper empire, and it should cease because it has created unhealthy interdependencies as well as the potential for self-dealing conflicts.

In addition, other self-dealing antidotes include a ban on mutual funds buying securities underwritten by a related person or company; a ban on investment advisers or management firms recommending the purchase of securities underwritten by a related person or company; a ban on life or casualty insurers underwriting coverage for a related person; and a ban on securities underwriters warehousing stock with related persons or companies.

Self-dealing has also occurred when entities have owned both financial assets and other assets, called "real economy" assets by economists. Such cross-ownership is forbidden under the Bank Act, which wisely prohibits banks from owning more than 5 per cent of any real economy company, a ruling circumvented by the Toronto-Dominion Bank and Oxford Development. The TD owns 5 per cent of Oxford's voting shares, but 40 per cent of its non-voting share equity. In keeping with the spirit of the law, if not the letter, the TD should divest its 40-per-cent interest in Oxford immediately. The banking ban should also extend to trust companies, many of which also own real estate companies.

If laws fail to disallow owning both types of assets, self-dealing rules should be enacted to forbid financial companies from conducting any transactions with their real economy cousins, whether providing or accepting evaluation advice, providing intermediary services, or buying real economy assets. Such rules would have prevented Peter Pocklington from selling highly speculative properties to his trust company; when the properties collapsed in value, the trust company was forced out of business.

Bankruptcy Act changes proposed by consumer minister Michel Côté should be passed as soon as possible to better protect smaller borrowers, who are often harmed when big banks make bad loans to big customers. The changes provide protection for all customers, as exists in the U.S. In Canada, only the biggest customers are now protected. The new bankruptcy rules would allow courts to give companies time to restructure their affairs by keeping banks and other creditors at bay. This gives them breathing space and gives their non-bank creditors time to bargain for a fair share of proceeds, if any.

Without such legislation, banks have been able to pull the plug on small companies, leaving owners and other creditors high and dry. In many cases, owners have deliberately boosted inventories, knowing they were about to go bust, so that inventories would be sufficient when banks marched in to cover bank loans. The creditors owning the inventories were left with a choice of writing off their losses or buying their own goods back from the bank. While such horror shows have happened continuously in Canada, big companies, like Dome, never have the plugs pulled on them by their banks.

Another area needing reform in light of the degree of concentration is taxation. It remains a fact of life in Canada that it is easy to stay rich, but difficult to get rich. In the spring of 1985, with Quebec's abandonment of its death and gift taxes, Canada became the only developed country without special taxes on the flow of wealth from one generation to another. The wealthy will argue that death duties would be onerous and unnecessary because upon death, Canadian estates must pay capital gains tax on half the increase in assets since the valuation date of January 1, 1972. They argue that imposing death duties on top of that would cause the forced sale of most private family businesses, possibly at fire-sale prices as estates scramble to come up with cash for Revenue Canada.

Canada's wealthiest citizens should pay more taxes, because it is fair and because they can afford to. This is the underlying principle behind all taxes on income or wealth: that the greater proportion of the tax burden must be shouldered by those who can afford to do so. After all, lower-class and middle-class people pay an annual "wealth tax" in the form of property taxes on their principal assets, their homes. Even those who rent end up paying this wealth tax for their landlords. The wealthy, on the other hand, pay property taxes on their mansions but nothing on their principal assets, as those less privileged must do.

The best option is to adopt the Carter commission's suggested "accession" tax, as opposed to succession duties. With accession tax, the beneficiaries are taxed, taking into consideration their means, rather than the estate itself being taxed, as it is with succession duties. This would mean, for instance, that $1 million bequeathed to 100 relatives would be taxed at a lower rate than would $1 million bequeathed to one person by three estates in one year. In addition, gift taxes would be required in order to prevent beneficiaries from ducking accession taxes by receiving tax-free gifts from living relatives before their death.

Without any death or gift taxes, concentration is speeded up as money passes from generation to generation without any tolls. However, that tax measure would have a minuscule effect compared with another tax change, which could profoundly arrest concentration: cancellation of the deductibility of interest on loans obtained to make takeovers. Interest deductibility was allowed in the early 1970s, and it greatly contributed to the enormous take-over activity that followed.

Unfortunately, Canada ends this privilege at its own peril. It was instituted because the U.S. permitted such deductions, and Canadian players merely shifted their activities south. They would again. Some suggest that deductibility be allowed only for those takeovers that are "in the public interest." However, such a policy would give civil servants and politicians far too much discretion. It would be so arbitrary that companies would not dare take a chance, because if deductions were disallowed the economics of a transaction would profoundly change. It would become a de facto ban on deductions, and capital would leave the country.

Taxation policies may not be able to discourage the paper entrepreneur, but they may be used to encourage the type of entrepreneur who builds projects, who creates and exports new goods or services. In the past, governments have handed out grants or tax breaks to encourage exploration or research and development. Manufacturers and exporters get some tax breaks now, in the form of fast write-offs, slightly lower corporate taxes, and no sales taxes on exports, but more can and should be done.

Studies have shown that Canadian manufacturers and exporters are not at any tax disadvantage compared with British or American manufacturers. But they do not have advantages either. And advantages are necessary to offset the fact that Canada has a domestic economy too small to act as a springboard for low-cost exports. The result is a branch plant economy consisting of small foreign-owned subsidiaries, making small amounts of many products for a tiny Canadian market.

Canada needs to foster Canadian manufacturers and to encourage our branch plants to obtain "world product mandates" from their parents, allowing them to specialize, lower their costs, and export more goods. Such manufacturers, like Canadian Westinghouse, often outshine their American parents and export Canadian-made products back to the U.S. (Westinghouse has a world product mandate in great part because it has specialized in making components for Canada's federally supported nuclear industry.)

What is needed is huge tax breaks, or even tax holidays, for these types of entrepreneurs. Breaks give rise to criticism from other business sectors, such as service industries, but all would ultimately benefit as many major multinationals would find world product mandates to be viable alternatives. That, in turn, could lead to more world product mandates, more exports, and more research and development here in Canada. Such tax breaks would increase the debts of our already deficit-ridden governments, but they would be a bold industrial strategy that could contribute to the nation's wealth.

The connection between taxes and concentration is being examined in a study now being conducted by the federal government into whether corporations should be allowed to "consolidate," subtracting losses from one company against the profits of another without wholly owning either. If allowed, consolidation will greatly increase the amount of concentration. Currently, the only way losses can be transferred from one partially owned company to another is through wind-ups or amalgamations. Even though financiers like Conrad Black have become masters at such manoeuvres to avoid tax, they are an expensive and often controversial strategy. With consolidation, more empires will be able to more easily shelter even more tax, and will grow exponentially as a result. This should not be allowed.

Oddly enough, some of the issues surrounding pension reform also relate to concentration of ownership. Among the biggest social rip-offs in this country are the laws governing private company pension schemes, affecting about 60 per cent of the country's workforce of 10.5 million. The laws must be changed because they allow corporations to skim off surpluses made by those pension funds. For instance, in 1986 Conrad Black and his nearly defunct Dominion Stores were able to take $62 million out of the pension funds of Dominion employees, mostly because so many had been laid off.

This opportunity arose — and the same blow has happened countless times to millions of other workers — because after Black sold most Dominion stores, many employees were laid off before their individual pensions were "vested." (A pension is vested after the worker has been with the company for a certain period, usually ten years, allowing the worker who quits to take with him the employer's pension contributions as well as his own, with interest.) This meant that, in actuarial terms, there was more money in the pension fund than was needed to look after vested employees, so Black and his company were entitled to the extra money. Hijinks such as these contribute to the growing concentration of power, particularly during times of high interest rates when conglomerates could help themselves to millions of dollars worth of so-called surplus earnings, rather than let the surpluses stay in the funds, collecting interest for the eventual benefit of their workers.

Another problem involves public pension schemes such as the Canada Pension Plan and the Quebec Pension Plan. These two funds have given birth to a great deal of concentration of power in the area of public enterprise, or people's capitalism. The operation of the plans is currently under review in Ottawa, where officials are considering recommendations to double contributions to these schemes because both will be broke by the turn of the century. They are running out of money because the population is aging: by the year 2000, there will be three workers for every pensioner; today there are nine to one.

Beginning in 1987, the two pension plans will pay out more money each year than they take in, and as the funds shrink, the provinces — to which this money is lent until it is paid out — must begin to repay the funds. So politicians are eager to hike contributions.

This should not be done. Canada's two pension funds are nothing more than open-ended slush funds for provincial politicians, allowing them to run up huge tabs and deficits for years. In light of the frightening debt and feather-bedding that has taken place, the two funds should be wound up and run as a pay-as-you-go fund, with only enough money coming in to meet obligations going out. This is the method used in most countries. The wisdom of such a policy is that the slush funds will dry up, forcing provincial governments to spend their money wisely. And provinces should not be allowed to run deficits or incur foreign debts without the permission of the federal government; neither should municipalities.

Another reform needed to stem concentration is the phasing out of the "90-per-cent" rule, which forces pensions and other institutional investors to invest 90 per cent of their money in Canada. This has fostered the type of paper entrepreneurship that plagues Canada: takeover artists have a captive audience from which they buy and to which they sell shares. Typically, when Company A is taken over, institutions make profits on the shares of Company A taken over by Company B. Then Company B sells more of its own shares, common or preferred, to these same investors, in order to pay for its takeover of Company A. The pension funds do this kind of investing because there are few choices yielding such high returns. But it is an artificial and parasitical game. It does not create meaningful economic activity, but diverts capital to paper, rather than real, entrepreneurs; it bids the price of Canadian securities up higher than they should be, and it encourages too many takeovers and too many debts.

The institutions should be allowed to invest in smaller, more entre-preneurial companies and to seek better returns outside the country. However, foreign investments should be taxed by the federal government, as an incentive to keep the money here at home. That would encourage some foreign entrepreneurs to set up shop here to tap these funds, which are tax-free if invested in Canada. There should also be more incentives to invest in high-tech, manufacturing, or exporting businesses. The Tories made a start in this direction by relaxing the 90-per-cent rule for investments in small entrepreneurs, on a dollar-for-dollar basis; for every dollar investors put into a small Canadian entrepreneur, they can invest a dollar offshore. But more is needed, more quickly.

Other anti-concentration measures that need immediate attention involve concentration of ownership in the media and in telecommunications. Ottawa should immediately adopt the suggestions of the Kent commission into concentration in the newspaper industry, which included a freeze on the size of newspaper chains, retroactive to the year the commission sat; a directive to the Canadian Radio-television and Telecommunications Commission ordering it to refuse to renew licences of broadcasters also owning newspapers in the same market areas, unless they divest one or the other; and the separation, in terms of ownership, of the *Globe and Mail* and the Thomson newspaper chain, because Thomson-owned newspapers dominate forty communities in Canada. In telecommunications, Bell Canada Enterprises should be forced to compete for long-distance rates in order to give newcomers opportunities, and it should divest all its minority interests in other telephone monopolies in Canada.

Last, but far from least, Canada's level of concentration requires more vigilance to ensure that economic power cannot buy political power. A lobbyists' registry and guidelines governing acceptable lobbying activities should be imposed. This has been promised by Prime Minister Mulroney. It would go a long way towards helping politicians and civil servants to evaluate representations as well as curbing abuses such as lavishing publicly paid decision-makers with gifts, trips, and other benefits. It is inappropriate, for instance, for Paul Desmarais to give free flights to the prime minister's advisers or to cabinet ministers.

Equally important, campaign contribution ceilings and disclosure rules should be enforced in all provinces and in all forms of elections: municipal and provincial races, school board elections, and leadership contests at provincial and federal levels. Current rules are spotty and do not apply everywhere. New rules should ensure the integrity of our electoral system. Voters have as much right to know what developers have contributed to a mayor's campaign as they have to know what tycoons, if any, bankrolled John Turner's bid to become Liberal leader.

Clear-cut conflict-of-interest guidelines must be put into effect everywhere, at all levels of government. And the assets — as well as the debts — of all elected officials and of their spouses or children should be disclosed to the public. Many jurisdictions now require disclosure to party leaders on a confidential basis, but this is inadequate. While it may seem to invade privacy, disclosure is an accepted price that public officials pay in many democracies. With the degree of concentration that exists in this country, we can demand no less.

Concentration of power, and what to do about it, has been the black hole of Canadian public policy even though it has affected all of us, as consumers, investors, workers, depositors, and taxpayers. It has also weakened our competitive position as a trading nation. With so many widespread effects, there is little wonder that it has not been addressed. I hope this book has underscored the need for solutions and proposed remedies that apply a scalpel, and not an axe, to these problems. Concentration, after all, is not an evil in and of itself. But, if left mostly to its own devices, it can be dangerous. And if it is left completely unbridled, it will cost us our freedoms.

ACKNOWLEDGEMENTS

Controlling Interest is simply the latest book to deal with concentration of power in Canada, the black hole of Canadian public policy. I was first alerted to the problems of concentration years ago when studying the seminal work on the topic, C. Wright Mills's classic *The Power Elite*, which inspired generations of sociologists around the world. Here in Canada, *The Vertical Mosaic* applied Mills's theses to the Canadian landscape, and Peter C. Newman popularized the business players involved in running the country with his *Canadian Establishment* books.

These concerns last came to a head for the nation in 1978 when the federal Royal Commission into Corporate Concentration reported that concentration existed, but was inevitable in a country as small as Canada. Without question, that commission listened mostly to big business arguments and failed miserably to fulfil a mandate to address the public policy questions raised by this phenomenon. Hopefully, this book won't fail.

Controlling Interest is a private-sector, one-woman royal commission. I have criss-crossed the country, scoured the literature, and conducted several hundred interviews to document the new, faster-growing forms of concentration as well as to describe its abuses and potential abuses, and the ramifications for the rest of us in terms of jobs, the nation's wealth, opportunities, and political freedoms.

Among the many who provided insights and encouragement for this book from business and academe were Henry Knowles, John Duby, Bernie Ghert, William Stanbury, and Robert Kerton. Also, special thanks to many wordsmiths who have encouraged or helped me along the way, sometimes unknowingly: Peter Newman, Jack McArthur, Catherine Ford, Joann Webb, Sandy Ross, Michael Enright, Larry Zolf, John Bryden, Helen Henderson, Dick Wright, and Peggy Wente. I am also indebted to researchers Arlene Arnason and Beryl Wetstein as well as to my agent, Beverley Slopen, for steering me through the maze of book publishing. And my children, Eric and Julie, and my husband, Frank, are to be congratulated for putting up with an occasionally intense and obsessed writer.

I thank most of all John Honderich, former business editor of *The Toronto Star*, for his encouragement and help, as well as Farley Faulkner, wherever you are.

INDEX